ANNALS OF THE NEW YORK ACADEMY OF SCIENCES

D0777912

INFRASTRUCTURE
MAINTENANCE AND REPAIR OF PUBLIC WORKS

Edited by Alan H. Molof and Carl J. Turkstra

The New York Academy of Sciences
New York, New York
1984

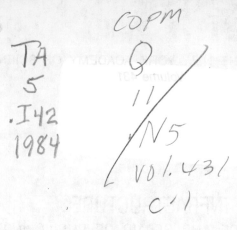

The cover photograph shows the intersection of William and Wall Streets, New York City, around 1917; courtesy of the Port Authority of New York and New Jersey.

Library of Congress Cataloging in Publication Data

Main entry under title:

Infrastructure: maintenance and repair of public works.

(Annals of the New York Academy of Sciences, ISSN 0077-8923 ; v. 431)
"Volume is the result of a symposium . . . held on December 5–7, 1983 and sponsored by the Department of Civil and Environmental Engineering of the Polytechnic Institute of New York, the New York State Legislative Commission on Science and Technology, and the New York Academy of Sciences"–P.
    Bibliography: p.
    Includes index.

    1. Public works—Maintenance and repair—Congresses. 2. Public works—New York (State)—Maintenance and repair—Congresses. I. Molof, Alan H. II. Turkstra, Carl J. III. Polytechnic Institute of New York. Dept. of Civil and Environmental Engineering. IV. New York (State). Legislature. Legislative Commission on Science & Technology. V. New York Academy of Sciences. VI. Series.
Q11.N5 vol. 431 [TA5]   363'.09747   84-25405
ISBN 0-89766-256-3
ISBN 0-89766-257-1 (pbk.)

CCP
Printed in the United States of America
ISBN 0-89766-256-3 (Cloth)
ISBN 0-89766-257-1 (Paper)
ISSN 0077-8923

ANNALS OF THE NEW YORK ACADEMY OF SCIENCES

Volume 431

December 5, 1984

INFRASTRUCTURE[a]
MAINTENANCE AND REPAIR OF PUBLIC WORKS

Editors and Conference Organizers
ALAN H. MOLOF and CARL J. TURKSTRA

CONTENTS

[a] This volume is the result of a symposium entitled New York Conference on the Infrastructure: Maintenance and Repair of Public Works held on December 5–7, 1983 and sponsored by the Department of Civil and Environmental Engineering of the Polytechnic Institute of New York, the New York State Legislative Commission on Science and Technology, and The New York Academy of Sciences in cooperation with the American Society of Civil Engineers, the Business Council of New York State, the New York Chamber of Commerce and Industry, the New York City Partnership, the New York State Society of Professional Engineers, the Office of the Governor – State of New York, the Office of the Mayor – City of New York, the Office of the Speaker – New York State Assembly, and the Port Authority of New York and New Jersey.

Part III. State Legislative Initiatives for Infrastructure Maintenance
Joseph Ferris, *Chair*

Part IV: Impact of Infrastructure Maintenance and Repair on Current Standards
Satoshi Oishi, *Chair*

Part V. Establishing Maintenance Policies
Charles M. Smith, Jr., *Chair*

Part VI. Impact of Emerging Technologies on Civil Engineering Education and Research
William S. Butcher, *Chair*

Financial assistance was received from:
• CONSTRUCTION INDUSTRY FOUNDATION • WESTCHESTER AND PUTNAM
    COUNTIES
• MARINE MIDLAND BANK
• O'BRIEN AND GERE ENGINEERS, INC.
• L. F. ROTHSCHILD, UNTERBERG, TOWBIN

Introduction

ALAN H. MOLOF

Department of Civil and Environmental Engineering
Polytechnic Institute of New York
333 Jay Street
Brooklyn, New York 11201

The prefix "infra" defined as "below" does not indicate the scope of the word "infrastructure." As used here, infrastructure is public works — sewers, water pipes, roads, rails, bridges, and buildings. Aging and/or lack of maintenance has resulted in the critical situation of a decaying infrastructure. The purpose of this conference, the first of its kind, was to bring together the present and future decision makers involved in maintaining, repairing, and rebuilding our infrastructure.

The importance of the infrastructure to any governmental unit can be seen from incidents such as water pipe breaks, sewer overflows, road potholes, bridge failures, train derailments, and building ceiling collapses. The solution to these infrastructure problems is ultimately money.

However, it is important to note that the financial program component is only part of the ultimate solution. In this conference the technological program component is given the major role since the design of any segment of the infrastructure will of necessity include techniques for reducing maintenance, repair, and rebuilding costs.

This conference is a first step in bringing this technological component to its proper role along with the financial and governmental components to provide cost-effective solutions to our infrastructure problems. A vibrant and productive discussion of all the above components was an integral part of the conference.

The three day conference resulted in the dissemination of valuable information. The first day concerned government policies and perspectives, financial considerations, and maintenance initiatives by state legislatures. The first day also featured governmental input at the state level with Governor Mario Cuomo as the keynote speaker and Mayor Edward Koch at the city level as the luncheon speaker. The second day changed the focus to a technological emphasis and covered the effect of infrastructure maintenance and repair on current standards and policies, and the effect of emerging technologies on civil engineering education and research. The third day covered more applied technology such as reconstruction descriptions and innovative solution case studies. The third day also featured the field of civil engineering by having Dr. Russell Stearns, president of the American Society of Civil Engineers, as the luncheon speaker.

There has been a joint sponsorship of the conference by (1) the Department of Civil and Environmental Engineering, Polytechnic Institute of New York, (2) the New York State Legislative Commission on Science and Technology, and (3) the New York Academy of Sciences. The outstanding cooperation of all three organizations enabled the program to represent the significant levels of government, finance, and technology — all vitally necessary to solving our infrastructure problem.

Rebuilding Our Infrastructure
Keynote Address

MARIO M. CUOMO

Office of the Governor
The State of New York
Two World Trade Center
New York, New York 10047

I do not know the exact route most of you took here this morning, but those of you who came down the Franklin D. Roosevelt Drive or across the Manhattan Bridge or on the subway have already received as eloquent an argument as there is for rebuilding our infrastructure.

Other routes would have been just as convincing. You could have taken the Fifty-ninth Street Bridge from Queens or come down the Hutchinson River Parkway from Westchester. The point does not have to be belabored.

It is clear that many of the familiar structures we have taken for granted for so many years cannot be neglected much longer.

And what is true here in the city holds all over the state. Everywhere—in the North Country and the Southern Tier, on the Island, across the state in Albany, Syracuse, Rochester, Buffalo, in every county, town, and municipality—there is work that needs to be done.

The dimensions of the job are monumental but hardly more intimidating than the problems that faced those who first planned and built our roads and bridges and canals and water systems—people in government like Governor De Witt Clinton whose vision went beyond the next election and others in the private sector like the Roeblings. Nothing could stop their bridge—neither seemingly insuperable engineering obstacles, nor personal tragedy, nor crippling illness.

The Brooklyn Bridge was 13 years under construction. The Erie Canal—Clinton's Ditch—took 8 years to complete. The second Croton aquaduct system, the source of much of the city's water—including the dam still standing at Kensico—also took 13 years.

Today, the task of maintaining and, where necessary, rebuilding the infrastructure requires of us the same determination and long-range vision that it took to conceive and create these projects in the first place.

For many of us—especially those of us in government—learning to take the long view will mean a conversion. It will mean thinking and acting in a way that is, or has been, foreign to government. Since at least the 1930s almost every governor and legislative leader has recognized the need for long-range planning. Yet, we have remained a government that mostly deals with problems on an *ad hoc* basis, that reacts to crises rather than trying to anticipate and prevent them.

Because of the failure to plan and because of the resulting inability to

1

take preventive action, we find ourselves trying to catch up with our problems instead of controlling them, running, like the Red Queen in *Alice in Wonderland*, as fast as we can just to stay in the same place.

Fortunately, that situation is finally changing.

This year we created the State Council on Economic and Fiscal Priorities. The council brings together, for the first time, leaders from business, labor, and academia to help us develop a long-term planning horizon against which we can determine, in a more rational way, what will be needed and where and when.

The plain truth is that we cannot meet all the perceived needs indiscriminately, or simultaneously and immediately. Nor can we do it all alone. The federal government has an unfulfilled obligation to assist states with this task.

Yet failure at the federal level to invest adequately in assisting states with infrastructure repair should not be taken by us as an excuse for inaction or further delay. In New York, it will not be.

In November 1983, the voters showed their willingness to invest in New York's future when they approved the Rebuild New York Bond Issue. It will allow us to begin a program of rebuilding that is unmatched in any other state. It will allow us to end the pattern of "deferred maintenance" and continually postponed reconstruction responsible for the slow undoing, over the years, of the very system of roads and rails and ports that has made New York the international center for so many industries and businesses.

New York had already begun the work of reconstruction with passage of the 1979 Transportation Bond Issue and the Five-Year Capital Improvement Program undertaken in 1981 by the Metropolitan Transportation Authority. Just this spring, we expanded the MTA program to a total of $8.6 billion.

Recently, too, Governor Kean of New Jersey and I announced another program to preserve essential systems in the metropolitan area. Under this joint program, the Port Authority of New York and New Jersey will, in the next decade, finance more than a billion dollars in capital projects, including the redevelopment of waterfront areas on both sides of the Hudson River.

Still another initiative is our proposal for creation of a water finance authority to assist local governments in financing needed improvements. New York State has an abundant supply of water, but many of its water delivery and sewer systems are overburdened and deteriorating. In Buffalo and Poughkeepsie, for example, nearly half the water that flows through their antiquated systems is lost. And many rural water supply systems cannot even meet the basic need of fire protection.

The economic as well as the physical health of our state is dependent upon an adequate, safe water supply—one of the most critical community resources industry considers in deciding to expand or relocate its operations.

These initiatives, together with better management practices in state agencies and more realistic assessments of maintenance needs, are a beginning to the long-range preservation of the infrastructure already in place.

While maintenance and preservation remain our primary emphasis, there is another element. We will also need to develop new facilities to meet emerging needs of new industries and businesses. Here, too, development cannot be indiscriminate. We must plan carefully to anticipate future demands.

The Council on Fiscal and Economic Priorities has already identified some broad areas in which new investment will be critical. Air cargo capacity must be expanded to accommodate the growth of service and manufacturing industries that specialize in high-value, low-density products. Our ports, both upstate and downstate, must be made more accessible and efficient. Modern telecommunications facilities are essential for retaining and attracting financial and service institutions.

State capital spending can also help foster new industrial growth in the area of joint industry-university research and development. It is now widely recognized that a partnership among industry, government, and the universities is prerequisite for industrial innovation. New York has committed more than $30 million to the development of a new center for industrial innovation at Rensselaer Polytechnic Institute in Troy. Other centers for advanced technology are being developed at universities across the state.

A final element of our capital development strategy must be the creation of new employment and new opportunity for those who need them most. It is clear that the recovery that is apparently beginning will not be the traditional postrecession expansion of the entire economy. This recovery, when it occurs, will leave many older industries in a state of collapse. It will leave a record number of workers without jobs, the victims of what is called "structural unemployment."

Temporary programs, one-shot expenditures, and short-range recovery policies aimed at increasing total gross national product growth will not solve this problem. What is needed is a commitment to changing the structure of opportunity: to creating new business opportunities in minority and low-income communities; to providing transitional jobs — jobs that train people as well as employ them. The objective of these efforts should not be "make work" but the integration into the mainstream economy of people left outside it, and the reintegration of those, like the steelworkers of Lackawanna, who suddenly find themselves shut out after years of hard work.

That, as briefly as I can put it, is our program — a long-range program of rebuilding New York's magnificent system of public works, of investment in areas of new growth, of investment especially in those areas and for those people most devastated by recession and a changing technological base.

It has been estimated that the final price tag for infrastructure repair in New York alone will be over $35 billion, and despite all that is being undertaken, despite all New York is doing on its own, we simply do not have the resources to accomplish everything that must be done.

We need the long-term help and commitment of the federal government. Not a handout. But a partnership, a joint effort where the federal government acts as a catalyst for reconstruction much as it did in the 1930s and 40s when it set in motion the public works and public investments that led to the rise of the so-called Sun Belt.

Some have suggested that this help should take the form of a reconstruction finance corporation, along the lines of the institution that proved so successful in pulling America out of the depression. There are other forms that federal aid and assistance could take, and all of us should be ready to consider them.

Certainly, at least as an interim step, there should be a cohesive, unified national planning strategy for public works to replace the current hodgepodge of federal programs. The adoption of a federal capital budget system should be a priority.

The simple truth is that the work of construction and reconstruction will not wait. The rebuilding of our infrastructure is a task that transcends ideology or political philosophies or social theories.

It is an economic fact of life, a foundation that we all depend on equally, Democrat and Republican alike, upstate and downstate, rural and urban, an indispensable ingredient of our common future.

It is time to get on with the job.

Federal Perspectives on
Public Works Infrastructure[a]

One Person's View from the Executive Branch

DAVID G. MATHIASEN

Executive Office of the President
Office of Management and Budget
726 Jackson Place NW
Washington, D.C. 20503

My assignment here is to look at the issue of public infrastructure from the
point of view of the executive branch of the federal government. In doing
so I should state at the outset that the views I will express are my own, not
those of the Office of Management and Budget and certainly not those of
the administration.

1. The competition for budgetary resources not only continues to exist,
   but has become more intense.
2. Whatever our views on the need for increased public investment in infrastructure, some budgetary facts of life must be faced if we want to
   carry on a reasoned debate.
3. It may seem mundane, but we need a hard look at the criteria for making
   budget decisions, including public works.
4. Public policy in this area involves not only an analysis of what we need,
   but how best to pay for it.

These propositions are not new or original. Indeed, some just anticipate
subjects that will be discussed more fully in later sessions. But they are often
conveniently ignored, and that we cannot afford to do.

COMPETITION FOR BUDGETARY RESOURCES

The federal budget is often viewed as a leviathan. It seems to grow inexorably.
That part in which an individual or a group is interested seems relatively understandable. Teachers do not find the need for federal education money hard
to grasp. To a retiree, an annual adjustment in social security benefits for
inflation is no mystery. An engineer can readily see the need for rebuilding

---

[a] The views expressed are those of the author. They do not represent a statement of policy
of the Office of Management and Budget or of the United States government.

5

old roads. To most of us it is the "other" part of the budget that seems excessive, inefficient, and most certainly less important. Unfortunately, each of us defines the "other" part in our own terms.

However, for those of us who live in the fiscal emergency room, the view is very different. The budget seems to be an almost unreconcilable combination of solemn and deeply felt commitments to the nation's people (often summed up by the term "social contract"), high-priority emergencies, and absolutely essential investments—the postponement of which will only make our problems worse. Some of the rhetoric we encounter daily illustrates the problem. Will Rogers said he never met a man he didn't like. In Washington, you never meet a need that is not only "national" but "critical." We have, it seems, only high priorities. We cannot afford to balance the budget on the backs of the poor, the aged, the sick. Without an adequate national defense, our very freedom is in danger. Public investment is likewise critical to rebuild our cities, educate our children, preserve the environment, protect the small farmer, or promote exports.

But make no mistake. The common justifications for public spending have extremely strong political appeal. You probably know them as well as I. For example:

- Major flooding causes hardship for hard-working people through no fault of their own, and a wealthy nation should provide disaster assistance for them.
- Poor quality education in math and science is causing us to fall behind other industrialized countries and threatens our ability to maintain a strong national defense.
- Structural unemployment of the disadvantaged in our central cities and many rural areas creates a loss to society that will become permanent unless effective training and employment programs are expanded and improved.
- Medical care is not only a matter of compassion, but an investment in human welfare and, for many, productivity.
- Child nutrition and head start programs are essential investments in our most valuable commodity—future generations.
- Supporting assistance for countries overseas is essential to our national security by lessening regional instability and the likelihood of war.
- The space program and other research and development efforts are critical to maintaining a cutting edge in high-technology industry.
- Loans for export development and promotion permit us to maintain our competitive position in world markets, which is particularly important during a period of a highly valued dollar and a ferociously competitive marketplace.
- Payments to our retired people through social security represent benefits they have earned over 45 or more years of their working lives.
- Compensation, pensions, and health benefits for veterans represent the least a grateful nation can do for those who have fought our wars.

These justifications for competing demands for the federal dollar are not meant to be taken as either cynical or lighthearted. We know from repeated public opinion polls that most or all of these are considered legitimate and often important claims on federal resources by many, if not most, voters. We know from observing the political process that most legislators and executive branch officials want the total budget to be smaller, but the pieces — especially, their piece — to be bigger. And they do not understand why a huge budget cannot accommodate their wishes. This sentiment is largely behind the expansion of federal spending from 20% of the gross national product (GNP) a quarter of a century ago to 25% today.

In the environment of the fiscal emergency room it is not the easiest thing in the world to defend putting federal funding for the resurfacing of bridges at the head of the list.

BUDGETARY FACTS OF LIFE

Aside from competing claims, what are the facts of life?

- The deficit for the last fiscal year came in just a shade under $200 billion. Under the president's policies — which require congressional agreement — these deficits are still likely to be in the $100 to $200 billion range through 1987.
- In contrast, three of the most widely used economic forecasting services — Chase, Data Resources, Inc., and Wharton — show annual net operating surpluses of state and local governments for 1983 and 1984 in the $14–24 billion range. These operating surpluses *exclude* investments in pension funds.
- Defense has been a long-neglected budget priority. In 1983, defense outlays were 6.5% of a recession-reduced GNP. That compares with an average of 8.6% during the entire decade of the 1960s, and is a modest increase from the 1978–79 level of 5% of the GNP, the lowest in over 30 years.
- In the last two decades, federal investment in nondefense physical infrastructure — *adjusted for inflation* — doubled. Nondefense outlays, measured in 1972 dollars, were $8 billion in 1960, $10 billion in 1970, and $15 billion in 1980. As a percent of the GNP, direct federal investment has not changed in 15 years. Grants to state and local governments for physical investment have ranged between seven-tenths and nine-tenths of a percent of the GNP since 1964, with no discernible trend.
- The present commitment to physical infrastructure under existing administration and congressional policies is still strong. Last July's projections under current law through 1986 for water projects and navigation, highways, mass transit, airports and airways, and water-treatment plants show that the level in 1982 of $23 billion will grow to $29 billion (in nominal dollars), with total investment during the 1982–1986 period of just under $130 billion.
- Meanwhile, the economic base of the country has been restored. We

have now fully recovered from the recession and are experiencing nonin-
flationary, postrecessionary expansion of 6% to 7% in real terms.
- State and local tax-exempt borrowing for public purposes grew very rapidly in 1982 and has remained high, suggesting an ability by states and
localities to finance capital projects.

CRITERIA FOR BUDGET DECISIONS

We need, as always, to question the basic premises of our thinking. By question I do not mean reject; rather, I mean that we should not blithely accept
the notion that any federal or state and local payment — whether for infrastructure or health — is *prima facie* essential or even beneficial.

Let me raise briefly four other questions that illustrate the kinds of issues
we need to consider in developing a public works policy:

- To what extent does public investment promote economic growth?
- How should we incorporate constructively discussions on federalism that
have taken place over the past one-and-a-half decades?
- Are we using the best analytic tools for decisions — and using them
honestly?
- Have we given adequate consideration to the skeptics — those who question the basic premise that public works investment is clearly in need
of enhanced support?

Consider the first issue. Does physical infrastructure promote economic
growth? If so, how much and under what conditions? How do we define
"needs" and "standards"? Have we, for example, taken into account some
of the experience of other industrial countries — many of which have had
thriving economies despite narrow roads, small railcars, sky-high fuel taxes,
and home water heaters that go on only at night? Japan is currently the topic
of widespread discussion when the subject of economic growth comes up.
It is, of course, famous for the bullet train. But note that, because of budget
constraints, work on the planned expansion of the train has been postponed.
Moreover, as I read the literature, most current analysts attribute Japan's phe-
nomenal economic growth to cultural patterns that produce very high savings
rates, managerial techniques emphasizing worker participation and quality,
and high levels of technical education. How do these factors stack up relative
to the need to build or rebuild public works? I do not suggest we accept the
standards of Japan or anywhere else, but perhaps we can learn from them.
Furthermore, we need to be explicit about the infrastructure that really does
promote efficiency and growth and that which raises our standard of living
through convenience or even by increasing the choices we have of where to live.

We need to examine again the premise of modern United States federalism. For years, we have heard governors, mayors, and other state and local
officials argue strenuously against strings attached to federal grants. We are
told that they are inefficient and distort resource allocation. States can get
along with fewer dollars if they are not encumbered by lengthy regulations

mandating maintenance standards, matching shares, design and engineering standards, contracting procedures, etc. Similarly, there is concern that the federal grant mechanism has favored capital at the expense of maintenance, and new construction at the expense of rehabilitation. Yet the data suggest that federal funds may merely have *replaced*, not increased, state funds for infrastructure. And the General Accounting Office, for one, has suggested stronger regulation of grants to states so that federally funded facilities are properly maintained.

Legislation recently reported by the Senate Committee on Environment and Public Works would authorize $5 billion of federal funds for public works, but require:

- State matching on a dollar-for-dollar basis.
- Federal approval of detailed state plans for maintenance.
- Federal approval and continued monitoring of detailed state plans for *financing* further infrastructure development and maintenance.
- Federal approval for, among other things, provision of child-care facilities for people employed on public works projects.

My purpose here is not to object to these or other federal controls but, rather, to plead that we should face this dilemma honestly. Do we need strict state and local fiscal standards to maximize the degree to which federal grants for public works really are additive? Do we need tight criteria on rehabilitation and maintenance? Or should federal regulations be reduced, as the current administration believes, so that the funds can be used more flexibly and efficiently? We cannot have it both ways.

As always, we need the best possible analysis, but also the realization that analytic techniques alone—whether benefit-cost analysis or quantitative models—will not provide automatic answers. Few who have been involved in budgeting for very long claim to have a magic tool that compares the benefits of health research with an improved national airway system. In some cases, we need to learn some modesty from the past. I am sure we all have our list of well-justified projects that turned out wrong—or the opposite. On my list is the inner-loop highway system for Washington which was almost built in the 1960s. We now know that we did not need it—indeed, ultimately did not want it. Public facilities shift from being underutilized to overutilized and back again. As our shared experience would suggest—and as many budget hearings clearly demonstrate—the kind of comprehensive analysis that leads to optimum public policy decisions is imprecise at best. On the other hand, I recall an instance where I was discussing a new free downtown bus service with the head of a major metropolitan transit authority, and discovered that while he proclaimed it a great success, he had not bothered to calculate its cost. We cannot afford that kind of indifference to analysis.

Finally, we need to question our assumptions. Achieving a consensus on infrastructure needs among believers is easy. But the skeptics deserve due consideration. The Advisory Commission on Intergovernmental Relations (ACIR)—a body known more for quiet scholarship than for political controversy—just last month [November 1983] discussed preliminary findings that question the premise that America is seriously underbuilt. The ACIR study, which is being considered by members of the commission later this week, states: "The infrastructure problem is manageable. It has not reached crisis proportions. Neither is there an imminent 'infrastructure crisis.' "[1] The Congressional Budget Office — widely described as nonpartisan, as indeed it must be serving masters of two different parties in the two houses of Congress — published a study in April 1983 that recognized the need for investment in public infrastructure as essential for long-term economic growth, but found evidence for an immediate crisis lacking.[2] Further, it stressed the importance of financing infrastructure in ways that promote economic efficiency. A more recent study on the federal system states that "the original rationales" for a major federal role supporting public works infrastructure "may no longer apply," and "a number of infrastructure programs were designed to achieve important development goals that have now largely been met — such as building a national network of highways, fostering the growth of Western agriculture, and constructing a system of locks and dams."[3] As you begin your deliberations, this is not the time to take sides on this issue, but it is the time to recognize there is more than one.

PAYING FOR INFRASTRUCTURE

It may be clear from these remarks that — given competing priorities, the history of federal aid for infrastructure, and the general consensus that the deficits shown by our present budget projections are unacceptably high — no one should build great expectations for substantial infusions of additional funds from the United States Treasury. Let me quote again from the ACIR study. "The enormity of the 1983 federal budget deficit of $195 billion is underscored by a stunning comparison — it is about $25 billion larger than the 1983 tax collections of all state governments combined. In fact, it is necessary to go back to World War II to find another year when the federal budget deficit was greater than total state tax collections."[1] Thus, as you deliberate on the need for new and renewed infrastructure, you will be concerned with not only how to build it but how to pay for it. There are three concerns that may be worth noting.

- Budget policies should highlight, not obscure, the competition for resources among many public policy objectives. Let me be quite specific. We should oppose the use of capital budgeting techniques if their purpose — intended or not — is to obscure public policy choices. It may be wise to finance some public infrastructure throughout its useful life. Certainly, benefit-cost analysis and other techniques need to evaluate the long-range benefits of alternative investments. But it is equally important to realize that the real resources in the economy are used when a structure is built and that we must compete with other demands for real resources. To be specific, bond financing may make financial sense, but it should not be permitted to obscure the impact of increased government borrowing on today's financial markets, or the potential inflationary impact of shifting economic resources from private to public use. Nor should it take the place of explicit policy choices between alternative public goods.

- Unless we are prepared to alter our basic income and social insurance tax structure, any major increases in public works are going to be paid for by local taxes or some self-financing mechanisms. User fees not only provide a source of funds, but help to ensure efficient utilization of resources. Similarly, variable rates for utilities may be used to encourage off-peak use of public resources, creating a market structure that increases efficiency.
- In addition, and again your program anticipates this, financing and budgeting techniques need to avoid perverse incentives. Among these are too much new construction at the expense of maintenance and rehabilitation, and the exchange of future costs for current ones through unfunded labor contracts that promise early and generous retirement.

These considerations lead to what may appear to be a paradoxical conclusion. On the one hand, we need to broaden our scope of analysis and question our assumptions. On the other hand, neither a detailed and specific federal public infrastructure *policy* nor a national *plan* seems desirable or feasible. Of course we can, and should, define our public works needs better. But this should be done in the context of such other competing claims as defense, human resource development, and private sector investment. I would modestly suggest that the federal budget continues to be an excellent vehicle for this process. Of course the budget process is slow, inefficient, complex, and political. But in a free society that is the price we pay for democratic choices. It is in this sense that I do not want to exclude public infrastructure policy from the national debate; rather, quite the contrary, to include it. During the rest of this conference strong arguments will be made for a greater commitment to infrastructure and, I would expect, more federal dollars as part of that commitment. If the cause is just and the arguments convincing, there should be no temptation to avoid the normal budgetary process. Those who have some lingering doubts may look elsewhere for guidance. As Woody Allen once said, "If only God would give me some clear sign! Like making a large deposit in my name at a Swiss bank."[4]

REFERENCES

1. ACIR. 1983. Financing Public Physical Infrastructure. U.S. Advisory Commission on Intergovernmental Relations. Washington, D.C. (Draft report.)
2. U.S. Congressional Budget Office. 1983. Public Works Infrastructure. Policy Issues for the 1980s. U.S. Government Printing Office. Washington, D.C.
3. U.S. Congressional Budget Office. 1983. The Federal Government in a Federal System: Current Intergovernmental Programs and Options for Change. U.S. Government Printing Office. Washington, D.C.
4. PETER, L. J. 1980. Peter's Quotations. Bantam edit.: 155. William Morrow and Company, Inc. New York, N.Y.

Look Ahead, Never Back

RICHARD J. SULLIVAN

Committee on Public Works and Transportation
United States House of Representatives
2165 Rayburn Office Building
Washington, D.C. 20515

I was going to say I am from the federal government and I am here to help you, but I think I had better classify myself after a character in that well-known space series: *Star Wars*, *Return of the Jedi*, and *The Empire Strikes Back*. You, my friends, may call me Darth Vader because for 27 years of my life I have been counsel to a distinguished committee in Washington whose title may be a misnomer today. It is the Committee on Public Works and Transportation. We thought all those years in our misbegotten way that we were developing this country for a greater good of each and every one of you, for your children, and your grandchildren to come. We thought, when we authorized the highways that linked this nation and developed its economy making it the greatest automobile center in the world, that we were achieving some good for the country. When we attempted in our own feeble way back in the 50s, despite administration pressure, to develop a needful water program so you and your children would not die of polluted water, we thought we were helping the nation.

When we were developing our nation's port system including your great port of the city of New York, when we poured millions of dollars into clearing up your rotted ports in this area and developed a highway system to link this state from one end to the other, we thought we were doing some good.

Today suddenly in 1983 we find a new word—infrastructure. There is nothing new about infrastructure. It is simply the fundamental basis on which this country was built—public works.

I heard a distinguished public servant of your state stand up here and say: This is too costly. It was overbuilt. The charge of keeping it is too great. I deny each and every premise that gentleman made. He is totally incorrect. If we had not built this country beginning with the Atlantic and going to the Pacific coast and from one border to the other, you would still be on the shore of Manhattan Island. Let me tell you why.

If we were like God, had godlike vision, then those people 100 years ago that were trying to develop this country could have planned differently. They did not have the vision. They did the best they could. Do not tell me about Cleveland, Ohio, now that people are moving out. Do not tell me about New York because people are moving out. Do not tell me about deteriorating subway systems or sewer systems. Right across the river in Hoboken, in Patterson, and other parts of the country, those systems were built to help the

12

development of the country at the time and they achieved the purpose. Do not tell me the cost is too great. No cost is too great when you bring to a nation's people social and economic ease that helps them live as better human beings. We are still struggling to do that today. Do not tell me that cost is too great. I gainsay it. I deny it.

Do not tell me the cost of maintenance is going to be too great because we in Washington, if you study what we are doing, have been recognizing that factor for a long, long time. Let us talk about the U.S. Army Corps of Engineers projects, the much maligned "pork barrel"—a misnomer. Misnamed by those who do not understand what the projects do or their meaning.

The planning that helped the south, the north, the east, and the west of this country had a meaning and an effect. Those projects built by the Corps of Engineers saved thousands of lives, saved millions of dollars in properties, and now today, they are considered pork barrel. Nonsense. I do not intend to be defensive. It is not my style. But I sat here and I was amazed. I was aghast to hear these comments of this distinguished gentleman. Do not talk to me about the Bureau of the Budget. We have been fighting the Bureau of the Budget for 27 years, a great organization and badly needed because without the Bureau of the Budget we could not control the financial way this country runs. We in Congress followed their process and set up the committees on the budget in the House and the Senate.

I say to each and every one of you at the beginning of this conference, there is one thing you have got to understand. Find the way to get your local people and your state people and your federal people to get involved and give them the message that the need for public works still exists. I will tell you why the need still exists. However, I want to get to one more point before I do and it is simply this.

I want to point out to you with pride that we have built almost 41,000 miles of interstate system in this country. It linked all our major cities, over 50,000 in population. Go talk to the people in southern California. Talk to the businessmen, to the industries. How would they like the highway system taken out of southern California. Go to those parts or at least those sections of the country never linked before and ask the people in the trucking business, the automotive business, and any other form of business how they would like it taken out of their area.

For two years our chairman, Jim Howard, the ranking Republican member of the Transportation Subcommittee at the time, Congressman Schuster, and the Secretary of Transportation, Drew Lewis, fought with the present administration for an increase in the gasoline tax. We got an additional five cents. For what purpose? To build new systems? No, there is no need to build a larger interstate system. There is a need to maintain the system so it does not deteriorate. Do not talk to me about the fact that we do not recognize the need to apply cost factors because part of the benefit-cost ratio of the Corps of Engineers projects involves upkeep by local people, maintenance and local contribution. A major bill is about to be reported from the Public Works Committee, the first meaningful water bill in seven years, which embodies all the points mentioned above. Let me point out that through administration after administration, we have ignored one of the greatest problems in this country, and that problem is the proper use of water. Since the beginning of time there has only been so much water on this earth. We pollute it. We contaminate it. We misuse it. If we do not address ourselves to it shortly we will find ourselves in one hell of a box.

That is what this legislation addresses.

We do indeed recognize cost factors, benefit factors, and maintenance.

These same standards developed for every program in the committee apply to our airport programs, public buildings program, and every item under jurisdiction.

I was not going to get into these comments. I came with an entirely different tenet in mind, but I have to let you know there is another side to the coin and I am here to tell it to you.

I hold in my hands a series of bills that have been introduced in Congress over the last couple of years, going from a capital program to public works development to local participation to block grants to studies covering one subject—infrastructure.

Since the beginning of this country to today, almost a trillion dollars have been spent in various forms of public works. There has been no inventory of that program; no real look at what happened to it, or where it goes. One of the things we want to try to do is take a look at where we have been, so we can look to the future and see where we are going and where we must go.

Will future programs still be federal, part federal, or all state? These are the issues that I think will be addressed in the remaining days of the 1980s.

I think eventually we will evolve some sort of a legislative process that will recognize the need to maintain and to operate and to continue the infrastructure that we have created. How much more has to built is problematical. I leave that to the experts—to the engineers, to the scientists; and remember, research is a major portion of what is going to come in the future. I leave it to all of these to discover the answer.

The future is ours. The vista is endless. The challenge is great, but the task is ours. So is the reward.

Part I: General Discussion

Federal Perspectives

Moderator: EDWARD V. REGAN

Office of the Comptroller
The State of New York
A. E. Smith Building
Albany, New York 12236

B. BIRDSALL (*Steinman Engineering Firm, New York, N.Y.*): It's very good to hear that there will be, in the future, legislative and institutional requirements providing funds for maintenance. The continuation of those requirements presumably must depend on a continuation of public awareness and support. I would like to know if we also have a program going to discover a way to maintain public awareness of the need for maintenance funds.

R. J. SULLIVAN (*Committee on Public Works and Transportation, U.S. House of Representatives, Washington, D.C.*): The answer is yes, in the sense that the legislation we've been passing lately, as I talked about before, such as our highway program, now requires funding specifically for the four Rs — rehabilitation, repair, reprovement, and restoration. That's number one. Number two, in the new water bill that's coming out, we specifically require for the first time, prior to being made eligible, that the local people or the state people contribute a user fee of some type. And for the first time in a number of years we require in a major port bill that after a certain depth is reached and federal funds come into the picture, user fees also come into the picture by the local people. Finally there are many organizations in Washington, allowed to have their own form of developing programs, that stress the very point you are talking about.

W. C. WRIGHT (*Metropolitan Studies Program, Syracuse University, Syracuse, N.Y.*): There's been a lot of talk and increasing public debate about privatization as a response to some of the problems that we're having with the infrastructure. In other words, going to the private sector to either purchase or lease facilities that the public now owns and then operate them. I'd like to have some legislative viewpoint on what you feel about the privatization issue.

R. J. SULLIVAN: You're talking about private funding coming in to the extent that it will replace federal money?

W. C. WRIGHT: No, actually I'm talking about the private sector operating, maintaining, and taking over public facilities, such as a wastewater treatment plant, and maintaining the parks.

R. J. SULLIVAN: My answer to that will be a simple one: if the cost would be no greater than the public charge would be, I'm all in favor. The more the private sector comes into the picture I think the less federal funds have to be expended. We have a leasing program now in the Public Building Program that basically gets the private sector in that way. We've given a lot of thought to what you're saying, but we have to. You have your own program right here in New York. Wasn't that an issue that was brought up recently about your convention center and private factoring? Your point, I think, is to go back to some state or local government control.

Our concern is if you get into the private sector, what will the cost be to the general public? Otherwise it's a commendable thought. I don't know how good an answer that is, but that's what it is at the present time.

D. G. MATHIASEN (*Office of Management and Budget, Washington, D.C.*): I really have nothing to add to that. I think that, without going to the theory of public goods, there are some things that must be financed through government because they are shared and cannot be easily split up.

On the other hand, I would like to point out one of my favorite examples—speaking as an economist and a student, not as someone who believes in public versus private sector in an ideological sense. Most developed countries, all so far as I know, have telephone systems that are public. We have one that's private, and it seems to be the best there is, which I think is an interesting illustration of the fundamental point. There may be some public goods that do not have to be.

UNIDENTIFIED SPEAKER: I address my question to Mr. Sullivan. Could you give us a relative timetable as to what you see as the potential track on a water bill? And do you see any of the block-grants concept that was discussed being included in anything that may come out?

R. J. SULLIVAN: The committee has reported out the water bill; it has to go to the Interior Committee, to the Ways and Means Committee, and maybe to one other comittee, Merchant Marine. The senators moved their own water bill. That's already out: hopefully we could be on the floor with the legislation in March of 1984, and we're really going to attempt to get a bill through by the end of the year. As I said before, first, without it we're in serious trouble in our whole water program. This is going to tie in with the Water Pollution Bill by the way. Second, we're seven years behind, and if we go any further, as was pointed out by the opening speaker, the cost is going to be astronomical. As to tying in with block grants, I think in some way—because the Senate's position is really strong on that—you could get up to some form of block grants in some shades of the program. That's basically as I can see it now.

B. ROGAN (*Brooklyn Union Gas Company, Brooklyn, N.Y.*): With all these infrastructure rehabilitation programs and the fundings, we're concerned with the relocation expenses. That's costing us as a utility an excess number of dollars that we have to pass on to the rate payers. Is there any funding in there where the utilities can be reimbursed for these relocation expenses?

R. J. SULLIVAN: I guarantee to you they will be reimbursed in some form; they're very effective. In the 1956 act, we took care of them as we will in these other programs. In addition to which, the average citizen and the small businessman is going to be taken care of. In 1970 we passed the Uniform

Relocation Act. It's been fairly effective; we're reviewing it now with the support of the budget people. I might add, it has already passed the Senate, and I think will pass the House next year and be signed by the president. That will take care of your small businessman and your ordinary citizen. Utilities will be taken care of too, I think.

    B. ROGAN: About when?

    R. J. SULLIVAN: I can't tell you when, but I tell you, you will be.

Preserving New York State's Transportation Infrastructure

JAMES L. LAROCCA

Office of the Commissioner
Department of Transportation
The State of New York
1220 Washington Avenue
Albany, New York 12232

I do appreciate the opportunity to address this distinguished gathering, but at the same time I must admit to some misgivings about my assigned topic.

I have been asked to speak on "preserving New York State's transportation infrastructure." My misgivings stem not from unfamiliarity with the subject — which may or may not be the case, depending on who you talk to — but from my self-imposed task of trying to sound a fresh note after many months of talking about little else.

Infrastructure . . . I do not particularly like the word. To some ears it may sound elitist and perhaps a bit intimidating. I would like to see us go back to talking about public works. Or transportation facilities. For many years, in fact until 1967, my predecessors in this post were known as state superintendents of public works.

But lay that aside. My prime message to you today is that, after many years of neglect, and after months of effort to inform the voting public, we now have the means — the Rebuild New York Bond Issue — to *begin* to correct massive deficiencies in our roads, bridges, and other elements of the "whatch-amacallit."

Notice that I say "begin." The $1.25 billion in bond funds approved by the voters a month ago [November 1983] will serve as the nucleus of a five-year, $7.4 billion Rebuild New York Program.

This is all very well and good, but a study released last summer by Senator D'Amato pegs our public works restoration needs in New York — including water and sewer systems and all jurisdictions — at a daunting $35 billion over the next several years.

As I say, we can now mount a good beginning to the herculean task we face. Rebuild New York bond funds will enable us to attract the maximum in newly expanded federal aid without resort to increased state taxes or the draining of other state programs.

The $7.4 billion rebuild program will include some $6.5 billion for state and local roads and bridges, $520 million for transit facilities, $61 million for railroads, $170 million for airports, and $96 million for ports and waterways. Federal funds will constitute more than half the total, or $4.2 billion.

To give you an idea of the scope of the work ahead, I would like to focus for a moment on just one aspect of our endeavors — on bridges. Here in New York City especially, with four of its five boroughs on islands, bridges comprise one of the most compelling examples of the public's dependence on serviceable transportation facilities. Serviceable, but for how long, without heroic measures?

One factor that is causing a steady increase in the number of deteriorated bridges, not just in New York City but throughout the state, is their age distribution. There were two peaks to bridge building in New York. The growth of auto and truck traffic in the 1920s led to the first great bridge-building period, which reached its apex during the depression. Over 1800 bridges were built in New York between 1925 and 1939. They are reaching the end of their design life now. While many in this group have been replaced, we will be dealing with the remainder for the rest of the decade and beyond.

Our best estimates indicate that even the record program levels that will be made possible by the Rebuild New York Program will not enable us to keep pace with deterioration of bridges, much less allow us to reduce the backlog of structurally deficient and functionally obsolete bridges. Starting with a current need of $1.8 billion, if the rate of deterioration and planned rehabilitation continues, at the end of 1986 our bridge needs will have *increased* to $2.1 billion.

Moreover, if we are not able to arrest through improved maintenance the deterioration rate of the large number of interstate bridges built in the 1960s, we may be headed toward the shutdown of major portions of the highway system in the years ahead.

These gloomy statistics are reflected in Federal Highway Administration reports. The latest available FHWA bridge report shows that New York has more deficient bridges on the federal-aid system than any other state. The report lists 3308 of our bridges as deficient, or 38%, which is 1000 more deficient bridges than in the next closest state. Another tabulation shows that New York has almost twice as many structurally deficient interstate bridges as any other state — about 30% of the total. In the next worst state, only 16% of the interstate bridges are deficient. FHWA estimates that over $500 million is needed to rehabilitate New York's interstate bridges alone. This is almost four times the amount needed by any other state.

How can New York State extricate itself?

For the moment — or rather, for the next five years — we have the $7.4 billion program sparked by the Rebuild New York Bond Issue. Let me repeat, for emphasis, this is a good start. Last year only 1% of the state's resources were allocated to make the highway and bridge improvements required to sustain commerce and industry throughout the state. If state policy were changed to devote only 2% of its resources to the highway system, an additional $200 million annually could be made available for needed highway improvements.

Various other funding mechanisms apart from periodic bond issues have been mentioned. These will certainly be scrutinized as we attempt to sustain the momentum of the five-year Rebuild New York Program.

Without indicating any preference, here are some approaches:

- Increasing highway use taxes and fees. The Automobile Association of America urges that such revenues be specifically dedicated to highway purposes.
- Issuance of bonds by the Thruway Authority for nonthruway use. This has been done already, on a small scale.
- Pledging assured federal aid toward support of new state highway bonds. The Metropolitan Transportation Authority now sells bonds on the strength of the state's commitment to funding transit capital programs. This is called service contract bonding.
- Retaining the state gross receipts tax on oil companies, now scheduled to expire in 1985, and dedicating these revenues to transportation projects.

These are not new ideas. But old or new, we must in this decade decide how we shall meet the never-ending challenge of decaying pavements and structures. Hand-to-mouth and year-to-year measures will not do.

The Rebuild New York Program is fine for the near term. But let us start to look beyond it. Let us look hard at the long term.

That, I think, is the fresh note I said at the beginning I might attempt.

Infrastructure
Local Government Role

CARL S. YOUNG

Office of the County Executive
Government Plaza
Post Office Box 1766
Binghamton, New York 13902

Local government has a unique and important role in the construction, reconstruction, and maintenance of the infrastructure system in America. This level of government has the responsibility for virtually every type of infrastructure and can accurately relate to the important needs of the local citizenry.

Our nation's deteriorating infrastructure, which has recently received considerable publicity, has a significant impact on county, town, village, and city governments. To address its infrastructure needs, local government must define the problems, develop a plan, implement the plan, and institute a maintenance and preservation program. Objectives can be best met by extensive communication with the federal and state governments as they establish infrastructure policies and by integrating local policy, programs, and funding with those of the respective governments.

BROOME COUNTY GOVERNMENT

By way of background, Broome County is located in upstate New York directly south of Syracuse on the northern border of Pennsylvania. The county has a population of 213,000 as of 1980, with Binghamton its largest city. Broome County, in many ways, is a typical county in the Northeast with a blend of urban, suburban, and rural areas.

The county government employs 2000 people full time and will have a 1984 budget of approximately $130 million. Broome County has major responsibilities for infrastructure systems including roads, bridges, an airport, all county jails, mass transit, community-college facilities, parks, flood-control dams, and many public buildings. Water and sewer systems are maintained by separate water districts.

Like many local municipalities, Broome County is facing the decay of many of its infrastructure systems. On February 6, 1983, our major newspaper, the *Binghamton Press*, did a 20-page supplement in their Sunday issue on the county's infrastructure problems.[1] They estimated that it would take $678 million to repair the existing infrastructure systems adequately. This broke down as follows:

21

Roads, sidewalks, guide rails—$284 million.
Sewers and storm drains—$197 million.
Bridges—$77 million.
Water systems—$48 million.
Refuse disposal—$40 million.
Public buildings—$32 million.

This works out to a cost of $8690 per family in Broome County, and about six times the county's total annual budget.

DEFINE THE PROBLEMS

Although there has been much publicity on the needs and costs of addressing the infrastructure problems on the national level (cost estimates for the remainder of the decade range from a low of $400 billion to a high of $1-3 trillion),[2] the magnitude of the local problem, severity of condition, and extent of cost must be defined by the local governmental owner.

Problem definition may be accomplished by utilizing internal technical staffing, private consultants, intergovernmental sharing of resources, and *ad hoc* committees, including membership from the private sector. Another method is to enlist the aid of any established planning or technical organization. For example, the local Municipal Planning Organization (MPO), under a program of the Federal Highway Administration (FHWA), is known as the Binghamton Metropolitan Transportation Study (BMTS). The BMTS has staff expertise on transportation planning and, by working in conjunction with the local New York State Department of Transportation staff planners and engineers, is a valuable resource on transportation matters including highway, bridge, and drainage problems.

Broome County government has established condition-inspection programs utilizing internal technical and professional staffing. Road, bridge, and building condition inspection is performed periodically with conditions documented. Problems requiring specialized expertise are developed into a scope of service, and outside consulting firms are retained to analyze and define alternative solutions further.

As a result of the problem-definition effort in Broome County, we realize that the task of addressing infrastructure needs is enormous. As an example, the county maintains 337 miles of roads and it is estimated that 80% of this system needs rehabilitation. The cost of repairing and upgrading the roads varies from several hundred thousand dollars per mile to two million dollars per mile, depending on the condition of the road and related factors.

DEVELOP A PLAN

A logical and important sequential effort to problem definition is plan development. Local governmental officials have a responsibility to decide what needs rehabilitation or replacement and to determine the necessity and importance of additional or expanded infrastructure based on local need.

Factors such as safety, essential services, environmental impacts, financial impacts, and social impacts must be considered in developing alternatives for problem solution. In addition, the needs must be given priority ranking, with the most urgent problems addressed first. All local governments have fixed or limited resources, and it is neither possible nor prudent to attempt to address every need immediately.

An informal method used by Broome County is to classify needs into three categories: immediate, short term, and long term. Immediate needs are those that cannot be postponed, for example, a safety issue such as a structurally deficient bridge on a critical highway or replacement of certain sections of guide rail in critical areas. Other immediate needs may relate to environmental reasons, for example, the collection, containment, and treatment of landfill refuse leachate to preclude impact to groundwater. Still another immediate need may derive from financial considerations, i.e., to repair or replace a deficient roof to prevent extensive damage to a public building and its contents.

Short-term needs (1–3 years) are problems that are important but do not need to be done immediately — for example, roadway rehabilitation to preclude further deterioration — or that, if left unattended, will lead to a future safety problem.

Long-term needs relate to items that can be systematically addressed and planned as a rehabilitation, replacement, or expansion project and that will not need implementation in the short term. For example, Broome County is planning a resource recovery program which is intended to be a cost-effective and environmentally safe system for refuse disposal.

As a culmination of this effort, Broome County has a 6-year Capital Improvement Program which is reviewed and modified annually as part of the budget process. Each major component of county responsibility is listed with a brief project description, total cost estimate, and breakdown of anticipated funding from federal, state, and county sources. A specific component of this process is our 10-year plan for repair and replacement of bridges for which the county has responsibility.

Available funding is a vitally important ingredient in establishing priorities. It is in this area that the integration of federal, state, and local policies and programs must be realized. As indicated previously, local government has limited resources. As a practical matter, current means of raising revenues at the local level are, with few expections, by property assessment and local sales tax.

User fees are not a means of raising revenues in Broome County, with minor exceptions being park-entrance fees and bus fares. Typically these only supplement operational budgets. Given the current means of raising revenue, local government officials must do everything possible to increase the tax base.

Local government and its representatives need to become part of the process to influence federal and state policies. The National Association of

Counties (NACO),[a] at its conference in February of 1983, adopted an interim policy resolution on infrastructure needs, which is summarized as follows:

- Local government infrastructure needs are too large for local governments to handle solely with their own resources.
- County governments have the responsibility for major portions of our nation's infrastructure system and should be involved from the start with the development and implementation of national policy.
- Rural and urban needs should be taken into account in an equitable manner in the development of national policies and programs.
- Local governments should qualify for public works grants and loans primarily on the basis of their infrastructure needs, but also including unemployment factors.
- The federal government should move to consolidate infrastructure grants and loan programs with the goal of maximizing local government flexibility, decision making, and priority setting.
- The tax-exempt status of municipal bonds should not be changed in any aspect of infrastructure financing legislation.
- Local government matching requirements should be minimized especially for economically depressed areas with a demonstrated inability to pay.
- Federal seed funds for infrastructure banks should supplement rather than replace existing grant programs.

This national organization is supportive of an increased federal role in assisting all levels of government to meet our nation's infrastructure needs. Of all levels of government, the federal government is probably the most fragmented in its approach to the infrastructure problems and this results in problems and inefficiencies among the other levels of governments. NACO generally supports federal efforts to survey our infrastructure needs on a state-by-state basis, thus assuring the involvement of local government officials, increased federal funding for infrastructure projects, better coordination of public works programs among all levels of government, and a voluntary system of infrastructure banks at the state level with assurances of local government official representation.

One strong effort that the Broome County community is working on is a proposed $10,000,000 industrial park. This effort is in conjunction with both federal and state programs [for example, the Economic Development Administration (EDA) and the recently approved New York State Transportation Bond Act]. This proposed industrial park will create several thousand jobs and will increase the county tax base.

---

[a] The National Association of Counties is the only national organization representing county government in the United States. Through its membership, urban, suburban, and rural counties join together to build effective, responsive county government. The goals of the organization are to improve county governments; serve as the national spokesman for county government; act as a liaison between the nation's counties and other levels of government; and achieve public understanding on the role of counties in the federal system.

IMPLEMENT THE PLAN

As the infrastructure plan is being formalized, it is necessary to consider how it will be implemented. A realistic schedule should be established that considers the limits of financial resources and the availability of personnel resources (including technical and administrative personnel). Also, it is important to consider "life cycle costing," to the extent possible, in addressing the problems. Perhaps infrastructure systems will have to be built, or rebuilt, to a higher standard than previously contemplated. Short-sighted economic conditions coupled with poor workmanship, inadequate materials, and design errors have led to the deterioration of many infrastructure systems before their design life was achieved. It is vitally important to have sound professional design, quality materials, proper construction techniques, and thorough inspection to insure that the public is receiving the most benefit for the money invested.

MAINTENANCE AND PRESERVATION

Perhaps the most important phase of the infrastructure issue, but one that usually does not receive notable attention, is the perpetual maintenance of the infrastructure system. As previously mentioned, the local government has every type of infrastructure and it is imperative that it preserves what it owns. Expensive rehabilitation or replacement is too costly an investment to ignore or neglect.

Local government must commit the necessary resources to carry out the maintenance function. Adequate resources, including the proper personnel, equipment, and supplies, must be coupled with proper maintenance techniques that emphasize training and state-of-the-art methodology.

Methods of financing must be considered when addressing the operational and maintenance functions required to preserve the initial capital investment. Lawmakers should not arbitrarily cut operational and maintenance budgets, but should provide administrators with sufficient resources to maintain an enormously large investment.

Each local government has the responsibility to maintain and preserve its infrastructure and should take the responsibility seriously. Local governmental officials must institute programs for regular and scheduled condition inspections, for scheduled proper maintenance, for timely repairs performed professionally, and for necessary replacement performed professionally with "life cycle costing" considered.

In conclusion, let me underscore the need to develop a plan, and then to *carry it out*. It is frequently tempting, when preparing an annual budget, to allow political considerations (i.e., too great a tax rate impact) to lead to "postponement" of projects. A second or a third such postponement usually follows. Ultimately, you then find yourself facing an "infrastructure crisis," and spending more in the long run than would have been the case had you adhered to your plan.

Lest we blame the politicians too much for this shortcoming in the system, let us keep in mind that *all* of us, taxpayers and officeholders, are the ones who insist on those lower taxes. We must *all* appreciate the fact that there simply is *no free lunch.* If we want good roads, bridges, sewers, industrial parks, we will have to pay for them. And in paying for them *today*, we assure ourselves of our long-term economic vitality, as well as maintaining a system that is safe.

While we must all seek ways to control taxes and make the delivery of services more cost effective, I think New Yorkers should stop apologizing for their taxes and start boasting about our quality of life. From the quality of our education system to our system of transportation, New York is a leader in this country. Continued investment will keep us a leader.

REFERENCES

1.   1983. The Road to Ruin. Binghamton Press (February 6).
2.   1983. Infrastructure estimates slashed. Engineering News Record (May 5): 10–11.

Infrastructure Issues Facing the City of New York

ROBERT F. WAGNER, JR.[a]

Office of the Deputy Mayor for Policy
The City of New York
City Hall
New York, New York 10007

For New York City, rebuilding our infrastructure is a problem that ranks in importance only behind the city's fiscal health in the immediate future and that in the long term may prove more difficult to solve.

The city's capital plant is the platform on which our economy rests; it is the basis for delivery of municipal services; it is the anchor of neighborhoods. When it breaks down, essential activities come to a halt. When it is neglected, there is not only inconvenience but also the possibility of real danger. The collapse of the Mianus Bridge in Connecticut dramatized just how real the possibility of danger can be. We in New York City saw a similar event back in 1974 when a major section of the West Side Highway collapsed, though fortunately no lives were lost. And just last summer, water main breaks in midtown Manhattan closed streets and subways, caused a blackout, and seriously disrupted business.

New York's capital needs are enormous. The extent and variety of our infrastructure are extraordinary:

- 47 waterway bridges and 2057 highway bridges and elevated structures.
- A water supply system that delivers 1.45 billion gallons of water a day from a reservoir system of 1956 square miles. It delivers water through two tunnels (a third is under construction), 32 million linear feet of trunk and distribution mains, and 20,000 trunk valves.
- 6100 miles of sewers, 12 operating water pollution control plants and two more under construction, 80 sewage pumping stations, and 450 combined sewer overflow regulators.
- 6200 miles of paved streets which cover approximately 30% of the city's land.
- 6700 subway cars which ride on 232 miles of track (137 miles underground, 72 miles elevated, and 23 miles open bed) and 4560 buses.
- An estimated 3500 acres of landfill, and nine marine transfer stations.
- Over 25,000 acres of parkland.

Just as the extent of the capital plant is extraordinary, so has been its ne-

---

[a] Present affiliation: The Twentieth Century Fund, 41 East 70th Street, New York, N.Y. 10021.

glect. In 1978, the Koch administration found a pattern of neglect almost frightening in its extent. The desirable rate for repaving streets is once every 25 to 50 years, depending on usage. In 1978 the city was repaving streets at the rate of once every 200 years. Engineers say a water main will require replacement probably every 100 years. In 1978 we were replacing water mains at the rate of once every 296 years. in 1978 the state found 135 waterway bridges and highway structures to be in poor condition and requiring major reconstruction. The same pattern would apply to all other parts of the city's physical plant.

One of the major aims of the Koch administration has been to reverse this pattern of neglect and decay, and I believe with some success. In fiscal 1977, the city's capital program — which provides funds for building and rebuilding streets, highways, bridges, sewers, water mains, mass transit, and other city assets — totaled $349 million, of which $168 million were city funds. In 1983, for the second year in a row, the capital program exceeded $1.6 billion. Of this amount, city funds were approximately $1.2 billion in each year.

Overall, between 1979 and 1983, New York initiated capital projects totaling more than $6.4 billion — almost two-and-one-half times what had been done in the five previous years. If the portion of the New York City Transit Authority's (which is responsible for operating bus and subway systems in the city and is a constituent agency of the Metropolitan Transportation Authority, a state agency responsible for coordination of the regional transit system) capital program not reflected in the city's capital budget is added, the record is even more impressive — $8.5 billion or over three times what had been committed in the previous five years. (Prior to fiscal 1982, the entire Transit Authority capital program was funded through the city's capital budget. Since then, the Metropolitan Transportation Authority has begun to raise its own capital funds for Transit Authority projects.)

In developing its policy for capital investments in 1978, the current city administration established two basic priorities: reconstruction and rehabilitation of existing assets, as opposed to new construction, and improvements to the city's infrastructure that support, improve, or reduce the cost of city operations.

In addition to setting clear overall priorities, the city has, over the last several years, extended its planning horizon and developed a 10-year capital plan to improve planning for the future and to identify the magnitude of need for capital investments. As far as I know, New York is the only city in the United States that attempts to plan its capital budget decisions on a 10-year time horizon. Our planning effort attempts to establish standards for annual capital investments that ensure that, within the limits of available financing, appropriate replacement cycles are maintained and operational changes and needed investments are planned to meet future demand. The current 10-year plan contemplates almost $35 billion in capital investments over the next 10 years. Over 75% of this amount is anticipated to be spent for improvements to the city's infrastructure. Although the amount is large, it nonetheless represents a compromise between what New York can afford based upon our assessment of available financing over the 10-year period, and what we believe we could usefully spend, which we have estimated is about $55 billion over the decade. the city believes that if it can raise the expected $35 billion from federal, state, and city financing sources, significant progress will be made in rebuilding the city. But at the same time it has to be kept in mind that even with all that has been done, even assuming the city will be able to fund its ambitious $35 billion program, there will be significant capital needs not met.

Since 1978, the city has been able to raise the necessary funds to meet its capital program largely through the Municipal Assistance Corporation (MAC) (organized in 1975 by the state of New York to provide financing assistance for the city) and $1.6 billion in federal loan guarantees secured in 1978. Future success in financing the city's capital requirements depends upon the city's continuing market expansion beyond the $1.052 billion that New York has been able to borrow since reentering the public long-term credit market in 1981. Our current plan anticipates issuances of general obligation bonds in excess of $1.1 billion annually beginning in fiscal 1986. In addition, legislation has been proposed to create a state water finance authority, which would provide a mechanism to raise an additional $300 million annually through water and sewer bonds backed by user fees.

We have also taken some additional steps to finance our capital program, many of them using aspects of federal tax policy. For example, during 1982 the city, consistent with the "safe-harbor" leasing provisions of the Economic Recovery Act of 1981, entered into a tax benefit transfer agreement with a private corporation with respect to two new ferry boats. The transaction netted the city approximately $1.4 million. The city continues to evaluate whether traditional leverage leasing should be considered for other types of equipment and facilities.

We are also exploring other possible financing approaches. The city recently selected a financial advisor in connection with the $226 million Brooklyn Navy Yard Resource Recovery Project. One of the principal financing objectives will be vendor or third-party equity participation in the project to minimize the amount of city bond financing required.

We are reviewing the use of vendor financing to purchase certain office and computer equipment. We plan to introduce an amendment to the state constitution which would allow the issuance of term (sinking fund) bonds for any purpose for which serial bonds may be used. Right now, under state law, term bonds can only be used to finance water, docks, and rapid-transit projects, so that this change would provide us with greater flexibility to meet the demands of the market. With the help of our financial advisers, we are examining the possibility of using tax-exempt commercial paper similar to MAC's successful $250 million commercial paper program.

The city is committed in its determination to rebuild its physical plant, particularly its infrastructure. We have made progress—in our planning, in our spending, and in our financing. We are determined to build on this record. But, to achieve the goals we have already set as well as to meet the real needs not included in the city's 10-year plan, we will need the help of the federal government.

Earlier I mentioned that we believe that over the next 10 years we can advance a $35 billion capital program. As we see it today, $17.4 billion would come from city sources, $7.2 billion would come from sources such as fare-backed bonds and Triborough Bridge and Tunnel Authority (a state authority responsible for seven toll bridges and two tunnels within New York City) bonds, $1.4 billion from state sources, $696 million from private sources, and $7.9 billion from the federal government. The bulk of federal support would come in two traditional areas of federal infrastructure assistance—transit and water pollution control. Achieving the anticipated level of federal support, while far from impossible, will require steady increases in funding over the next several years.

Based on our assessment of the city's physical plant, an additional $20 billion would be required to satisfy all the needs that we have identified. Additional federal expenditures for infrastructure would allow us to begin to deal with these needs as well as to allow states and localities to increase and accelerate local capital programs.

I believe there is a compelling case for the federal government to increase its direct assistance for local and state capital needs. I also believe the federal government has a very definite role to play in developing financing mechanisms to assist state and local governments in their own borrowing efforts.

What has become clear over recent years is that the problems confronted by an older city like New York are shared by the rest of the nation. Throughout America—perhaps because as a nation we have always looked to the future rather than the past—maintenance has been deferred, rebuilding put off; instead we have concentrated on new projects and new construction. Time has caught up with us. Now report after report has appeared documenting the state of America's bridges and highways. A problem once thought of as belonging only to the Northeast and Midwest has now become a problem of the Sunbelt as well.

Let me cite two recent studies that give a sense of just how extensive the problem is. According to a recent study by the Council of State Planning Agencies, 8000 miles—or 20%—of the nation's interstate highway system are in need of immediate repair. Another study, conducted by the United States Department of Transportation in 1982, concluded that 45% of the nation's 248,500 bridges are structurally or functionally deficient. And just as the extent of the problem is great, so will be the cost of solving it. Dr. Amitai Etzioni in his recent *An Immodest Agenda: Rebuilding America before the 21st Century* has even suggested that the United States will have to spend $3 trillion over the next 10 years to deal with its infrastructure needs. That means we should spend $300 billion a year.

To put it simply, a national issue of such scope certainly requires federal leadership. What I am arguing for is not federal assumption of the local and state share of infrastructure costs, but rather expanded federal participation. There are more than enough projects to go around. What precisely the federal role should be deserves serious consideration. While clear lines of responsibility generally exist only on organization charts, it is important, in considering greater federal participation, to sort out what level of government should have responsibility for what kinds of projects.

In this context it would make sense for the federal government to adopt the idea of a national capital budget. There is currently no comprehensive framework for taking inventory of public facilities, evaluating their condition, and assigning them priority levels. A federal capital budget would provide such a framework. Sensible budgeting procedures would seem to dictate such an organized method.

Traditionally in the Northeast, the federal government has concentrated its efforts on water pollution control and transportation, including mass transit. More recently, it has expanded into the area of bridge rebuilding. All three are totally appropriate areas for federal involvement. In other areas of the country, particularly in the Southwest, water projects — for irrigation, recreation, flood control, and water supply — have received federal support. There should be a more equitable national policy that would assist those parts of America with water supply systems in place as well as those needing new projects.

Serious consideration should be given also to increased federal involvement in the area of solid waste, particularly the construction of resource recovery plants. Solid waste has become increasingly a regional problem, and that, taken together with the technological complexity and cost of resource recovery plants, would seem to justify a greater federal role.

For those who feel as I do about an expanded federal role, there is reason for some concern these days. In at least one major area of federal activity — water pollution control — we have seen actual reductions. We have also seen decisions that can only make the problems of the infrastructure worse. For example, the federal government's relaxation of trucking regulations with regard to allowable sizes and weights will only accelerate road and bridge deterioration.

Even when positive actions have taken place in Congress, the administration has shown a reluctance to be supportive. The best example of this came with passage of the Five-Cent Gas Tax Bill. Only a month after the bill was signed, the president's 1984 budget proposals threatened to undermine the gas tax benefits. Congress appears to have won the day, but the simple fact that a fight was necessary is hardly reassuring.

Now there is the issue of H.R. 3110, the governmental leasing act of 1983, which would impose more expensive tax treatment of sale-leaseback transactions involving government and other tax-exempt entities. Two issues are troubling about this proposed amendment. One is the issue of fairness; this legislation only applies to the public sector. The other is its potentially very damaging impact on the MTA's ability to continue successfully to use this financing technique as well as what it could do to the city's plans in such areas as resource recovery.

Fighting to keep what we have is hardly what is called for when much more is needed. Part of what we in New York need is an increase of funding in traditional areas of federal capital support — water-pollution control, mass transit, bridge rebuilding, and highway reconstruction. All are areas where there are enormous unmet capital requirements. As I mentioned before, increased financial support in the area of water projects would be desirable. For New York City, it could make an enormous difference. For example, to complete all four stages of the third water tunnel (a total of 60 miles extending from the Kensico reservoir in Westchester, N.Y., to the Red Hook section in Brooklyn) will cost an estimated $4.5 billion (in 1983 dollars). Some level of federal support for this project would free up city capital dollars for other essential programs.

An expanded federal role in the area of solid waste would also be very helpful. We are close to a garbage crisis in New York — not in terms of collecting it but of disposing of it. We have almost run out of places to get rid of it. To deal with this, the Department of Sanitation has put together a plan to build between 7 and 10 resource recovery plants over the next decade. The cost of these plants will be over $2.1 billion.

Before moving off the subject of funding, I should touch on the subjects of mandates and the local share required to obtain federal dollars. The federal government still too often imposes mandates on state and local governments without providing the dollars to cover the cost. Even when it does provide the dollars, it often accompanies those dollars with mandates that keep local governments from dealing with their most urgent needs. Take the case of water pollution control facilities. Because of federal requirements, New York concentrated on the construction of two new facilities — the North River and Red Hook plants — at a time when it should have done much more to upgrade its older facilities, particularly those at Owls Head and Coney Island. As a result, last year the Coney Island plant was within a few minutes of total collapse, an event that would have meant that basements of 250,000 Brooklyn residents would have been flooded with sewage.

As for requiring local matching funds, this is an understandable policy given Congress' concern for local maintenance of effort. However, it can also serve to divert local capital dollars away from the areas of greatest local need. I would hope that the federal government would review the issue and reduce the number of areas where this approach is followed.

Obviously the level of direct funding is important, but helping to make it possible for state and local governments to borrow the dollars required at reasonable rates is also a major issue of concern. The rapid increase in the number of debt-issuing public authorities and the use and abuse of industrial revenue bonds have resulted in a long-term tax-exempt credit market that grew from $42 billion of issuances in 1979 to $75 billion in 1982, an increase in 79% in just four years. This has put local and state governments at a disadvantage in competing for the limited dollars in the public credit markets. It has been hard for those poor, older localities that have the greatest needs. It has meant deferring bond issues or paying excessively high interest rates.

The federal government should reevaluate current tax and fiscal policy to define more clearly the range of qualified tax-exempt issues. This would help prevent state and local governments from being crowded out of the marketplace. The availability of alternative tax-shelter mechanisms for major institutions should also be reexamined. Part of the problem faced by local governments in borrowing has stemmed from commercial banks and property casualty insurers shifting from the tax-exempt market to these alternatives. Obviously, reduced federal borrowing would help open up opportunities for local borrowing.

A new agency, perhaps similar to the Reconstruction Finance Corporation, or some form of federal infrastructure bank should be created to provide capital for the revitalization of American industry and the nation's roads, bridges, and other components of the public plant. Such an agency could provide seed dollars as well as low-interest loans for appropriate projects.

Another area of real potential is in loan guarantees. This approach, which was of extraordinary importance to New York City, could be used to help troubled localities to borrow, providing they met strict federal requirements. One particular guarantee now under discussion concerns allowing the Federal Housing Authority (FHA) to back the bonds of public hospitals. For years this form of financing has been available to voluntary hospitals. Extending it to public hospitals would seem only fair. For New York City it would be of real assistance.

This hardly represents a definitive discussion of how the federal government can make financing easier for local governments, but it does set out two clear policy directions which should be followed: reform of the public credit market (which would also benefit federal revenues) and the creation of several ways to provide money to local governments at a low cost.

Finally, the federal government can help by streamlining rules and regulations that govern infrastructure projects and which all too often result in cost-inflating delays. This is particularly true of environmental regulations which in some cases have become so complex that they cease to serve the goals for which they were adopted and can delay a project in endless legal actions. New York's Westway is a good example of this phenomenon. Last summer, Mayor Koch proposed that Congress enact legislation that would set definite but reasonable limits on the time and actions that can be taken for reviews, hearings, and legal remedies relative to infrastructure projects subject to environmental review. This approach is similar to that adopted by Congress when the Alaska pipeline was built. Avoiding delays saves money, and those savings can go to rebuild more infrastructure.

The condition of the infrastructure of this country is a disgrace, a disgrace from which until very recently we averted attention. Fortunately, that is no longer the case. We have begun the long process of rebuilding our city, of reversing decades of neglect and misguided priorities. But the truth is that we cannot do it alone. We need the help of the federal government. I also believe we deserve it.

Part I: General Discussion
State and Local Government Perspectives

Moderator: EDWARD V. REGAN

Office of the Comptroller
The State of New York
A. E. Smith Building
Albany, New York 12236

B. HABER (*Hardesty & Hanover, New York, N.Y.*): I'd like to make one quick observation first. A theme has come out of this conference from our elected officials and appointed officials, and that is that cutting a ribbon at a new public building is more important than taking credit for painting a bridge. I chair a community planning board in northeast Queens — with a population of approximately 150,000 people — and I can tell you categorically that the people in the community appreciate the fixing of potholes and the rehabilitation of sewers much more than the cutting of a ribbon for a new school. My question very simply is, When considering gasoline prices throughout New York State, and within any given community where the variation can be as much as 10¢ or 15¢ a gallon, is the state considering a small, dedicated tax on gasoline for transportation maintenance?

J. L. LAROCCA (*New York State Department of Transportation, Albany, N.Y.*): I'm not sure how you related the variation of prices to whether or not there would be dedication. This dedication issue was raised throughout the bond issue campaign, and it can be very deceptive. In those states with a dedicated tax coming out of a unitary tax on gasoline where we've seen a stabilization of gasoline consumption, or in other states where the tax is related to the value of gasoline and gasoline prices have come down, there was no stability for the financing that came out of that tax because it still had to go to other sources to deal with inflation and the growth in the size of the programs. So dedication alone does not assure attention to the needs to be served by the dedicated fund. It creates a floor, there's no question about that. But in a state like New York we have a floor anyway. We spent more money last year on these matters than we raised from our highway user taxes.

The specific question is, Is it under consideration? The answer is no, not right now. But some time during the next five years, while we have this Rebuild New York Program in place, we're going to have to deal with the longer term. And one of the things we should look at is a dedication — but a dedication that is related to something that accounts for growth, something that accounts for the flexibility, because if you tie it simply to consumption or value and those things change, you haven't avoided the budgetary problem that we face now every year.

M. S. JETHWANI (*New York City Department of Environmental Protection, New York, N.Y.*): Deputy Mayor Wagner, you mentioned a lot of things about a capital budget process, specifically, that the federal government should have a capital budget process. As you know, in New York City, we have had that process, and our process is no better. But the process we're now talking about concerns the money for future maintenance. Has any thought been given to setting aside a certain percentage of the construction costs — say 5% or 10% — and putting it in a sinking fund for future rehabilitation?

R. F. WAGNER, JR. (*Office of the Mayor, New York, N.Y.*): The issue you raise is a very valid one. I think that the idea of setting aside part of the funding isn't possible given the fact that it would not be eligible for borrowing. Maintenance would not fulfill the legal requirements on periods of probable usefulness for borrowing.

Increasingly, as we put together our capital budget, we've attempted to focus on the issue of not just its impact in terms of capital allocations but what would be required to maintain it. We have in the last year, particularly in terms of bridge maintenance, increased the allocation in the hopes that we can avoid the kind of problem that we had through years of deferred maintenance for those bridges that are now rated in good or excellent condition. We have been doing that with street maintenance as well. We have a ways to go in terms of water pollution control and water main maintenance, but the commissioner in that area is an effective advocate, and hopefully during this year's budget it will get even greater consideration.

Probably within the whole area of the capital plan where this becomes the biggest issue is an area like parks. There we have a vast amount of parkland and yet there have been major cutbacks in terms of maintenance. My guess is that that would have to be the most critical area we will have to deal with. While in the last six years we poured in $242 million, there is still real concern that a lot of that money will be wasted without maintenance to keep it going.

G. A. FOX (*New York Building Congress, New York, N.Y.*): I'd like to address my question to Mr. Wagner. There's a general agreement that the cost of financing is enormous in connection with these projects. Given the complexity of the process and the long time that it takes to get these projects under way, it is apparent that anything you can do to shorten the process (and you referred to the mayor's effort in connection with the approvals) is desirable. Would one of the elements in that regard be assigning on major projects a chief of operations whose sole focus of attention would be to get the third water tunnel built or Westway, or the Metropolitan Transportation Authority program, in order to cut through as much as possible of the bureaucratic jungle and process thicket?

R. F. WAGNER, JR.: It's actually critical in those major projects and even some of the smaller projects that we have an emphasis on project management. This is something we've done much more, in both the city and the Metropolitan Transportation Authority, over the last several years than we did before. In addition to that, we created the Office of Construction in New York City, which has been helpful in terms of moving the projects along. I know that you have worked with Charles Smith, and I think it's been a very productive relationship.

Where the issues become more difficult is on issues such as Westway that go across a whole variety of different agencies and run into a whole variety of different environmental considerations. I think we should look harder at the kind of management structure we have used, and that should be an issue addressed over the next several years.

C. S. Young (*Office of the County Executive, Broome County, Bing-hamton, N.Y.*): I just have a word of supplement to what Mr. Wagner said. For those municipalities that are represented here, I'd strongly recommend that when you have your project managers, keep them somebody whose throat will always be reachable. We in Broome County built a memorial arena, and we hired an outside firm to be our resident Clerk of the Works. The same firm was Clerk of the Works when we built our new office building. And five years later, when the roofs were all leaking and a tremendous cost had to be borne to repair them, lo and behold the firm was defunct as a corporation. There was no way that we could get anything out of them, so the tax-payers have borne nearly $900,000 of repairs that never should have had to be made in the first place.

New York City's Infrastructure

Luncheon Address

EDWARD I. KOCH

Office of the Mayor
The City of New York
City Hall
New York, New York 10007

Welcome to New York City. Nowhere else is infrastructure so vital to the economic prosperity and even survival of the community. We are a city of more than 7 million, encompassing five boroughs held together by the sinews of infrastructure. When I took office in 1978 "infrastructure" was not a household word. Our city capital expenditures, exclusive of federal and state grants, were only $200 million. We could not borrow in the public markets: our credit was no good. Maintenance was deferred, and the natural problems that plagued an infrastructure up to 100 years old began to push service delivery toward collapse.

Today I am proud to say that the city's capital program for 1984 will exceed $1.8 billion, of which $1.3 billion are city funded. Between 1978 and 1983, the city committed $7.2 billion in capital construction, $4.7 billion of which were city funds.

The two principal credit agencies have both given the city investment-grade ratings. Our bonds have consistently been sold at interest rates comparable to higher-rated credits.

I think this background is important because our aggressive capital actions are visible — sometimes causing inconvenience, but visible. People can see what is happening in New York. They know that we are working to do the repairs that were left undone for so many years.

Here is a list of some of the things we have done or are in the process of completing between 1978 and the end of the city's 1983 fiscal year.

Using 100% city funding:

- 300 miles of water mains to expand (25%) or replace (75%) our water supply delivery system were committed to construction at a cost of about $230 million.
- 150 miles of sewers, including new construction in southeast Queens and Staten Island and replacements in Brooklyn, were committed to construction at a cost of about $535 million.
- 2300 lane miles of streets were resurfaced.
- 500 lane miles of streets were totally reconstructed.
- 5 million square yards of repairs were done to the roads (potholes and strip paving).
- $480 million were committed to the third water tunnel.

37

Using partial city funding:

- Over 48 bridges had reconstruction work done on them, for a total of $221 million, $89 million of which were city funds.
- Construction and reconstruction of water pollution control plants were carried out at a cost of $811 million, of which $132 million were city funds. This included five major treatment plants.

Our mass transit system, with a combination of fare-backed revenue bonds, major state appropriations, and some city funds, has completed or ordered:

- 1375 new subway cars, purchased at a cost in excess of $1.4 billion, representing approximately 25% of the current fleet. As you know the first 10 cars arrived last week [November 1983].
- 2324 new buses, all but 170 of which have already been placed in service, representing 50% of the current fleet, were purchased at a cost of $300 million.
- 20 subway stations have been or are being modernized, representing 5% of all stations, at a cost of $50 million.

Only a month ago [November 1983], the voters of this state were asked to approve a $1.25 billion Rebuild New York Bond Act. Observers said it would not pass. As you know, it passed, the first bond act to do so since 1979. (We all know the voters traditionally reject referendums to create additional debt even when a sound purpose can be demonstrated, such as the Prison Bond Act referendum in 1981.)

Why did it pass? I will tell you why. It passed because the voters in New York City have seen what we have done in the past six years. With a margin of more than 70% of the city vote, we were able to overcome the upstate rejection. We did not need the Mianus River Bridge collapse to awaken us — we had already responded to the infrastructure challenge. It takes time to implement a dormant capital program, but we are in high gear.

On a national basis, what we have done in New York must be replicated — but first let me deal with one of the stumbling blocks that we have encountered.

Since the time of the founding fathers, Americans have wisely taken the view that government has an important role to play in maintaining the foundation upon which a thriving private economy can be constructed. But government has neglected its responsibility, and today that foundation is in serious disrepair.

Simply put, we must have a master plan for public improvements — what today is commonly referred to as infrastructure. Our infrastructure, which I define broadly as the basic installations and facilities on which the continuance and growth of a community depend, such as streets, highways, bridges, water tunnels, waste-disposal facilities, and transit systems, is crumbling. My description of the gravity of the situation is quite literal for any one of the tens of millions of people in the northeast corridor who traveled the West Side Highway or the Mianus River Bridge before they collapsed.

The cost to rebuild our infrastructure nationwide is estimated at between

$900 billion and $1 trillion. And, without proper maintenance, the infrastructure just falls apart — literally collapses.

In recent years the nation's approach to this problem has been complicated by its attempts to protect the environment. As a former member of Congress, I strongly supported environmental legislation, and still do. However,
the goal of protecting the environment through environmental impact assessments has often led to conflicting and counterproductive regulations that in-
flate costs dramatically. An unlimited range and number of issues can be
brought to bear on a project to prevent it from ever moving forward. The
environmental acts and seemingly endless legal actions that can be taken by
special interest groups, in some cases, cease to serve the goals for which they
were adopted. In the end, little goes into solving the problem at hand.

We must learn from our mistakes. We must streamline the process in order
to keep our infrastructure safe. Congress must enact legislation that will set
reasonable but definite limits on the time and actions that can be taken for
reviews, hearings, and legal remedies relative to infrastructure projects subject to environmental review. This legislation should clearly set forth requirements for project initiation and early review, as well as precise time frames,
to insure adequate and prompt response. Also, the legislation must identify
the circumstances under which legal or administrative remedies can be sought
in an effort to avoid delay and limit potentially harassing litigation. Such legislation will serve to alleviate our nation's infrastructure woes. Just remember
that the Alaskan pipeline might have lingered like Westway but for the com-
monsense time limitations that Congress imposed on potential litigation.

Let me give you an example — with a solution.

As a result of these procedures, the construction of Westway, a $2 billion
project, has been substantially delayed, costing the city valuable time and
increasing the eventual cost of the project to the taxpayer. It has been estimated by project engineers that even an alternative plan would require the
lengthy and expensive environmental review process to start all over again.
Meanwhile, traffic continues to be snarled for want of this vital missing link
in New York City's transportation network.

Among the most critical problems facing communities today, and which
is certain to be exacerbated in the future, is waste disposal. The environmental
considerations raised by these facilities, without question, are among the most
difficult and elusive. Federal powers through legislative action must be brought
to bear on the decision-making process in planning and constructing these
facilities.

How can the majority of our citizens, then, be assured that major projects,
whether in Texas, New York, or California, will be carried out in a timely
manner with a minimum of costs?

Congress in the past has enacted specific legislation when issues of national importance have been delayed and stymied beyond any reasonable time
limit for a final decision to be made. In two important situations concerning
our energy resources, Congress was compelled to act. In November 1973, by
passing the "Trans-Alaska Pipeline Authorization Act," Congress decided as

a matter of national policy that an adequate review had been conducted, limited further review, and granted the Department of Interior the discretion to issue a permit that would allow the pipeline's construction. Similarly, in 1976, in anticipation of national debate, Congress passed the "Alaska Natural Gas Transportation Act" to provide a process for arriving at a sound decision to select a transport system for delivery of gas to the rest of the United States.

In anticipation of setting national priorities on infrastructure, I believe the foregoing examples should serve as models for legislation that will insure timely initiation and completion of infrastructure projects where such projects are:

- federally funded in whole or in part; or
- locally funded but subject to federal laws requiring issuance of permits or similar approvals.

The legislation should establish a legal and administrative framework within which requirements for project initiation and early reviews are clearly set forth and, in conjunction with these reviews, precise time frames are established to insure adequate and prompt response. The legislation also must identify the circumstances under which legal or administrative remedies can be sought. Such remedies would also be subject to time limits for commencement and subsequent decision. The courts, similar to the provisions of the Trans-Alaska Oil Pipeline legislation, would not be permitted to enjoin a project, and judicial review would be clearly defined as to the following:

- Limit to the time to commence an action challenging the decision to proceed with a project.
- Upon commencement of an action, give preference for adjudication to these actions over all other matters on the court's docket and assign a hearing at the earliest possible date.
- Limit requests for injunctive relief allowed during the proceeding to final adjudication or settlement.
- Require that appeals be made directly to the United States Supreme Court.

If such steps are taken, we can expedite the process to repair and rebuild.

I would also like to emphasize the need to implement long-range planning and identification of the requirements that are needed. The city adopted in 1982, as part of its capital budget and 4-year financial plan, an analysis of capital needs over the next 10 years. This tool allows us to assess our needs as well as look at our resources. We can make well-informed decisions based on facts. I am happy to see that in 1983 New York State enacted a 5-year capital planning process that, beginning in January 1984, will be part of the state budget process.

While Congress has held hearings on the need for a federal capital budget or plan, no legislation has been seriously considered. I think it would be useful to establish long-range planning at the federal level as well. The "ad hoc" way in which capital projects are appropriated leaves a lot to be desired.

Finally I urge that in the planning process we raise our sights to the cities and states of tomorrow. This is not a world's fair "futurama" idea but a realization that we must begin to shape our capital planning into the next century. We must use the planning process to determine what we should consider as alternative delivery systems. We must use our ingenuity to design efficient systems that will improve service, last longer, and cost less.

That is your challenge and mine!

Introduction

PETER C. GOLDMARK, JR.

Office of the Executive Director
The Port Authority of New York and New Jersey
One World Trade Center
New York, New York 10048

The subject of this session is financing the nation's infrastructure requirements. Many of you have been aware for some time that this is a subject that has gradually pushed its way to the front of America's consciousness. It has, in the past 18 months, been on the covers of *Time* and *Newsweek*, and also *Business Week*. It has affected the consciousness of editors' judgments about what is important in a way that I do not think any of us would have predicted three or four years ago. We also have just come to the end of a decade — 1970 to 1980 — when some alarming figures began to pour in. We looked at this record and we saw that, in fact, it was a period of declining investment in many of our core infrastructure systems. This problem and this stage of infrastructure deterioration have now triggered conferences such as this all over the country.

But the most timely bit of news I bring you today in introducing this session comes fittingly enough from the *Wall Street Journal*. In an editorial on November 16 that absolutely astonished me, the *Journal* summarized facts about what happened in terms of bond issues around the country on this 1983 election day. Voters in six states and five local governments approved a total of $2.88 billion in tax-exempt financing, which was by no means a list of all the bond issues that were on ballots in the nation. The *Journal* pointed out that for the second year in a row, more than 85% of all bond issues passed. That was a sharp turnaround from the 1970s. The *Wall Street Journal* also noted that this was the highest proportion of bond issues approved since the year 1960. And although they did not quote a figure, they stated it was clear that the overwhelming majority of these bond issues related in one way or another to repairing our existing capital stock. The *Wall Street Journal* concluded: "It's apparent that voters are listening to calls to replace infrastructure. There's no question that roads, bridges and just about everything else had been neglected in the last 20 years." And this from the *Wall Street Journal* — hardly the trumpet of affirmative government in our society. An editorial worth taking note of and a trend and a vector in the map that I think may be very, very significant.

Before the authors present their papers, I want to take a minute and bring you up to date on one development in terms of financing infrastructure that I think will have relevance for New York and for the Northeast in general. One of the questions that has troubled us all, which Dick Sullivan addressed here earlier and Governor Cuomo alluded to in his speech, is now that we have recognized that there is a massive job to be done, and even though we know most of that job must be done by state and local governments, what is the proper federal role in this task of rebuilding the nation's infrastructure and how do we define it and how do we address it?

In this regard, I simply want to describe to you very briefly an idea that is emerging from a national advisory committee created by the Joint Economic Committee of Congress over a year ago and on which I serve. This idea, in addition to the proposal for a capital budget, has begun to take its place in federal budgetary deliberations. The idea is that Congress should create a national infrastructure corporation. (Congress, you know, has the right to charter independent national corporations.) This national infrastructure corporation could be empowered to raise debt funds and make the proceeds available as loans to state and local governments, either through capitalizing the infrastructure banks some of them are setting up or through financing existing state and local capital programs. Thus, the federal government would seed and catalyze the massive part of the job, the larger part of the job, that will have to be undertaken by state and local governments. The idea here is that a pot of capital, a nut for each state to work with, would be created. The interest on that nut or that seed loan would be borne by the federal government through its annual appropriations process and as part of the federal debt for the period of the program — 20–30 years — whatever it turns out to be; that would be the form of the federal subsidy.

What has attracted several governors and mayors around the country to this national infrastructure fund proposal is the idea of a modest federal loan, sustained and predictable in its dimensions, that takes us outside the annual roller coaster of appropriations and regulatory changes. Last of all is the idea that it would be structured as a capital vehicle to address a capital problem in support of the massive state and local reconstruction efforts that will have to take place. One additional intriguing dimension of this idea, so far, is that it is emerging from a group that includes governors and members of Congress from the western states. The western states have said to those of us in the East that they would be prepared to make a common political alliance with us in trying to work something like this out with Congress. And to those of us in the Northeast, that should be music to our ears. We should finally be willing to take "yes" for an answer. It has been a while since the political leadership in any part of the West has been willing to say, We want to find a common basis with you in which to work out a political alliance to get the federal government to help with the infrastructure reconstruction role.

For those of you who are a little surprised by the idea of a national infrastructure corporation, I simply want to remind you that there are, in fact, many precedents for this in our history. One of them cited by Henry Reuss, former chairman of the Joint Economic Committee and chairman of our National Infrastructure Advisory Committee, is the old reclamation program where the federal government provided the loan capital and carried the interest for all those years. But I want to remind you that at many points in our history, the federal government has turned to the device of a federally chartered corporation to focus our energies and direct the resources and the will and the talent and time of the country toward a specific task. Rebuilding our capital stock is clearly a job that will take us from now to the end of this century. We have in the past created these federal entities for special specific long-term jobs. For example, all the cheap power in the Northwest was created by the Bonneville Power Authority, a federally chartered corporation, and the Tennessee Valley Authority did the same thing in the East. More recently, we are seeing Congress create the Communications Satellite Corporation (COMSAT) because it wants a corporation to operate outside the day-to-day fluctuations in the appropriations process and to be able to raise the debt and manage the nation's effort in putting up commercial and civilian satellites. And I think a national infrastructure corporation can accomplish the same purpose. People we have talked to about it so far subscribe to this infrastructure fund as long as it sticks to the key provision that it represents capitalization of state and local efforts. In other words, the federal government should not pick or fund any single project, any single dam, or any single sewer or water system, but the fund should lend its effort and its long-term financing strength to state and local efforts.

Financing the Nation's Infrastructure Requirements

ROGER J. VAUGHAN[a]

Gallatin Institute
1120 Connecticut Avenue
Washington, D.C. 20036

INTRODUCTION

The nation confronts a crisis precipitated by years of underinvestment in the maintenance of its public works. But beyond the clamor in the press and the tragic bridge collapses, we know very little concerning the extent of the problem. One study has estimated that we will need to spend an additional $3 trillion during the next decade simply to arrest the rate of deterioration.[1] This would entail a 40% increase in all state and local taxes — a move that would be legally impossible in many jurisdictions and politically impossible in all of them.[2] The Congressional Budget Office has estimated our national needs more conservatively at a little over $500 billion.[3] It is clear that the problem is much more than money.

Even if the federal government were to provide additional funds to state and city governments to repair and replace deficient bridges, roads, water systems, sewers, and public buildings, few of the recipients would know how to spend the money wisely. They lack the planning techniques, inventories of what needs to be done, and the capital budgeting procedures to assure that money would flow where it is most needed and in a manner that makes best use of scarce public dollars.

But lack of money is part of the problem. Between 1965 and 1980, the share of the gross national product (GNP) devoted to investments in public works fell from 5% to only 2%. The list of deficient structures and major problems has grown. Of the nation's 564,999 bridges, 17% are in "critical or basically intolerable structural condition."[b] Eight percent of the interstate highway surfaces are "substandard." Boston loses 43% of its water supply through leaks. There are numerous bills circulating in Congress that would attempt to deal with the infrastructure problem. The purpose of this paper is to analyze how we got into this crisis, and to determine what can be done to arrest the rate of deterioration and to meet future infrastructure demands. The appropriate remedies can only be prescribed when the causes of the ailment have been diagnosed.

---

[a] Address correspondence to Post Office Box 822, Gray, Maine 04039.
[b] For a long list of the symptoms of the underinvestment in infrastructure, see Reference 1, Chapter 1.

HOW DID WE GET INTO THIS MESS

The absence of record keeping is a prime culprit in explaining how we have been able to underinvest in our public capital for so long. A private corporation that attempted to balance its books and demonstrate a favorable cash flow by ignoring the depreciation of its plant and equipment would, very quickly, attract the attention of the Security and Exchange Commission (SEC) and provoke the ire of its stockholders. Yet that is precisely what state and local governments have been, and still are, allowed to do. Some have even managed to offer tax cuts — financed by accounting practices that would be shunned by businesses. Until all levels of government agree to present capital budgets that include careful documentation of the rate of depreciation of public capital, we will not be able to resolve the basic infrastructure problem.

There are other causes of the present crisis. We have emphasized expansion and growth rather than the prudent use of public resources. With the massive population movement westward during the nineteenth century, the shift from rural to urban areas during the first half of this century, and the rapid suburbanization since World War II, our public works problems have been those of accommodating growth. Federal grants — from the land grants to the railroads to rural electrification and wastewater treatment projects — have reflected this focus. We need to develop a more balanced public investment strategy that weighs the need to build for growth with the need to conserve what we have already built.

The short time horizon of most public officials is also to blame. Public facilities have a longer expected useful life than the expected political lives of most elected officials. The consequences of deferred maintenance will be visited upon some future mayor or governor. Repair projects are not sufficiently glamorous. A major new project offers convenient media opportunities. A highway resurfacing does not.

If these factors have contributed to a chronic underinvestment problem, other factors have created a crisis in recent years. The combination of rapid suburbanization, the energy crisis, inflation, and prolonged recession have robbed state and local governments of the revenues needed to make capital investments. If New York City and Cleveland suffered the most publicized brush with bankruptcy, many other jurisdictions were not far behind. Irate taxpayers placed constitutional or legal lids on the amount their governments could spend, borrow, or raise in revenues. Capital projects were the most vulnerable budget item. It is much easier to cancel a project to relay a sewer pipe than to lay off teachers and police.

The federal government has contributed to the problem, often not in ways intended by Washington's lawmakers. During the 1960s and 1970s, Congress seemed ready to come to the assistance of cities if they could document a severe problem. Between 1970 and 1980 the share of state and local governments' capital budgets that was subsidized by federal grants rose from 20% to 40%. Such a generous and undemanding benefactor did not encourage careful investments by grateful governments.

The federal government encouraged wastefulness not only by its willingness to create new categorical grant programs but by the way it handed out the money. Most of its programs paid only for new construction and major rehabilitation, leading many recipients to neglect maintenance until the public works had decayed badly enough to be eligible for federal funds. Federal-aid highway grants pay for 90% of the costs of construction of interstate highways, 75% for primary, secondary, and urban roads, and 80% for bridge replacement. State officials told the staff of the United States General Accounting Office that some states deliberately allowed their roads to deteriorate to a point where federal funds were available.[4] The bias runs across many federal programs. In a survey of state and local governments conducted by the American Public Works Association, 90% of the respondents indicated that federal capital funds cause them to lower the priorities they attach to maintenance and repair (see Reference 4, Chapter 5). Additional federal money will not solve the problem.

Recently the municipal bond market—through which states and localities fund about half of their capital expenditures—has been an increasingly hostile environment.[5] Real interest rates remain at record levels, even though market rates have declined somewhat. The advantages of tax-exempt financing have shrunk as the market has been squeezed by two forces. Demand for municipal bonds has been reduced by the 1981 Economic Recovery Tax Act, which lowered tax rates and provided potential investors with other mechanisms to shelter their income. At the same time state and local governments have dramatically increased the volume of bonds offered for sale. In 1981 less than half of the revenues from the sale of long-term tax-exempt bonds were used for traditional public works projects. The rest were used to subsidize private sector investments in health-care facilities, pollution-control equipment, and industrial plant and equipment.

In short, we have a backlog of needed public investments that may run into trillions of dollars. We have acted myopically and kept no records of our waste. We have designed federal programs that contribute to the problem rather than help ease it. We seem unwilling to spend enough on public infrastructure. Where do we go from here?

PAYING THE PIPER

The challenge is enormous. It will not be met by marginal changes in a few programs. There is no simple solution. It will require state and local governments to develop comprehensive public investment strategies that include commitments to long-range capital planning, capital budgets, radical reforms in the way public facilities and infrastructure systems are managed, the establishment of state infrastructure banks, increased reliance on user fees to back revenue bonds, reduction in the use of tax-exempt bonds to subsidize private development, the rationalization of responsibility for infrastructure funding between federal, state, and local governments, and raising some taxes to cover maintenance and repair expenditures. None of these steps will be easy to undertake, but all are necessary for a complete solution to a very pressing problem. Although the focus of this paper is upon the financing components of this strategy, it is important to recognize that financial initiatives are only part of the total picture. While politicians typically focus on where the dollars are, unless there are complementary reforms in planning and management procedures, there will be no long-run solution. In the following two sections, policies to be pursued at the federal and the state level are analyzed.

The Federal Role

In spite of recent budget cuts, the federal government will remain the dominant influence on public capital spending. Its broad taxing powers, the fact that many infrastructure systems are in the national interest, and the sharp differences in fiscal capacity among states dictate a continued federal presence. But future programs must correct the harmful aspects that have pervaded previous federal initiatives. Four federal initiatives should be contained in any national program: (1) decentralization of responsibility for public works investments compensated for by federal assumption of income maintenance programs; (2) establishment of state infrastructure banks partially capitalized by federal funds; (3) enactment of the taxable bond option; and (4) federal coordination of state and local planning and budgeting procedures.

A New Federalism

Both the National Governors' Association and President Reagan have proposed initiatives that would "sort out" the allocation of fiscal responsibilities between federal and state governments. This is urgently needed. The guiding principle should be for the federal government to assume responsibility for programs that aid people — which are national programs — and for state governments to assume greater responsibility for financing and administering public works projects and programs — which have, primarily, a local impact. The logic is unexceptional and has been endorsed by the Advisory Commission for Intergovernmental Relations.

It is impossible for state governments to assume full responsibility for public works without some fiscal offset. A swap would allow this to happen. Since this sorting out would reduce the probability that Congress would initiate a new infrastructure program to bail out states and cities, it would encourage these jurisdictions to take better care of the systems that they already have in place.

State Infrastructure Banks

Decentralization of both fiscal and administrative responsibilities for infrastructure construction and maintenance will only work if state governments have both greater discretion over the type of projects they fund and the administrative mechanism to make it effective. One way to effect this is for states to pool their resources in state infrastructure banks. The federal fiscal responsibility would be to "decategorize" those capital grant programs that would remain after the swap—suggested above—has been carried out so that these block grants could be used to capitalize the state banks. The federal government would maintain responsibility for establishing and enforcing air- and water-quality standards, highway-condition standards, and other regulations to ensure that the national interest was recognized in the state-administered infrastructure systems. Two of the most important program areas would be water and highways.

Most major water projects concerned with inland freight transportation are totally funded and managed by the United States Army Corps of Engineers. Water projects concerned with electricity generation, irrigation, and municipal water supply have mostly been undertaken by the Board of Reclamation. Studies by the United States General Accounting Office have found that some of these projects are not cost effective. When no local funds are involved, localities have little incentive to identify and undertake only those projects that are economically viable. Senators Moynihan and Domenici have proposed to convert water projects into a state block grant under which state matching funds would be required for any project funded. This proposal is consistent with the administration's own new federalism. State administration of these funds would be through a state infrastructure bank or a statewide water authority that would issue bonds, backed by user fees, to undertake major projects and to lend money to localities. All federal water-related programs should be made available to states through block grants (if not swapped outright).

Highway programs could be treated in the same way. Repairing the deteriorated interstate system will be one of the major infrastructure programs during the next decade—financed through the additional five-cents-a-gallon gasoline tax that went into effect earlier this year [1983]. But a more comprehensive solution to road transportation problems should include the decentralization of responsibility. States should establish their own trust funds which would combine federal monies with state revenues from gas taxes, tolls, and other highway-use taxes and vehicle registration fees. Allocations to the state trust funds would be made in a manner similar to present procedures, with state matches required to lever federal contributions. But states would have greater flexibility in determining the projects they wished to undertake. They would choose which incomplete sections of the interstate system they wished to build, which bridges they wished to repair, and which sections to upgrade. This would end the time-consuming and highly political negotiations that currently attend these decisions. All states would be required to set up trust funds by some prescribed date, and all federal gasoline-tax revenues would be channeled through these institutions (they could be part of the state infrastructure bank). States would be able to conduct long-range planning because their federal fund allocations could easily be predicted. The present prohibition of the imposition of tolls on the interstate system would be relaxed—tolls are an efficient and equitable way of raising revenues to finance highways and bridges.

Some proposals circulating in Washington call for a federal infrastructure bank to make loans to state and local agencies to fund major infrastructure programs. This proposal should be rejected. It would create another bureaucratic layer that would be subject to the same delays and problems that have bedeviled most federal discretionary programs. The combination of federal block grants and the taxable bond option (discussed below) provides state and local governments with the fiscal resources they need to make necessary infrastructure investments.

Taxable Bond Option

During the last decade, there were several proposals, both by congressional committees and by analysts of the municipal bond market, to provide state and local governments with *the option* of issuing taxable bonds for which they would receive a direct subsidy for part of the interest costs from the United States Treasury (this issue is discussed fully in Reference 6). The proposal was supported for two reasons:

First, the exemption of interest on municipal bonds from federal taxation is unnecessarily expensive. Some research indicates that as much as one-third of the $6 billion not collected by the United States Treasury goes not to municipalities but to high-income holders of the bonds.

Second, a taxable bond would compete in a much broader capital market than tax exempts, which would avoid fluctuations in the relative interest rates of taxables and tax exempts.

The recent changes in the tax code and the recent behavior of the tax-exempt market merit reconsideration of this proposal (see Reference 5, Chapter 8).

The proposal would be simple and inexpensive. State and local governments and public authorities would be empowered to issue taxable bonds and would receive an annual cash payment equal to 35% of their annual interest costs. Since the marginal tax rate of bond holders is probably equal to 35%, the tax revenues collected by the Internal Revenue Service would be about equal to the subsidy. For example, if the long-term taxable rate were 10%, the postsubsidy cost to the locality would be 6.5%, below the present rate differential. Taxable bonds could only be issued for traditional types of public investments—including public education facilities, roads, bridges and highways, sewer and water systems, and ports and terminals. It would explicitly exclude bonds whose revenues were used to subsidize private investments, or facilities with private tenants.

The interest subsidy would be an open-ended entitlement. It should not be subject to the vagaries of the annual appropriation process. Any attempt to cap the number of bonds that could be issued in any one year would create a wasteful race for subsidized issues, deter long-term capital planning, and generate uncertainty.

Federal Assistance for Planning and Management

We have already stressed the critical importance of sweeping changes in planning and management practices by state and local governments. The federal government must both set an example and assist in the design and implementation of appropriate systems. At the very least, the federal government should develop its own capital budget which includes careful accounting of the depreciation of the capital assets that it owns and manages. The techniques it develops in doing this should be shared with state and local governments.

Establishing generally accepted procedures is best done by a federal agency and then adopted by state governments, rather than allowing the development of many different and competing systems.

The State Role

During the next decade, the greatest increase in fiscal and administrative responsibility for public capital will fall on state governments. Not only will states have to change their own planning and financing techniques, but they will also have to provide increased assistance—fiscal, technical, regulatory, and administrative—to local governments. Many of the state functions will be unfamiliar—financing water supply systems, entering into leasing arrangements with private firms, or managing hazardous waste disposal sites, for example.

The first step will be to develop comprehensive state capital budgets—modeled on federal efforts, it is to be hoped. These must be much more than a wish list of future projects. They should include an assessment of the condition of existing facilities and systems; a review of the allocation of responsibilities between the public and private sectors for infrastructure; projections of future economic and social factors that will influence the demand for public works; estimates of the projected rate of depreciation of existing systems; analyses of the impacts of proposed new projects on future operating budgets; and an evaluation of the costs of alternative financing techniques for proposed projects.

The second step will be for states to commit the necessary resources to careful capital planning. Good planning leads to the selection of cost-effective projects—a process that will be reflected in lower bond interest rates. Good planning will require the personal commitment of the governor. Only the governor can co-opt the business and labor leaders who must participate, can ensure that all agencies cooperate, and can lobby for the components before the legislature.

To finance the increased investments in public facilities, states must make much greater use of user fees. Charging those that use public facilities and services for the privilege is the most equitable and efficient way of paying for public works. If residents must pay for each gallon of water that they consume, they will use the water frugally—which will reduce the need to expand the capacity of the supply system. Some opponents claim that this will penalize low-income households. But they are penalized even more heavily by many present systems that impose a uniform charge for water regardless of the quantity consumed or, even less equitably, by systems that offer declining block rates so that large users pay a lower average cost than do small users.

There are many opportunities for raising more revenues from user fees or through taxes that act like user fees; these are listed in TABLE 1. A sound user price system can provide sufficient revenues to finance most needed public works. Critics of this approach often cite the fact that revenue bonds tend to command higher yields in the tax-exempt market and therefore increased use of revenue bonds will raise the cost of financing public works. The difference in cost is more apparent than real.[7] After allowing for differences in bond quality, underwriting practices, and other factors, revenue bonds would command only slightly higher yields than would general obligation (GO) bonds issued by a given locality for a given project. The slight difference in yields would be more than offset by the other advantages of revenue bonds and by the preservation of the jurisdiction's GO rating for projects that cannot be financed through revenue bonds. Techniques such as creating double-barrel revenue bonds — with state grants-in-aid being earmarked for debt service should the primary revenue source prove insufficient — can further reduce the cost of revenue bond financing. The state infrastructure bank could be an ideal mechanism to implement these new financing mechanisms.

Some of the infrastructure costs should be met by increased use of the private sector. Residential developers can be required to install streets and sidewalks and utility hookups — a practice that is becoming increasingly prevalent in California in the wake of Proposition 13. Some services and facilities

TABLE 1

Type of Infrastructure	Possible User Fees
Roads	• Ad valorem registration • Gasoline taxes • Sales taxes on equipment • Tolls
Research and higher education	• Tuition paybacks • State match to private research and development grants • Tax incentives to private donations • Technology user fees
Transit	• Increased fares (especially during peak hours) • Subsidy from commuter gas tax • Para transit licensing
Water supply	• Metered water use • Full costing for hookups • Seasonal pricing
Wastewater treatment	• Industrial and commercial effluent charges
Recreation	• Seasonal pricing • Special district property taxes

can be turned entirely over to private operators. Probably too much has been said about privatization, but for some facilities a private operator may be able to build and operate at much lower costs than a state or local government could.

Too much has also been said about the various innovative financing techniques that were spawned by the 1981 Economic Recovery Tax Act. Congress now appears to be moving to limit the tax advantages of leasing, and so it is difficult to predict how useful this activity will be to state and local governments.

States can also take steps to help local governments. New Jersey and North Carolina help small local jurisdictions establish budgetary and accounting procedures and authorize local bond issues – activities that have led to substantially lower interest rates on local issues. States with many small local jurisdictions should consider setting up bond banks to lend their superior bond ratings to localities (this function could be incorporated in the state infrastructure banks).

CONCLUSIONS

The initiatives outlined above provide an ambitious menu for the nation. A long-term solution requires long-term, and drastic, measures. It would be a mistake to view the financial components of this strategy as separate from the other necessary measures. More important than increased federal aid is the sorting out of intergovernmental responsibilities so that public works will not continue to deteriorate as highly paid lobbyists try to find a federal program to bail out states and cities.

REFERENCES

1. CHOATE, P. & S. WALTER. 1981. America in Ruins: Beyond the Public Works Pork Barrel. Council of State Planning Agencies. Washington D.C.
2. VAUGHAN, R. 1980. Inflation and Unemployment: Surviving the 1980s. Council of State Planning Agencies. Washington, D.C.
3. Congressional Budget Office. 1983. The Condition of the Nation's Infrastructure. U.S. Government Printing Office. Washington, D.C.
4. VAUGHAN, R. & R. POLLARD. 1983. Rebuilding America. Volume 1: Planning and Managing Public Works in the 1980s. Council of State Planning Agencies. Washington, D.C.
5. VAUGHAN, R. 1983. Rebuilding America. Volume 2: Financing Public Works in the 1980s. Council of State Planning Agencies. Washington, D.C.
6. VAUGHAN, R. 1979. Federal policy and state and local fiscal conditions. In The Urban Impacts of Federal Policies. Norman Glickman, Ed. Johns Hopkins University Press. Baltimore, Md.
7. KIDWELL, D. & T. KOCH. 1982. The behavior of the interest differential between tax exempt revenue and general obligation bonds: a test of risk preferences and market segmentation. J. Finance 1: 73–86.

Creative Financing of the Infrastructure

ROBERT A. LAMB

L. F. Rothschild, Unterberg, Towbin
One Penn Plaza
New York, New York 10119

CONCEPTS AND CONTEXT OF CREATIVE FINANCING

The weak national economy, between 1974 and 1975, and 1979 and mid-1983, combined with many efforts to reduce state and local taxes, led to the downgrading of many states' credit ratings.

To understand why, remember that states and localities contribute greatly to social program costs. As these costs escalated, the revenue side was not keeping up. States began to borrow heavily in the short-term market for cash-flow needs. The fiscal picture was exacerbated by several tax-cut propositions which limited the tax-collecting ability of the state or locality. When budgets had to be trimmed, infrastructure maintenance was a politically easy, although costly, target. Rapid inflation has escalated the cost of this neglect very substantially—any infrastructure-needs discussion uses billion-dollar benchmarks.

Twelve states were downgraded in the latest recession, some twice. This is important because states are increasingly concerned about the debt burden they carry. Therefore, they have shown an interest in financing strategies that are by nature not general obligations of the state. Thus, rule number 1 in creative financing is that credit-rating protection is an issue in any creative financing scenario.

Many states, like New York and New Jersey, created public authorities to assist them in financing needed public programs that would be revenue supported. Public authorities have grown strong, in part because of their independence from the state. They have also shown strength in spite of recent economic downturns. It is natural that the states that created these authorities would want to utilize their strength. For example, Triborough Bridge and Tunnel Authority surplus revenues go to support the Mass Transit Capital Program of the Metropolitan Transportation Authority (MTA); the Municipal Assistance Corporation may help support the convention center in New York. I will go into one example in detail below. The concept I want you to understand is that creative financing strategies may utilize the strength of the public authority for the benefit of non user-fee payers. Rule number 2, then, is that fiscal strength is an issue in creative financing, as well as who pays the tab.

There are four major infrastructure systems in this country—a federal system, a state system, a municipal system, and a privately owned system.

The Congressional Budget Office and others have stated that they are on target for spending on the system the federal government is concerned with. States have bitten a tough bullet in the last few years to raise taxes to meet expense requirements. Some states have plans to accelerate infrastructure reinvestment. New York's bond issue is but one example. A substantial effort is under way to develop multiyear capital plans. Capital planning is a very significant part of an overall strategy to finance the infrastructure. In many states it will take 10 years to finance improvements sufficiently to bring the infrastructure system to a state of good repair. The importance of developing an *overall financial plan* for infrastructure renewal is that a planned mixture of financing strategies can be tailored to a state's cash availability requirement. The other significant point in developing a multiyear capital plan is that it becomes a measure of the state's progress in infrastructure renewal. Rule number 3 is that before one gets into "creative financing," one should have a good idea about the overall financing needs and how this strategy fits with it.

The local municipal system is also mature (translated: declining rapidly). The problem with the local system is that it is hard to obtain reliable figures to determine the size of the problem. However, because of the shrinking percentage of local budgets that have gone to public works spending, massive capital spending is required. This will require, in most cases, tax increases or intergovernmental revenue sharing. The states are frequently asked to help out as a crisis emerges. For example, New York State supports local highway improvements as well as a portion of the capital program of the MTA, which by lease is a city responsibility. Therefore, the fourth issue in creative financing is that the local problem can become a state problem when a crisis develops. This is also true at a state level — a state crisis can become a federal problem.

THE FINANCING MECHANISMS

Bank for Regional Development

The Port Authority, New York State, and New Jersey in a three-way agreement have developed a mechanism to fund local infrastructure improvements using the strength of the Port Authority. The Port Authority was given a toll and a Port Authority Trans-Hudson (PATH) Train fare increase, and New York State agreed to move out of its space in the World Trade Center and rerent the space at three times the state's cost, taking the increment and putting it into the bank. The bank has a capitalized value of $775 million plus private dollars, of which $200 million are earmarked for PATH system improvements. The balance is available for grants and loans. Loans are a better deal because the money becomes leverageable, helping to support up to $3 billion in capital spending.

Infrastructure Banks

In general, these are structured in two ways — as a revolving fund or as a capitalized value structure. The former is relatively straightforward — set up a pool of funds for low-interest loans, reloan the repayment stream; they are better than grants to get the job done. Leverage is about 1.5:1 over 10 years. Loans are made by one level of government to another.

The capitalized value strategy involves the use of a pool of money to reduce the cost on another pool of money—a resource-sharing concept. One pool of money earns interest, which can be applied to another pool of funds which are borrowed and reloaned. Leverage on the first pool of funds can be as high as 7:1 using a 200 basis point discount, 5:1 using a 400 basis point discount. The cost to the local unit of government is reduced.

Conversion of Interstates to Tolls

The United States government built a network of major highways which stimulated suburban development. However, these roads are in need of repair—an obligation of the highway trust fund. These are major arteries. Many states are calling on the Federal Highway Administration and Congress to allow tolls on these roads as part of an overall plan to finance highway improvements. It looks relatively painless and could generate substantial revenue. There are liabilities, however. The strength of the interstate system, as a limited access highway, is due to the federal investment of billions of dollars. Will it be repaid? Also, will each exit be tolled? This would represent a major operating expense. Will the highway have to be upgraded to toll standards? This will also be costly. It is a program that is appealing, potentially a revenue strength sharing program in concept. User fees will support construction and rehabilitation programs that are off that user fee system under a pooled relationship.

Use of Authority Surpluses

New Jersey just passed a referendum which allows the state to gain access to the surpluses of their public authority system. It will mean a lot of business for financial houses because a lot of outstanding bonds must be refunded to expunge existing bond covenant restrictions on the use of surpluses.

The surpluses from all the public authorities can be used to finance projects off their respective systems. This is another example of sharing of fiscal strength. The fee payers on the systems are subsidizing the taxpayers—an unusual twist. Fee payers have determined by their behavior that cost to use the toll highways is not as important as other considerations, such as time savings. Thus, the fee schedule for the toll roads appears to be somewhat inelastic and can be used to generate funds for other public purposes.

Tax-Oriented Financing

Forced, Indirect Federal Revenue Sharing

Sale-Leasebacks. Sale-leaseback has been popular because it has offset early costs, generating present value savings to government in an inflationary period. Basically, a municipal unit of government sells a property and leases it back, giving the tax benefits to private owners. Then it retains the right to repurchase the property in less valuable dollars, with no guarantees on the repurchase cost. There have been problems of abuse because it is a forced, indirect federal revenue sharing. Congress is trying to take away the benefit of the depreciation if property is leased to local government. The proposed legislation by Senator Dole goes too far, penalizing local government, if it enters into long-term rental agreements, by raising the costs to the owner through reduced tax shelter benefits.

Service Contracts. Service contracts allow private ownership and control over property under a performance contract with a government. Equipment is financed in this way. It is not a lease because of a greater service focus and other responsibilities assumed by the contractor. This is also under attack in Congress because of the lost revenue to the treasury.

Liquidation/Decapitalization

One way to make a program more affordable is to reduce its size. A recurring pressure in government has been to build new projects. This has been reflected in federal policies until very recently. Comptroller Regan and Mr. Mathiasen have clearly stated the issue of build versus repair. Spot overcapacity has also become a problem.

The cost to properly maintain the massive infrastructure in New York State is staggering. There are no reliable numbers, only large numbers. Liquidation of non-public-purpose or marginal public-purpose facilities to private ownership reverses a long-standing trend – a needed reversal. The funds generated by a liquidation strategy may not be great, but the fact of liquidation has the benefit of a reduced maintenance burden. This is when some real savings will be realized to the state.

Cost-Reduction Strategies

Many strategies can be employed to reduce costs to states and localities. If someone else will pay, then cost is reduced. This may not contribute to an efficient investment strategy, however.

There are some strategies that can be employed to reduce the high real interest cost in today's market. Basic strategies would include:

1. Do not bond all capital expenses (limited to over 10 years).
2. Require the investment to be maintained.
3. Develop an overall financing plan.
4. Assess method of financing and who will pay.

Some methods are relatively less expensive:

1. Put bonds.
2. Other variable-rate paper — which is indexed to short-term rates and allows the issuer to take advantage of those short-term rates.
3. Tax-exempt commercial paper.
4. Credit enhancement is another method of reducing the cost of borrowing in the markets, largely by shoring up issuer credit ratings.

My advice to you as engineers is to work with a financial advisor to do a facts and circumstance evaluation and develop an overall financial plan.

Nonfinancial Cost-Reduction Strategies

As a final thought, we should work to improve engineering standards and change the award process so that low-maintenance-cost projects get designed and built. To the extent that we can reduce the maintenance costs, the competition for state dollars will be lessened and more money made available to rebuild the infrastructure.

Financing New York City's Infrastructure

MARK PAGE

Office of Management and Budget
The City of New York
Municipal Building, Room 1209
1 Centre Street
New York, New York 10007

I am going to talk about how New York City gets the part of the money supporting its capital program that in fact comes from the city's borrowing. Unfortunately you are once again going to hear about the city's fiscal crisis, because it has a lot to do with the city's financing problems now. Without the fiscal crisis the city might not have the exemplary financial management and budget planning that we have; we would also probably not have the problems of market access for our bonds that are still with us. Improved management and planning were going to solve the limitations on our market access. Perhaps they eventually will, but there are other technical steps, which have been taken already and should be taken in the future, that can also help us to borrow.

You are aware of the $35 billion capital program planned for the city's infrastructure over the next 10 years. You have also probably heard that the city believes that optimally this program should be $55 billion. It is not at the $55 billion level because we are not confident that we can borrow enough to fund a program at that level.

Expense budget resources are adequate to pay debt service both at the current level and substantially higher. Since the fiscal crisis the percentage of the city's budget going for debt service has declined, and under the assumed $35 billion program the percentage will continue to decline.

Our problem is who will lend us the money. For a $35 billion program, the city is obliged to fund just over half from its own sources of financing. At this time a major increase in the size of the program would mean a major increase in the amount of capital funds borrowed by the city.

The existing program relies on funding from city credit of approximately $650 million this year, increasing to $1.2 billion in 1985, $1.7 billion in 1986, and $1.8 billion in 1987. We already see these amounts as a possible problem. Last year we borrowed $450 million; so far this year we have borrowed $275 million. We are confident that the debt service on city borrowings can and will be paid. But in the end it is the investor's confidence that we must have. How do we get and hold the investor confidence that will let us count on market access in the planned or larger amounts in future years?

As a municipality in the state of New York, New York City borrows money under a legal structure last basically revised in the 1930s. That structure defines and constrains the purposes and amounts of bonds issued by cities, but then tries to provide absolute assurance that debt service will be paid. Debt service legally has first claim on all city revenues, property tax can be levied without limit to pay debt service, and state aid to municipalities must first go to make up any shortfall in provision for debt service by the municipality.

So why doesn't this do it?

For New York City it did, until 1975. In 1974 the city borrowed about $1.5 billion in the public credit markets. In current dollar value this would equate to $2.8 billion today.

What happened? Investors lost confidence that their legal first priority for payment would hold. They realized that their payment depended on the capacity and will of management to maintain basic services and meet legal obligations when due, and they lost faith it would then. In the end, buying a bond due 30 years from now requires faith. What can we really know now about New York City government then?

The process governing investor confidence in a general obligation (GO) credit as complicated as the city's is sometimes described as theology. In fact the city never failed to pay interest and principal when due on city bonds, even at the height of the fiscal crisis. So clearly an unblemished record of debt service payments on bonds is itself not enough for the city to hold investor confidence. Ironically, only city note holders were even required to wait for their money, and city notes have now achieved the top rating from one rating agency and the city's market access for notes has been adequate for its needs since 1981.

If steady payments, even in acute budget adversity, do not hold investor confidence, what will not just hold it but win it back?

Since the fiscal crisis, accounting, management, and budget planning has become very good in the city. Although the process of identifying and allocating resources engenders much debate, it happens with enough lead time and accuracy so that the actual administration of each budget year is orderly. From 1978 to 1981 under accounting standards dictated by state law, and since 1981 under generally accepted accounting principles, the city's audited financial results for each year have shown results better than planned. There have been no nasty surprises. And yet with an annual capital cash flow of over $1 billion and growing, the city has not yet succeeded in borrowing half that amount from the public in one year. This year we hope for $650 million.

Now at last we have investment-grade credit ratings from both rating agencies. These investment-grade ratings are minimum investment grades. This is helpful, but what more can we do to establish confidence in our orderly management and the fact that debt service will be paid? How do we make our ratings come up? And in a related process, although not locked to ratings, how do we regain the degree of investor faith that let us sell the equivalent now of almost $3 billion in general obligation debt in 1974? Even with the best will and performance on our part, the process seems simply to take a long time to reestablish faith. Meanwhile, a minimum investment grade is a serious obstacle in alternative financing, such as IDB's. To the extent projects depend on contractual payments by the city, they are still generally rated below investment grade.

While waiting for time hopefully to cure the rating and faith problem for City GOs, what can be done?

One can attempt to change the nature of the credit structure underlying city bonds. An obvious and dramatic example is the federal guarantee of New York City bonds. A less dramatic but effective federal presence has been federal mortgage insurance available to satellite borrowing entities such as the Housing Development Corporation. Recent federal legislation should make it possible for the Health and Hospitals Corporation to augment its city capital funds by issuing its own bonds backed by Federal Housing Authority insurance.

One can also try to simplify the structure of the entity issuing bonds, so that it is easier to quantify the sources of funds and the uses of funds that could compete with debt service on the bonds being issued. In effect, this kind of structuring reduces the "faith factor," for lack of a better word, in credit judgments. If the credit is simple to quantify, objectively, there is less room for theology. And we think the underlying facts are with us.

The Municipal Assistance Corporation for the City of New York (MAC) is the original and continuing example of this approach in connection with the city. In 1975 investors would not buy city general obligation bonds, despite their legal claim on all city revenues including the sales tax and other revenue streams later pledged to MAC. New York City was apparently too large and complicated an entity, with too many competing needs and no orderly method to sort among them, for investors to be confident of payments in accordance with their right.

MAC is close to as simple as a bond-issuing entity could be for purposes of credit analysis. The city's sales tax and certain other tax revenues flow to it. The only significant claim on its resources is debt service on its bonds. So there is no competition for the investors to worry about. Only after discarded by MAC is the city's sales tax revenue subject to the other competing needs of the city. Although economic and political factors may affect MAC's revenues, it has a large coverage margin and the appearance of MAC as a debt issuer has screened out the obvious presence of political forces. MAC continues to have a better credit rating than the city and access to a portion of the credit market the city has not entered. It should also be noted that MAC has the state moral obligation. What this is worth now, or when MAC was created just after the state let UDC default on its debt, I am not certain.

MAC's enhanced credit remains important to the city. We need MAC to give us the benefit of its market access over the next year. MAC's market access needs to support the financing assumptions in our capital plan by making capital funds available in future years.

The Metropolitan Transportation Authority (MTA) transit revenue bonds are a more recent example of a specified revenue stream supporting a particular group of bonds which go to finance a capital need previously carried by city GO bonds. In the case of the MTA, unlike MAC, the cost of running the service is paid by the same entity that pays debt service. However, that entity also controls the source of revenue in that it sets the fare. It is obliged, under the terms of the bonds, to set the fare at a rate sufficient to pay debt service and operating costs.

Similarly the city is pursuing legislation that would allow its water and sewer services to function effectively as a separate entity. The entity would be able to fund its capital needs from the proceeds of bonds it issued, paid for, along with the service itself, from water and sewer rates. Even though these bonds would be payable from one revenue, as compared to city bonds which are payable from all city revenues, we believe water and sewer revenue bonds would probably be rated higher than city bonds now are, and would effectively extend the city's market access. Again the entity would be simpler to analyze and quantify than the city as a whole: the cost of one service competing with the cost of the bonds for one revenue stream, controlled by the entity and required under the terms of the bonds to be set at a rate to pay costs and debt service.

Water and sewer revenue bonding takes me to my last point, which is that although fashions in the credit market have changed, the New York State laws governing financing by municipalities have not. The city is basically authorized only to issue GO debt. In 1974, 60% of the tax-exempt market was GO bonds, 40% was revenue bonds. Those proportions have more than reversed. New York City itself needs to be able to issue revenue bonds. Cities in other states have water and sewer revenue bonding entities. They are current and respectable and therefore there is some predisposition in the marketplace to have faith in and buy bonds issued by such an entity. State law needs to be revised to let us do it and to enable municipal issuers greater flexibility in general to do revenue bonding. People who invest in tax-exempt bonds do not seem to like bonds, or bond issuers, that do not seem to adhere to the current norm. A part of the current norm is revenue bonds.

In the long run the presence of MAC in the marketplace as an issuer of revenue bonds for the city is probably not desirable, although it has been and is now vitally necessary. The original reason for MAC as a bail-out mechanism is remembered.

There are other state laws governing the way we issue general obligation bonds that, on the margin, could make these bonds more appealing. Only New York, among the cities in the state, may issue term bonds instead of serial bonds, and even we are very limited as to the purpose for these bonds. Our underwriters tell us term bonds issued with a pattern of maturities reflecting demand in the marketplace, instead of serial bonds dictated by the state constitution, would sell better. Our limited experience with term bonds supports their conclusion. Better market reception translates into cheaper and more secure borrowing, so why not provide for the issuance of term bonds by municipalities in the state? Municipalities could be required to set aside an amount annually to avoid an extraordinary budget expense in any one year.

The advice we get is similar with respect to selling bonds at deep discount or notes at variables rates. Other issuers, including state authorities, can take advantage of these marketing tools, why not the cities?

In the end we are selling a product in a highly competitive marketplace. The product is bonds which must have terms and underlying credit structure, which can, in aggregate, appeal to the broadest possible market of potential investors. For the foreseeable future, the bulk of the city's capital needs are likely to be financed through the issuance of GO bonds. Any adjustment to the terms of such bonds to make them more attractive to the marketplace would help, along with the long-term effort to demonstrate consistently prudent management to the point where credit analysts can no longer support an equivocal position. At the same time we will continue to pursue opportunities to vary the underlying credit structure through revenue bonding. And explore whatever alternate sources of financing we can find.

Part II: General Discussion

Moderator: PETER C. GOLDMARK, JR.

Office of the Executive Director
The Port Authority of New York and New Jersey
One World Trade Center
New York, New York 10048

M. KARAMOUZ (*Polytechnic Institute of New York, Brooklyn, N.Y.*): As Mr. Sullivan and Mr. Young mentioned this morning, there is a need for further research in infrastructure development. Is there any place for research funds in capital budgeting? And how can we allocate research funds?

M. PAGE (*New York City Office of Management and Budget, New York, N.Y.*): There probably is such a need. When you look at New York City's infrastructure right now, it's huge and realistic standards for what replacement cycles really ought to be, or really must be, are very vague. Nobody has developed a replacement cycle that makes sense for masonry crosstown sewers that were built at the end of the nineteenth century. Basically they seem to do fine until they collapse. What kind of standards do you apply to infrastructures of that kind? And the same thing is true for any number of parts of city infrastructure.

If some objective standards that made sense could be developed, that would be a great help.

R. J. VAUGHAN (*Gallatin Institute, Washington, D.C.*): I think they also have to look at ways of translating replacement standards in the existing capital stock into some estimate of value on the rate of depreciation, so that it can be included in the capital budget.

P. C. GOLDMARK, JR.: I'd just add one word to that. I think that the Port Authority is convinced that research is a very important component of the infrastructure effort and that it has been generally neglected. We probably spend more on research ourselves than any other public sector organization, at least certainly that I'm aware of, as a proportion of our total funds.

One of the reasons research is important is if we go into a large infrastructure reconstruction effort and we do not do it using a more modern set of technologies and a more competitive set of approaches, we will not have the positive effect on the economy that we desire. We will not be able to make the overall function of the American economy more competitive, which should be one of our primary goals. The point is not merely to restore those Civil War sewers to their previous condition; it is to do it in a way that is economically efficient; to make sure the overall economy is competitive. To make the economy competitive, you've got to do it in a modern, technologically up-to-date way that allows and facilitates regular and cost-effective maintenance — and that means research.

M. GOTSCHALL (*The Bond Buyer, New York, N.Y.*): I have a question for Mr. Vaughan. You endorse federal taxation of tax-exempt municipal bonds. What about the increasing number of small investors who are buying tax-exempt municipal bonds? It seems to me that municipal bond dealers in America have enticed a lot of small investors into the bond market by offering a variety of new products, such as diversified bond funds, deep-discount zero-coupon bonds, and put bonds to name a few. Now by taxing tax-exempt municipal bonds, won't you be penalizing these small individuals as well as the larger high-income investors that you spoke of?

R. J. VAUGHAN: The taxable bond option is not the imposition of taxes on tax-exempt municipal bonds. It is an option that allows municipalities to issue taxable debt. It does not change the status of anything that has been issued to date. It would stabilize the relationship between the tax-exempt and taxable markets, which has been highly unstable in the last 5 or 10 years. We are not suddenly penalizing the tax-exempt market. We're allowing a new financial instrument to be issued — one presumes, at the advice of investment bankers and other advisors to state and local governments depending upon market conditions. It will improve arbitrage between the taxable and the tax-exempt markets.

M. LANG (*Camp Dresser & McKee, New York, N.Y.*): There are two points I wish to bring up here. One was Mr. Vaughan's statement about giving free water — which proves to me, as a native New Yorker and a former city official, that if New York City didn't exist, someone would invent it to attribute all the ills of mankind to it. Even a well-informed analyst like Mr. Vaughan was somehow seduced by these cliches about the city.

The other was a question from Dr. Karamouz about research and Mr. Goldmark's comment. In my talk, I will want to point out that in some areas at least, New York City did stay and probably still is staying at the cutting edge of development of some new techniques. I'd like to point out though that in those days, we were doing these things we talked about with a research and development budget of zero. But I'd like to point out that even the lack of a formal research and development budget is not necessarily a deterrent to in-house research and in-house operational development.

P. C. GOLDMARK, JR.: I trust Mr. Lang will let me say in defense of Roger Vaughan that, while I think all of us know water is not free in New York City, I think there are few of us who would point to New York City's water fee system as a model of effective pricing and modern management.

Introduction

JOSEPH FERRIS

Legislative Commission on Science and Technology
The State of New York
Two World Trade Center, Suite 5026
New York, New York 10047

This session will focus on state legislative initiatives for scheduled maintenance of the infrastructure.

The Legislative Commission on Science and Technology, of which I am chairman, has been involved in this problem for the past two years as a follow-up to work done by our New York State Assembly Speaker, Stanley Fink, and his Infrastructure Task Force.

From the efforts of the task force, the Speaker's bill on capital planning, budgeting, and reporting was developed and was enacted last summer. This legislation focuses on the matching of revenues and expenditures for five years into the future and mandates precise and regular accounting on where the state stands on each of its capital projects.

The bill developed by the commission, A.6084A, on which Speaker Fink has also joined me as a cosponsor, addresses the other side of the coin: the scheduling and budgeting required for the continuous maintenance of the infrastructure into the future.

The background and need for this measure are clear to all of us: New York State is endowed with the most massive, densely built up, and sophisticated complex of public facilities in the nation—and indeed, perhaps in the world. It is also one of the oldest and most in need of repair.

You have heard much about all of this already today. A large proportion of the state's existing bridges are in urgent need of repair. In Manhattan alone water mains have burst, sections of Franklin D. Roosevelt Drive and the West Side Highway have collapsed, and cables have snapped on the Brooklyn Bridge—all in a single season.

The cause is deferred maintenance. Maintenance is deferred on public facilities for the same reason it is deferred on railroads in the private sector: declining revenues and increasing demands for every budget dollar. In brief, fiscal crisis.

But in government, it is fiscal crisis compounded by the nature of our political system.

That political factor is the natural human tendency of an elected official to respond to those demands where pressure is greatest and most immediate— crime in the streets or the education of our children—or to those projects where the accolades are greatest — such as opening a new playground or cutting the ribbon on a new project.

Repairing a road or repainting a bridge not only lacks that kind of glamor and reward; it can often be put off for a year without any *noticeable* ill effects — or public outcry.

The result has been an almost continuous rollover of urgently needed maintenance in one jurisdiction after another.

As the conservationists used to say when fixing the blame for the deterioration of our environment, "We have met the enemy, and the enemy is us."

The syntax may not be perfect in that quotation, but the idea is clear. We who are elected officials are responsible for the condition of our public facilities — but the system in which we operate has encouraged the neglect and deterioration we have allowed to take place. Now we must shape up on this issue.

The bill we propose — A.6084A — is an attempt to change this system; change it so that those public officials who protect our state's physical assets hopefully will be rewarded by the editorial writers and the voters, and those who neglect those assets can be held accountable.

The specific provisions of this bill are as follows: The State Finance Law would be amended by adding a new Section 26 requiring that the chief executive officer of every state department and agency would provide the governor with a schedule of future dates and costs for maintenance whenever a capital project in excess of $5 million is initiated.

A professional engineer, as well as the chief executive officer of the state department or agency, would certify the schedule and explain how it was calculated. Future budgets would include such maintenance in the years when it is due except that such maintenance could be postponed by the governor for fiscal reasons, or for technical, nonfiscal reasons when the schedule is amended with the approval of a licensed professional engineer.

The Division of the Budget would keep a record of all maintenance on projects covered by this section. Starting with the fiscal year beginning on April 1 of the third year following enactment, certain existing facilities will be brought under the law provided they remain viable parts of a master plan. These are projects where a continued postponement of maintenance would threaten the public safety or force an imminent shutdown of the project, or projects valued at more than $25 million that were built since January 1, 1958.

A final section of the bill requires the contract on all new capital projects costing more than $2 million to provide for comprehensive manuals covering the operation and maintenance of the entire system.

A legislative hearing on the bill was held on April 20, 1983 in Albany. Out of this testimony came a request for an amendment to the bill, which was incorporated into our amended version, A.6084.A. This amendment, which added subdivisions 3(B) to Section 26, provides for maintenance schedules on *all* the facilities covered by the Department of Transportation. While this broadens the bill's coverage, it will also make it easier for the Transportation Department to administer.

You will note that the bill is only a first step and that it *phases in* gradually this scheduled maintenance activity. It starts with only new construction—a relatively small proportion of our total infrastructure. It then allows three years before it picks up the existing infrastructure—and then only those facilities that were built since 1958 at a cost of over $25 million, or are currently threatened by either breakdown or danger to the public.

Even then coverage of the bill is still limited. Only facilities owned by *state* agencies are included. That leaves out all of the properties owned by our counties, cities, towns, and villages, including New York City. State authorities and public corporations *are* included; but the Port Authority, as a bistate agency, is not. Parenthetically, I would say that this is as it should be; the Port Authority has had the money and management to maintain its own facilities adequately over the years.

Looking down the road I would hope that this first attack on the problem would prove successful and that, once debugged, we could then include smaller facilities and extend it not only to all existing facilities owned by the state but also to those *financially assisted* by the state—our schools, for example—and ultimately to all levels of local government. But we must walk before we can run. And I know that this bill, while simple in concept, represents some very considerable administrative problems for the Division of the Budget.

One advantage we have had in tackling this problem is the recognition and support we have received for the bill. Pennsylvania has adopted it word for word in a bill they are pushing. Massachusetts has included our concept and wording in a bill they have introduced. Most important, we have had backing from leaders of both parties here in New York State. Speaker Stanley Fink and State Comptroller Edward Regan have long been deeply committed to this concept and Governor Cuomo and Lieutenant Governor Del Bello have pledged their support. This kind of encouragement makes it easier to be both tough-minded and flexible as to the details and language of the bill. We at the commission would welcome your suggestions as to how to improve it.

Legislation Needed for the Construction, Operation, and Maintenance of Our Public Buildings

JOHN C. EGAN

Office of General Services
The State of New York
The Corning Tower
Empire State Plaza
Albany, New York 12242

I am pleased that your program has incorporated "public buildings" into the overall picture represented by the term *infrastructure*. I appreciate this opportunity to share some thoughts that merit the same concern and response as that presently afforded to transportation and other public work endeavors.

THE STATE'S PHYSICAL PLANT

To provide a more comprehensive term for the "public building" portion of this address, I am substituting the words "physical plant." This terminology is more inclusive for all aspects of the support requirements for the conduct of all agency programs. The physical plant is the building environment and supporting facilities for the functional needs of each agency, such as furnishing office space, prison facilities, and health-related institutions. The physical plant activities directly impact upon all programs. While I will be addressing the concerns of the state's physical plant, the same attention should be addressed by private enterprise.

To place the magnitude of this portion of the state's infrastructure into proper perspective, the state's physical plant consists of approximately 12,000 buildings, including their ancillary facilities, such as:

1. Support services, including heating plants, sewage treatment plants, and potable water treatment plants, along with their underground piping distribution systems serving all buildings on a campus or institution.
2. Parking lots, outdoor lighting, site roadways and sidewalks, landscaping, and outdoor recreation facilities.
3. Electric substations and electrical power distribution cables.

These buildings, both individual office buildings and those at multibuilding complexes, are located at over 850 sites throughout the state, having today's replacement cost of more than $20 billion, exclusive of their real estate value. They require construction work for additions, alterations, improvements, and repairs. These buildings and sites provide the physical needs for the state's line agencies programs, including, but not limited to, the following:

1. Correctional institutions and facilities for youthful offenders.
2. State University campuses.
3. Division of Military and Naval Affairs armories.
4. State police headquarter buildings and barracks.
5. Department of Transportation maintenance shops and district engineer headquarter buildings.
6. State education schools for the blind and the deaf.
7. Department of Health's Roswell Park Memorial Institute and other health laboratories.
8. The Office of General Services' (OGS) 25 individual office buildings and two large multibuilding complexes (the Governor Nelson A. Rockefeller Empire State Plaza and the Albany State Office Building Campus), the Capitol, and the Governor's Mansion.

The Office of General Services is in a unique position in that we not only have the operation and management responsibilities for the physical plant represented by the state-owned office buildings for our tenant client state agencies, but we are also "agents" for most other state agencies for the planning, design, and construction of their facilities throughout the state, both new and rehabilitation work. As an example, we are also modifying the state's existing underutilized mental hygiene facilities for adaptive reuse for correctional facilities. Some examples of OGS design and construction work, including alterations, improvements, and repairs of the state facilities, include:

1. Add-on stand-alone correctional facilities at existing correctional sites, utilizing the original facility's modified common heating, sewage, water, and electric power services.
2. Alterations and improvements to all of the state's 85 large central heating plants, serving multibuilding complexes.
3. Heat recovery modifications to the 23,500-ton central air conditioning plant at the Empire State Plaza for energy conservation.
4. Repair and replacement of roofs at State University of New York (SUNY) campuses.
5. Emergency replacements or repairs involving health and life safety, such as immediate correction of electric outages at any state facility.

The recitation could continue with a number of other state operating agencies, but I believe we have established the credibility of our concern for the proper ongoing operation of the state's physical plant. Regardless of the extent or size of any client agency program, the same basic elements are present. Each program's effectiveness, continuity, and growth are interdependent upon the supporting conditions provided by the physical plant. The program needs and physical plant upkeep are equal partners. This is not to say that other factors of the program are not equally important, but primarily to place greater credence on the role played by *dependable*, efficient, and ongoing physical plant support services.

I submit that the effective and efficient operation of the physical plant is a commitment, for any effective program. This commitment represents not only the initial investment for buildings and their support facilities, but also a systematic funding for repairs, replacements, alterations, and improvements when required, with annual maintenance accountability, rather than the present costly *deferred* rehabilitation funding. This can be accomplished by sound initial planning that translates program needs into physical plant requirements. These requirements must include the "life" implications of the required operational needs, as well as the initial cost indications, which will define the support needs for the program. Many of these endeavors have been ignored or overlooked in the past, but prudent management has placed greater emphasis upon achieving maximum utilization of the state's physical plant capabilities. Quality is not only applicable to material and equipment, but also to physical plant activities in minimizing the development of "potholes" that affect program productivity and in establishing smooth environmental conditions for program continuity and growth. The realization of this commitment requires resources for planning and sustainment of plant activities. This includes both monetary and qualified personnel resources that are dedicated to producing the ongoing support functions necessary. Physical plant activities are too often taken for granted, since it has been a rare occasion when we are inconvenienced when the "lights go out" or the "heating system fails," but when it does occur, it becomes bad news. Having been directly involved previously in physical plant operation, I would prefer to preclude any occasion of inconvenience; fortunately our many talented and resourceful staff personnel have been and are diligently working to this end. However, there is no magic to this endeavor, and the effectiveness of physical plant services requires a carefully developed plan of operation and the resource support indicated in the plan development.

MAINTAINING THE STATE'S PHYSICAL PLANT

I have attempted to provide an overview of the magnitude of what can be classified as the "state buildings infrastructure operations," and I submit that it is a most significant part of our total infrastructure picture. I would like to share with you some steps that should be implemented to upgrade physical plant conditions consistent with the program commitments. The first step is planning. This is a very important endeavor since it defines the overall commitment and resources for the project. Fortunately, we now have expertise to apply accepted techniques that can develop comparative analyses for decision-making assistance. Such activities as life cycle cost analysis will provide insight into the continuing commitment that will be required to support ongoing operating requirements. Our present dilemma is predominantly, in our opinion, caused by the absence of maintenance funding. The initial construction cost of a project should be determined in its planning phase by professionals. Such analyses to identify ongoing needs for proper maintenance planning should become a known factor at the inception of a project, and with provided future resources, physical plant system deterioration can be curtailed to the extent of normal service life of each type of equipment or structure. Replacement of system components is also considered in these life cycle costing analyses and becomes another factor in the development of the sustainment resources required by the project.

The preceding presents some of the considerations that are used in a life cycle cost evaluation that has been the subject of several New York State legislative drafts, but they have never become law. New York was one of the first states to consider the life cycle costing concept, but it is now among the 30% of the states that have not progressed this principle into law. The inclusion of this activity will assist in the decision-making process and would not only produce a more complete picture of the total commitment, but also indicate the ongoing support required in staffing, maintenance, and operating resources to properly maintain the state's physical plant condition. I believe that legislation requiring this effort is long overdue. Required activity of this nature for future capital projects would present an applicable tool for preventing its future deterioration, a concern that we all have to deal with at this time. We do however have to remain pragmatic by realizing that such analyses are factors for decision making, but commitment by the legislature for resource support has to be defined and then the needed support resources for ongoing physical plant service continuity must be provided. This will assure the furnishing of proper physical rehabilitation needs simultaneously with the agencies' program installations. Legislative bill 6084-A presently under consideration includes some of this subject matter. A life cycle cost analysis procedure would solidify the ongoing commitment implications and augment the expressed intentions of this bill; this can be accomplished by separate legislation or by modifying this bill.

The preceding remarks will be beneficial for future capital projects and major rehabilitation endeavors. However, it does not address the needs of the major portion of our *existing* physical plant at the state's 850 sites. Such items as an old boiler with only a 5-year service life left, a water chiller with a 10-year service life, the roof of a 10-year-old building, a 15-year-old electric network transformer and switchgear, the brick exterior of a 50-year-old building, steam traps, valves, insulation; the list of such components goes on and on. They are a major operating concern, which, when ignored, develops into the conditions that are being addressed at this seminar. There is a parallel condition in our physical plants to that indicated for our roadways and bridges, which, in most cases, are not as readily visible and therefore do not have the clarion effect required to indicate the urgency of the resolutions needed. However, this inability to maintain efficient ongoing physical plant conditions will have the undesirable cost effect due to increased energy cost, more frequent repairs and replacements, and possible service disruptions, which reduces each facility's program effectiveness. This trend must be *reversed*, but it requires reaffirmation of the continual commitment of required resources. I recommend that a dedicated budget item be established exclusively for ongoing maintenance, alteration, and improvement needs. Construction for a new project should be considered only after investigation by a qualified professional survey team determines that adaptive reuse of existing underutilized state facilities cannot fill the project program needs. However, when the project is completed, the ongoing life cycle needs established during the planning state should be included in this budget item. Likewise, routine operating expenditures would also be included elsewhere in the budget. The key word is "dedicated," as the funding provided must be used for the intended purpose and not siphoned off for some other program.

In addition, there is an urgent need to provide the proper operating staff. The unfortunate situation existing at most of our physical plant facilities is that the needed staff complement is established but, due to vacancies, the personnel available cannot perform in an effective maintenance manner to sustain optimum physical plant conditions. With the austere budget criteria that we have been faced with for the past decade, personnel services have been justifiably scrutinized and revisions in staffing patterns made. However, due to reduced maintenance and operation staffing patterns, as well as limited repair and replacement, little alteration or improvement has occurred, while the size of the state's physical plant has grown. There is an urgent need to provide a realistic staffing and physical rehabilitation of the state's physical plant consistent with the demands of its agencies' functional requirements. Monetary and staffing support should be a common provision, and while it is usually considered as overhead or even as a liability, an efficient physical plant does provide a payback as represented by improved program operation efficiency, greater operational consistency, reduced frequency for component repair and replacement needs, and reduced energy consumption. All of this equates to a properly operated and maintained facility infrastructure.

There is a widely quoted expression that is relevant to this specific concern: "Plan your work and work your plan." We all recognize the specter that must be addressed, and I trust that this brief overview has confirmed that methods are available for resolution. Let us take the next step to define the specific methods and commence with their applications.

Due to the large volume of new construction over the past three decades, rehabilitation of physical facilities is destined to become an increasingly important aspect of the New York State capital construction budget. We need a systematic approach to evaluate which state-owned buildings are to be rehabilitated due to the continued austere state fiscal situation. The term rehabilitation will refer to all physical work or changes needed in buildings and their ancillary support facilities after the completion of their initial construction, which are beyond the scope of normal facility maintenance capabilities.

In regard to rehabilitation, it is imperative to the discussion of rehabilitation of the physical plant that we define the two types of rehabilitation.

Physically required rehabilitation is typically necessitated by functional deficiencies in the building materials or equipment. These functional deficiencies in turn may have been brought about in a number of ways, such as:

1. Deterioration of building components due to:

      a. prolonged use;
      b. improper maintenance;
      c. exposure to weather and atmosphere conditions.
  2. Damage due to:
      a. fires;
      b. vandalism;
      c. floods;
      d. other accidents;
      e. tenant abuses.
  3. Defective components.
  4. Incorrect installation due to errors in:
      a. design;
      b. construction.

The second general category, *user (agency) determined rehabilitation*, that is, *program rehabilitation*, is necessitated by changes in function or performance as a direct response to users' needs or desires, caused by changes in the agency programs. The following causes would bring about program rehabilitation work:

1. Replacement of technologically obsolete, but still functioning, materials or equipment (e.g., updating a lighting system).
2. Installation of new equipment (e.g., air-conditioning system or computers).
3. Relocation of components or equipment due to change in building function (e.g., partition location changes).
4. Restoration or preservation of historically significant buildings (e.g., the Capitol).

The Rehabilitation Process

As the term is used in this talk, the rehabilitation process includes all of those activities that are directly related to the accomplishment of rehabilitation work for buildings and ancillary facilities owned by New York State. The process begins with the development of a need for rehabilitation work. The activities included in the rehabilitation process encompass determination of the need and the scope of work; arranging for the required funding for the project; scheduling for design and construction; accomplishment of the design; selection of contractors to carry out the work; and performing the construction work and its supervision. For a particular project, the rehabilitation process terminates with the completion of construction or other physical work involved. In the broader systems sense, though, the rehabilitation process should be viewed as a continuous means for obtaining the most efficient utilization of the state's physical facilities.

In any building project, there are three basic but interrelated variables that must be considered—*time, cost,* and *quality*. All are as important in rehabilitation as in new construction. *Time* includes the total period that elapses from the identification of the need for a project through its ultimate completion and beneficial occupancy. An important component of this period is the time involved in actual construction work, but the planning time before that is also a relevant consideration. Similarly, *cost* refers to more than simply the cost of doing construction work. It also includes the cost of planning and design, and the future cost implications for maintenance, upkeep, repair, replacement, and alterations. The third item, *quality*, refers to physical attributes including workmanship, type of materials, and the design that governs their arrangement.

In actual projects, the relative importance of these variables may be different. In the rehabilitation sector, for example, some cases are emergencies and time may be the most important consideration. In historical preservation work, the quality of materials, workmanship, and design may be the governing factor. In other cases, for budgetary reasons, cost may be the most influential variable. Theoretically, it is desirable to obtain the highest possible quality at the least cost and in the shortest period of time. In reality, however, it is usually necessary to *trade off* among these variables depending on the particular problem, project situation, or funding availability. The lowest-cost alternative may not be the most efficient solution, if it corresponds with such a low level of quality that work must soon be redone or repaired. Efficiency in the rehabilitation process may, therefore, be defined as obtaining an optimal mixture of the three basic variables in a particular building or facility situation. This may be stated in another way—to obtain the greatest value for dollars expended in light of budget constraints, user desires, and urgency.

Need Identification

To improve the rehabilitation process, the area of need identification will require substantial development. Need identification is accomplished by each central agency headquarters requesting the various agency institutions to submit project requests on the appropriate budget request forms. Thus, no comprehensive coordinated need identification program exists that is uniform for all state institutions, or even for all institutions within a particular agency. Need identification presently depends entirely on the capabilities, priorities, and interests of individual institution personnel.

One of the difficulties inherent in the current need identification method is that some institutions are better qualified than others to perform this activity. Larger institutions generally have higher skills and more diverse capabilities on their maintenance staffs. Even for the state's larger institutions, though, the degree of capability to identify needs adequately may be insufficient. Studies of several state institutions found that "potentially hazardous conditions were observed that were beyond the ability of the facility's safety department to detect due to lack of training in recognizing such conditions."[1] Thus, there may be dangerous situations that go unidentified under present procedures due to insufficient expertise applied to need identification.

There are, in addition, other disadvantages to the current need identification procedure. The nature of need identification tends to be *reactive* rather than *anticipatory*. That is, a need is not identified until it is present, at which time it is reacted to rather than its having been anticipated in advance and planned for. This reactive approach contributes to the overall process time problem because, in effect, funds are not budgeted until the year after they are needed to pay for the necessary rehabilitation. In addition, the lack of anticipatory information gives no indication as to future rehabilitation needs. Such information would be useful to the Division of the Budget and the legislature in allocating funds, as well as to each state agency's long-range facilities planning personnel.

Most physical need identification is accomplished by an institution's maintenance and operating staff, while user need identification is the responsibility of the administrative staff. In either case, it is unlikely that the needs identified are sufficiently oriented to the needs of actual institution users (students, patients, inmates, etc.). At best, the current identification procedures include some input from such personnel as doctors, nurses, administrators, faculty, wardens, guards, and so on, but even this is not inherent. There is no apparent overall methodology, for all of the state's agencies, for effectively gaining real user participation in rehabilitation programming. Under the present approach, there seems to be a bias toward the concerns and desires of the institution administration.

There are really two aspects of need identification. The first is to provide information to determine the budget for rehabilitation work, and the second to provide information to determine rehabilitation projects to be carried out with the money allocated. The information required for each is different, yet in the current overall rehabilitation process no distinction is made between the two. As a result, some of the information obtained in current need identification is more detailed than necessary for budgeting, while other parts are insufficient. In many cases, the information gathered initially is inadequate for design and must be followed up by a second need identification activity performed before commencing design work.

LEGISLATION

I am pleased that the legislature has passed Chapter 837 in the 1983 regular session, an act to amend the State Finance Law in relation to capital planning, budgeting, and reporting. This act includes in the definition of infrastructure not only roads, bridges, ports, airports, and canals, i.e., the transportation sector, but also *public buildings* and *their ancillary facilities*, i.e., the state's physical plant. The act specifically includes prisons, educational facilities, park and recreational facilities, and other capital assets that are in need of repair, expansion, and replacement. The physical rehabilitation needs I have previously described pertain to these. This law is long overdue, and we fully concur with it.

The *deterioration* of the existing physical plant has been occurring for the last three decades. There has been a large expansion of new buildings and supporting facilities—such as, in the 1950s, the Department of Mental Hygiene; in the 60s additional State University campuses; in the 60s and 70s, new office buildings; and now in the 80s, the rapid expansion of the Department of Correctional Services prison facilities to increase inmate housing and their support facilities. In the latter case, program support includes visitation areas, health and dental facilities, indoor and outdoor recreation, administration, and vocational areas, etc. In addition to these user or program needs, there are physical needs for the facilities. These include adaptive reuse of underutilized mental hygiene institutions for correctional use, including modification of shared support facilities such as heating, sewage, potable water, and electric power systems. In spite of the recent increase of the state's physical plant, much of which was done under bonded money under the public benefit authorities and corporations, the funding for physical rehabilitation needs was neglected. Physical rehabilitation work is predominantly accomplished by capital funds. Large rehabilitation work such as alteration and improvements of the state's physical plant was funded by individual line items in the capital budget. Contract small maintenance and repair work was funded by lump sum minor rehabilitation allocations. Physical rehabilitation resources are increasingly deferred by the competing demands for other state services and program alterations; thus a systematic methodology is required to spend the limited state funds, be they bonded or capital funds, for both the physical and program rehabilitation needs.

I talked before about a $20 billion state physical plant. If this plant was in good condition today, the annual funding required to keep it maintained in its current functional condition is estimated to require 1% for physical rehabilitation needs and 1% for agency program needs. This is a total expenditure of $400 million a year after the physical plant is brought up to the proper maintenance level for efficient operating conditions. In addition to this large sum of money, there is the money required for adaptive reuse of underutilized state facilities for both Department of Correctional Services and Division for Youth facilities for their expanding housing needs. Before any future new construction is considered, there should be a study by professional architects and engineers to adapt the existing underutilized state sites to new projects. This should prevent the continuation of new buildings and ancillary facilities while leaving underutilized sites to fall into disrepair.

In addition, the existing 12,000 buildings will have to be maintained in a complete functional environment for the operating agencies so they can perform their functions. By function or program needs, I am talking about furnishing an appropriate physical environment for correctional adult inmates, youthful offenders, and mental patients. Recreation facilities are required for many State University campuses, all of our correctional and youthful offenders facilities, and, of course, the state parks. Office spaces are required for all state agencies to perform their administrative and operational program functions. Because of the state's limited financial resources, a prioritized system for state funds will have to be dedicated to public facilities' capital improvements.

It is important to provide separate, independent funding for the physical rehabilitation needs and for the program rehabilitation needs, since all too often in the past, the program needs progressed rapidly but unproportionally to the physical rehabilitation needs. A mathematical model, using historical data and information, should be developed to determine the allocation of the total funding available by systematically dividing the funds among the various state facilities. There cannot be "orphans" of a low-priority client agency building vs. the high "wealthy" visible type of client agency building. A building is a building, and each will always require maintenance, repairs, alterations, improvements, and replacement of some of its components.

For the long-range plans for all line agencies and public benefit authorities and corporations, a five-year time period is most significant. For example, for a State University campus there is hard dollar funding under State University of New York appropriations, as well as State University Construction Fund bonded monies. Both of these will have to be identified collectively for the agency, rather than independently. The same analogy applies to the Facilities Development Corporation, the Office of Mental Health, and the Office of Mental Retardation. This method will allocate *all* available funds between the ongoing specific needs for the state's individual buildings or facilities. A professional architectural and engineering team should visit each site, in order to determine both its physical and program rehabilitation needs and its estimated construction cost. The priority of its physical maintenance or repairs should be also identified if it is evident that it is reaching a critical stage of deterioration so that the facility cannot perform its program functions. Of course, there will always be emergency repairs and these should be from a lump sum funding source. This latter category can easily be identified *collectively* from historical documents and then individually allocated as each need surfaces.

In our OGS Design and Construction Group, we have a 15-person Bureau of Plant Rehabilitation consisting of architects and engineers. They visit assigned client agency facilities for site investigations. They perform studies for each of their assigned client agency's projects for their budget documentation. For each project they write the technical definition of the project's scope and its estimated construction cost. They perform work for over 40 client line agencies, public benefit corporations, and authorities. Some of their major clients are the OGS state office building facilities, Department of Correctional Services, Division for Youth, State University of New York, State University Construction Fund, Facilities Development Corporation, Office of Mental Health, Office of Mental Retardation, Division of Military and Naval Affairs, Parks and Recreation, Department of Transportation, etc. Note that for the Department of Transportation, we perform all planning, design, and construction work for their new and rehabilitated buildings; they, of course, are responsible for their highways and bridges. You can see that the Bureau of Rehabilitation Planning staff is merely a "drop in the bucket" required to perform the function of budget survey identification for all of the above agencies. This is one of the state's problems. Not only is our architectural and engineering staff for project need identification and definition limited, but also the staff for our assigned design and construction work.

Likewise, maintenance and operation work at the various state facilities is similarly understaffed.

Most of the state's facilities perform only deferred maintenance or emergency "breakdown" repairs, rather than also performing preventive maintenance, because of understaffed site maintenance personnel resources. Bonded monies often resulted in new buildings or facilities, but then subsequent capital hard dollar funding was not made available for their annual physical rehabilitation needs. You do not run your personal new car into the ground without normal lubrication, oil changes, and tune-ups, yet this in essence is what the state has done in many cases for its physical plant. Large monetary resources would not be required for major repairs or replacements if ongoing small annual maintenance funds were made available.

Another element, the building mechanical and electrical systems, has shared limited maintenance forces. If required calibration and maintenance is not performed, a facility's energy consumption goes up dramatically over the years. For example, we have nine combustion control specialists visiting the 85 large central heating plants serving multibuilding complexes. They have saved a net cost avoidance in energy consumption during the last six years of over $30 million. However, similar energy conservation efforts on a prioritized basis for the state's other buildings to save the "big bucks" have not been implemented due to lack of resources. A continuous preventive maintenance program should be implemented for all our mechanical and electrical systems. In fact, it is required for *all* building systems. A roof is a good example of progressive deterioration — if its water leakages are not fixed within a few years, the fiberglass insulation rapidly deteriorates for the complete roof area, which then has to be replaced in subsequent years at many, many times the cost of its annual inspection and minor repairs. A similar analogy can be made for parking lots, tennis courts, etc. The allocation of funding has to be updated annually for expansion of the physical plant, for readaptive reuse of underutilized facilities, for program changes, for neglected repairs requiring replacements, etc. Legislation alone will not correct this problem for the state's annual physical plant maintenance needs, but it is a partner in effective reduction of progressive deterioration. Recently passed legislation correctly states that the state's comprehensive capital planning and budgeting process must incorporate long-range plans of all state agencies and public benefit corporations to insure that important projects receive their proper allocation of limited resources. Particular projects of a facility or client agency that are program oriented cannot be implemented at the expense of its needed physical maintenance needs. Once again, as I mentioned before, these needs will have to be identified *separately* in each project's budget request and allocation. This is not to say that program needs are not required, but they should be funded separately and not at the expense of maintenance and repairs.

I would also like to comment on proposed assembly bill 6084A, introduced by Assemblymen Ferris, Kremer, Fink, and others. This bill we wholeheartedly endorse as a supplement to the previously mentioned passed law. It does include many areas not covered by the previous law of Chapter 837. This bill also identifies that corrective deferred maintenance items are non-productive due to both inflation and *progressive deterioration*. Note the words "progressive deterioration"—the analogy I gave before on roofs is a good example. It highlights the "breakdown" principle whereby replacements are made only when a building component ceases to function or deteriorates to an intolerable level so that it cannot perform its function. The bill states the need for forecasting of needed maintenance. I would substitute the words "physical rehabilitation of the state's physical plant" for the word "maintenance." Future budgets should collectively analyze both bonded monies and "hard dollar" capital funds. We concur with this proposed bill's reference to the requirement for life cycle costing analyses, although it did not identify this by name.

Let me define that life cycle costing of a project consists of the total cost of the project. For example, for a new building it would consist of the initial cost; the staffing requirement costs over the life of the building; and the maintenance, repair, and replacement costs of the building's materials, systems, and equipment over the life of the building. The life of a state building would normally be from 30 to 50 years, depending upon the particular project and method of funding. For a new building, the architectural/engineering consultants should furnish a life cycle costing analysis, but their fee would have to be increased proportionally for this item. The fee for design of a new building is in the range of 5 to 6% of its construction cost, but it is less than 1½% of the total life cost of the building. So it is prudent to include extra cost for the design, including life cycle costing analyses as well as an integrated maintenance and operation manual of the completed facility. I use the word "integrated," because usually what we have received for our projects are maintenance manuals for the individual equipment or systems for each of at least five contracts per project required by public bidding laws. For the building example, there would be a construction contract; a heating, ventilating, and air-conditioning contract; an electric contract; a plumbing contract; and a site work contract. But within these contracts we receive numerous manuals on each contract's equipment and systems. Since a common maintenance force has to do *all* maintenance and operation, an integrated common maintenance manual is required, with a complete schedule of maintenance for such items as lubrication, testing of emergency generators, etc. This manual is valuable, especially for the building's mechanical and electrical systems that are energy oriented. They are available from design consultants at a very nominal fee.

We have provided the State University and many other major client agencies with roof maintenance manuals and training courses so that their maintenance personnel can early identify minor leaks in the roofing systems and have them repaired before they require major repairs or complete replacement. We are performing training of heating plant operators on their combustion control systems. Much greater efforts in training of maintenance and operating staffs of the physical plant in other areas are required.

The highlighting of deferred maintenance in both of the aforementioned legislative bills is important so that maintenance needs do not slip through by deference from year to year due to the state's austerity periods.

I would like to mention another concept that has been used limitedly in the state, that is, a revolving fund for energy conservation. If we could reallocate say 50% of the money saved in energy expenditures documented by a facility for a particular fiscal year, this money could be used for future energy conservation projects at the facility having relatively short payback periods. This "priming of the pump" is a technique that should be investigated as a methodology to assure sufficient funds for energy conservation. The same approach can be utilized for other maintenance needs. For state purpose and capital budget expenditures, scheduled physical plant rehabilitation work can be identified; those that are not funded one year should be included in the subsequent following year. This would prevent any specific item constantly slipping through the budget cycle for more than two years. These bills are both important, as they place the accountability on all of the governing bodies: the Governor's Office, the Division of the Budget, and the client agencies. The legislative intent of these two bills for a systematic facility rehabilitation approach on a priority basis consistent with funding is good intent, but will function only if supplementary monetary and personnel resources are made available. Management reports are required to identify all funding and resulting accomplishments. More important, they should also identify those areas that are constantly being deferred in regard to much needed physical rehabilitation.

Although the legislation refers to both physical rehabilitation of and manuals for *mechanical* and *electric* systems, it should refer to *all* building and facility systems, including construction and site work. However, the mechanical and electric systems are probably the most important for a large building, because they are energy oriented. Oil and gas prices are escalating at a higher rate than the normal consumers index or material and labor inflation rates; so it would be prudent to emphasize physical rehabilitation of mechanical and electric systems, but not at the cost of other elements such as roofing, landscape, parking lots, etc. As I reflect, during my tenure with the state for the last 35 years, I have lived with this problem from my early days to the present. This includes my assignment as Chief Stationary Engineer for the Albany State Office Building Campus, Director of Facilities Planning and Operation Group for all OGS state office building operations, and subsequently my present position as commissioner of OGS. I commend the legislature's "Commission on Science and Technology" for including in this all-encompassing conference consideration of efforts to solve the problem of the state's deteriorating physical plant.

REFERENCE

1. Environment Systems International. 1971. Saref, Systems Approach for Rehabilitation of Existing Facilities. Office of General Service. The State of New York. Albany, N.Y.

Legislation Needed to Rehabilitate Our Water and Sewer Infrastructure

HENRY G. WILLIAMS

Office of the Commissioner
New York State Department of Environmental Conservation
50 Wolf Road
Albany, New York 12233-0001

I appreciate the opportunity to be here today to discuss what has become an increasingly important water resources management need — water and sewer infrastructure rehabilitation. You know there is an old Russian proverb that goes something like this: Don't spit in the well; you'll be thirsty by and by. I would say that if we have not spat in the well yet, it is a sure bet that we are about to. If not, you can bet the pump is broken.

But what I want to talk to you about today is this: our water infrastructure is an economic asset and the foundation of our future. Right now, it is in serious disrepair. In New York, the repair bill is a multi-billion-dollar dilemma. The problem is not going to go away by itself. There are no magic buttons to push to make it disappear. There simply is no way to stop wear and tear on existing systems. It is inevitable. Furthermore, we cannot depend on the federal treasury to rebuild our public works. Washington has shown some interest but no action. We have to do the job. Indeed, we must commit our state to infrastructure rehabilitation and improvement. The question is, how?

As you might imagine, we have given a lot of thought to the subject, considering ideas from federal assistance to state bond acts to privatization and everything in between. The infrastructure problem is basically a financing problem. To finance the rehabilitation and get commitments from localities to operate, maintain, rehabilitate, and improve it, as they are needed, is a tough assignment. Yet, I think, it is doable. Here is why.

Let me go back a minute and review some political, institutional, and social facts of life. The first and most important is that the provision of water and sewer services is an essential enterprise that is revenue producing. Furthermore, according to a United States Commerce Department survey, the most critical community attribute that industry looks for in deciding where to relocate or expand is the availability of fire protection. That means the most important asset a community can develop is a reliable water system capable of delivering water at a sufficient pressure and flow. This is much more valuable and important to industry than tax incentives are. Yet states and localities continually compete with one another to ruin their tax bases. As this same survey indicates, taxes make little difference in the final relocation or expansion decision. This means we have a valuable asset that is worth fixing.

Second, there are probably not going to be major federal grants for water supply. As a result, solutions will have to be oriented toward state and local financing capabilities.

It is also our strong belief that New York State taxpayers cannot be asked to pay higher taxes to resolve the problem. Nor should they be subject to further debt liability because of unforeseen circumstances that may result in municipal default. There is no reason for the people of Yonkers to pay or be obligated to pay for water improvements in Syracuse. Clearly, the citizens of New York State do not need additional taxes or the prospect of more tax liabilities to support what is essentially a revenue-producing utility.

Another factor is that the New York State Constitution has effectively prohibited the use of revenue bond financing by cities where we have our most serious problem. This has occurred because of the structuring of debt limits, and because of certain constitutional prohibitions on the establishment of public corporations. While we may argue that these are unjust or inappropriate requirements, they exist and we must face them. We must work within our constitutional framework.

Also, the revenue generated by our state's water utilities is sometimes used to help support other municipal services. We respect those local decisions. Yet, to the extent that these monies can be reserved to operate, maintain, refurbish, and improve the water utility, the better off a water system will be. That is the object on a statewide basis of the Ferris bill.

From a state viewpoint, any institution that is created to resolve this dilemma must have the incentive and ability to seek federal funds to help localities finance refurbishments and improvements. And there should be provisions for the development of a coherent state expenditure and regulatory policy. While we do not want to restrict or control local decisions, the expenditure of billions of dollars should be made under some consistent statewide framework. Such a policy will make the entire state more attractive to business and industry.

I believe that the New York State water finance authority legislation proposed by Governor Cuomo can effectively deal with the physical and financial needs of localities. It does this by meshing our water infrastructure needs with the political and institutional realities just enumerated to create an institution that is capable of meeting each locality's water system priorities. In addition, it will enable the municipality to capitalize on emerging opportunities as they occur.

The water finance authority would do this by providing $4 billion of bonding capacity for water and sewer system rehabilitation and improvement. It would also provide a means for establishing a self-sustaining water utility. There is provision for development of a coherent state expenditure and regulatory policy. And finally, there is a means to seek and apply for federal grants to help finance water improvements.

How will the authority work? From a municipal perspective, the most pressing questions relate to financing options and project priority selections.

Let me briefly speak to the three financing options. Let me emphasize that all of these options are strictly voluntary.

The first is a loan option. Basically, the loan works like a home mortgage. Municipalities decide what they want to build and apply for a loan. Payback terms are reached by mutual agreement. Locally, either real estate taxes or a user charge can be used to cover the liability.

The second option is a leaseback approach. Under this arrangement, the municipality builds and then leases the facility, say, a water treatment plant, from the water finance authority. The asset is owned by the authority until it is paid in full. This protects the authority in the event of bankruptcy because the authority will own a revenue-producing asset to repay investors. A user charge and reserves are established within the municipality to cover operation, maintenance, and debt service.

The third alternative open to public municipal water purveyors is the revenue bond option. It is by far the most attractive. Here is how it works.

Once again, the municipality establishes its water system infrastructure priorities. A contract between the water finance authority, the local water board, and the municipality is drawn to accommodate the local priority project. The board must be established to comply with the state constitution. It requires an act of the legislature. It, in effect, is a water revenue accountant and bagman for the municipality. The board collects all service revenue to pay off the debt to the authority, and they see to it that there is enough money to operate and maintain the utility. The surplus revenue can be returned to the general revenue fund. Because the board is separate from the municipality, revenues are protected in the event of general municipal default. This not only accommodates the state constitution but also Wall Street, which is a tough combination to satisfy, I might add. The municipality continues to be the owner and operator of the water utility.

The advantages of the revenue bond financing alternative are many. The first is that revenue bonds are often more favorably rated than the municipality's own general obligation debt. And they ensure that water and sewer utilities are put on a self-sustaining basis. Additionally, revenue bonds are more attractive to investors than is general obligation debt. Since 1970, the proportion of new bonds sold as general obligation bonds decreased from 66% of new market issue to less than 30%, while revenue bonds have increased from 33% to over 70%.

Secondly, the increased debt capacity helps a municipality maintain a more favorable debt position for general obligation borrowing.

The third is that general obligation borrowing capacity can be saved for projects that are not revenue producing. This happens because the accumulation of debt for water supply is not restricted by the constitution.

And finally, communities can, if they so choose, refinance up to 20% of existing debt through this funding option. This increases their general obligation capacity. It also can reduce absolute project costs by reducing financing payback periods at lower rates of interest.

That, in a nutshell, describes the financing alternatives and their advantages. I might add that, in each case, existing mandated statutory reviews by the Department of Health and the Department of Environmental Conservation must be made.

From a state perspective, there are additional advantages. The first and most obvious is that we would have a credible institution in place that can help localities reconstruct, refurbish, and improve the state's water and sewer infrastructure systems. The attendant benefits include the jobs produced, the attraction of industry by such an asset, and lower-interest financing for everyone because centralized borrowing will not necessarily bid up interest rates.

In addition, the state taxpayer is not obligated for debt, thus protecting the state in the event of default.

Also, the bill allows local control over the water or sewer utility.

Through the development of water resources management strategies — also part of the bill — and resultant system refurbishment, the ability to use our water resource as an economic incentive is enhanced. This will be an economic benefit for the state.

In summary, I believe that the water finance authority is an innovative financing and management mechanism for New York State and is urgently needed to assist municipal and private water purveyors in financing water and sewer system rehabilitaton. It would also allow New York State to evaluate local water projects in a statewide and regional context. Because of the special structure of the bill, the authority would not obligate New York State taxpayers for debt. It would provide assurance to investors for payment in full in the event of a municipal default, and it would allow local control over water and sewer system operations. It would not only provide several innovative financing alternatives for water and sewer system rehabilitation and improvements, but it also would provide a mechanism to develop a coherent state expenditure and management policy through development of statewide and regional water resources management strategies required by the legislation. And finally, we need your support because the program will only benefit those who want to help themselves.

Part III: General Discussion

Moderator: JOSEPH FERRIS

Legislative Commission on Science and Technology
The State of New York
Two World Trade Center, Suite 5026
New York, New York 10047

W. C. WRIGHT (*Metropolitan Studies Program, Syracuse University, Syracuse, N.Y.*): I have a question for Mr. Egan. Earlier, Robert Lamb talked about decapitalizing government—and that really involves selling nonessential buildings. I wonder, is this something that you're trying to inventory? And will you as a policy measure get rid of these buildings you consider to be nonessential?

J. C. EGAN (*New York State Office of General Services, Albany, N.Y.*): Yes, under the Public Lands Law the Office of General Services is responsible for the inventory of all state-owned real properties; and indeed that very thing has occurred, though I regret to say we haven't emphasized it to the media. There are a number of facilities that have been surplused by the state.

One of the most prominent ones is in the New York City area, the former drug addiction control facility at Ridge Hill. We were able to decommission it under a long-term lease, rather than a sale lease, to the Lorell Corporation, which is a high technology electronics firm. Thus it was taken off the state's list of facilities and put into the private sector for very specific economic development purposes. There are a number of other facilities like that. A second one in New York City is 55 Hansen Place, a former YMCA in Brooklyn. We're looking at the possibility right now of selling that facility, then possibly leasing it back for office space as we move out of the World Trade Center.

A third one is the former Homer Folkes facility at Oneonta, New York. We rent that facility to the federal government for use by the Job Corps, and we've sold off a significant amount of that property.

My guess is that within the next month there may be an announcement indicating the amount of real property the state has sold during the past 12 months. I don't want to use the dollar figure, but there's a significant amount of revenue that has accrued to the state over the last 12 months from the decapitalizing of our plant.

My personal opinion is that we have to do more—we have to recognize that perhaps the state is getting smaller.

J. DEDYO (*Metcalf & Eddy, New York, N.Y.*): My question is to Mr. Burns [New York State Department of Environmental Conservation] and to Mr. Ferris. We talked about alternative financing on a number of occasions here, and earlier someone mentioned privatization and asked a question about it. I don't recall whether there was a specific response, but at this session I didn't hear anyone mention anything about the need for any changes in legislation that would permit privatization. I guess the meaning of the word privatization is getting private financing into the ownership, construction, and operation of facilities such as municipal water treatment plants, sewage treatment plants, and other facilities.

I was wondering whether or not the legislature has considered any of this or has the Department of Environmental Conservation [DEC] considered any of these legislative changes that might be required? I can think of a couple: (1) procurement; (2) long-term contracting and the possibility of private ownership of what may be a municipal facility right now.

J. C. EGAN: Within the DEC we've considered privatization particularly for sewage treatment plants. We really haven't looked at it in any detail for water supply. The government now is going to develop and has developed some task forces to look at various innovative mechanisms for financing infrastructure. Privatization is one of those being considered. There is no legislation on the state level for privatization that I'm aware of.

J. FERRIS: I would add, since you posed the question to me also, that I think it's a matter of philosophy. You do have some water systems in this state that are privately owned, and some that are publicly owned. My concern is that it's a very fragmented arrangement throughout the state. Water is one of the most important natural resources that our state has and there has to be an overall plan for its use. Yet, I really don't know how that can be done in such a way, in a state the size of New York, that you maintain both the system and the quality of water to be delivered through that system for the people, the industries, and the commercial enterprises.

It's been posed as an intriguing alternative to public ownership. What you're talking about is the use of citizens' assets. Very near to my district is a city-owned building that is no longer utilized. That's one type of privatization that might make very good sense. There are other examples. For instance, we've moved away from the day when roads were privately controlled. I think a good part of a session could be spent on this question. I think it's something we should look at both from the standpoint of people's philosophy and also some of the practical applications of the need for resources, i.e., revenues and capitalization. I would keep an open mind on it.

W. C. WRIGHT: Mr. Wagner today expressed a need for federal money in the water industry. As a practicing engineer and involved in academics at this time, I see the performance of the federal grants system as somewhat suboptimal. The American Water Works Association is very much against federal involvement in the water industry. I just wonder what your opinion is on having a large federal involvement in the water industry at this time.

J. C. EGAN: We would like any kind of federal money that we can get to help subsidize what is a large state need in water supply. How that money comes to the state, whether it be in grants or in the form of a low-interest loan, is what we're debating at the moment.

At the federal level I think there's no chance to get a grant like a sewage treatment plant grant for water supply; rather we're looking at perhaps a bank that would give us low-interest loans.

J. Rowen (*State Capitol, Albany, N.Y.*): I have a question for either Commissioner Egan or Assemblyman Ferris. One of the things about the maintenance budgeting bill is that it is reporting and budgeting public accountability. If a system like that is in place, either by administrative means or by Assembly Bill 6084A, and we get better reporting, what do you think the next step or the next problem is going to be in taking care of the state agencies' physical plant maintenance?

J. C. Egan: I think one of the things that concerns me is not overpowering people with paper and not overpowering them with information. You know it is the information age, and we can accumulate an awful lot of data that people get discouraged with. I think the right amount of information is what we're looking for, and we're looking for consistency, and we're looking for standards. At the present time standards in my judgment are lacking, and that's probably the most important thing we can actually do. The governor said this over and over when talking about where the money was needed most. I mentioned earlier having been in the Corrections Department when it really wasn't a popular department, and we didn't spend any money on maintenance so the whole place crashed and broke down.

What we're saying is that the physical plant belongs to all the people of the state and that maintenance standards should be consistent regardless of the agency and that the monitoring process should be consistent, whether it's for energy conservation or whether it's for roof maintenance or building maintenance in general. But above all, it has to be professionalized because the state has a tremendous investment.

J. Ferris: I would just like to add to what Commissioner Egan said. I think really what it does is impose a discipline upon us which has not been there. It also requires us to begin to plan with a view that maybe long after we have left the scene, there will be an ongoing continuity. This is one of the things I have seen emerge in my own experience in the legislature. People are beginning to talk about doing things in some kind of continuous way. When planning capital projects, the budgetary process is now including the idea of maintenance projections. In some areas we're no longer simply waiting for something to happen or for it to be politically alluring. We do maintenance in a way that's consistent and understandable by our constituencies. I think this has not been part of the normal political discourse, and it has not been in the public consciousness. I've tried in my own district to bring this to the fore so the people would understand that a water tunnel is important and the maintenance of public facilities is something that you just don't take care of when something happens, but that you do it on a regular, consistent basis.

I think it's critical to create the consciousness, to create the discipline, to create the strategy in terms of planning and capitalization both in terms of building, rebuilding, and maintaining.

I would just like to add that the beginning we have made here at this conference has been excellent. We've had thoughtful, intelligent input from every level of government. This forms the foundation for us to have a logical, coherent position to develop so that we may draft and implement legislation that will resolve the problem of maintaining and repairing our infrastructure.

Introduction

SATOSHI OISHI

Edwards and Kelcey
Engineers and Consultants
53 Park Place
New York, New York 10007

Before beginning this session, I thought it might be useful and informative for me to exercise my prerogative as chairman by appending a few words of overview and introduction to the subject of standards and their role and impact on the repair and maintenace of infrastructure.

There are two different sets of standards or goals that govern the planning, design, and construction of public works.

One set of standards are expressions of public policy. Written into laws and legislation, they express our desires to attain such goals as cleaner air and water; energy conservation; a higher quality of the natural environment; more choices in transportation; and protection from natural and man-made disasters. We have instituted great and costly programs in the pursuit of these goals. And for the most part, we rely on the skill and competence of the technological and professional communities to implement these programs.

Coming into play in the process of implementation is a second set of standards, which assure the public that satisfactory levels are met in regard to safety, performance, and equity. These standards are the codes, specifications, and practices, usually written in great detail by professional societies or associations and intended to reflect the currently accepted state of the art. They are compiled, viewed, and revised periodically according to evidence collected from experience, performance, research, and the general advance of technology.

In the first years of our national attention to the repair and maintenance of infrastructure, we are finding, not surprisingly, that current codes and specifications are not helpful in many situations. The main body of the codes and their focus are addressed to new construction — not enough to repair and rehabilitation. Many problems involving conflicts between old and new standards are being met and solved on an *ad hoc* basis, using the best judgments available on that occasion; tests and research are being conducted on new materials for specific, perhaps one-time-only applications; innovative construction techniques are being used to repair or upgrade facilities without interrupting their use; and new analytical techniques are being used for evaluation. In the beginning of this national effort of infrastructure renewal, new standards are being created at the same time that the work is going on. The experience and data being gained are not being gathered and recorded systematically.

In this transitional period, the experiences and observations regarding the impact of standards on repair and reconstruction will be discussed by three outstanding engineers who are working in the forefront of this activity — Bernard Haber, Martin Lang, and James Pielert.

Bridge and Highway Standards

BERNARD HABER

Hardesty & Hanover
Consulting Engineers
1501 Broadway
New York, New York 10036

When a pin falls out of a link bar suspension bridge as happened in December 1967 resulting in the collapse of the Silver Bridge between Ohio and West Virginia and killing 46 people, or a span of a major highway bridge suddenly collapses as occurred in June 1983 on the Connecticut Turnpike killing 3 people, we all become concerned over the safety and integrity of our nation's transportation system. It is hard enough to accept the present-day risks and perils of derailments, aircraft crashes, tank explosions, and nuclear plant failures, but we do not accept the failure of our infrastructure especially in our transportation system.

After the 1967 Silver Bridge collapse, the federal government undertook a massive inventory, inspection, and evaluation program of the nation's more than 600,000 bridges. Major attention was focused on the specifications and standards that were used for the design of our bridges and highways. As a result, a flurry of revisions and additions have been made to the most-used specifications such as the Bridge and Highway Specifications published by the American Association of State Highway and Transportation Officials (AASHTO) and the American Railway Engineering Association's Specification for Railroads and Railroad Structures (AREA).

BRIDGE SPECIFICATIONS

The major changes in bridge specifications have dealt with fatigue and life cycle consideration and with details of steel design. The early AASHTO specifications, under which our interstate highway system has been designed, dealt with fatigue only in alerting the design engineer to evaluate alternating stresses in his design of structural steel systems. They required that if alternating stresses occur in succession during one passage of live load, the maximum positive and negative stresses should each be increased by 50% of the smaller and the connections of such a member should be proportioned for the sum of the net alternating stresses.

In the early 1960s, AASHTO specifications paid little attention to criteria for stress range, cycles of loading, and details to minimize stress concentrations and fatigue in steel design. Subsequent specifications and research focused on the effects of repetitive loading on bridges and resulted in a better

91

understanding of bridge fatigue behavior. Substantial changes were made in fatigue provisions in the 1965 AASHTO and the 1969 AREA bridge design specifications. These revised specifications for the first time addressed the fatigue problems from secondary and displacement-induced stresses.

Present fatigue specifications provide criteria for redundant and nonredundant load path structures. Redundant structures are those with multiload paths where a single fracture of a member cannot lead to collapse, such as a single-span multistringer bridge or a multilayered riveted or bolted connection. Nonredundant structures are those with a single load path where a single fracture can lead to a catastrophic collapse, such as flanges or webs in a one- or two-girder span bridge or in a single-element welded connection.

In current specifications, major stress reductions are required for 2,000,000 or more load cycles. Many of our existing urban bridges and highways are subjected to more than 2,000,000 cycles of maximum load annually. These existing bridges were designed with much greater allowable stresses than would be permitted in current criteria.

Other major changes in bridge specifications dealt with details of steel design, strength requirements of bridge railing, increased allowable stresses in reinforcing steel and structural steel, protection of substructure over navigable waters, pile foundation design, concrete decks, and reinforcing steel placement to name a few. The recent increase in the allowable live loadings of almost 10%, to an 80,000-pound vehicle, will have a most significant effect on our bridge and highway system.

Standards in bridge deck design have changed greatly. In the past 20 years, certain types of bridge deck construction have fallen in and out of favor. Included in these are monolithic concrete decks, orthotropic decks, composite decks, and concrete decks with latex or asphalt overlays. Most bridge deck reinforcement now consists of epoxy-coated steel bars to minimize corrosion and deterioration of concrete. Current specifications place much more emphasis on design of bridge joints, bearings, drainage, waterproofing, and on the design of the details of bridges.

HIGHWAY SPECIFICATIONS

Major changes in highway design have also occurred over the past 15 to 20 years. The changes deal mainly with making our highways safer for our present faster, larger, and heavier vehicles. These changes include such design requirements as:

1. Wider lanes.
2. Longer acceleration, deceleration, and weaving lanes.
3. Construction of median barriers and stronger railings.
4. Elimination of gores by use of impact attenuators.
5. Increased horizontal and vertical clearances to hazards such as bridge structures, poles, and natural obstructions.
6. Highway shoulders for disabled vehicles.
7. Break-away poles.

8. Signing, lighting, and reflectorized pavement markings.
9. Oversized traffic-signal lenses.
10. Scarified pavements for skid proofing.

Since design speeds dictate minimum highway curvature, superelevation, and stopping sight distance, our new highways have longer vertical and horizontal curves, pronounced superelevation, and flatter grades. Present standards are more stringent. Often in the past, decisions were made based on political expediency rather than design criteria. Many older highways have dangerous drop-off lanes, parking cutouts instead of shoulders, narrow lanes (11 feet and under), substandard clearances, sharp curvatures, steep grades, and superelevation not consistent with operating speeds. These highways are now considered functionally obsolete and are prime candidates for reconstruction in our present national effort for infrastructure rehabilitation.

BRIDGE AND HIGHWAY REHABILITATION DESIGN

The result of specification changes has been structures that are more conservatively designed than those of the 1950s and 1960s. Therefore, the deterioration that has been uncovered during the federally mandated inspection and evaluation program most likely will prove a lesser problem in 10 or 20 years when structures designed in the 1970s and 1980s are well into their life cycle. Likewise, our highways designed today are safer and more durable to withstand the loads and traffic they are subjected to. But one of the major problems that today's engineer is experiencing is making the rehabilitation and repair of our bridges and highways conform to present specifications, that is, applying present specifications to structures and highways designed and built 20, 30, or more years ago.

In many cases, applying present standards would require the removal or closing of an existing bridge or highway and complete reconstruction of the facility. Obviously, most times this is not possible. Therefore, substandard features must be reduced to the best of the engineer's ability.

A typical case history where problems were encountered in trying to apply present-day specifications to a rehabilitation design was for the 3.5-mile, high-level Pulaski Skyway between Jersey City and Newark, New Jersey. This structure is composed of a series of stringer, girder, and truss spans with major cantilever structures over the Hackensack and Passaic Rivers. It is probably the longest continuous viaduct structure in the Northeast. It was designed between 1925 and 1930 and built in the early 1930s. The specifications that were used were those of the American Association of State Highway Officials (AASHO) dated 1924, 1928, and 1929. Those specifications as well as subsequent ones (until the early 1960s) allowed exterior stringers to be proportioned for the actual dead load and live load they carried. Present-day AASHTO specifications state that the outside stringers shall not have a capacity less than interior stringers.

In analyzing the Pulaski Skyway for the present-day criteria, exterior stringers were found to be substandard, requiring reinforcement or replacement. The cost of this work was prohibitive. After much discussion and further investigation, it was decided that the specifications that the bridge was designed under will be the ones used for rating the exterior stringers, since the exterior stringer will never be subjected to load greater than it was designed for, nor was widening of the structure contemplated or possible. Thus the exterior stringer will never become an interior stringer (see FIGURE 1). This rating proved to be satisfactory and negated the need for any rehabilitation. The experience proved that careful evaluation is required before proceeding on expensive rehabilitation programs which may be required by specification. In this instance, using working stress analyses and applying only the actual loads to be carried by the exterior stringers resulted in an acceptable rating.

Present-day standard specifications should be used if physically and economically feasible. However, if this cannot be done, then extreme care should be exercised in designing the repair or replacement elements. As an illustration, riveted or bolted bridges require accurate analysis of the base metal if repairs by welding are indicated. In general, engineers believe that field repairs by welding should be minimized.

Many items for bridge rehabilitation such as drainage, joints, bearings, lighting, and barriers are not necessarily affected by specification changes. However, bridge geometrics involving substandard lane width, obstruction offsets, superelevation, safety curbs, and underclearances can pose a serious problem. Bridges are expensive, and therefore the ingenuity of the engineer in improving or eliminating substandard features is most valuable.

Another difficult problem is the rating and posting of bridges and highways for specific loadings. The engineer must carefully consider the type of traffic the bridge or highway carries. An occasional truck on a passenger vehicle parkway such as the Grand Central Parkway or Henry Hudson Parkway in New York City or the Merritt Parkway in Connecticut is not sufficient reason to post a parkway structure even if, under analysis, it cannot sustain the specified truck loading. On the other hand, the Long Island Expressway (I-495) and the Connecticut Turnpike (I-95) must have the capacity to carry the maximum specified truck loadings.

Highways must be reconstructed to meet current criteria and modern design. Communicative signing, high occupancy vehicle lanes, collector-distributor roads with controlled access, service interchanges between freeways and arterial streets, system interchanges between freeways, adequate length of acceleration and deceleration lanes, safety design and appurtenances, elimination of obstructions, and pavements having the structural capacity for longer and heavier vehicles are all examples of current criteria and modern design to be considered in highway rehabilitation. Obviously, many of these improvements require addition of right-of-way which may or may not be available. Highways such as the Pennsylvania Turnpike, one of our oldest toll roads, can only accommodate a few of these improvements. Here the judgment of the engineer requires that he evaluate all factors (cost, land acquisition, community impact, etc.) to make the highway conform as best as possible to current safety and design standards, knowing full well that all substandard features cannot be eliminated and that all current criteria cannot be met.

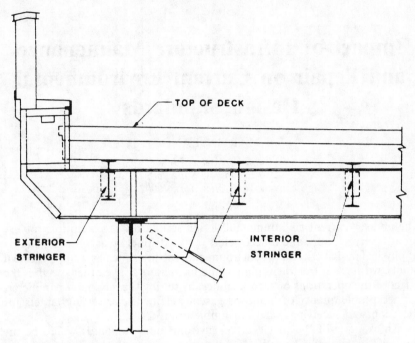

FIGURE 1. Typical girder span section. Exterior and interior stringers are shown.

Present estimates of public construction needs throughout the nation indicate that rehabilitation, reconstruction, and repair of bridges will cost approximately $50 billion. Reconstruction of highways will cost approximately $320 billion. Some existing and new sources of funding that could pay the bill are dedicated taxes, infrastructure bank, transportation bonds, and trust funds. Much will be learned during this enormous expenditure. Unlike new construction, which is well documented, rehabilitation and repair design and construction have little history. The experience encountered in this work should be recorded and made available to all agencies throughout the United States. We need a federally controlled information system for recording details of bridge and highway repair and rehabilitation projects. The information gathered should help government and private agencies to assure the integrity and safety of our transportation system.

In summary, bridge and highway specifications have become more conservative. This development creates major problems for the engineer in the rehabilitation of bridges and highways. Yet, substandard features must be mitigated wherever possible, which will require the ingenuity of the engineer. The efforts put forth, though, should not be lost to future generations, and therefore a national information system should be developed for recording the methods and details of repair and rehabilitation of our bridges and highways.

Impact of Infrastructure Maintenance and Repair on Current Environmental Design Standards

MARTIN LANG

Camp Dresser & McKee
250 Broadway, Suite 2601
New York, New York 10007

The phrase "current environmental design standards" is susceptible to very broad interpretation, and indeed refers to two distinct areas. One is the body of physical design criteria for environmental facilities such as water treatment plants, wastewater treatment plants, and incinerators. The other specifies the effect of the operations of such facilities, by setting the minimum parameters for acceptable quality of liquid or gaseous effluents, or setting targets for the quality of receiving waters or ambient air.

An example of the first type of environmental standards would be the body of the Federal Clean Water Act requirements, which would affect the design of, for example, the North River water pollution control plant on the Hudson River in New York City.

An example of the second type would be the Interstate Sanitation Commission's requirement for the minimum level of dissolved oxygen to be maintained in the Hudson River in New York City.

We will discuss each type separately, since they have different impacts and require different responses.

The very word "environment" itself embraces such a wide spectrum of meaning that it would be prudent to confine this discussion to a more specific arena. It is quite true that I once attempted to define the "total environment" as the entire ambience affecting humankind — that, of course, included pure air, pure food, and pure water and also included housing, employment, energy, transportation, and recreation. However, basic urban infrastructure problems usually involve facilities and programs involving land, water, and air.

We can sharply focus on typical urban infrastructure maintenance problems by using urban water pollution control programs and their current status as an example. An overview of these programs illustrates the effect of both kinds of environmental standards, since:

1. They have been steered by a proliferating and changing complex body of standards both for treatment itself and for the receiving waters.
2. Their funding ranges from a vast federal program to penurious local budgets.

3. The technology ranges from sewers, some of which would look familiar to the ancient Romans, to highly sophisticated automated advanced waste treatment plants.
4. The maintenance history ranges from grossly malign neglect to effective computerized preventive maintenance programs.

Confronted with a doomsday scenario of disintegrating cities, the National League of Cities and the United States Conference of Mayors conducted a survey of about 700 cities, sampling a population of 60 million, to at least approximately quantify the infrastructure status and needs of cities. This was published as *Capital Budgeting and Infrastructure in American Cities: An Intitial Assessment* in April 1983.

Of 19 different categories of urban infrastructure, 3 were:

Stormwater collection and drainage.
Wastewater treatment and interceptors.
Sewage collection.

It is noteworthy that when these cities ranked their capital budget priorities, these 3 items were ranked second, third, and fourth of the 19 infrastructure parameters.

In this tremendous sample, probably the best currently valid data base available, the cities were required to rate the status of the various components of their infrastructure:

1. Of 738 cities responding, 74% cited "stormwater collection and drainage" in need of major rehabilitation.
2. Of 696 cities responding, 58% cited "sewage collection" in need of major rehabilitation.
3. Of 582 cities responding, 48% cited "wastewater treatment and interceptors" in need of major rehabilitation.

What are the prospects of these cities for accomplishing this major restoration of these vital support systems? The cities were asked to assess their ability to finance this work. The credibility of the responses may be indicated by the fact that only 25% of some 600 cities responding indicated that they needed any significant outside help to fund water supply rehabilitation. However, 77% required such help for wastewater treatment and interceptors, 54% for stormwater collection and drainage, and 52% for sewage collection. (There is an interesting sidelight to this. Cities had never looked to outside help, in the past, for water supply aid. For the last decade, cities have been hooked on federal funding for water pollution control.)

There is then compelling evidence that water pollution control facilities represent a major part, and a high-priority part, of urban infrastructure needs.

This is after $30 billion have been committed under the Clean Waters Act. This is a decade after Congress passed the prototype act, PL 92-500, over the president's veto. Now that the federal funding is being phased down, it is reasonable to estimate that it will take the remaining 17 years of this century for the upgrading and rehabilitation of these three components of the urban life-support system.

Before we draw any conclusions as to the cause of the present state of these systems, it would be prudent to review their history, particularly the last decade, which was marked by a ferment of design and construction in water pollution control.

1. For the past century, until the environmental movement heightened the public consciousness, sewer maintenance, in some cities, as well as wastewater treatment, was viewed as some unsightly and malodorous function, out of the public sight and mind, and to which the untrainable residue of political patronage could be assigned.

2. In some cities, a high degree of engineering talent was utilized to design and construct wastewater facilities, but that same level of expertise was rarely deployed in operation and maintenance thereafter.

3. The massive funding to design and construct was actually easier to get, in some instances, through bond issues and federal aid than was the local funding that had to be scrimped together to operate and maintain.

4. The late 1970s were marked by the allegations that many of the facilities recently built under Environmental Protection Agency (EPA) funding were not operating to regulatory standards or design intent. There were multiple causes, but a significant one was the belated local recognition that the local community had made a commitment in perpetuity to staff, operate, and maintain, out of local funds, the shiny new facility built largely by federal funds. Furthermore, the skills required for a relatively sophisticated installation called for a relatively higher pay than anticipated. The town mayor's half-witted brother-in-law could not cope with an automated physical-chemical advanced treatment process. In any event, the local community did not fully assume that fiscal obligation to staff, supply, operate, manage, and maintain properly.

5. EPA failed to enforce their own regulations, which called on them to only make grants contingent on their verification of the community's capability to assume its share of the capital costs and ongoing operation and maintenance costs. Only now, in 1983, is EPA strengthening this policy and preparing to enforce it.

These five points tend to show that design standards, of themselves, were only a minor aspect of this situation. The "easy big bucks to build" and "scarce pennies to operate" point to the budgetary problem of deferred maintenance. Typically, a recent article in *Engineering News-Record* was headlined "High Tech Junk Litters Water Pollution Control Landscape." The so-called high tech was not that unusual or innovative. In a modern synthetic chemical plant it would be in routine use. The real significance is that wastewater facilities, strapped for operating resources, did not hire the new breed of technician that could operate, maintain, and respond to computerized and instrumented processes.

However, highly idealized standards of treatment did contribute to this disillusionment. For example, in the 50s and 60s New York City pioneered in successful, large-plant-scale operation of a series of variations of the activated sludge process. A series of reliably operating and economical types of intermediate treatment became feasible. It was no longer necessary to choose between rudimentary plain sedimentation and the high capital and operating costs of the conventional activated sludge process. Typically the Newtown Creek plant — for modified secondary treatment, with a capacity of 350 million gallons per day (MGD), coupled with sludge digestion and power generation — has been on line in Brooklyn since 1967. At a cost of $60 million and compressed into 30 acres, it is a model of tight design. However, in subsequent years the EPA began to insist on the same high degree of treatment on a tidally flushed saltwater estuary as it did for potable freshwater streams. Here is a case where objective *scientific* assessment should be used. It may well be that if such scientific findings prevailed, the present mode of intermediate treatment might be deemed acceptable. Pragmatically, a reliable year-round intermediate treatment might have a better impact on the receiving waters, in some cases, than an intermittent and troubled effort to yield a higher degree of treatment.

In the course of design for new construction, or rehabilitation and expansion of existing facilities, in the past there has frequently been a lack of adequate "regenerative feedback" between operating and design personnel. There is no substitute for "hands-on" experience to insure "operability" and "maintainability." Over the years I have heard the complaint of operators throughout the country, "They give us the lemons, and we have to squeeze them." I would like to cite a few from my own experience. I remember bringing the design engineer down to the Oakwood Beach water pollution control plant (WPCP) in Staten Island to show him a plunger pump for sludge, placed next to a wall. I defied him to show me how anybody who was not a contortionist could clean the pump. In a more serious matter, proper design calls for inverted siphons for raw sewage to be protected by grit separation chambers. These should be accessible, amenable to ventilation and designed for material removal. In many instances inadequate structures that are more death traps than grit traps are provided. It means, of course, that these siphons never get maintenance until they are all plugged and the area floods. Every time it rains heavily in New York City, the Franklin D. Roosevelt Drive is flooded in the vicinity of the Mayor's Mansion. As one-time Commissioner of Water Resources, I found it hard to explain to a succession of indignant mayors that the inlets and piping draining stormwater from the drive were losing several feet of head instead of inches of head.

I do not want to belabor this point, but where there are equipment failures, particularly where government employees are involved, there is an almost Pavlovian reflex in stating, "They didn't maintain them properly." In the 1950s and 1960s at the Jamaica, Bowery Bay, and Coney Island WPCPs, there was a series of failures of major rotating equipment, engines, generators, motors, and blowers, in all cases from major manufacturers. Prolonged and bitter disputes ensued, but in all cases investigation showed some design failures.

In the case of sewers we are dealing with facilities that should have a real life of 100 years. In the case of plants, a 50-year life is absolutely realistic. The Wards Island plant, in the East River, should, after current expansion, round out a century of service to the city.

With such a life expectancy, a *scientific* and multidisciplinary evaluation of potential causes of even incipient failure is well warranted. For example, I have seen cast-iron components that have undergone graphitization after about 40 years of service. Over years, some types of stainless steel can fail by carbon segregation at intergrain boundaries. Changes in traffic patterns and the cumulative effects of ground currents and point stresses can lead to pipeline failures. An interesting aspect of the city's expanding water pollution control program is the return of the teredo, the marine borer, which must be factored into projected life of wooden marine structures. Sometimes conventional engineering practice does not take cognizance of these long-range implications. A classic example is provided by failures of building facades, and the emergence of scientific input to engineers on the expansion forces generated by the increased volume of products of corrosion. Hence the need for chemists, metallurgists, and experts in other disciplines, where a useful life of 100 years is projected.

I have already mentioned the flippant phraseology about "high tech junk." Inevitably the entire environmental area will be increasingly pervaded by on-line sensors and ancillary instrumentation, but this should be preceded by verification of the applicability and maintainability of that array. Almost 30 years ago I spoke at an engineering meeting in New York City about the "white elephants" of misapplied instrumentation in the wastewater field.

There is another area of environmental standards that affects the public credibility of environmental facility design. This is the requirement to achieve some standard that cannot be reliably and continually measured. I was once confronted by the ultimate absurdity, when I was required to verify the particulate emission of an air pollution control device on a refuse incinerator. I found that the regulatory agencies were untroubled by the fact that there was then no on-line equipment for reliable real-time readout of particulate emissions. The watchdog agencies could, and did, accept a test made by manual sampling on one day by a consultant team as indicative of the environmentally acceptable performance of the incinerator for an extended period of operation. I could only conclude that the figures on highly publicized incinerator stack particulate output throughout the country were then just a charade.

There are really two factors I would like to advance as most important in the prolongation of life and enhancement of performance of infrastructure. These are improvement in construction inspection and the increased use of "value engineering," coupled with scientific expertise.

Our profession was once characterized by *meticulous professional* inspection of all phases of construction, and *professional* electrical and mechanical engineering competence in the selection and inspection of equipment. Too often, in recent years, we have seen millions of dollars of construction left in the hands of one or two harried all-purpose inspectors. In these days of "risk analysis," adequate inspection is one of the cheapest forms of insurance.

I recall seeing a huge aeration tank floated several feet upwards, with a misplaced water stop contributing to this catastrophe. I found final settling tanks at one plant with incorrect dimensions. Whatever restorative measures were made, the life of these units was shortened, and their maintenance made more difficult. Sometimes even more is at stake. A misplaced bulkhead in the construction of the Bowery Bay interceptor was associated with the death of three men at the site.

In this instance, instead of some exotic new technique, I am suggesting a reversion to the stodgy practices of the past where a powerful, knowledgeable, and tough resident professional engineer headed a team of specialists to insure compliance with specifications.

If we combine scientific analysis and innovative thinking for inherent maintainability and operability, and forego slavish repetition of past practices, we will realize the epitome of true value engineering. New York City's water pollution control program can cite some spectacular successes from that practice.

Some years ago some of us began to worry about the costs of parts, replacements, and energy for the collection of sludge from final settling tanks. In the city plants, at that time, this was done by heavy waterlogged redwood flights, riding on cast-iron shoes, dragged along by malleable iron chain. There were *100 miles* of chain in motion for this purpose throughout the city. This was the normal practice throughout the world. Now this was for sludge, a light slurry readily swept along the tank floor by the slightest current. We said: "Maybe we can cut the tremendous cost of chain replacement, sprocket wear, shoe wear, and rail wear. We don't need this tremendous tonnage of steel and wood to move sludge that's 97% water." In our own simple fashion, we added buoyancy cells on the flights. Within a year, equipment manufacturers began to make buoyant plastic flights. Today the equipment shows feature plastic flights and plastic chain.

About 18 years ago, the Newtown Creek plant was under construction, with the longest final settling tanks east of the Mississippi River. In equipping these tanks with rails, pillow blocks, and shafting for the drive chain and collecting flights, the normal practice here and elsewhere was installation by millwrights. The results were uniformly poor, with always some degree of misalignment. I postulated that in a tank about 300 feet long, one should not assume that the tank was perfectly rectilinear, that the walls were 90° vertical, or the floor horizontal and uniformly sloped. Further, trying to keep bottom rails perfectly aligned and parallel in the floor of the tank as the huge concrete pour was made would be like trying to hold rubber bands in place. I called for instrument, rather than millwright, precision. The space for the bottom rails was boxed out during the pour, and they were set in a separate operation parallel to a center line set in the tank by surveying instruments. They became our first tanks to operate smoothly at first start-up.

Perhaps the epitome of successful, immediate, and economic application of innovation was the institution of "high-rate" sludge digestion by W. W. Torpey, then Division Director of Sewage Disposal Operation. Throughout the world, as in New York City, the anaerobic digestion of sewage sludge was being practiced. These digesters were built in the United States essentially to the "Ten States Standards," in effect providing 1 cubic foot of digester for every 0.03 lbs. of volatile matter fed per day. Torpey reasoned, and subsequent investigation yielded confirmation, that these huge tanks were partly encumbered by scum accumulation, partly filled by sand and grit, that the real biological activity took place in only a part of the tank, and therefore the true rate of sludge digestion was much higher than the design basis. Therefore a properly mixed and uniformly heated tank should be capable of much higher loading. Suffice it to say that, within a year, routine operation was demonstrated at five times the previous loading rate. Typically, the Jamaica plant had eight digesters and was to be expanded. It was planned to build eight more digesters. Instead, by exploiting the verified true rate, the plant was expanded, no additional digesters were built, and one of the existing digesters was converted to a gas holder and another to a storage tank. By now, this work has influenced design throughout the world.

The ultimate irony is that this in-house developmental work was done on a nice round figure of a research budget — zero. The author may be betraying his age and cynicism when he notes that if somebody were asked to tackle this sort of problem today, Phase 1 would be a request to EPA for $1 million to generate a plan of study.

Now, can a similar mix of scientific and engineering expertise be brought to bear to challenge simplistic regulatory fiats on effluent and water quality? We have already cited the case of intermediate treatment at Newtown Creek, which is still pending. However, a number of case histories can be cited in New York City, where decisions were influenced by a multidisciplinary approach. Assessing treatment and pollution impacts on the harbor waters eventually involves sanitary engineering, oceanography, marine chemistry, mathematical modeling, and marine biology, including many specialities such as ichthyology and protozoology.

It was the city of New York that sought and obtained a grant to perform the first total study of an arm of the harbor, in Jamaica Bay, and then reduce it to a mathematical model whose credibility was then verified in successive major field tests.

This work catalyzed the New York Bight Study performed over the past six years by the National Oceanographic and Atmospheric Administration of the Department of Commerce.

The findings of the Jamaica Bay study, even before it was complete, were sufficiently compelling that a select committee of the national academies supported the author in his contention that building a solid runway from Kennedy Airport to Jo Co Marsh in Jamaica Bay by the Port Authority would irretrievably degrade the eastern part of the bay. This dispute had polarized the top city management, but is now forgotten after the runway was built on piles — and the airport flourishes.

Similarly, the Port Authority was earlier deterred from building a solid runway on land fill from LaGuardia Airport towards Rikers Island.

Meanwhile the U.S. Army Corps of Engineers proposed to proceed with a "hurricane barrier" at the single entrance and exit from Jamaica Bay, at Rockaway Inlet. Their concrete scale model at Vicksburg purported to show no deleterious effect on circulation within the bay. The findings of the mathematical model showed that gross impairment would take place of the already weak circulation pattern of the bay. The barrier was not built, and the corps itself adopted the New York City model.

Similarly, in 1972 when a hostile federal administration served a "180-day" notice on New York City, with unsubstantiated allegations of failures in pollution control, a careful and quantified response was readily forthcoming, based on such scientific studies, coupled with an annual harbor survey, and in-house research on the origin and distribution of metals in New York City sewage.

A major move to substitute verifiable data for anecdotes and to quantify pollution and treatment impacts on the harbor was the award of the largest "Section 208" grant under the Clean Water Act to New York City in 1974, for extending the Jamaica Bay study concept to the entire harbor.

The point to be made is that externally imposed environmental standards can be challenged to a degree, but only when in-house expertise is at hand.

Returning to the present status of environmental facilities, as typified by water pollution control, deterioration in maintenance is to a degree attributable to the fact that the top talent in our field has been utilized to design new facilities. As federal funds dwindle, it is to be hoped that some of this skill will be redeployed to protect the huge capital investment already in place.

To conclude, environmental standards have had relatively minor impact on the maintenance of environmental facilities. The problems of physical deterioration of this life-support system were pervasive and of long duration long before the Clean Water Act. The infusion of $30 billion into these programs still leaves a generation of backlogged rehabilitation and restoration. Several responses are required to these problems. One is that environmental facilities should look to the water utilities as a model, as they move toward self-sustaining enterprises. Another is a return to vigorous professional inspection techniques. Some top engineering talent must be redeployed to the protection of the built capital investment. Value engineering is as applicable to rehabilitation as to new work, but in environmental enterprises should embrace other disciplines.

Structural Standards Activities Related to the Infrastructure

JAMES H. PIELERT[a] AND CHARLES G. CULVER[b]

National Bureau of Standards
Washington, D.C. 20234

INTRODUCTION

Roads, bridges, water supply and sewage systems, buildings, airports, railroads, waterway systems, mass transit systems, and other structures represent a substantial portion of the nation's wealth. This "infrastructure" supports a variety of activities that are vital to the efficient operation of the economy. Over half the nation's wealth is invested in buildings and other facilities that shelter and support most human activities and enterprises. Construction of buildings and other facilities is one of the nation's largest industries, usually amounting to about 10% of the gross national product. The deteriorating nature of the infrastructure in this country has been well documented, and it suffices to say that a considerable expenditure of time and money will be required to upgrade its condition.

Structural standards and related quality control mechanisms provide a means of achieving safety and economy in design and construction activities affecting improvements in the infrastructure. These standards may address materials, components, or systems and may be referred to by a variety of descriptive titles including "specifications," "recommended practices," "recommended criteria," "design guides," "design specifications," "building code requirements," and "codes."[1] The principal use of structural standards is for the design and regulation of new construction or modifications to existing construction. While materials standards, such as those developed by the American Society for Testing and Materials for concrete, steel, and other construction materials, are not structural design standards in the strictest sense, they provide information that must be considered during the design and construction process. This is often accomplished by referencing materials standards in structural design standards.

Many organizations in the United States are engaged in standards development. Those that play a major role in structural and related standards include industrial associations and manufacturers, professional societies and technical organizations, organizations of governmental officials, federal agencies, and standards organizations. Some of these organizations are:

---

[a] Materials Reference Laboratories, Building 226, Room A-365.
[b] Structures Division, Building 226, Room B-268.

- Aluminum Association (AA, Washington, D.C.)
- American Association of State Highway and Transportation Officials (AASHTO, Washington, D.C.)
- American Concrete Institute (ACI, Detroit, Mich.)
- American Institute of Steel Construction, Inc. (AISC, Chicago, Ill.)
- American Institute of Timber Construction, Inc. (AITC, Englewood, Colo.)
- American Iron and Steel Institute (AISI, Washington, D.C.)
- American National Standards Institute, Inc. (ANSI, New York, N.Y.)
- American Plywood Association (APA, Tacoma, Wash.)
- American Railway Engineering Association (AREA, Washington, D.C.)
- American Society of Civil Engineers (ASCE, New York, N.Y.)
- American Society for Testing and Materials (ASTM, Philadelphia, Pa.)
- American Welding Society (AWS, Miami, Fla.)
- Brick Institute of America (BIA, McLean, Va.)
- National Concrete Masonry Association (NCMA, Herndon, Va.)
- National Forest Products Association (NFoPA, Washington, D.C.)
- Steel Joist Institute (SJI, Richmond, Va.)
- Truss Plate Institute, Inc. (TPI, Frederick, Md.)
- Federal agencies (U.S. Army Corps of Engineers, Bureau of Reclamation, Federal Highway Administration, etc.)

These organizations use various standards-making procedures designed to suit their own scope, objectives, and purposes.

Standards development is a continuing process consisting of formulation of new standards, revision of existing standards, and the carrying out of research needed to provide the technical basis for standards.

The remainder of this paper will discuss selected structural standards activities related to the infrastructure, examples of relevant research activities at the Center for Building Technology (CBT) of the National Bureau of Standards (NBS), and technical needs for structural standards.

STRUCTURAL STANDARDS RELATED ACTIVITIES

Concern about rebuilding the nation's infrastructure and the adequacy of existing standards is receiving national attention both within government and in the private sector. The selected activities discussed in this paper are concerned with the application of uniform standards and criteria for design and construction, techniques for the evaluation of existing construction, and maintenance and repair procedures.

Federal Highway Administration (FHWA)–U.S. Department of Transportation (DoT)

FHWA is assessing procedures for assuring the effective use of Federal highway funds as required by the Surface Transportation Assistance Act of

1982. Specifically, Section 110(c) of the act directs DoT to coordinate a study with the National Bureau of Standards, the American Society for Testing and Materials, and other organizations as deemed appropriate to determine:

1. The existing quality of activities associated with highway and bridge projects and programs.
2. The need for uniform standards and criteria, including those related to personnel training and implementation of enforcement techniques.
3. The needs and costs of developing a national laboratory evaluation and accreditation system.

FHWA held the Conference on Quality Assurance of Highways and Bridges at NBS in August 1983, which addressed these issues. A report summarizing the findings will be prepared by FHWA and sent to Congress by the end of 1983.

American Society for Testing and Materials (ASTM)

ASTM develops a large number of standards applicable to structural materials, components, and systems. A partial list of ASTM committees engaged in this work includes:

A-1   Steel
C-1   Cement
C-9   Concrete and Concrete Aggregates
C-27 Precast Concrete Products
D-1   Paints
D-4   Road and Paving Materials
D-18 Soil and Rock
D-6   Performance of Building Constructions
E-17 Travel Service Characteristics

ASTM held an exploratory meeting on May 19, 1983 in Philadelphia to determine if there was a need for additional standards for bridges and transportation systems. After considerable discussion, it was decided there was no need for another ASTM committee. Current standards activities under way by ASTM and new ones being planned within existing committees are adequate to address materials, testing and evaluation procedures, and methods of practice.

There are two ASTM activities particularly concerned with rehabilitation of buildings. Committee E6.24 on Building Preservation and Rehabilitation Technology is developing a standard procedure for improving overall building performance as opposed to individual consideration of materials, components, and subsystems. Committee E6.14 on Structural Performance of Completed Structures is currently planning the development of a guideline on "inspection and evaluation of structural condition of existing buildings."

American Society of Civil Engineers (ASCE)

ASCE became an American National Standards Institute accredited organization for standards-generating purposes in 1977. The principal objective was to fill the need for standards where gaps exist and to improve the
development and coordination of standards in the field of civil engineering.
The four standards committees currently operating are composite steel deck
slab; foundations and excavations; masonry structures; and structural condition assessment of existing buildings.

NBS provides the secretariat to the Committee on Structural Condition
Assessment of Existing Buildings, which began work in October 1982. The
scope of this committee is "to identify needs and to develop consensus standards for the condition assessment of existing buildings including the overall
evaluation process and specific considerations of building materials, components and systems."[2] Research conducted by NBS[3] and by the U.S. Department of Housing and Urban Development[4] will provide the technical basis
for the standard currently under development.

American Concrete Institute (ACI)

One of the most important ACI activities is the preparation of codes,
specifications, and recommended practices for concrete construction. There
are currently over 30 ACI standards pertaining to most areas of concrete
practice.

ACI Subcommittee 364 on Rehabilitation of Structures is considering the
development of design requirements for rehabilitation of concrete structures.
A proposed standard will deal with concrete structures in the areas of condition assessment, analysis and design, and construction requirements. This proposed standard is in the preliminary stages of development.

American Association of State Highway and
Transportation Officials (AASHTO)

The purpose of AASHTO is to foster the development, operation, and
maintenance of a nationwide integrated transportation system. Membership
consists of transportation officials from the states, Puerto Rico, the District
of Columbia, and the DoT.

AASHTO develops technical standards for highway transport and other
modes of transportation through various standing committees dealing with
administration, planning, aviation, highway traffic safety, highways, public
transportation, railways, and water transportation. State highway departments
generally utilize standards developed by AASHTO or ASTM. In many cases
AASHTO and ASTM standards are the same or have only minor differences.
The Standing Committee on Highways develops major engineering standards

for the highway program, including those for road and bridge design, materials, construction, and maintenance. As an example, the Highway Subcommittee on Materials annually publishes specifications for materials, standard methods of sampling and testing materials, and information on the performance of materials evaluated by member departments. AASHTO also publishes technical manuals and guidelines related to the design, repair, and maintenance of transportation systems.

NBS ACTIVITIES RELATED TO STRUCTURAL STANDARDS

The NBS is the nation's central measurement laboratory. The Center for Building Technology of NBS conducts laboratory, field, and analytical research to develop knowledge on the performance of building materials, components, and systems and on related measurement techniques.[5] CBT does not develop or promulgate building codes or standards. CBT does provide an objective source of technical information for standards-developing organizations such as those listed in this paper. CBT research provides in many cases the technical basis for standards. Research is often conducted in cooperation with others such as university and industry research organizations. Current activities in CBT will serve to illustrate NBS contributions to developing and implementing improved standards. These vary from basic studies of materials properties to programs that provide for quality control of materials-testing laboratories.

Strength Gain Characteristics of Concrete

Studies are being conducted to investigate strength gain characteristics of concrete at early ages. Basic research on cement is under way to improve understanding of the physics and chemistry of cementing reactions. This research will also provide a basis for computer-based predictions of the performance of cement and concrete in actual use. NBS researchers have developed a preliminary mathematical model for the hydration of tricalcium silicate (the major constituent of portland cements) and are testing it using data obtained with a precise multiple microcalorimeter built at NBS.[6]

Fracture Characteristics of Mortars

Studies on the fracture of mortars are seeking relationships between the microstructure of mortars and their microcrack characteristics.[7] New models to explain cracking will be based on factors such as porosity, the constituents of mortar, and moisture content. Previous studies of fracture mechanics of plain and polymer-impregnated mortars performed at NBS showed that variables such as water-to-cement ratio and curing time had no significant effect on fracture mechanisms of the impregnated mortars. The effect of impregnation of the mortars with polymers was to hinder crack initiation and lead to greater fracture stress. The influence of maximum pore size and cement-aggregate bond on the fracture of mortars has also been investigated at NBS. This work has shown that, for the normal range of maximum pore sizes, the fracture is sensitive to the aggregate-cement bond as well as to the maximum pore size. This basic technical work is intended as a foundation for the development of improved laboratory test methods and nondestructive field test methods for assessing the quality of concretes and other cement-based materials.

Nondestructive Evaluation (NDE) of Concrete

Laboratory tests can assure the quality of materials delivered to the construction site, but there is also a need for proper on-site evaluation of the quality and uniformity of hardened concrete and reinforcement. Standard test methods are available for assessing the characteristics of concrete prior to placement. However, the quality and uniformity of hardened concrete are also affected by construction practices, workmanship, and curing conditions. Concrete inspectors are responsible for determining whether the contractor is adhering to acceptable practices and design specifications, but inspectors generally form only subjective conclusions that depend on their level of training and experience. NBS research has evaluated nondestructive evaluation (NDE) approaches to the quality control testing of hardened concrete.[8] The development of criteria for selecting NDE procedures is part of a larger project supporting improvement of construction safety standards.

Coated Steel Reinforcing Bars

Proper design, construction, and inspection procedures can safeguard a concrete structure from collapse, but corrosion of reinforcing steel remains a substantial threat. Many concrete decks of bridges built in the 1950s, particularly those of the interstate system and those crossing large rivers in major northeastern cities, have deteriorated more quickly than expected because of the corrosion of reinforcing steel in concrete bridge decks caused by deicing salts. It is estimated that corrosion of steel in concrete bridge decks contaminated by chlorides costs the American economy more than $200 million annually.

NBS, in conjunction with FHWA, conducted the pioneering research on coatings for steel reinforcing bars, developing the performance criteria and testing procedures that became ASTM standards.[9] Subsequently, epoxy-coated rebars have become commercially available and a new industry has developed. Federal and state highway departments are now using protective coatings for the reinforcing bars in many northern states where deicing salts are used.

ANSI A58 Standard

The American National Standard A58 *Minimum Design Loads for Buildings and Other Structures* is the only United States national voluntary consensus standard that deals with structural loads. CBT staff serve as the secretariat to the A58 committee and provide administrative and technical support. The new version of the standard issued in 1982 incorporates many findings from research programs conducted at CBT.

The new ANSI A58 standard was developed by a committee representing the numerous interests in building construction: consulting engineers and architects, professional and trade associations, researchers, code officials, and the federal building community. The new standard, for the first time, enables consistent safety levels to be specified for the principal construction technologies. The live load provisions contain a new load reduction procedure which draws upon survey data gathered and analyzed as part of NBS research on structural loads. Revisions to the A58 wind speed map, gust factors that account for turbulence, and wind pressure coefficients for low-rise buildings were based on NBS measurements on full-scale structures. Several features of the new earthquake provisions are taken from model seismic regulations for buildings that were developed in a collaborative program between CBT, the National Science Foundation, and design professionals from throughout the United States. An expanded commentary on general structural integrity reflects CBT efforts to model the occurrence of accidental loads and to develop provisions to prevent progressive collapse.

Developing loading requirements for the design of buildings has been a major thrust of CBT in recent years. The work includes wind loads, snow loads, earthquake loads, and live loads. This research involved the development of instrumentation and experimental techniques for both field and laboratory wind load/response measurements in model and full scale, the measurement and characterization of load spectra and extreme-value distributions used to establish load criteria for serviceability and ultimate limit states, the development of mathematical models for response prediction which incorporate nonlinear stiffness and damping parameters and which allow for the variation of loads in both time and space, and the application of reliability theory in developing the serviceability and safety criteria. The work has been carried out in cooperation with academic and professional groups.

Materials Reference Laboratories

NBS research on cements and concrete is complemented by the NBS-managed activities of the ASTM-sponsored Cement and Concrete Reference Laboratory (CCRL), which carries out inspections of testing laboratories and distributes proficiency test samples.[10] Materials included in the CCRL programs are cement, concrete, and aggregates. Established at NBS in 1929, the CCRL inspects almost 600 cement and concrete testing laboratories, which request the service approximately every two or two and one-half years. Under the CCRL Proficiency Sample Program, participating laboratories in the United States and several other countries periodically receive two samples of a concreting material from different sources or lots. The laboratories perform specified standard tests on the samples and report the results to CCRL. Confidential reports are provided by CCRL to the individual laboratories, comparing their test data with those from other laboratories. This gives participating cement and concrete laboratories a uniform procedure for checking the quality of their test results. Committees of ASTM on cement and concrete receive information from the CCRL activities, which may provide a basis for improvements in standards.

The AASHTO Materials Reference Laboratory (AMRL) is also located at NBS and is similar to CCRL in its basic functions except that AMRL is concerned with bituminous materials and mixtures, aggregates, soils, and friction trailer calibration verification. The state materials laboratories are the major participants in the AMRL inspection program, though the program is available to private laboratories. Many private laboratories participate in the proficiency sample program.

These examples illustrate how NBS research impacts structural standards that can be used to improve this nation's infrastructure.

SUMMARY

There is a large family of structural standards developed by a diverse group of organizations which can be used in upgrading the nation's infrastructure. This paper provided an overview of many of the organizations and the current status of their involvement. Since a firm technical base is needed for the formulation of structural standards, research activities at NBS that resulted in improved standards were highlighted.

The following technical needs related to structural standards as applied to the infrastructure have been identified by CBT work on existing structures and can be summarized as follows:

1. Techniques for evaluating the condition of existing structures including the cause and extent of damage.
2. Guidance for selection of appropriate materials and repair methods.
3. Method for identifying, ranking, and scheduling required maintenance and repair.
4. Improved technical base for standards criteria.
5. Methods for predicting remaining service life of materials and systems.

REFERENCES

1. GROSS, J. G., J. C. SPENCE & R. A. CRIST. 1980. Development and use of structural design standards. Consulting Engineer (January): 86–90.
2. American Society of Civil Engineers. 1984. Official Register: 169. ASCE. New York, N.Y.

3. LERCHEN, F. H., J. H. PIELERT & T. K. FAISON. 1980. Selected Methods for Condition Assessment of Structural, HVAC, Plumbing and Electrical Systems. Report No. NBSIR 80-2171. National Bureau of Standards. Washington, D.C.
4. U.S. Department of Housing and Urban Development. 1982. The Guideline for Structural Assessment. Report No. HUD-PD&R-632. Washington, D.C.
5. RAUFASTE, N. & M. OLMERT, Eds. 1983. 1982–1983 Building Technology Project Summaries. NBS Special Publication 446-7. National Bureau of Standards. Washington, D.C.
6. POMMERSHEIM, J. & J. R. CLIFTON. 1979. Mathematical modeling of tricalcium silicate hydration. Cement Concrete Res. **9:** 765–770.
7. KNAB, L. I., H. N. WALKER, J. R. CLIFTON & E. R. FULLER, JR. Fluorescent thin sections to observe the fracture zone in mortar. Cement and Concrete Res. (In press.)
8. CLIFTON, J. R. & N. J. CARINO. 1982. Nondestructive evauation methods for quality acceptance of installed building materials. Nat. Bur. of Stand. J. Res. **87**(5): 407–438.
9. CLIFTON, J. R., H. F. BEEGHLY & R. G. MATHEY. 1975. Nonmetallic Coatings for Concrete Reinforcing Bars. NBS Building Science Series No. 65. National Bureau of Standards. Washington, D.C.
10. LOCKE, J. W. & J. H. PIELERT. 1983. Evaluation and accreditation of construction materials laboratories. *In* Conference on Quality Assurance of Highways and Bridges, August 30–31, 1983. Federal Highway Administration. Washington, D.C.

Part IV: General Discussion

Moderator: SATOSHI OISHI

Edwards and Kelcey
Engineers and Consultants
53 Park Place
New York, New York 10007

E. JONES (*American Society of Civil Engineers, New York, N.Y.*): Looking over the program, I see this as one of the most important sessions because I perceive in my own mind a very great impact on current standards by the infrastructure problems. But I don't really see that my concerns are shared by the speakers. I'd like to make a statement and then ask for some comment on it.

I've looked at standards as a very big problem in that much rehabilitation work is being done to modern-day standards. I don't see that it's necessary to do rehabilitation work to bring facilities to current-day standards—I believe there should be some level of serviceability between the condition the structure is in now and current-day standards.

In fact, as I see it, this also adversely affects the estimates of cost of restoring the infrastructure. We hear talk of trillions of dollars, and yet many of those estimates are based on bringing the facilities up to current standards, which again I'll say I don't believe is really necessary. There's got to be some level of serviceability, and in my opinion, there should be standards established to set that level of serviceability.

B. HABER (*Hardesty & Hanover, New York, N.Y.*): I believe I tried to bring that out, and unfortunately there wasn't enough time. I agree with you wholeheartedly; it isn't the intent of rehabilitation to bring the infrastructure up to the standards that we have today, since they are changing every day. In fact the new AASHTO specification is just being published now. The changes in the AASHTO will make it different than it was last year and the year before, so we can never really catch up to the most current standards.

The example I gave of the Pulaski Skyway was a good one because there we couldn't meet current-day standards. Another good example is the rehabilitation of the Long Island Expressway, which has been a major problem in New York City. It will now be upgraded, but not to current-day standards. As an example, current-day standards require 10-foot shoulders, while all that can be achieved on the Long Island Expressway are 4-foot shoulders. Obviously we can't meet those standards that are dictated today for new construction, but we can do the best that we can in our rehabilitation. I think that is the intent and the charge to every engineer—that he must use his ingenuity in trying to make the best of a bad situation. It wasn't my intent to give you the impression that we must meet current standards and specifications in the rehabilitation program.

E. JONES: One more question along the same line. We've heard a little bit of this regarding highways and bridges and building codes. How about water and sewers?

M. LANG (*Camp Dresser & McKee, New York, N.Y.*): The thrust of what I was saying was at a much more basic level — mainly just to insure basic operability and viability of sewers, water mains, and wastewater treatment plants. Since their deficiencies in such operability stem largely from sheer limitation of resources and adequate talent to maintain them, I felt that the standards themselves, while important, were less important than actually providing the basic manpower and resources.

S. OISHI: I'd like to underscore a couple of points that were brought out during the discussion. I think that the impact of standards on repair and rehabilitation is really unknown at this point. As Mr. Haber suggested, what is needed is a sustained, permanent effort to collect information on all experiences, put it together in one place, and evaluate their impacts, especially as they affect maintenance and operations, and their budget needs in the future.

No commonly accepted standards exist in this area. The Port Authority maintains their bridges to a different standard than does New York City, for example. The profession needs to supply the politicians with a basis for budgeting acceptable levels of maintenance, based on standards. Out of this session, I would like to see an effort started, as Mr. Haber suggested, for the profession to give more attention and to be more vocal about the need for this.

B. HABER: Since the Mianus River Bridge collapsed in June of 1983, every agency in this entire area and probably throughout the United States is concerned about bridges that have links. There are many bridges like this all over the New York City area, and everybody is going around inspecting links and doing rehabilitation. The support of a link while you're doing the inspection requires an intricate device so that you can maintain traffic while you are examining the link or taking it apart. I would like to see as an example a state agency, either with consultants or without consultants and with their own in-house staff, develop a standard for this type of detail — for inspecting a link.

J. DEDYO (*Metcalf & Eddy, New York, N.Y.*): Mr. Lang, you may be aware that New York City has undertaken a study of its infrastructure — water, sewers, etc. — and is taking that first step to find out what it really needs and what standards will have to be developed and implemented in the future. So this may be a lead that other cities can follow that are having problems with their infrastructure.

M. LANG: Yes, I am aware of it; and like Mr. Haber, I say that we must institutionalize the procedures for operation and maintenance. And of course, the beginning of wisdom is the initial inventory to find out what you have and what its status is.

C. TURKSTRA (*Polytechnic Institute of New York, Brooklyn, N.Y.*): I'd like to make a very detailed technical comment and then a more general comment with a question. First of all, I think this concept of redundancy is a two-edged sword. It is certainly true that the bridge collapse in Mianus involved a lack of redundancy. However, the ceiling collapse in New Jersey involved a very highly redundant structure and opinion seems to be that it was too redundant. When it did come down, it involved a much larger area of the ceiling than it should have.

In general, I think that redundancy brings its own problems including greater sensitivity to secondary stresses, for example. There has to be a careful analysis of every situation.

In some situations, such as a design of a bridge pier, there is no way to have redundancy. If a ship takes out the pier, that's the end of the bridge and there's little you can do about it.

There is in the literature the useful concept of "robustness." This is a more general concept which includes progressive collapse as well as the question of redundancy.

The second comment I'd like to make relates to the problem of insuring adequate maintenance and inspection after a structure has been completed. The political people yesterday seemed very clear about the need for this and admitted they had not done what they should have done. They did not put in the money they should have because there was no political "juice" in it in comparison to new construction. This morning Mr. Lang mentioned this again.

I would like to know why we let this happen and if there is not something we engineers can do about it so that it doesn't happen again.

It seems clear that when programs are mandated, society finds the money to pay for them one way or another. Examples include environmental protection, medical care, and legal aid. In the case of nuclear energy, vast amounts of money go into maintenance and repair as well as the evolution of operating procedures. In these cases the expenses are mandated by an agency that simply says that things must be done and they are done.

It seems that in public works, engineers have generally been content to do the designs and hand them over to the owner. It has not been necessary to mandate later inspection policies. When one begins to think about the complete lifetime of a project, the concept of a performance plan or a quality insurance plan arises. Those concepts are used in the nuclear regulatory agencies and also in Europe for other types of construction.

For example, in Switzerland one must present detailed plans for the use of structures or other facilities detailing how they will be maintained and inspected along with the plans and specifications. This is part of accepted procedure and is mandated by a standard or set of standards.

Is there no movement anywhere in any of our standards agencies that would give design engineers some control over what happens to their systems after they have been built? If not, would it not be a good idea to start one?

S. OISHI: Is that a question, Dr. Turkstra?

C. TURKSTRA: Yes! I'd like to know if there is any movement to give engineers some sort of legal control of their works after completion. Otherwise there will be no contraints on what happens to a system after it is built.

M. LANG: Dr. Turkstra, I did briefly allude to my kind of visceral yearning to go back to the past of a standard of particular, professional inspection during construction — at least it would be a light. I'm looking around at this array of engineers, I think many of you can cite huge jobs sometimes left to the discretion of a few harried all-purpose inspectors and the consequences that flow from that sometime. This regrettably does happen in government construction, and sometimes some irrevocable errors are made then that will haunt us for a long time. I remember crawling through a channel under an aeration tank that floated several feet in the air for lack of a properly placed water stop. That was a Jamaica plant here in New York. I remember that Coney Island plant where the final tanks were constructed so that the dimensions were absolutely incorrect due to only superficial inspection. Even though you try to remedy some of these things, you obviously are going to shorten the life of those structures. So in response to one part of your question, again I make that pitch for reversion to some of the standards that used to prevail. But maybe in that different era, we had more top talent that could be assigned to such things as construction inspection.

B. HABER: Let me suggest something. This is close to my heart because it is something that I've been engaged in for the last 15 years, and that is public participation in government. New York City has 59 community boards. I'm one of the few engineers who chair a community board, and I'm very concerned with the infrastructure of New York City, especially in my area which is northeast Queens. I and my community board advocate maintenance, and as I have said before, the ribbon-cutting days for new buildings and new structures are really not the thing that the community and the public want. I know in my own community the people are more concerned about the potholes and the condition of the Long Island Rail Road station and looking underneath the Bell Boulevard Bridge and seeing that the structure is deteriorating. It's those kind of things that we're concerned with, and I think it's important that the engineer gets involved in public affairs if he wants to make an impact on making sure our structures are maintained. He can't just sit behind his drafting board and make the drawings and do the plans and then walk away. He must be concerned over what happens in his community. He must get involved in the political arena to make sure that we do have a maintenance program.

I believe someone asked a question earlier, why not attach a rider to a design insisting a maintenance program must be provided. I think it's a great idea, I think it's terrific. How do you get that? You get that through politics and through legislation. You can't do it just because we engineers want to say, hey, this is a good idea. It won't just happen. You've got to get involved in the political arena. Maybe it will happen if we do that.

S. OISHI: Assemblyman Joe Ferris has a bill in Albany, which has passed one branch, that requires a statement of maintenance requirements for every capital project that's proposed under the state budget.

J. ROWEN (*State Capitol, Albany, N.Y.*): One of the things that comes up when standards are discussed in a very general sense regarding the infrastructure crisis is an anecdote ridiculing "gold-plated" standards. I have heard it goes something like this: one of the major components in the inventories for highway and bridge construction is inadequate deck geometry, which means the bridge is narrower than the approach roads, this is one of the reasons we've got such a big price tag on some of this infrastructure. I'm wondering if that is in fact the case.

The second question I have is that in upstate New York every winter, you see damage to the roads from the salt. I'm wondering why salt has continued in use and what the trade-offs are between protecting the physical plant and protecting the user safety, the driver.

B. HABER: You're right. Of the 600,000 bridges that are inventoried in the United States, approximately 250,000 are considered structurally deficient or functionally obsolete. It's that latter category of functionally obsolete that you're talking about — and that represents about half of the 250,000. These are just rough numbers. Say you are in a country lane and you have an 18-foot-wide bridge or a 20-foot-wide bridge, why do you need to have two 12-foot lanes requiring the demolition and rebuilding of that bridge? I agree with you, and I think when people set their priorities of what's to be done first, it's that element of the reconstruction of our infrastructure that will probably take last place. When we've done all the rehabilitation of those bridges that I've shown you that have deteriorated stringers and top flanges, and bearings that are ready to collapse, when all that is done, I think we will then deal with the functionally obsolete structures.

The only thing I can say about the salt is that there is a tremendous salt lobby in Washington, and they have done a tremendous public relations job. There are other substitutes that are being investigated. It's much easier for New York City to spread salt in an icy condition than to spread sand because the sand eventually has to be cleaned up and has to be taken out of the catch basins and so forth.

Many states, by the way, do use sand; some states have eliminated the use of salt. If we could do that, that would be a tremendous plus for saving our structures. Not only highway and bridge structures, but our sewers and our water systems and everything else that's below the ground, because the salt impacts everything that we have in our public works program.

S. OISHI: A committee of the Metropolitan Section of the American Society of Civil Engineers last year asked nearly all departments of transportation in the country regarding the salt problem. We got responses from 35. Everyone is looking for and testing substitutes for salt. Salt is used because it acts faster than sand and is cheaper than any other chemical as a snow melter. The Triborough Bridge and Tunnel Authority is the only agency in the New York area that holds off the use of salt until the last possible moment, which often elicits complaints because cinders and sand don't clear the roads as quickly as the salt used by the city on contiguous roads.

B. HABER: I'm the engineer to the Niagara Falls Bridge Commission, an international bridge commission between the United States and Canada. They own the Rainbow Bridge. The commission does not allow salt application on its bridge, but it's very interesting to note that half the bridge is deteriorating and the other half is not because the salt is tracked from the United States to about halfway across the bridge. The half in Canada, where they don't allow any salt on the approaches, is pretty clean.

A Consultant's Response to Mandated Maintenance Policies

Or Developing Maintenance Strategies to Protect Facilities Investments

ROBERT R. RUHLIN

Syska & Hennessy, Inc.
Engineers
11 West 42 Street
New York, New York 10036

The title of this three-day meeting is "New York Conference on the Infrastructure." It is difficult to conceive of a single factor that has a more dramatic effect on the overall life of our highways, tunnels, utility systems, or buildings than the efforts and related cost attributed to their operation and maintenance. In 1981, David Rosoff, of Building Economics Research, published a number of statistics relative to facilities construction and long-term costs. As a point of interest, the operating and maintenance costs for a high-rise structure equate to more than 40% of the total, which comprises design, construction, and finance as well as operating and maintenance (O&M) expenses. Are you surprised? Most audiences are! Couple that thought with the number of failures that have been brought to our attention within the recent years, and you wonder as to "how well we have been spending our 40%." Failures that I speak of comprise bridge collapses in Greenwich and Bridgeport; highways and road surfaces in New York; stadia in Connecticut and South America; and utilities in New York City.

And certainly we have seen a spate of government activity on the state and federal level directed toward these areas. Massachusetts requires designers to provide O&M programs for public structures; Nebraska and Utah have had ongoing commissions to address "deferred maintenance." New Jersey has been very aggressive in implementing long-term O&M strategies. And we know that New York has a pending bill that will address the maintenance issue at the designer's level.

All physical facilities or plant property is susceptible to failure (breakdown) or deterioration due to natural causes of age or the effects of use. Causes of deterioration or failure may be internal or due to external factors. Failure results in expense to replace or repair the facility itself as well as possible losses in services if output is critical or maintenance excessive. Costs may also be due to resulting idleness of allied equipment or personnel. Steps may be taken to maintain a level of maintenance of the facilities that will reduce the likelihood of failure to a minimum. (Note that no degree of maintenance will prevent failure; for example, start-up or infant failure may be reduced by zero-defect and preventive maintenance programs, but cannot be totally eliminated.) However, maintenance to prevent failure — usually designated as preventive maintenance — involves significant expense itself. If the only objective is to prevent failure, excessive monies may be spent to conduct the preventive maintenance program and the cost of prevention will exceed the cost of failure. However, as with most, if not all, cost-oriented plant activities, there exists a break-even point on the failure-maintenance cost curve which establishes the optimum balance between the level of preventive maintenance provided and the effect of failure.

In establishing a strategic plan that will result in the most cost-effective approach to O&M, one must be aware of the various operational facets that must be maintained or capable of being executed within the plan. Developing a strategy is easy if there are no constraints. Various operational decisions that must be considered by those drafting legislation or developing a management plan include:

1. Preventive versus failure maintenance philosophy.
2. Work performed by internal or external service personnel.
3. Repair versus replace philosophy.
4. Replacement parts inventory schemes.
5. Depth of maintenance job assignment control.

Although these branches of a decision tree are nowhere complete, these do represent some of the critical areas that designers, consultants, government legislators, and owners must consider when developing strategies for upgrading O&M practices. Of the five previously mentioned items, only the first two questions, i.e., whether to require preventive maintenance actions and whether to perform work with one's own staff, do not have a significant impact upon how O&M is actually performed, monitored, and evaluated.

For instance, should one contend that preventive maintenance is too costly and, as a result, decide not to require actions that will anticipate breakdowns, then one is committed to a course of reacting to circumstances. Failures will occur at a greater rate, or at least when least expected, than with a functioning preventive maintenance program. However, this could be the mandate — "let it crumble." And then there is no need to monitor performance; failure will be self-evident.

Likewise, deciding who will perform O&M services, i.e., contractors or internal staff, does not bear significantly on the design of a program to prolong the life of a bridge. The system, however, must be geared to the level of skill that is to be provided, irrespective of the source from which it is supplied.

Now let us discuss the remaining strategies and see how they should fit into our governmental mandates or daily operations.

Repair versus Replace

Again, we are basically faced with a problem of economics. In developing a strategy for care of highways or major utility systems, one could demonstrate that the cost of replacement is a better choice than the periodic roadway resurfacing or pipeline and valve repair activities that are commonplace. The clinker in this strategy, however, is the loss of service and revenue to many parties. The loss of the Mianus Bridge span for two months created an inordinate amount of problems, but repair did return service prior to a total breakdown of community relations. An abandonment and replacement decision would not have been tolerated.

On the other hand, continued replacement of tollgate barriers with "wooden arms rather than of a metal alloy" is more economical, conducive to traffic flow, but not a deterrent to a potential violator. We never did say that better O&M would be the cure-all to poor design.

Irrespective of your choice, repair or replacement activities must be monitored, and these mandates and legislature should ascribe to these needs. If we are to make intelligent decisions regarding the use of O&M or capital funds, then we must be aware of our O&M expenditures.

Replacement Parts Inventory

Replacement parts inventories have the same costs associated with them as do raw stores or finished parts inventories, e.g., parts costs, space costs, ordering costs, and carrying costs. In addition, there is the cost of failure to have a part on hand when needed. This last may be sizable at the time of individual occurrence since the cost of failure to have the part may be the summation of all the costs associated with lost production. Various economic order quantity formulas have been presented in many texts and will not be repeated here; rather we will look at incorporating those considerations important to the spare parts problem.

The problem with most of our maintenance organizations today, irrespective of whether they represent the public or private sector, is that they (a) keep the wrong items in inventory, (b) do not keep anything, (c) have excessive security relative to 80% of the inventory, and (d) have no methodology for cataloguing or cross-referencing items of inventory to end uses. From a strategic point of view, only (b) above is of significance. If we decide that we will not stock spare parts for our infrastructure and buildings, then there is no need to mandate identification and supply procedures. As a matter of fact, the remaining three situations will then not be of concern, since there will be no stockage.

From a more practical point of view, we know that spare parts for maintenance of significant items are a necessity. The problem remains as to what and to what level should inventory be maintained. Should this be a concern of our mandate developers? Yes! There is no reason why designers of infrastructure and providers of equipment are not required to stipulate the quantity of spare required. Further, each plant in the private sector and public agency should be charged with developing control systems that establish minimum stock levels, usage rates, and cross-referencing catalogues for use by their respective source personnel.

This then leads us to the last leg of our strategic planning decision.

Maintenance Job Assignment Control

Although times for maintenance operations are more variable than for production or routine jobs, standard times have been established and successfully used by a number of progressive organizations. The state of New Jersey adapted such a level of performance in 1981. Measures of efficiency on individual jobs must recognize the limitation of basing standards on average content, but if weekly or monthly performance indexes are established this variation is minimized and control meaningful.

Now how does that relate to a strategy for the future? Where does it fit into the development of mandates?

The strategy of the future requires that the maintenance staff should be provided with those tools, programs, and systems that will optimize their effectiveness as well as increase their utilization. Electing such a strategy requires rethinking many of our O&M methodologies as well as contractual provisions for architect/engineer (A/E) design services. We are now at the nub of the dilemma. What can government do to protect its investments and resources (people and structures)?

We suggest that there are two major considerations that governments should investigate for inclusion in designs, construction, and service contracts: the furnishing of complete—manual or computerized—maintenance programs, and the furnishing of operating and maintenance manuals. Either and in some cases both of these "management tools," to be employed by the maintenance artisan, should be provided by any organization responsible for the design and construction of infrastructure or public facilities. In the case of maintenance service contractors, contracts should be awarded on the basis that government O&M procedures, provided to the contractor, not written by the contractor, will be the performance criteria.

Let us discuss the makeup of each of these two provisions, which eventually will be in all new design and construction contracts.

Complete Maintenance Program

Irrespective of whether the A/E or general contractor is required to provide a manually administrative or computerized system, the system should include:

- Nameplate data and spare parts information storage and retrieval.
- A preventive maintenance work order program.
- Support for planning and scheduling of all maintenance efforts.

```
MSI # 007        AHU        003      MSI 1
BUILDING   BIRCH
LOCATION   ROOF                ITEM NAME   HVAC NO. 3
OPERATED WITH MSI#  007-REF-003        NO. OF COMPONENTS  2
AREA SERVED   DORMITORY
-------------------------------------------------------------------------
COMPONENT TYPE   MOTOR             MANUFACTURER   CENTURY
SERIAL #                          MODEL #                    TYPE   OPEN
CONDITION   1                     DUTY   2                ENVIOR.   2
-------------------------------------------------------------------------
COMPONENT TYPE   AIR CHANGER       MANUFACTURER   TRANE
SERIAL #                          MODEL #   PCC-10          TYPE
CONDITION   1                     DUTY   2                ENVIOR.   2
-------------------------------------------------------------------------
OPEN LINE   YEAR INSTALLED 1980
OPEN LINE

STEAM COIL (Y/N)          # OF COILS    2

RPM    1750/2072          CFM     6700          GPM

PSI                       RATIO                 VOLTS    208

H.P.   7.5                FRAME   213 T         AMPS

NEMA DESIGN               CODE                  INSUL. CLASS

KW                        KVA                   SF

TONS                      TYPE DRIVE    BELT    BTU/HR
```

FIGURE 1. MSI name plate data maintenance screen.

- The status of all work requests (work orders).
- Storage and retrieval of work order history.
- A spare parts and maintenance inventory control program.
- Management reports.

```
CODE #   00000    WORK ORDER TYPE   PU              SCREEN #  1

MATERIALS & TOOLS REQUIRED    DRAFT GAUGE

                    **** ENTER TEXT INFORMATION ****

*1. REPORT WORN, NOISY OR OVERHEATING BEARINGS

*2. REPORT ANY LEAKS IN FLEXIBLE CONNECTIONS AND DUCTWORK

*3. CHECK DIFFERENTIAL PRESSURE DROP ACROSS FILTER, IF IT
    EXCEEDS MANUFACTURERS RECOMMENDATIONS, REPLACE FILTER
    OR INDICATE ON THIS WORK ORDER THAT IT IS TO BE REPLACED

*4. CHECK OPERATION OF FILTER DIFFERENTIAL PRESSURE GAUGE
    (IF INSTALLED) CHECK AND ADD FLUID IF REQUIRED

*5. INSPECT COMPLETE UNIT FOR PAINT CONDITION REPORT

         ENTER N FOR NEXT, P FOR PREVIOUS
            S FOR SEARCH, M FOR MORE COMMANDS
         PRESS RETURN WHEN DONE: .:
```

FIGURE 2. Partial preventive maintenance work order.

REPORT NO. W01   PM WORK ORDERS ISSUED STATUS REPORT - ANCORA PSYCHIATRIC HOSPITAL
                  FOR WEEK NUMBER 41   RETURN BY FRIDAY OF WEEK NUMBER 42

WORK ORDER NO.	MSI NO.	LOCATION	ESTIMATED HOURS	COMMENTS
PU410001	7740-001-EEL-001	CENTER	0004.1	-----
Pu410002	7740-001-EEL-002	MALE SIDE	0004.0	-----
PU410003	7740-001-EEL-003	F SIDE	0004.1	-----
PU410004	7740-002-DYR-001	CENTER	0002.0	-----
PU410005	7740-002-DYR-002	NW WALL	0002.0	-----
PU410006	7740-002-DYR-003	CENTER	0002.0	-----
PU410007	7740-002-DYR-004	STAFF ROOM	0002.0	-----
PU410008	7740-002-DYR-005	STAFF ROOM	0002.0	-----
PU410009	7740-002-DYR-007	STAFF ROOM	0002.0	-----
PU410010	7740-002-DYR-008	CENTER	0002.0	-----
PU410011	7740-002-EXT-001	BETWEEN WASHERS	0002.0	-----
PU410012	7740-002-FIR-001	WEST WALL	0002.0	-----
PU410013	7740-002-FIR-002	WEST WALL	0002.0	-----
PU410014	7740-002-FIR-003	WEST WALL	0002.0	-----
PU410015	7740-002-FIR-004	NE WALL	0002.0	-----
PU410016	7740-002-FIR-005	WEST WALL	0002.0	-----
PU410017	7740-002-FIR-006	NE WALL	0002.0	-----
PU410018	7740-002-FLD-001	WEST WALL	0002.0	-----

FIGURE 3. Preventive maintenance work orders issued status report.

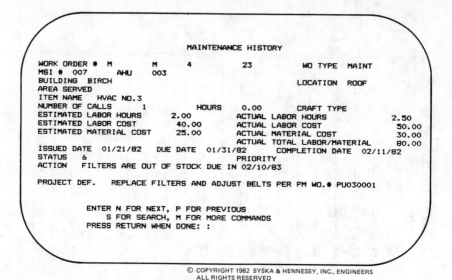

```
                        MAINTENANCE HISTORY

  WORK ORDER #  M          M       4         23        WO TYPE  MAINT
  MSI #  007       AHU    003
  BUILDING  BIRCH                                     LOCATION  ROOF
  AREA SERVED
  ITEM NAME    HVAC NO.3
  NUMBER OF CALLS      1          HOURS     0.00       CRAFT TYPE
  ESTIMATED LABOR HOURS       2.00      ACTUAL LABOR HOURS              2.50
  ESTIMATED LABOR COST       40.00      ACTUAL LABOR COST             50.00
  ESTIMATED MATERIAL COST    25.00      ACTUAL MATERIAL COST          30.00
                                        ACTUAL TOTAL LABOR/MATERIAL   80.00
  ISSUED DATE  01/21/82    DUE DATE  01/31/82    COMPLETION DATE  02/11/82
  STATUS    6                        PRIORITY
  ACTION    FILTERS ARE OUT OF STOCK DUE IN 02/10/83

  PROJECT DEF.   REPLACE FILTERS AND ADJUST BELTS PER PM WO.# PU030001


               ENTER N FOR NEXT, P FOR PREVIOUS
                 S FOR SEARCH, M FOR MORE COMMANDS
               PRESS RETURN WHEN DONE: :
```

FIGURE 4. Specific work order maintenance screen.

The above-listed elements would be appropriate for a structure, utility, highway, bridge, airport, hospital, or plant. The following gives a nontechnical understanding of what such a system will provide. By understanding this, you will readily recognize that we are not suggesting that the A/E provide something strange—but only something that has been commonplace in the private sector for years.

All systems should be designed to store and provide, via the computer screen or by report via a printer, nameplate and related data and information (FIGURE 1). Information should be entered or updated via interactive screens using simple commands. When data are initially entered, the program compares the data with those in a library of tasks which specifies description code or codes, time standards, and frequency of preventive maintenance (PM) efforts for each maintenance-significant item (MSI). The frequency of PM work orders is specified by using a number that corresponds to times such as monthly, bimonthly, or annual inspections.

The PM work orders are issued weekly upon request. When they are printed, the PM work order issued status report is also printed, indicating the schedule of PM work to be done (FIGURES 2 and 3). When the PM work orders are issued, they are automatically placed in the open work order file. Upon their completion, the work order file is updated by utilization of the work order maintenance screen (FIGURE 4). At the end of the week the PM work order status report is requested (FIGURE 5). This provides information about the work completed and items requiring further work.

The work order maintenance program is utilized to support the planning

PM WORK ORDER STATUS REPORT - ANCORA PSYCHIATRIC HOSPITAL

Week Number 41

```
Work Orders Scheduled    206
Work Orders Completed    170    Work Orders not Returned/Completed  36
Total Hours Utilized      34    Work Orders Requiring Further Action 4
```

MSI'S Requiring Additional
Maintenance Action:

Work Order	MSI Number	Defect or Action Required:
PU410048	7740-008-AHU-003	Replace Belts & Filter
PU410053	7740-008-CRP-002	Noisy Bearings - Replace
PU410131	7740-011-GEF-002	Replace Bearings
PU410195	7740-016-GEF-012	Replace Belts

Work Orders Not Returned/Completed:

Work Order	MSI Number	Location	Estimated Hours
PU410001	7740-001-EEL-001	Center	4.1
PU410002	7740-001-EEL-002	Male Side	4.1
PU410003	7740-001-EEL-003	F Side	4.1
PU410004	7740-002-DYR-001	Center	2.0
PU410005	7740-002-DYR-002	NW Hall	2.0
PU410006	7740-002-DYR-003	Center	2.0
PU410007	7740-002-DYR-004	Staff Room	2.0
PU410008	7740-003-DYR-005	Staff Room	2.0
PU410009	7740-004-DYR-007	Staff Room	2.0
PU410010	7740-005-DYR-008	Center	2.0
PU410011	7740-002-EXT-001	Betw. Washers	2.0
PU410012	7740-002-FIR-001	West Wall	2.0
PU410013	7740-002-FIR-002	West Wall	2.0
PU410014	7740-002-FIR-003	West Wall	2.0
PU410015	7740-002-FIR-004	NE Wall	2.0
PU410016	7740-002-FIR-005	West Wall	2.0
PU410017	7740-002-FIR-006	NE Wall	2.0
PU410018	7740-002-FLD-001	West Wall	2.0
PU410019	7740-002-FLD-002	Center	2.0
PU410020	7740-002-FLD-003	Center	2.0
PU410021	7740-002-FLD-004	Front Area	2.0
PU410022	7740-002-FLD-005	West Wall	2.0
PU410023	7740-002-MGL-001	Center	2.0
PU410024	7740-002-MGL-002	Center	2.0
PU410025	7740-002-WHR-001	Wash Room	.7
PU410026	7740-002-WHR-002	Wash Room	.7
PU410027	7740-002-WHR-003	Wash Room	.7
PU410028	7740-002-WHR-004	Wash Room	.7
PU410029	7740-002-WHR-005	Wash Room	.7
PU410030	7740-002-WHR-006	Wash Room	.7
PU410031	7740-002-WHR-007	Wash Room	.7

FIGURE 5. Preventive maintenance work order status report.

and scheduling of all maintenance efforts and to provide information about all types of work orders. The work order maintenance screen is utilized to enter and update information about all work orders. When the work orders are completed, the entry of the completion data information will cause the information to be added to the maintenance history, which can be obtained via a screen or a report (FIGURES 6 and 7).

As suspected, the inventory control program should be utilized to provide information about spare parts and materials (FIGURE 8).

ANNALS NEW YORK ACADEMY OF SCIENCES

```
              WORK ORDER HISTORY  MSI NO. 007-AHU-003


  WORK ORD  ACTUAL  ACTUAL  ACTUAL   TOTAL    ISSUED      DUE     COMPLETE
   NUMBER    HOURS   LAB $   MTL $    COST      DATE      DATE       DATE

   PU420008   1.0    20.0    0.00    20.00   10/09/81  10/16/81  10/16/81
   PU460004   0.7    14.0    0.00    14.00   11/06/81  11/17/81  11/16/81
   PU500002   0.5    10.0    0.00    10.00   12/04/81  12/11/81  12/11/81
   PU030001   9.2   180.4   25.00   205.40   01/15/82  01/22/82  01/20/82
   MM040023   2.5    50.0   30.00    80.00   01/21/82  01/31/82  02/11/82
   PU070002   0.7    14.0    0.00    14.00   02/12/82  02/19/82  02/22/82
   PU110016   0.6    12.0    0.00    12.00   03/12/82  03/19/82  03/17/82
   PU160002   0.7    14.0    0.00    14.00   04/16/82  04/23/82  04/28/82
   PU200007   0.8    16.0    0.00    16.00   05/07/82  05/14/82  05/15/82
   PU240013   0.6    12.0    0.00    12.00   06/04/82  06/11/82  06/10/82
   PU290011   6.0   120.0   20.00   140.00   07/02/82  07/09/82  07/08/82
   MM300014   2.0    40.0   35.00    75.00   07/10/82  07/20/82  07/15/82
   PU330005   0.5    10.0    0.00    10.00   07/30/82  08/06/82  08/13/82
   PU370005   0.5    10.0    0.00    10.00   09/27/82  10/03/82  10/03/82
   PU420010   0.6    12.0    0.00    12.00   11/02/82  11/09/82  11/15/82
  ** TOTAL **
             26.9   534.4  110.00   644.40
```

FIGURE 6. Work order history screen.

In an inventory control program, each item in the material and spare parts stock room should be identified and given an inventory number. This information, along with the quantity on hand, expected annual usage, unit cost, reorder point, and storage location, is then entered into the program. Subsequently, disbursements, receipts, and purchase order information are also entered. When these actions are accomplished, the program will provide the inventory availability information and specify items to be reordered.

This type of a program is utilized to provide predetermined listings of information, various predetermined management reports, and to generate any custom reports that are desired.

Now what does such a system or program do? Well, it tells us where we are headed, what to expect, and what we have experienced—all the elements of good decision making. For the sake of brevity, we will highlight the more significant elements.

Labor efficiency report. This report will indicate the hours of planned maintenance work performed, the hours of preventive maintenance work performed, the hours of project work performed, the hours of "do it now" (DIN) work, and the hours of emergency work that have been performed during the period. It will also include the total hours budgeted, total overtime hours, total vacation, medical, and other hours, total other hours unavailable, total hours available, and the total hours accounted for and the total hours not accounted for during the period (FIGURE 9).

Cost control report. This report is issued in combination with the labor

REPORT NO. 004

MSI WORK ORDER HISTORY

```
Building Birch
Location Roof
Operated With MSI No.
Area Served Dorm        Item Name  HVAC #3        MSI No.  7740-007-AHU-003
```

WO. NO.	ISSUE DATE	DUE DATE	COMPL. DATE	HOURS	ESTIMATED LAB. CST.	MAT. CST.	HOURS	ACTUAL LAB. CST.	MAT. CST.
MP030001	1/15/82	1/22/82	1/20/82	9.2	.00	.00	9.2	.00	.00

PM Work Order Information: 00000 00017

WO. NO.	ISSUE DATE	DUE DATE	COMPL. DATE	HOURS	ESTIMATED LAB. CST.	MAT. CST.	HOURS	ACTUAL LAB. CST.	MAT. CST.
MM000023	1/21/82	1/31/82	2/11/82	2.0	40.00	35.00	2.5	50.00	40.00

2/10/82 ACTION TO EXPEDITE: BELTS OUT OF STOCK DUE IN 2/4/82 RECEIVED NOTICE IN STOCK

PROJECT DEFINITION: REPLACE BELTS PER PREVENTIVE MAINTENANCE WORK ORDER MPO30001

WO. NO.	ISSUE DATE	DUE DATE	COMPL. DATE	HOURS	ESTIMATED LAB. CST.	MAT. CST.	HOURS	ACTUAL LAB. CST.	MAT. CST.
PPG70002	12/12/82	2/19/82	2/19/82	.6	.00	.00	.7	.00	.00

PM Work Order Information: 00000

FIGURE 7. MSI work order history report.

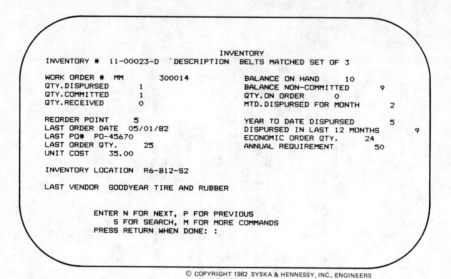

FIGURE 8. Inventory data screen.

efficiency report and will indicate the labor hours, labor dollars, and material dollars that have been expended during the period on PM work, DIN work, project work, emergency work, and repair work. Costs will be provided by MSI and building and totaled by building (FIGURE 10).

Maintenance and project work order status report. This report will indicate the current information for non-PM work orders in the in-planning stage, in the awaiting-material stage, in the to-be-scheduled stage, and in the in-progress stage. It will also indicate work completed (work orders that have been completed during the report period). PM work orders when printed will be indicated in the "to-be-issued" stage until they are completed. The report includes a listing of "actions to expedite" and "project definition." All work orders will be listed and totals provided by status, type, and primary shop (FIGURE 11).

The remaining outputs of such a system provide performance data that will assist management in "repair or replace" decisions as well as measuring the overall performance of the servicing organizations.

There should not be construction starting in 1985 without the above program required of the design team.

Operating Manuals

And now for the remaining "gadgets" that should be available to facility managers from their central agencies. Each new structure, roadway, bridge,

REPORT NO. MO4   LABOR EFFICIENCY REPORT - ANCORA PSYCHIATRIC HOSPITAL
                              FROM 09/03/82 TO 10/22/82

TOTAL HOURS BUDGETED STRAIGHT TIME-- 480

TOTAL HOURS BUDGETED OVERTIME-- 88

TOTAL HOURS VACATION, MEDICAL-- 40

TOTAL OTHER HOURS UNAVAILABLE-- 66

TOTAL HOURS AVAILABLE--- 462

TOTAL HOURS ACCOUNTED FOR-- 420

TOTAL HOURS NOT ACCOUNTED FOR-- 41

HOURS PLANNED MAINTENANCE WORK BUILDINGS AND BUILDING MECHANICAL SYSTEMS------ 110.5

HOURS PLANNED MAINTENANCE WORK BUILDING EQUIPMENT AND OTHER EQUIPMENT---------- 0.0

HOURS OF PROJECT WORK--- 0.0

HOURS EMERGENCY WORK BUILDING AND BUILDING MECHANICAL SYSTEMS------------------- 0.0

HOURS EMERGENCY WORK BUILDING EQUIPMENT AND OTHER EQUIPMENT-------------------- 0.0

HOURS DIN WORK BUILDINGS AND BUILDING SYSTEMS----------------------------------- 110.0

HOURS DIN WORK BUILDINGS EQUIPMENT AND OTHER EQUIPMENT-------------------------- 0.0

HOURS PREVENTIVE MAINTENANCE WORK BUILDINGS AND BUILDING MECHANICAL SYSTEMS----- 200.0

HOURS PREVENTIVE MAINTENANCE WORK BUILDING EQUIPMENT AND OTHER EQUIPMENT-------- 0.0

                                        END OF REPORT

FIGURE 9. Labor efficiency report.

COST CONTROL REPORT - ANCORA PSYCHIATRIC HOSPITAL
FROM 09/03/82 TO 10/22/82

	TYPE OF WORK	MSI NO.	LOCATION	------ACTUAL------			
				HOURS	LABOR	MATERIALS	TOTAL COST
CEDAR	PREVENTIVE	008-SAC-001	MECH RM	1.0	0.00	0.00	0.00
CEDAR	PREVENTIVE	008-SAC-002	MECH RM	0.8	0.00	0.00	0.00
CEDAR	PREVENTIVE	008-SAF-005	MECH RM	0.5	0.00	0.00	0.00
CEDAR	PREVENTIVE	008-TEF-001	RM 4	1.0	0.00	0.00	0.00
CEDAR	PREVENTIVE	008-TEF-002	RM 7	3.0	0.00	0.00	0.00
CEDAR	PREVENTIVE	008-TEF-004	RM 18	0.5	0.00	0.00	0.00
CEDAR	PREVENTIVE	008-USS-001	ELECTRICAL RM	3.0	0.00	0.00	0.00
CEDAR	PREVENTIVE	008-VCR-001	MECH RM	1.0	0.00	0.00	0.00
CEDAR	PREVENTIVE	008-VCR-002	MECH RM	3.0	0.00	0.00	0.00
			Building Totals	45.0	19.00	0.00	19.00
GARAGE	PREVENTIVE	010-SAC-001	COMPRESSOR SHED	7.0	0.00	10.00	10.00
GARAGE	PREVENTIVE	010-WSP-001	PIT	4.0	0.00	10.00	10.00
			Building Totals	11.0	0.00	10.00	10.00
SWIMMING POOL	PLAN MAINT	014-SPF-001	ARC	0.0	0.00	0.00	0.00
SWIMMING POOL	PLAN MAINT	014-SPF-001	ARC	0.0	0.00	0.00	0.00
SWIMMING POOL	PREVENTIVE	014-SPF-001	ARC	3.0	0.00	0.00	0.00
			Building Totals	3.0	0.00	0.00	0.00
SPRUCE	PREVENTIVE	017-CAC-001	MECH RM	3.0	0.00	0.00	0.00
SPRUCE	PLAN MAINT	017-CAC-001	MECH RM	25.3	250.00	30.00	280.00
SPRUCE	PREVENTIVE	017-CRP-001	MECH RM	9.0	0.00	0.00	0.00
			Building Totals	37.0	250.00	30.00	280.00
WILLOW	PLAN MAINT	022-CAC-001	MECH RM	5.0	100.00	50.00	150.00
WILLOW	PREVENTIVE	022-CRP-001	MECH RM	8.0	160.00	0.00	160.00
WILLOW	PREVENTIVE	022-CRP-002	MECH RM	7.0	140.00	0.00	140.00

FIGURE 10. Cost control report status report.

REPORT NO. MO2   MAINTENANCE & PROJECT WORK ORDER STATUS REPORT

FROM 09/03/82 TO 10/22/82

DATE 10/28/82

Due Date	Issue Date	Work Order No.	—Status—	MSI NO.	Estimated			Actual		
					Hours	Labor $	Materials $	Hours	Labor $	Materials $
11/01/82	10/08/82	AE000001	IN PLANNING	7740-014-SPF-001	20.0	200.00	.00	.0	.00	.00
11/01/82	10/08/82	AE000002	IN PLANNING	7740-017-CAC-001	20.0	200.00	.00	.0	.00	.00
			TOTAL FOR WORK ORDER TYPE AE		40.0	400.00	.00	.0	.00	.00
11/01/82	10/08/82	AE000003	AWAITING MA	7740-017-CRP-001	20.0	200.00	100.00	.0	.00	.00
11/01/82	10/08/82	AE000004	AWAITING MA	7740-017-CRP-002	20.0	200.00	150.00	.0	.00	.00
			TOTAL FOR WORK ORDER TYPE AE		40.0	400.00	250.0	.0	.00	.00
10/21/82	10/08/82	AE000005	TO BE SCHED	7740-023-MAU-001	20.0	200.00	75.00	.0	.00	.00
11/01/82	10/08/82	AE000006	TO BE SCHED	7740-023-MAU-002	20.0	200.00	175.00	.0	.00	.00
			TOTAL FOR WORK ORDER TYPE AE		40.0	400.00	250.00	.0	.00	.00
10/15/82	10/08/82	PU41000001	TO BE ISSUED	7740-001-EEL-001	4.1	.00	.00	.0	.00	.00
10/15/82	10/08/82	PU41000002	TO BE ISSUED	7740-001-EEL-002	4.1	.00	.00	.0	.00	.00
			TOTAL FOR WORK ORDER TYPE PU		8.2	.00	.00	.0	.00	.00
10/29/82	10/15/82	ME000020	IN PROGRESS	7740-016-CWP-001	16.0	320.00	150.00	.0	.00	.00
10/31/82	10/01/82	ME000022	IN PROGRESS	7740-001-AHU-003	8.0	160.0	50.00	.0	.00	.00
10/15/82	10/14/82	ME000025	IN PROGRESS	7740-001-SAF-001	16.0	320.0	100.00	.0	.00	.00
			TOTAL FOR WORK ORDER TYPE ME		40.0	800.00	300.00	.0	.00	.00
			TOTAL FOR IN PROGRESS STATUS		80.0	1200.00	650.00	.0	.00	.00
10/20/82	09/29/82	MM000049	COMPLETED	7740-003-HHU-004	16.0	320.0	150.00	16.0	320.00	160.00
10/18/82	10/01/82	MM000055	COMPLETED	7740-004-SAF-007	24.0	480.0	175.00	20.0	400.00	180.00
			TOTAL FOR WORK ORDER TYPE MM		40.0	800.00	325.00	36.0	720.00	340.00
			TOTAL FOR COMPLETED STATUS		92.0	1840.00	650.00	83.0	1610.00	660.00
			STATUS TOTAL		383.2	5390.00	4200.00	83.0	1610.00	660.00

(Please note that this is an abbreviated example)

FIGURE 11. Maintenance and project work order status report.

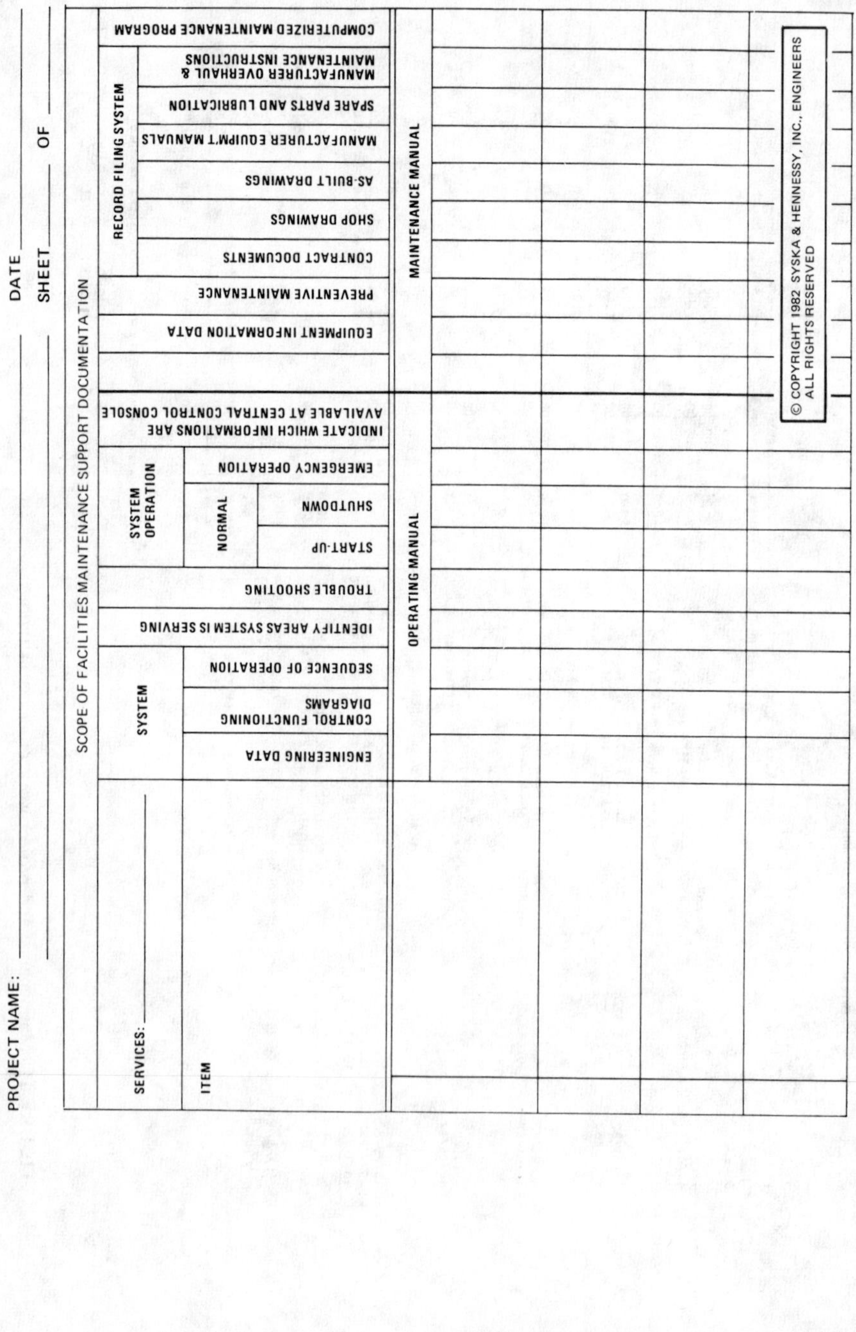
PROJECT NAME:
DATE
SHEET
OF
SCOPE OF FACILITIES MAINTENANCE SUPPORT DOCUMENTATION
SERVICES:
ITEM
SYSTEM
ENGINEERING DATA
CONTROL FUNCTIONING DIAGRAMS
SEQUENCE OF OPERATION
IDENTIFY AREAS SYSTEM IS SERVING
TROUBLE SHOOTING
SYSTEM OPERATION
NORMAL
START-UP
SHUTDOWN
EMERGENCY OPERATION
INDICATE WHICH INFORMATIONS ARE AVAILABLE AT CENTRAL CONTROL CONSOLE
EQUIPMENT INFORMATION DATA
PREVENTIVE MAINTENANCE
RECORD FILING SYSTEM
CONTRACT DOCUMENTS
SHOP DRAWINGS
AS-BUILT DRAWINGS
MANUFACTURER EQUIPM'T MANUALS
SPARE PARTS AND LUBRICATION
MANUFACTURER OVERHAUL & MAINTENANCE INSTRUCTIONS
COMPUTERIZED MAINTENANCE PROGRAM
OPERATING MANUAL
MAINTENANCE MANUAL
© COPYRIGHT 1982 SYSKA & HENNESSY, INC., ENGINEERS
ALL RIGHTS RESERVED

FIGURE 12. Sample O&M manual scope sheet.

PROJECT NAME: NORTHWESTERN EXTRUSION COMPANY
MILWAUKEE, WISCONSIN

DATE NOVEMBER 23, 1983
SHEET 5 **OF** 27

SCOPE OF FACILITIES MAINTENANCE SUPPORT DOCUMENTATION

SERVICES: EXTRUDING
ITEM 14" PRODEX EXTRUDER

ITEM	OPERATING MANUAL — Engineering Data	Control Functioning Diagrams	Sequence of Operation	Identify Areas System is Serving	Trouble Shooting	Normal Start-Up	Normal Shutdown	Emergency Operation	Indicate Which Informations Are Available at Central Control Console	MAINTENANCE MANUAL — Equipment Information Data	Preventive Maintenance	Contract Documents	Shop Drawings	As-Built Drawings	Manufacturer Equip't Manuals	Spare Parts and Lubrication	Manufacturer Overhaul & Maintenance Instructions	Computerized Maintenance Program
6.0 Barrell & Screw Machine Overall System	X	X	X		X	X	X	X	X	X	X			X	X	X	X	X
6.1 Drive System	X		X		X	X	X		X	X	X		X		X	X	X	X
6.2 Powder Feed System	X			X														
a) Conveyors		X	X		X	X	X	X	X	X	X				X	X	X	X
b) Color Injection		X	X		X	X	X	X	X	X	X				X	X	X	X
6.3 NIB Collectors	X									X				X				
a) Shakers		X	X	X	X	X	X	X	X	X	X				X	X	X	X
b) Blowers			X	X	X	X	X	X	X	X	X				X	X	X	X
c) Storage										X								

FIGURE 13. Completed scope sheet indicating items to be included in a manual.

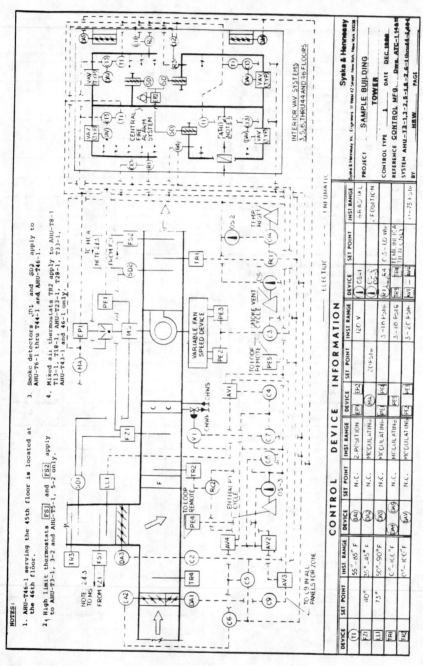

FIGURE 14. Sample O&M manual flow diagram.

SAMPLE BUILDING	PAGE H-26
TOWER	DATE December 1980
SYSTEM: ___Interior___ **OPERATING SEQUENCE**	CONTROL TYPE: ___1___

AHU-T3-1, 3-2, 5-1, 5-2, 6-1 through 44-1 and 46-1

2.3.1   CONTROL TYPE 1

    A. MANUAL START

        1. Place safety disconnect switch of supply fan motor into "ON" position.

        2. Place Hand-Off-Automatic ("H-O-A") selector switch of fan motor at the motor control center (MCC) into "HAND" position. Providing freezestat FZ1 or the system related smoke detectors SD1 and SD2 are not sensing an alarm condition, supply fan will start.

        3. When the supply starts the related automatic control system will be energized.

        4. Variable air volume (VAV) boxes are individually controlled by room thermostats which will modulate the VAV box damper. (For operating sequence and flow diagram see Control Type 22).

        5. As fan starts, automatic dampers and control valves will assume the system "ON" position as indicated on the schedule "Normal Position of Control Devices". Dampers DA1 , DA3 , DA4 , DA5 , DAV and SD will open. DA2 will remain closed.

    B. MANUAL STOP

        1. Place the "H-O-A" selector switch at the motor control center (MCC) of the AHU fan motor into "OFF" position. The automatic control system will be de-energized, therefore all control devices will assume their "System Off" position, as indicated on the schedule "Normal Position of Control Devices."

        2. On power interruption or fan shutdown the variable fan speed device will position to minimum speed.

    C. AUTOMATIC START

        1. Place the safety disconnect switch of the supply fan motor into "ON" position.

        2. Place "H-O-A" selector switch of the supply fan into "AUTO" position.

        3. Providing the safety device FZ1 or the system related smoke detectors SD1 and SD2 are not sensing an "ALARM" condition the building operating control center (BOCC) will automatically start the system as programmed.

        4. When in the automatic operating mode an optimum START/STOP program will automatically start the fan at an optimum starting time prior to the daily occupancy.

        5. For the starting sequence and function of system components refer to section "Manual Start" Section 2.3.1.A.

FIGURE 15. Sample operating sequence (start/stop instructions).

building, etc., should not be considered complete and ready for commissioning until the A/E of design has provided an operating manual of the system (infrastructure, etc.) to the using agency.

Now you ask: What is an operating manual? How does it differ from what is provided by equipment manufacturers? Let us quickly define this for you and illustrate its contents. Keep in mind that the Department of Defense and the Veteran's Administration have both begun to include a specification for the supplying of these documents in A/E design and construction contracts.

When thinking of operating and maintenance manuals, the key word is "system," and they should cover the whole system, not only individual pieces of equipment. Relating this to a utility distribution system, we are talking about the generating plant and pipelines up to the point of use.

Operating and maintenance manuals are typically defined as:

> A text, complemented by graphics, that describes to the user the system design functions, suggested operating sequences and recommended maintenance procedures to be followed for system optimization.

In essence, O&M manuals are to acquaint the staff with design criteria and the designer's intent as to how to operate and maintain the process and the facility.

The need and usefulness of a manual is especially apparent during the early stages of operations of a new process line or facility. For this reason, the manual should be in the possession of the operating staff no less than three months prior to the first start-up of this equipment. Properly prepared operating procedures and maintenance programs will contribute to achieving the following major goals:

- Assisting in training and qualifying new staff.
- Optimizing equipment in system performance.
- Conserving energy.
- Minimizing operating cost.
- Providing troubleshooting procedures.
- Reducing breakdowns and costly repairs.
- Providing emergency procedures.
- Increasing the return on investments.
- Lengthening the life of the equipment.
- Reducing operating hazards to personnel and property.
- Improving maintenance procedures.
- Providing a historical record of the systems.

Independent of the type of system that is described, there are basic formats and items that should be included in operating and maintenance manuals. FIGURE 12 illustrates a "selection" matrix which basically provides the "scope of work" to be provided in any manual. FIGURE 13 depicts a matrix for a portion of an O&M manual that was developed for a plastics manufacturing plant. The X's indicate the manual elements to be described. The following describes what some of these sections in a manual would encompass:

Engineering data. This describes the engineering data for each system, its capability, and limitation such as system type, design criteria, and special features.

Flow diagram. This indicates in a single-line flow diagram all major components affecting the system performance in operation, such as a cooling tower, boiler plant, distributed steam, manholes, and return condensate

SAMPLE BUILDING			PAGE H-285	
TROUBLESHOOTING PROCEDURES			HVAC	
NO.	**PROBLEM**	**NO.**	**PROBABLE CAUSE & CORRECTIVE ACTION**	
3.2	NO AIR MOVEMENT IN AIR HANDLING SYSTEM (SUPPLY, RETURN OR EXHAUST)	1.	NO POWER AT FAN	
		a.	Are starter disconnect and local fan motor disconnect switch in "ON" position?	
		b.	Is the fan "H-O-A" switch in the proper position? Check if fan starts in "HAND" position.	
		c.	Press starter "Reset" button and try to start fan again.	
		d.	Are all power panel circuit switches feeding fan starter in closed position? (see schedule "NORMAL POSITIONS OF CONTROL DEVICES", control types 1 through 23).	
		e.	Are any of the safety devices FZ , SD sensing an alarm condition?	
		2.	FAN IS RUNNING	
		a.	Check for slipping or broken fan belts.	
		b.	Are fire dampers, control, or volume dampers blocking air flow?	
3.3	INSUFFICIENT AIR MOVEMENT	1.	IMPROPER EQUIPMENT CONDITIONS	
		a.	Is fan running backwards?	
		b.	Are automatic air dampers, smoke dampers, fan inlet vane control dampers closed due to jamming, loose linkage, faulty operators or other controls?	
		c.	Are VAV box dampers DAV , and terminal air blender dampers DAT working properly?	
		d.	Are filters very dirty? Check for clogged intake or exhaust bird screens or louvers.	
		e.	Are heating or cooling coils excessively dirty?	
		f.	Are fire dampers accidentally closed due to a broken fusible link? Replace fusible link using the temperature ratings as specified. (See specification page 15012-5, section F-6.)	
		g.	Check manual balancing dampers and splitter dampers for right setting.	
		h.	Are open casing doors short circuiting air?	
		i.	Has an access door in a main duct or riser been left open?	
		j.	Is there a rupture in a duct joint or seam?	

FIGURE 16. Sample troubleshooting procedures.

system components. These diagrams may or may not contain all of the sensing elements physically installed within a control scheme. FIGURE 14 illustrates a sample flow diagram for a variable speed air-handling system.

System operation. This provides a sequence of operation describing the individual function of each system component, its set point, and resulting action during different operating cycles or conditions. The sequences of operation shall explain manual and automatic start and stop procedures. Sample "start-stop" instructions are included in FIGURE 15.

Troubleshooting procedures. The troubleshooting procedures section describes typical problems with their cause and corrective actions. It outlines normal troubleshooting procedures as well as troubleshooting efforts that should be followed in response to an alarm. These procedures follow a simple "symptom-cure" pattern, as illustrated by FIGURE 16, that enables safe but efficient troubleshooting.

The need for operating and maintenance manuals and their scope of work must be determined by the using agency's facilities management team. Those responsible for the daily control of the plant operating and maintenance staff are normally the best judges of the required scope, depth, and text style. When this staff feels that manuals are appropriate, it is best to seek advice from an engineering firm experienced in the design and production of such operating and maintenance documents. In some instances it may be determined that a manual of relatively few pages with minimum operating instructions will suffice, while in other situations the manuals may be of many volumes and in great detail.

Well, there it is; all laid out for you. A modern philosophy directed toward the care and upkeep of our facilities and a road map as to what our legislators and committees should mandate. A consultant's response to a very serious problem; a consultant's response that is not ethereal, but tried, tested, and retested, and now acclaimed as the "only and best way" to do it.

All of this adds up to one simple fact. The design of buildings and infrastructure in the future may be dramatically different from that practiced in the past 20 years. Owners, architects, engineers, and manufacturers will collaborate closely on the development of programs, design criteria, energy use, construction schedules, new materials, and systems. But all of this will be for naught unless the manner and philosophy used to address the overall 40% problem are changed. I submit that the end users and those responsible for mandatory change look to the A/E community and seek their leadership in creating this change. Some recommended changes have been suggested for you in this presentation.

Infrastructure Maintenance Strategies[a]
Governmental Choices and Decision Methodologies

BRUCE G. STEINTHAL

Steinthal & Steinthal, Certified Public Accountants
One West 37th Street
New York, New York 10018

The infrastructure problem facing governments, at all levels, is so immense that even with significant increases in financial resources and technological capabilities, it will be with us for many years to come. If you agree with this premise, then you must also agree that management and decision-making techniques will have a dramatic impact on how effective our response to the infrastructure problem will be.

The maintenance strategies and decision methodologies I will describe here are all based on existing practices in one or more governments around the country. I will attempt to describe a coherent approach to managing the infrastructure problem. This approach focuses on three basic decisions:

1. What is the appropriate level of "maintenance" activity?
2. Which particular facilities require some form of "maintenance"?
3. What type of "maintenance" (e.g., replacement, rehabilitation, preventive maintenance, emergency repair, abandonment) is most appropriate?

My comments are based on detailed, on-site investigation of infrastructure maintenance practices in 10 jurisdictions, including New York City, and other related research conducted by Public Technology, Inc. and the Urban Institute as part of a two-year study of capital planning, budgeting, and financing practices in local governments funded by the United States Department of Housing and Urban Development. The study's findings are detailed in a series of reports published by the Urban Institute.[1-6]

BASIC MAINTENANCE STRATEGIES

Before tackling the more contentious issues of setting project priorities and analyzing project alternatives, it is imperative that officials develop an overall strategy and plan for addressing the infrastructure problem. In practice, governments rarely develop a formal maintenance strategy or plan. We can, however, describe six implicit strategies found in local governments (TABLE 1).

---

[a] Based on Reference 1.

TABLE 1. Basic Maintenance Strategies

1. *Do nothing crisis maintenance.* Do only that maintenance that has to be done. This is a purely reactive approach.
2. *Worst first.* Repair (or replace) those infrastructure facilities that are in the worst condition, thus basing choices primarily on information about the condition and level of infrastructure problems.
3. *Opportunistic scheduling.* Repair or replace deficient components when other related work is scheduled, thus saving maintenance dollars. For example, repairs to sewers and water mains would wait until street repairs are scheduled.
4. *Prespecified maintenance cycle "standards."* Select and follow a repair cycle. For example, repair arterial roads every 15 years. This strategy is deficient because age is a poor predictor of condition and risk, both.
5. *Repair facilities "at risk."* Identify and work on those facilities most likely to have major problems in the near future, even though their current condition is not known to be a significant problem. High-risk facilities should also have a high inspection priority.
6. *Preventive maintenance.* Install a preventive maintenance program designed to reduce the need for later, presumably more costly and disruptive actions. Such a program would involve regularly scheduled inspections and light maintenance (e.g., cleaning and flushing pipe, painting bridges to reduce corrosion, sealing road joints to delay the need for resurfacing).

What is recommended? A combination of the "worst first," "at risk," and "preventive maintenance" options is both practical and effective. Ideally, maintenance activity should focus on those facilities where the risk of failure in the near term and the consequences of such failure are highest. The current paucity of information on failure rates and predictors, however, necessitates a reliance upon condition information (i.e., the "worst first" strategy). Moreover, where the consequences of failure are not severe, it may not be cost effective to repair a facility in advance of its failure.

The "worst first" strategy is widely used. Its chief advantages are that information on the condition of individual facilities is both obviously relevant to maintenance decisions and readily obtainable. Dependence upon condition assessment information can be overdone, however. Other information such as numbers of citizens affected by a facility and the facility's importance to the economic strength of a community is also a relevant factor. It will also be more effective to allocate some funds for preventive maintenance, rather than "repair" of facilities in worse condition, when actions taken currently will prevent larger costs from being incurred in the future.

"Preventive maintenance," like the "at risk" strategy, is highly attractive, despite its surprising lack of practice in local governments. Its validity is supported by studies of the New York City water distribution system[7] and Savannah, Georgia's water and sewer systems,[8] both of which have indicated that a significant portion of sewer stoppages and water main breaks were accounted for by recurring problems in a relatively small portion of each system. The statistics imply that a program of preventive maintenance targeted at these "high-risk" segments would be an effective means of reducing future system problems.

Two examples of the preventive maintenance strategy have been found at the state government level. In Minnesota, the State Department of Transportation categorized bridges on the basis of deck condition and average daily traffic (ADT), as in TABLE 2. A simplified cost-benefit analysis was then used to establish funding priorities among the 12 cells in the matrix. The analysis considered the maintenance cost and the increased life expectancy of the bridge decks. As expected, the heavily traveled, critically deteriorated bridges came out with the highest priorities. Of surprise, however, was that the slightly deteriorated bridges (in both of the higher traffic categories) came next. It had turned out that "an ounce of prevention would in fact be worth a pound of cure. If a deck was in excellent condition with only a minimum amount of chloride contamination, then why not protect it from further salting and eventual deterioration by adding an additional two inches of special concrete."[9-11]

The Utah State Department of Transportation, meanwhile, estimated the rate of pavement condition deterioration and annual costs of repair under four different pavement overlay frequencies for primary, secondary, and urban roadways. Utah found that total (surfacing and maintenance) annual costs declined with increased overlay frequency. The report explains, "As a pavement deteriorates under loads, it requires a greater overlay thickness to restore it and extend the service life."[12] The increased overlay thickness considerably increases the repair costs. On the basis of its evaluation, Utah's Department of Transportation recommended increasing the frequency of overlays, estimating that the added investment cost would be recovered in a little more than four years because of reduced annual costs to the state and to highway users.

Of the remaining maintenance strategies, only "opportunistic scheduling" deserves much favorable comment. "Prespecified maintenance cycle standards" use age alone as a proxy for condition or risk of failure, and a poor proxy at that, and are rarely adhered to. "Crisis maintenance" is purely reactive and generally inefficient.

Many jurisidictions schedule water and sewer system repairs and sidewalk improvements in conjunction with street improvement projects. While this practice may result in cost savings, these savings often prove illusory when, as is frequently the case, work is performed sequentially — with temporary street patches between subsurface and surface repairs — instead of simultane-

TABLE 2. Minnesota State Department of Transportation Priority Assignment for Bridge Repair[a]

Deck Condition (% unsound concrete)	Average Daily Traffic		
	> 10,000	2,000 to 10,000	< 2,000
1. Slight (0–5)	3	4	10
2. Moderate (5–20)	6	7	11
3. Severe (20–40)	8	9	12
4. Critical (> 40)	1	2	5

[a] As expected, the heavily traveled bridges with critically deteriorated decks received the highest priorities. Surprisingly, however, bridge decks with only slight deterioration in both heavily traveled categories received the next highest priorities. (Adapted from Reference 9.)

ously. While "opportunistic scheduling" does minimize cutting up newly improved streets for other infrastructure repairs—a major source of citizen complaints as well as a detriment to the life expectancy of the new street surface—it appears that the strategy has frequently led to placing the proverbial cart before the horse in that some projects may be selected for little reason other than the existence of street improvement plans.

One other concept should also be mentioned with respect to maintenance strategies. Since maintenance needs are directly related to facility usage, reductions in facility usage should result in reduced wear and tear on the facility and reduced maintenance need—without reductions in service quality. Demand reductions can be achieved in a number of ways, including promotion of mass transit and car pools and the use of time- or location-based user charges.[13]

FAILURE ANALYSES

Failure analyses are at the heart of any governmental plan for implementing a chosen maintenance strategy. Failure analyses are examinations of the length of time between major work on facilities (i.e., their expected life) and the identification of the facility or environmental characteristics related to failures. They have three primary purposes, each of which is an integral part of strategic planning.

1. They permit governments to estimate future rehabilitation and replacement needs, in dollars, by projecting future failures based on the failure rate analysis and applying estimated unit costs for replacement and rehabilitation.
2. They permit governments to identify facilities with the at-risk characteristics identified by the failure analysis, and thereby enable application of appropriate measures in advance of a facility's failure.
3. The information on at-risk facilities can be used to develop condition assessment frequencies so as to focus limited condition assessment resources on those facilities that are most at risk. While our study did not find failure analyses used in this manner in America, it has been proposed by England's Water Resources Center. They recommended that information on low-risk facilities be gathered on a reactive basis while conditions on high-risk facilities be regularly monitored.[14]

Milwaukee's road pavement "life" analyses and related sewer and water main retirement analyses exemplify the use of failure analyses to estimate future resource requirements. "Survivor curves" that indicate the percentage of road pavement (or sewer or water main) surviving after each year of life (FIGURE 1), for each major type of road pavement, are the heart of this analysis procedure. These curves are derived from department records of paving history data that indicate when each road segment was constructed and "retired" (i.e., reconstructed or resurfaced). These historical data are then plotted and compared with standard "Iowa curves"[15] for projection purposes.

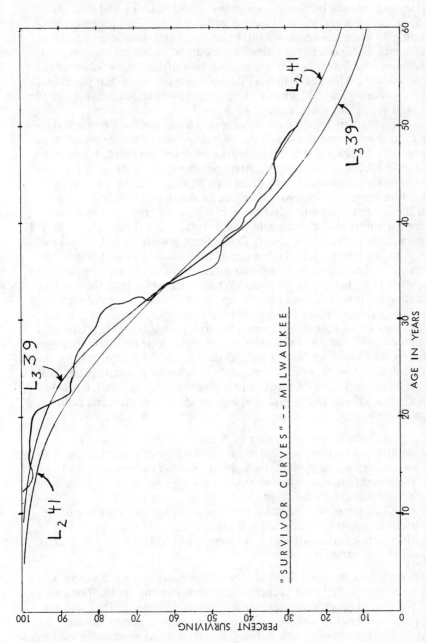

FIGURE 1. Milwaukee's survivor curves. By plotting the percent of street surface surviving, by street life (in years), and comparing this plot with standard survivor curves for industrial property retirements, the City of Milwaukee can project future street retirements and resultant capital needs. (Adapted from Reference 16.)

Using the standard Iowa curve that best matches the historical data for a particular pavement type, engineers project street repaving and reconstruction needs for 40 years into the future. Costs per square foot for reconstruction and resurfacing are developed on the basis of latest contract prices. These costs are then multiplied by the estimated amount of reconstruction and resurfacing needed each year to provide a projection of funding needs over the ensuing 40 years. Milwaukee found that various types of asphalt pavements average between 30 and 35 years of life, concrete lifetimes average 40 to 50 years, and macadam roads average 47 years.[16]

Some preliminary survivor curves were also developed for combined sanitary/storm sewers using the same approach described above. Application of this approach to sewer and water main retirements is hampered, however, by their longer lifetimes (compared to street pavements) and the need for 20% of the sewers or water mains of a given type and material category to be retired before a credible survivor curve can be developed.[17]

In the interim, Milwaukee has developed separate sewer and water main "retirement charts" to help estimate future replacement needs. These charts plot cumulative construction activity (linear feet), cumulative retirements (actual feet retired plus projected retirements based on the continuation of current trends and policies), and cumulative retirement based on an estimated average life (e.g., 125 years), by year.[18] While not as reliable as the survivor curve analysis, this "retirement chart" approach is easier to use. Moreover, it provides graphic support for the need for a facility replacement program.

New York City's water main break analysis is probably the most cited and best known failure analysis designed to identify at-risk facilities. Prepared in 1980 by the consulting firm of Betz, Converse, and Murdoch, Inc. for the U.S. Army Corps of Engineers,[7] the study consists of a detailed statistical analysis of the incidence of breaks in Manhattan, relating break frequency to such characteristics as age, pipe size, pipe location, pipe material, bedding, traffic over the pipe, and season of the year. The analysis indicated that:

- Age was not a principal cause of breaks.
- Small diameter pipe, particularly 6-inch to 12-inch pipe, was found to have unusually high break rates, primarily due to bedding problems. The system's 6-inch mains accounted for 37% of all breaks, yet only 10% of all water main pipe.
- A high correlation existed between the location and existence of unlined, cast-iron pipe and main breaks.
- Thirty-three percent of all breaks were found to be on pipe in contact with other structures.

Based on these findings, the study team recommended a replacement program for 6-inch, 8-inch, and 12-inch unlined cast-iron pipe in locations with heavy traffic and in certain locations with bedding problems. They also suggested a comprehensive leak detection program to both conserve water and minimize future erosion of pipe bedding, better coordination among utilities to reduce the frequency of street pavement cuts, and the establishment of a computerized data base of information on pipe and location characteristics. All but this last recommendation have since been implemented by the city.

Savannah, Georgia's analysis of sewer and water problems confirms many of the New York City findings while illustrating that similar analyses are not too difficult for local government staff to undertake themselves. The Savannah study focused on whether a preventive maintenance program could be effective for both the wastewater collection and water distribution systems. As TABLE 3 illustrates, analysis of sewer stoppages and water main breaks indicated that recurring problems, not random occurrences, dominated the work load. The study team concluded that this information "should be helpful in developing priorities for an inspection/preventive maintenance program,"[8] and recommended that the capital improvement program focus on correcting recurring problem areas.

The study also found that geographical considerations influenced the incidence of cave-ins in concrete sewer lines (possibly caused by concentrations of different soil types), that high water main leak areas tended to have highly corrosive soils and galvanized iron laterals, and that the greatest number of 6-inch main breaks occurred under roads with heavy truck traffic and medium-to-light traffic density (as was also the case in New York).[8]

PRIORITY SETTING

Having decided upon an overall maintenance strategy and developed a strategic plan, governments are then better prepared for selecting particular facilities for "maintenance." This priority-setting process involves decisions within each government agency and across agencies to select capital improvement projects each year.

By and large, most local government priorities are established in an unstructured group setting, usually after discussion among appropriate agency personnel and consideration of specific factors that vary, depending on the type of facility in question. While condition and importance are key con-

TABLE 3. Findings of the Savannah, Georgia Sewer and Water Analysis[a]

	Extent of the Problem		Concentration Measure
Sewers—1975[b]	35% of all stoppages	are concentrated in	7% of all locations
Sewers—1979[b]	45% of all stoppages	are concentrated in	9% of all locations
Water mains	47% of all breaks	are concentrated in	5% of the system[c]
Two-inch main breaks	30% of two-inch breaks	are concentrated in	10% of all two-inch mains[d]

[a] Adapted from Reference 8.
[b] Many of the same locations accounted for recurring problems in both 1975 and 1979.
[c] The 5% of the system consisting of two-inch mains.
[d] All in areas of corrosive soil.

siderations in most situations, "targets of opportunity" are also frequently considered. This concept involves taking advantage of opportunities created by other public or private sector projects in order to reduce capital costs, minimize community disruption, and coordinate improvements.

Most priority-setting procedures do not in themselves include any comparison of costs, nor do they directly compare different alternative ways of correcting whatever the problem is. Consideration of cost is typically done by estimating the cost to repair (rehabilitate or replace) each facility and then tallying the cumulative estimated total cost for any set of projects once projects are arranged in order of priority. The number of projects proposed for funding is based, to a considerable extent, on the agency's estimate of available funds.

Governments can improve their priority-setting procedures by moving toward more structured rating procedures. "Categorization procedures," where projects of comparable priority are assigned equivalent priority categories by some systematic rating procedure, are a step in the right direction. These procedures have the advantage that they are readily understood by decision makers and the general public, and provide systematic support and justification for capital budgeting decisions.

The following examples typify this type of priority-setting procedure:

- Dallas conducts an annual windshield survey of its streets, sidewalks, and curbs and gutters, using the following categories: streets — good, acceptable, fair, poor, unacceptable, poor repair (otherwise acceptable); sidewalks — good, fair, poor; and curbs and gutters — good, fair, poor. Specific rating guidelines, including the use of photos to help define each rating category, are relied upon to reduce inter-rater variability.[19]
- New York City uses information on the condition of bridge decks, primary members, abutments, and piers taken from state-mandated variants of federal bridge inspection forms to assign one of the following overall ratings to each bridge:[20] poor — requires major reconstruction or replacement; fair — requires modernization or rehabilitation; good — requires minor work; and very good — requires minimal work.
- Dallas ranks stormwater improvement projects based on categories defined by loss of life, flood water in homes or industrial/commercial structures, and flooding surrounding homes or to a depth that disrupts emergency vehicles.[1,21]

The step beyond categorization procedures requires well-defined evaluation criteria and rating guidelines, explicit or implicit weights for each criterion, and the calculation of a weighted summary measure used to rank competing projects.

King (Seattle) County's street rating procedures are probably the most elaborate example of such a systematic rating methodology in use by local governments today. The county's Planning Division employs 29 evaluation criteria and weights for each criterion that vary from 0 to 3, depending upon the type of project under consideration (TABLE 4). Specific guidelines are provided for assigning a project rating of from 0 to 3 to each criterion, with the ratings being based on road condition and type of road. The criteria ratings

TABLE 4. King County, Washington Criteria Analysis Sheet[a]

Project: Major Widening of Secondary Road

Criteria	Value/ Description	Weight[b]	Rating Guidelines 3	2	1	0	Score[c]
Condition Criteria							
Existing average daily traffic	9300	3	M[d] 20+ S 12+ C 7+ L 2+	20–15 12–8 7–4 2–1	15–12 8–4 4–1.5 1–0.5	<12 <4 <1.5 <0.5	6
Sight distance	good	2	very poor	poor	fair	good	0
Surface condition	—	0	M poor S} C} L} very poor	fair	good	excellent	—
Service Criteria							
Bicycle corridor	high	2	high-priority route	medium-priority route	low-priority route	no	6
Amount of relocation	minor	3	none	minimal	minor	major	3
Citizen support	high	3	high	medium	low	opposition	9
				Maximum potential (MP)[e]			39
				Total points (TP)			24
				Normalized ratio (TP/MP)			0.62

[a] This analysis sheet, expanded to include 29 evaluation criteria, is used to rank project applications for federal funding and to develop the transportation component of community plans. (Adapted from Reference 22.)
[b] Weights vary depending upon project type (0 = not appropriate), for each of nine project types (e.g., new construction, major/minor widening, etc.).
[c] Score = weight × rating.
[d] Road categories: M = major, S = secondary, C = collector, L = local.
[e] Sum of criteria weights × 3 (in this example, 13 × 3).

TABLE 5. King County, Washington Pavement Distress Ratings[a]

Paving Distress	% Area	Criteria			Rating Number
		Severity			
		0–⅛″	⅛–¼″	> ¼″	
Alligator cracking	0–5	7	4	0	
	6–15	6	3	0	
	16–30	3	1	0	
	31–50	3	1	0	
	> 50	2	0	0	

Paving Distress	% Area	Severity			Rating Number
		Slight	Moderate	Severe	
Flushing	0–20	3	2	0	
	21–35	2	1	0	
	> 35	1	0	0	

[a] Note the implicit weighting of these two evaluation criteria. "Alligator cracking," with a maximum rating of 7, has more than twice the weight of "flushing," with a maximum rating of 3. Pavement conditions are rated using eight such criteria, and the sum of the eight ratings becomes the pavement condition rating, one component of the county's (road) deficiency ranking index. (Adapted from Reference 23.)

are then weighted and combined into one overall rating, as illustrated in TABLE 4. The resulting value is used to rank projects competing for federal funds.[22]

The county's Road Division uses a different procedure to rank its projects. This procedure uses (1) ride ratings derived from mechanical ridemeters, (2) visual pavement distress ratings such as those illustrated in TABLE 5, (3) drainage ratings based on the geometry of the roadway and drainage system, and (4) volume/capacity (v/c) ratios calculated from observed roadway geometrics, traffic data, and national standards. An adjusted condition rating

TABLE 6. King County, Washington Deficiency Ranking Index[a]

Adjusted Condition Rating (ACR)
If v/c is greater than 0.75, then
  ACR = (1.75 − v/c) × (ride rating + condition rating + drainage rating)
If v/c is equal to or less than 0.75, then
  ACR = ride rating + condition rating + drainage rating
where: 1. Ride ratings range from 0 (poor) to 50 (good);
    2. Condition ratings range from 0 (poor) to 40 (good), calculated by summing the eight pavement distress ratings illustrated in TABLE 5;
    3. Drainage ratings range from 0 (poor) to 10 (good); and
    4. v/c = volume divided by capacity (volume/capacity ratio).

Deficiency Ranking Index (DRI)
  DRI = 0.20 × (100 − ACR) × (average daily traffic + 40)$^{0.25}$

[a] The county mathematically combines a mechanical ride rating, visual pavement condition ratings, a geometrically determined drainage rating, and traffic data to rank projects and develop a six-year road program and capital improvements plan. (Adapted from Reference 23.)

and a deficiency ranking index are then mathematically derived from these four components (see TABLE 6). Road projects are ranked on the basis of the deficiency ranking index. Additional factors such as citizen opposition and physical constraints may cause projects to be deleted from the list, but projects are never added to it.[23]

On a much simpler note, Seattle uses the following priority score to rank potential asphalt street paving projects:

Priority Score = (2 × Condition Rating) + Traffic Rating + Transit Rating

where street conditions are visually rated from 1 (good) to 5 (very bad), traffic ratings of from 1 to 5 are based on average daily traffic, and the transit rating equals the number of bus routes on the street.[24]

Similar approaches can also be applied to other types of facilities. Initial rankings of water main projects in Dallas and Milwaukee are based on "breaks per year per 1,000 feet" and "breaks per 100 feet," respectively.[25,26] Seattle has ranked its large water main projects based on a visual inspection of their lining condition (0–10 points), the effect of the lining on water quality (0–10 points), the degree of pitting in the pipe (0–10 points), their leak history over 10 years (0–5 points), and the necessity of the water main for area supply purposes (0–5 points). The five ratings are then added for an overall rating.[27]

The chief advantage that these systematic rating procedures have over the simpler categorization procedures is their ability to systematically and explicitly consider more than one factor in rating projects. They also produce a ranking of projects that might otherwise receive the same category rating. This is important for marginal projects. Moreover, by listing the overall ratings in ranked order and looking for natural break points in the ratings, one can develop natural, as opposed to arbitrarily defined, funding categories.

REPLACEMENT ANALYSES

The final question that must be answered in implementing a strategic capital maintenance plan is that of what to do with selected capital facilities. Should they be replaced, reconstructed, preventively maintained to minimize future deterioration, repaired on an emergency basis, or simply abandoned (i.e., removed and not replaced)? The answer necessarily varies from project to project. Nevertheless, it should always be based on an explicit consideration of the cost of each option and the effect of each option on service levels, including how long the improved levels of service are likely to last and the amount of service disruption that the recommended "maintenance" procedure will avoid. The key feature of these economic comparisons of alternatives ("replacement analyses" for short) is that they permit public officials to identify the trade-offs that exist between costs and benefits for the various options and thus permit officials to make selections they believe are best for the community as a whole.

How should governments approach this basic question? To start, they should break it into four components:

1. Is the facility needed, or can it be abandoned?
2. If it is not to be abandoned, is a repair or preventive maintenance effort sufficient, or does the facility need to be replaced or rehabilitated?
3. If the repair/preventive maintenance alternative is *not* sufficient, which of several replacement/rehabilitation alternatives is most appropriate?
4. Should preventive maintenance be used to reduce future costs and service disruption even if the facility is not in immediate need of repair?

While formal replacement analyses addressing these issues are rarely conducted, and regular recurring analyses are even rarer, the following examples indicate that their preparation is quite feasible. They can and should be conducted on a regular basis.

Dallas' water main worksheet (TABLE 7) represents one of the best examples of a formal recurring replacement analysis. Each main break is recorded on a "main break card" when it occurs. Then, whenever maintenance crews suspect that the main has suffered more than 1.8 breaks per year per 1000 feet of main, whenever engineering personnel suspect undersizing or corrosion problems, and whenever overlying streets are scheduled for resurfacing, the main break cards are pulled and the frequency of main breaks per year per 1000 feet is calculated. If the calculated value exceeds 1.8 then the cost of repairing the main over the next 20 years is calculated and compared to the 20-year cost of replacing it. This analysis uses a compound amount factor (based on an estimated fixed annual cost inflation rate over 20 years) to compute the cumulative 20-year repair cost:

$$\begin{array}{c} \text{Cumulative} \\ \text{Repair} \\ \text{Cost} \end{array} = \begin{array}{c} \text{Repair} \\ \text{Cost Per} \\ \text{Year} \end{array} \times \begin{array}{c} \text{Number of Breaks} \\ \underline{\text{Over Last 4 Years}} \\ 4 \end{array} \times \begin{array}{c} \text{Compound} \\ \text{Amount} \\ \text{Factor} \end{array}$$

and a capital recovery factor (based on an appropriate interest rate for 20-year bonds) to compute the cumulative 20-year debt service cost incurred by replacing the main:

$$\begin{array}{c} \text{Cumulative} \\ \text{Replacement} \\ \text{Cost} \end{array} = \begin{array}{c} \text{Replacement} \\ \text{Cost} \\ \text{Per Foot} \end{array} \times \begin{array}{c} \text{Feet of} \\ \text{Main to be} \\ \text{Replaced} \end{array} \times \begin{array}{c} \text{Capital} \\ \text{Recovery} \\ \text{Factor} \end{array} \times 20 \text{ Years}$$

A similar analysis can and should be conducted by all government agencies responsible for water mains and sewer lines. This procedure can even be improved by (1) regularly tallying the number of breaks (or stoppages) per year per standard length of pipe whenever a specific threshold is reached (e.g., eight breaks within four years), (2) by permitting an increasing break rate in the calculation of cumulative repair costs, and (3) by calculating the present values of the stream of repair and debt service (replacement) costs, as opposed to calculating cumulative costs.

Concerned over expensive bridge-replacement proposals, Milwaukee has taken a somewhat different approach to comparing repair and replacement

TABLE 7. Dallas' Water Main Worksheet[a]

Yr. Break / Main Size	71'	72'	73'	74'	75'	76'	77'	78'	79'	80'	81'
6"		′	′					′	‴	⧌	‴

Breaks Per Year   ☐ 16/4

Length   ☐ 250'

Repair Cost

$$360.34 \;\times\; 16/4 \;\times\; 75.477 \;=\; \boxed{108{,}789.53}$$
$$\text{(\$/break)} \quad \text{(bks./yr.)} \quad \text{(CAF)}^b \qquad \text{(\$)}$$

Replacement Cost

$$20.5 \;\times\; 250 \;\times\; 0.1095 \times 20 \;=\; \boxed{11{,}223.75}$$
$$\text{(\$/ft.)} \qquad \text{(feet)} \qquad \text{(CRF)}^c \;\text{(yrs.)}\;\text{(\$)}$$

Breaks/Yr/1000 Ft. $16/4 \div 0.25 = \boxed{16}$

Information Given at ☐ 12.4 % Interest and ☐ 9 % Bonds

---

[a] This worksheet is used to calculate the cumulative 20-year cost of both repairing and replacing a given water main whenever the water main break rate exceeds 1.8 breaks per year per 1000 feet of main (over the last four years). (Source: Dallas Water Utilities, Dallas, Texas.)

[b] Capital amount factor.

[c] Capital recovery factor.

costs. Replacement (or rehabilitation) costs are first estimated, translated into annual debt service costs, and summed over the life of the bonds to be used to finance the project. The "annual replacement cost" is then calculated by dividing the preceding total by the expected lifetime of the new (or rehabilitated) bridge—Milwaukee used 50 years. If the estimated annual cost of repairing and maintaining the bridge exceeds the resulting "annual replacement cost," then the bridge should clearly be replaced (or rehabilitated). A stronger case for replacement is necessary, however, if the annual replacement cost exceeds the estimated annual repair costs. The results of this strict cost analysis must obviously be tempered by technical considerations (Will the bridge be safe under the repair alternative?) and user inconvenience caused by the increasingly frequent service interruptions for necessary repairs.[29]

Milwaukee's pavement evaluation analyses address the third question raised above, comparing various street replacement and rehabilitation alternatives. Conducted by an outside contractor, these detailed condition assessments of selected streets incorporate the results of (1) a detailed surface condition study using a dual rating that measures the severity and frequency of 34 different surface problems, (2) a deflection analysis, (3) a traffic analysis, (4) an environmental analysis, and (5) a pavement section analysis. The results of these analyses are combined into an overall pavement condition rating for each 200-foot section under study. The contractor then estimates the improvement in each section's overall rating that is likely under various replacement/rehabilitation options. (Options chosen for evaluation typically range from a minimal surface treatment such as seal coating through several resurfacing strategies with varying materials and thicknesses to several reconstruction strategies.)[30]

Replacement/rehabilitation comparisons are also the subject of U.S. Environmental Protection Agency mandated infiltration/inflow analyses and sewer system evaluation studies, as well as Dallas' flood plains analyses. Usually conducted by outside contractors, these analyses are textbook cost-benefit and cost-effectiveness analyses. Other analyses of replacement of sewer lines vs. new sewer lining methods such as Insituform and slip lining have also been conducted, with mixed conclusions, by the Washington (D.C.) Suburban Sanitary Commission, Dayton, New York City, Savannah (Ga.), and Seattle.

As for the fourth question posed earlier, the efficiency of preventive maintenance actions, I refer you to the Minnesota bridge, Utah highway, New York City water, and Savannah water and sewer studies discussed earlier in this paper.

The first question posed above, and the final one discussed here, concerns abandonment as an option. Abandonment is feasible only when a facility is both in poor condition and sufficient service can be delivered through other means. Thus, abandonment analyses need be conducted only when some question of need does, in fact, exist.

CONCLUSION

Government officials need not wait for massive infusions of additional financial resources or for new technological capabilities to improve their response to the capital infrastructure problems facing all of us today. Management strategies and methodologies can be of immediate help. Failure analyses can help turn strategic infrastructure plans from a theoretical exercise into a reality by objectively defining future capital needs on a year-by-year basis, identifying specific facilities with a high risk of failure in the near future, and providing an objective basis for allocating limited condition assessment resources. Systematic rating procedures enable officials to establish valid priorities, based on multiple evaluation criteria, in an understandable and justifiable manner. Finally, the explicit consideration of various "maintenance" options integral to formal "replacement analyses" enables officials to identify trade-offs that otherwise might be overlooked.

The tools are there; use them.

REFERENCES

1. HATRY, H. P. & B. G. STEINTHAL. 1984. Selecting Strategies for Maintaining Capital Facilities. The Urban Institute. Washington, D.C.
2. HATRY, H. P. & G. E. PETERSON. 1984. Maintaining Capital Facilities (Executive Report). The Urban Institute. Washington, D.C.
3. GODWIN, S. & G. E. PETERSON. 1984. Infrastructure Inventory and Condition Assessment: Tools for Improving Capital Planning and Budgeting. The Urban Institute. Washington, D.C.
4. PETERSON, G. E., R. BAMBERGER, N. HUMPHREY & K. STEIL. 1984. Financing the Capital Budgeting and Maintenance Plan. The Urban Institute. Washington, D.C.
5. PETERSON, G. E., M. J. MILLER, S. GODWIN & C. SHAPIRO. 1984. Benchmarks of Urban Capital Condition. The Urban Institute. Washington, D.C.
6. HATRY, H. P., A. MILLAR & J. H. EVANS. 1984. Setting Priorities for Capital Improvements by Local Governments. The Urban Institute. Washington, D.C.
7. Betz, Converse, and Murdoch, Inc. 1980. New York City Water Supply Infrastructure Study. 1. Manhattan. Plymouth Meeting, Pa. (Prepared for the U.S. Army Corps of Engineers.)
8. Management and Auditing Department. 1980. Water and Sewer Operations Study. City of Savannah, Ga.
9. TRACY, R. G. 1980. Scheduling the Bridge Deck Repair Program. Public Works (January).
10. TRACY, R. G. 1978. Priority Assignment for Bridge Deck Repairs. Department of Transportation. Research and Development Section. State of Minnesota. St. Paul, Minn.
11. Department of Highways. Office of Bridges and Structures. Bridge Deck Task Force. 1976. 1976 Report on Policy for Production of Concrete Bridge Decks. State of Minnesota. St. Paul, Minn.
12. PETERSON, D. E. 1977. Good Roads Cost Less. Department of Transportation. Research and Development Unit. State of Utah. Salt Lake City, Utah.
13. DOWNING, P. B. 1981. User Charges and Service Fees. Public Technology, Inc. Washington, D.C. (An information bulletin of the Management, Finance, and Personnel Task Force of the Urban Consortium.)
14. ROUSE, M. J. 1981. Progress in Current Research. Water Research Center. Swinden, England.
15. WINFREY, R. 1967. Statistical Analysis of Industrial Property Retirements. Bulletin 125, Revised. Engineering Research Institute. Iowa State University. Ames, Iowa.
16. LASZEWSKI, E. J. 1979. Average Annual Funding Needs for Street Repairing and/or Reconstruction for Forty-Year Period 1979–2018. Department of Public Works. Bureau of Engineers. City of Milwaukee, Wis.
17. 1982. Interviews with Edwin J. Laszewski, City Engineer, and other staff of the Bureau of Engineers, Department of Public Works, City of Milwaukee, Wis., 19–22 January.
18. 1980. Sewer Replacement Program wall chart and Water Replacement Program wall chart. Department of Public Works. Bureau of Engineers. City of Milwaukee, Wis.
19. Department of Street and Sanitation Services. 1977. Instructions for Completing Street Inventory Data Collection Forms. City of Dallas, Tex.
20. 1982. Interview with John J. Lopuch, Deputy Director of Engineering Management (Division of Structural Design), Bureau of Highways, Department of Transportation, City of New York, N.Y., 6 April.

21. 1982. Interviews with Don Cranford, Supervisor of Administration, Department of Public Works, City of Dallas, Tex., 10 March.
22. Department of Planning and Community Development. Planning Division. 1980. Transportation Project Priority Planning Process 1979–80. King County. Seattle, Wash.
23. Department of Public Works. Roads Division. Traffic and Planning Section. 1978. Priority Programming for Urban Arterial Development in King County. King County. Seattle, Wash.
24. FIES, G. E. 1982. Memorandum re: Transportation CIP Program Evaluation. Department of Engineering. City of Seattle, Wash.
25. 1982. Interview with Roger E. Proza, Pumping Division Manager, Operations Bureau, Dallas Water Utilities, City of Dallas, Tex., 11 March.
26. Department of Public Works. Bureau of Engineers. Water Engineering Division. 1981. Water Main Failure Experience Index Based on the Number of Breaks/100 Feet. City of Milwaukee, Wis.
27. Seattle Water Department. 1977. Steel Pipe Inspection Report. City of Seattle, Wash.
28. STACHA, J. H. 1976. Repair or replacement? The decision is yours. The American City & County (November).
29. 1982. Interview with John Erickson, Assistant Superintendent, Bureau of Bridges and Public Buildings, Department of Public Works, City of Milwaukee, Wis., 22 January.
30. 1982. Interview with Donald L. Hardt, Vice President, Novak, Dempsey & Associates, Inc., Palatine, Ill., 26 February.

Strategies for Winter Maintenance of Pavements and Roadways

L. DAVID MINSK AND ROBERT A. EATON

Corps of Engineers
U.S. Army Cold Regions Research and Engineering Laboratory
Hanover, New Hampshire 03755

INTRODUCTION

The common physical properties of snow and ice are well known: a melting point of 32°F (0°C) at standard conditions, bulk density of bubble-free ice of 57.2 lb/ft³ (917 kg/m³), for example. But their political properties are perhaps less well appreciated. The heavy snowfall on February 9, 1969, a Sunday, which left Queens buried and paralyzed for nearly a week and proved a political liability to Mayor John Lindsay for several years, is a case in point.[1] The major snowstorms in Chicago in February 1979 are widely credited with being a decisive factor in the election of former mayor Jane Byrne. New York City's travail with the 1969 snowstorm is documented by a former city official in a paper with the beguiling title "The Political Properties of Crystalline H₂O: Planning for Snow Emergencies in New York."[2] The political properties of potholes are beyond dispute. The statistics on New York potholes are published nationwide in newspapers accompanied by very dramatic pictures and dollar figures. We outline in this paper several strategies for reducing costs associated with winter maintenance and perhaps minimizing the potential political fallout.

COSTS

The cost of snow removal is not trivial, needless to say. The 1969 winter cost New York City $12.1 million to clear the 30 in. of snow that fell; $5.3 million had been budgeted.[1] Pothole repair, though it is a year-round business, is not much different in cost: an annual average of 760,000 potholes are repaired in New York City at a citywide average cost of $7.70 per pothole, or an annual total of $5.85 million.[3]

A survey of state snow-removal practices, costs, climatic factors, and highway statistics was made by the U.S. Army Cold Regions Research and Engineering Laboratory (CRREL) a few years ago. Some of the results will be of interest and will serve to put the snow-removal task in perspective vis a vis the influencing factors. The costs represent only the direct cost to the state maintenance authority of performing the snow and ice control function; costs related to the use of sodium or calcium chlorides, such as corrosion of vehicles and structures, and the cost of cleaning up abrasives are not included.

It is intuitively obvious that the more frequent the snowfalls and the more miles of road that are cleared, the higher the total cost. FIGURE 1 relates these factors in cost vs. snowfall-days; New York State data are heavily influenced by the frequent upstate heavy snows and the high route mileage. Upon considering cost as a function of volume, a different picture emerges (FIGURE 2). Though total cost of snow and ice control is nearly the highest of all the states surveyed, the cost based on total snowfall volume and route mileage is around $11/in.-mile; 12 states show higher costs than New York and 30 show less (FIGURE 3). The midwest and northeastern states have the highest costs, and a mapping of the costs that New York State incurs falls right in line with all its surrounding states with the exception of Connecticut, a highly urbanized state (FIGURE 4).

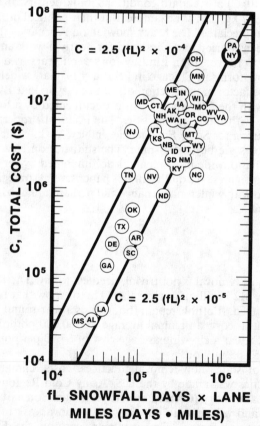

FIGURE 1. Total cost of snow and ice control on state road systems as a function of snowfall frequency and system mileage.

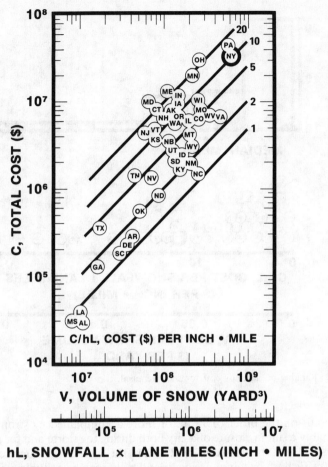

FIGURE 2. Total cost of snow and ice control on state road systems as a function of snowfall volume and system mileage.

STORM CLASSIFICATION

Snowstorms can be classified into two broad categories based on intensity, either by snowfall rate (in./hr) or total snowfall measured on a horizontal surface protected from wind scour or drifting. The division is arbitrary, but is selected with urban conditions in mind, where arterials and feeders carry heavy commuter traffic and commercial truck deliveries are critical. This division occurs at a snowfall rate of ½ in./hr or a depth on the ground of 2 in. Values exceeding these thresholds denote heavy snow; values less, a light snow. In a rural environment where traffic densities are low, the threshold between light and heavy would more properly be placed at 6 in. depth.

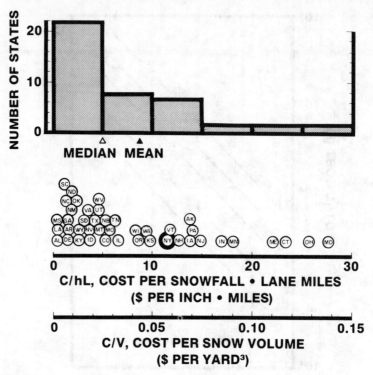

FIGURE 3. Ranking of states by cost for snow removal.

Snowfalls on the order of 12 in. or more accompanied by strong winds will invariably result in closure of a city both during the storm and for a period following it. Here visibility and drifting are the twin devils: these combine to tie up traffic both by minor accidents and by immobilizing vehicles in drifts. This in turn prevents snowplows from negotiating their routes. It is uneconomic for a community to equip its snow-removal fleet to handle the infrequent extreme snowfall, and so temporary road closures will have to be accepted as a consequence. However, the effects can be reduced by providing V-blade plows on smaller, maneuverable, all-wheel-drive trucks to clear critical routes or to open roads in advance of emergency vehicles on demand. Oversnow vehicles may at times be the only practicable means of emergency transport, as was demonstrated in the January and February snowstorm in Buffalo and southern Ontario in 1977.[4]

APPROPRIATE STRATEGIES

Two factors will have the greatest bearing on which strategy to adopt for snow removal: the snowfall rate (and/or the depth of snow on the ground) and the present air temperature and its trend. The choice of the appropriate strategy is conditioned on the observation that cold, dry snow falling on cold, dry pavement is not going to develop a strong adhesive bond, and therefore mechanical clearance methods will be effective. If the pavement is wetted, either because of stored earth heat or because deicing chemical has been applied, dry snow which otherwise might blow off will adhere. If it is not removed before the temperature subsequently drops below the freezing point determined by the concentration and type of chemical, a solid and possibly rough hazardous residue will remain. The temperature categories break at about 20°F, the point at which the melting effectiveness of salt (sodium chloride) is reduced such that excessive time is required for the solid chemical to go into solution. However, if the air temperature is 25°F and falling, the condition is considered as one of 20°F.

Four conditions are tabulated in FIGURE 5, combinations of the two factors of snow (two levels) and temperature (two levels). Various approaches are shown for the conditions. In all cases there is the choice of doing nothing, which may be appropriate in situations such as low traffic density, or in difficult or hazardous locations which may be allowed to fill with snow (e.g., mountain passes). In most situations some intervention will be required by the maintenance authority to avoid "losing the road," i.e., to prevent traffic from becoming completely obstructed.

When snow is light and temperature is above 20°F, salt may be applied if the conditions warrant. Until the last few years, when environmental concerns and an awareness of the delayed costs of salt use on pavements, utili-

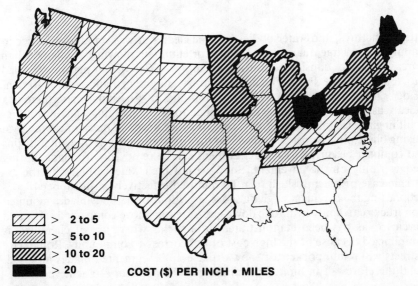

> 2 to 5
> 5 to 10
> 10 to 20
> 20

COST ($) PER INCH • MILES

FIGURE 4. Geographic distribution of annual snow and ice control costs as a function of snowfall and road (lane) miles.

CONDITION	APPROACH	DO NOTHING	PLOW	SAND	SALT
SNOW: LIGHT TEMP. > 20°F	1	✓			
	2		✓		
	3			✓	
	4				✓
	5		✓	✓	
	6		✓		✓
SNOW: LIGHT TEMP. < 20°F*	1	✓			
	2		✓		
	3			✓	
	4		✓	✓	
SNOW: HEAVY TEMP. > 20°F	1	✓			
	2		✓		
	3		✓		✓
SNOW: HEAVY TEMP. < 20°F*	1	✓			
	2		✓		

＊ OR 25°F AND FALLING

CLASSIFICATION	SNOWFALL RATE (in/hr)	DEPTH ON GROUND (in)
LIGHT	< ½	< 2
HEAVY	> ½	> 2

FIGURE 5. Approaches to snow and ice control based on coincidence of light or heavy snow and temperature above or below 20°F.

ties, structures, and water bodies became clearer, it was standard practice to apply salt in large quantities to reduce or eliminate plowing. In many urban areas it was not considered unusual to apply 2000 lb of salt per mile of road to "burn off" the snow. The contemporary enlightened approach is to consider salt as a tool to use with discretion and in situations where there is a clear case for it. Such a case can be made for freezing rain, which would result in glaze ice formation. In the case of snow, however, mechanical removal using blade plows must be considered the first option. Even snow that begins to compact because of its water content can be removed with blade cutting edges riding on the pavement. Snow with a high water content, in the extreme case producing slush, can be removed effectively with rubber blades contacting the pavement to give a squeegee action. Underbody blades mounted on trucks can apply hydraulic down-pressure to remove compacted snow and even ice, as has been demonstrated on airfields where use of chemicals is minimized because of the high cost of noncorrosive compounds. Rough city streets will retain pockets of snow or ice even if segmented blades are used, and therefore salt in limited quantities may be necessary to achieve an adequate coefficient of friction for traffic conditions. It is not commonly realized that a film of brine on the pavement surface in itself tends to lower friction coefficients and to prolong a wetted condition.[5]

A fundamental rule in mechanical snow clearance is to avoid rehandling the snow. Once disturbed, snow will rapidly develop intergranular bonds which increase the hardness of the mass and make subsequent clearance more difficult. Displacement (blade) plows necessarily have a fixed geometry and therefore will perform most effectively for a specific function according to their design, either high-speed operation for rural or expressway clearance where a long cast distance is desirable, or low-speed city clearance where long casts are not possible without burying or damaging roadside objects. In locations where maneuverability is restricted, a very effective plow carrier is an articulated front-end loader; some jurisdictions use wing blades mounted on front-end loaders as well as on trucks.

Sand or other abrasives will offer temporary increases in the coefficient of friction. Effectiveness will be increased if minimum snow or ice remains on the pavement at the time of application, and therefore plowing should precede application. It is important to bear in mind that abrasives are traction improvers and not deicers, and under some conditions their application can prolong the presence of snow and ice by insulating them from solar radiation or elevated air temperature. The effectiveness of abrasives diminishes rapidly with traffic action, as the particles are abraded into rounded form and do not embed in the snow or ice and therefore offer no traction improvement. In addition, traffic rapidly carries the particles to the side of the road where they do no good. Unless abrasives are cleaned up soon after application, they pose the threat of dust clouds which can obscure vision and which have even been known to exceed clean air standards. Fouling of drainage facilities is also a possible legacy of abrasive use, and windrows of sand on the shoulders can pond water and provide one of the conditions required for pothole formation. Nonetheless, their use for quick, short-duration traction improvement may prove necessary under emergency conditions.

The purpose of applying deicing chemicals or abrasives to pavement is to increase the coefficient of friction between rubber tire and pavement. The quantities required to achieve a desired coefficient in a specified time will vary with present surface condition (and ultimately temperature). Thus the optimum amount of either abrasive or chemical could be applied if the surface condition were measured just prior to distribution. This concept was incorporated in a recommendation made to the Federal Highway Administration in a maintenance needs study[6] to develop a pavement surface condition analyzer. The device would measure friction on a probe tire and, in real time, translate this into the amount of chemical required to achieve a desired coefficient of friction and adjust the distributor on the same truck accordingly. Such a device has not been developed yet, though it would have the potential for trimming excessive chemical use and for automating the selection of application rate.

POTHOLES

Is there any relation between snow and ice control operations and pothole formation? Are there seasonal factors involved? Three factors govern pothole generation: (1) there must be excess water present in the base material; (2) traffic must occur to apply cyclic loading to the pavement; and (3) the pavement must not act as a plate, i.e., it must be thin enough (less than 4 in. thick) for wheel loads to deflect the pavement and cause severe cracking.

Let us take each factor in turn. Water must reach the base material and remain there while traffic loading acts on the thin pavement. The most common method by which water reaches the base is through surface cracks. A regular crack-sealing program is therefore required to keep the roof sealed and water out. A poorly designed roadway that is not above surrounding grade or that does not have proper cross slope will retain water because of poor drainage. Unless a cyclic load is applied to the weakened road base by traffic, no failure is likely and no potholes will appear. A pavement that is thick enough to form a stiff plate and bridge local weak base areas will also preclude potholes. In practice, it has been found that a pavement with a minimum thickness of 4 in. will seldom develop potholes.

But to return to the question of seasonal influences on potholes. Remember that excess water is an essential ingredient in the failure mechanism. A road that is cleared of snow and subjected to freezing and thawing cycles will draw water from the water table, no matter how deep, and retain it in ice lenses. As long as the ice remains, the base will be rigid and will support traffic loads regardless of pavement thickness. But as soon as melting occurs, which is nearly always from the top down as the air temperature increases, the base material becomes weak and a thin pavement will crack, then fail (FIGURE 6). The winter conditions resulting in freezing and thawing will therefore accelerate pothole formation. It is ironic that freeze-thaw cycling will be reduced if a pavement remains covered continuously (both in space and time) with snow. Once this snow melts, however, it increases the water available to penetrate to the base material if any surface cracks exist. It is accepted practice in many rural areas of Scandinavia, other parts of Europe, and in fact some northern American states and Canadian provinces to allow snow to remain on roads all winter, plowing with the use of casters or shoes to avoid removal down to the pavement surface. This is obviously not a practicable approach in either a climate experiencing frequent daily temperature excursions above freezing, or on a heavily traveled road. Here the best practice is to remove all snow or ice as completely as possible to reduce the opportunity for water to penetrate to the base. The cutting edges of blade plows should ride in contact with the pavement. In areas where compacted snow or ice will form because of traffic action and where temperatures are low enough to prevent much free water below 25°F, hardened steel blades or tungsten carbide inserts to extend edge life are required. At higher temperatures, or where melting of the snow or ice has been accomplished by chemicals, a rubber cutting edge

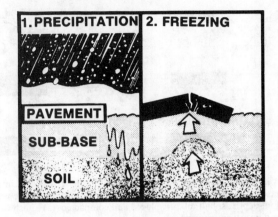

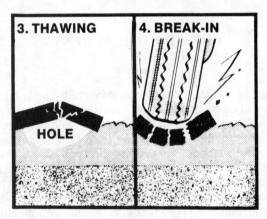

FIGURE 6. Pothole formation by fatigue cracking resulting from freeze-thaw action on the subbase.

can be used to squeegee the road surface. Experience in Washington State west of the Cascades, where temperatures seldom drop below 20°F, has shown that rubber blades, when properly used, cost less than half as much as steel cutting edges.[7]

Do deicing chemicals themselves aggravate the pothole problem? In moderate climates, typified by New York City, the base will generally not freeze deeply whether chemicals are present or not, so there is essentially no effect. In colder climates, where the base could be expected to freeze in its natural state, deicing chemicals can either thaw the frozen base or prevent it from freezing continuously, and thereby trap excess water with the potential of generating potholes, given the other two required conditions.

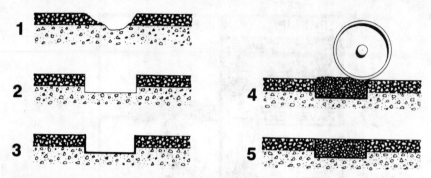

FIGURE 7. Steps involved in making good permanent pothole repairs. (1) Untreated pothole. (2) Surface and base removed to firm support, and edges squared and made vertical. (3) Tack coat applied. (4) Full-depth asphalt mixture placed and compacted. (5) Finish patch compacted to level of surrounding pavement, and edges sealed.

POTHOLE TREATMENT

Patching

A brief review of proper pothole repair is included here, but a more complete treatment will be found elsewhere.[8] FIGURE 7 depicts the procedure for making permanent repairs. Greatest emphasis should be placed on shaping the hole (step 2) and compacting the mix (step 4). The vertical edges minimize raveling at the joint, and roller compaction will prevent water intrusion. Hot mixed, hot laid asphaltic concrete should be used rather than cold mix to obtain maximum density. The mix should be placed in the hole prepared by removing loose material after squaring the edges, drying (with a propane torch if necessary), and applying a tack coat. Mobile equipment is now available for heating asphaltic concrete to the proper temperature and maintaining it while in the field.

Preventive Maintenance

Adequate transverse slopes of pavements, shoulders, and ditches need to be provided for obtaining good drainage. Drains must be kept open during the winter by clearing snow and ice or other debris. If subbase drainage is poor and remains saturated, underdrains should be installed. Surface cracks should be filled as soon as practicable to prevent water intrusion.

ALTERNATIVES

Chemicals are applied to pavement primarily to prevent buildup of a compacted snow mass tightly bonded to the surface. If some treatment on the pavement side of the interface could be found to reduce adhesion, then direct application of deicing chemicals could be reduced or eliminated. Attempts have been made to achieve this. One experimental approach which involved coating pavement with silicone rubber to which snow and ice adhered only slightly proved unsuccessful because of the short life of the coating, which was rapidly abraded and lost.[9] Two other approaches have met with somewhat better success and are in commercial application; both pavement modifications involve mix design and therefore require overlays. The first involves the mixing of rubber particles up to ¼ in. in the largest dimension as replacement for 3–4% by weight of aggregate. This provides a deformable surface which tends to fracture snow or ice bonds as it flexes. The material was developed in Sweden and patented under the name Rubit. It is marketed in the United States using the trademark PlusRide. Experimental road sections have been constructed in the Pacific Northwest and in Alaska.[10]

The second pavement system that has reached commercial development is Verglimit. This is asphaltic concrete into which calcium chloride pellets coated with linseed oil have been mixed. Traffic action abrades the surface and exposes the pellets, which go into solution when precipitation falls or humidity is high, winter or summer. A thin brine film is formed which will prevent a strong bond developing when subfreezing temperatures occur. The material was developed in Switzerland and has been used for several years in a number of European installations. Its use in the United States has been very limited, and because of the high cost of the mix this has been confined to bridge decks or other high-priority locations and to several test installations. It is most effective at temperatures close to 32°F, which represents the largest class of conditions justifying chemical use.

Though all deicing chemicals that act as freezing point depressants will have a physical effect on pavements as a consequence of the establishment of a concentration gradient with depth, nonchloride chemicals are available that will have minimal or no corrosive effect on metals. The most frequently used chemical is urea, a nitrogen-containing solid compound whose major deleterious effect is the stimulation of vegetative growth—it is a fertilizer. It is completely inactive at around 11°F and rapidly loses effectiveness below 25°F. It has been used for the most part on airfield runways, taxiways, and ramp areas because of its noncorrosive properties. Ethylene glycol, propylene glycol, isopropanol, and methanol have also been used, but to a much lesser extent because of their high cost. As liquids, they are best used as antiicing chemicals, i.e., for application to bare pavement prior to onset of freezing precipitation to prevent ice or compacted snow formation. Solid chemical, in contrast, is rapidly pulverized and blown away if distributed on dry pavement, and so solids are best used as deicing agents, i.e., for removal or bond prevention once freezing precipitation has begun to fall. Alcohols, however, will evaporate too rapidly to be used for antiicing except at very low temperatures.

A recent development has been the identification of calcium magnesium acetates (actually a mixture of calcium acetate and magnesium acetate whose Ca:Mg ratio will mirror the composition of the dolomitic limestone used as the raw material) as an apparently effective, environmentally innocuous, and noncorrosive compound.[11] Work funded by the Federal Highway Administration and by several states is under way to investigate the environmental effects of the material and to develop production methods that are less costly than the present pilot plant quantities. However, the projected cost even with large-scale production is not expected to fall below $400/ton, making the material economic only for limited areas posing special problems.

The kinetic energy of a fluid jet has been used to cut ice. High-pressure water jets—10,000 to 50,000 psi—have been shown by tests conducted at the National Research Council of Canada and by the Cold Regions Research and Engineering Laboratory to be an effective method of cutting through up to 30 in. of ice.[12,13] However, pressures this high will also cut into pavement—in fact, high-pressure water jets are used to remove reticulated rubber from airfield pavements. A lower pressure of 300 psi is being used by the Connecticut Department of Transportation on an experimental apparatus to apply sodium chloride brine from jets located underneath a tanker truck and directed forward at an angle of only a few degrees below horizontal.[14] In theory, less deicing chemical would be necessary because of the jet penetration into the interface between the snow or ice and the pavement. Tests are continuing in Connecticut.

REFERENCES

1. RANZAL, E. 1974. Snow no problem for city finances. New York Times (January 10): 41.
2. SAVAS, E. S. 1973. Management Sci. **20**(2): 137–145.
3. MYDANS, S. 1983. 700,000 potholes a year: city tries to cope. New York Times (November 1): A1.
4. ROSSI, E. 1978. White death—blizzard of '77. 77 Publishing. Port Colborne, Ontario, Canada.
5. MORTIMER, T. P. & K. C. LUDEMA. 1972. The effects of salts on road drying rates, tire friction, and invisible wetness. Highway Research Record **396**: 45–58. Transportation Research Board. National Academy of Sciences. Washington, D.C.
6. FWHA. 1975. Highway Maintenance Research Needs. Report No. FHWA-RD-75-511: 78–79. Federal Highway Administration. Washington, D.C.
7. ANDERSON, D. R., D. E. SLATER & A. R. CUNNINGHAM. 1974. Use of Rubber Snowplow Blades in Washington. Phase II. Report No. FHWA-RD-75-512. Federal Highway Administration. Washington, D.C.
8. EATON R. A., R. H. JOUBERT & E. A. WRIGHT. 1981. Pothole Primer. A Public Administrator's Guide to Understanding and Managing the Pothole Problem. Special Report 81-21. U.S. Army Cold Regions Research and Engineering Laboratory. Hanover, N.H.
9. AHLBORN, G. H. & H. C. POEHLMANN, JR. 1976. Development of a Hydrophobic Substance to Mitigate Pavement Ice Adhesion. Report No. EPA-600/2-76-242. Municipal Environmental Research Laboratory. Environmental Protection Agency. Cincinnati, Ohio.
10. ESCH, D. C. 1982. Construction and benefits of rubber-modified asphalt pavements. Transportation Research Record **860**: 5–13. Transportation Research Board. National Academy of Sciences. Washington, D.C.
11. DUNN, S. A. & R. U. SCHENK. 1979. Alternative Highway Deicing Chemicals.

Special Report No. 185: 261–269. Transportation Research Board. National Academy of Sciences. Washington, D.C.

12. MELLOR, M. 1973. Cutting Ice with High Pressure Water Jets. Report No. USCG-D-15-73. U.S. Army Cold Regions Research and Engineering Laboratory. Hanover, N.H.

13. COVENEY, D. B. 1981. Cutting Ice with "High" Pressure Water Jets. Mechanical Engineering Report MD-57 (NRC No. 19643). National Research Council. Ottawa, Ontario, Canada.

14. KASINSKAS, M. M. 1982. Evaluation of the Use of Salt Brine for Deicing Purposes. Research Report No. 396-F-82-6. Connecticut Department of Transportation. Wethersfield, Conn.

Part V: General Discussion

Moderator: CHARLES M. SMITH, JR.

Mayor's Office of Construction
The City of New York
52 Chambers Street, Room 205
New York, New York 10007

J. DEDYO (*Metcalf & Eddy, New York, N.Y.*): This is for Mr. Ruhlin. I got the impression from your talk that you felt that engineers and architects walked away from jobs. I don't recall whether you made some comments to support that — but "if it isn't in the contract nobody will do it." I think that this bill you are talking about realizes that as a necessity and is putting provisions in the contract language for providing maintenance manuals, operational instructions, and whatever else of that nature you consider as a part of the contract. I think if that was a problem in the past, it is something that should be resolved right now. As far as engineers and wastewater treatment plants go, over the years engineers have been asking their clients to permit them to provide follow-on service, which includes the operations and maintenance manual, operator start-up and training programs, and long-term advice. I believe the Environmental Protection Agency has finally come to the realization over the past years that this is needed and is including that as fundable under its grant program.

I just didn't want the public to feel that engineers and architects walked away from their contractual responsibilities, and I'm happy that the state has realized this and is including follow-on services in its engineering consultant contracts.

R. R. RUHLIN (*Syska & Hennessy, Inc., New York, N.Y.*): I'm not going to rebut what you are saying. The essence of what I was trying to get at is that we have been walking away from the construction site without being adamant enough in conferring with our clients that they know what they are getting into. Many of the firms or organizations that you just mentioned have, in the last five or six years, been providing this awareness to their clients as to what should be done. We shouldn't as a community, though, have had the need of pressing legislation to make us confer or discuss with our clients those issues that we feel they are in need of and that we have the ability to both perform and render to them. We should make ourselves further heard.

Educating Civil Engineers for Leadership Roles in Public Works

DOUGLAS WRIGHT

Office of the President
University of Waterloo
Waterloo, Ontario, Canada N2L 3G1

It is a great honor to be here, to be invited down from north of the border to talk to you about issues in which we have a common interest. I noticed at previous sessions that everyone on the program was busy telling you about their New York connections and thereby winning their bona fides. I can assure you that one branch of my family came south across the border quite a few years ago, and I have a whole bunch of New York policemen who are uncles and cousins and so on, too.

It is a unique experience, particularly, to have politicians and civil engineers on the same program. It is really a novelty. I have never seen it before in the same way, and I really do take off my hat to the Polytechnic Institute and to the New York Academy of Sciences for organizing and planning this meeting.

I noted before as well that the engineers in the audience were sitting and listening to the politicans talk. Now it is a bit more the turn of the engineers to speak, and I do not see too many of the politicians here to listen. That says something about power. I guess I would interpret the topic that I was asked to address, that is, to "talk about engineering education — educating civil engineers for leadership roles," as really an invitation to talk about power, so let me talk a bit about that. Especially as it relates to undergraduate education.

It is not especially new, but perhaps especially important now, that many engineers that I know, and not just students, are mystified by some of the issues that do arise, affecting them, and the ways in which they arise. I think the infrastructure issue provides us an important opportunity, perhaps even compelling. As I noted a moment ago, there really were not many engineers speaking at previous sessions, about the political dimensions of the infrastructure issue. I think the engineers feel a strange ambivalence. Look around at modern cities, multistoried buildings, elevators, transportation systems, aircraft, modern communications; everything that makes a modern large city possible is a result of the work of engineers. But somehow we are not there around the tables when the important decisions are made.

I am a great fan of Theodore von Karman. He once made a very nice and succinct definition, trying to differentiate scientists and engineers. He said scientists seek to understand what is; engineers seek to do what has not been done before. Engineers are doers.

Technology is, of course, compulsive. Skyscrapers are built because it is possible to build them. In the issue of *Engineering News-Record* dated November 3, 1983, there was reported a very interesting symposium in which people were saying that it is now possible to build 150- and 200-story buildings — and that they will certainly be built. The technology *is* compulsive. Just as the technology of a 32-bit VLSI is also compulsive — and will in fact overwhelm us, like Henry Ford's Model T.

Fernand Braudel has been probably the most important historian of the century; a Frenchman, he has given a great deal of attention to such matters in ways that, I am afraid, have not yet been discovered by historians in North America. He says, simply, that technology determines history, and proceeds in his own writings to show how that is.

Why then do we as engineers have so much influence and so little power? Why is there so much fuss about infrastructure? We all knew, all along, that pavements, bridges, and water and sewer systems need maintenance.

Well, I think there are several reasons. The first is that for us, and for the rest of the world, it has been easier to deal with new technologies because they tend to sweep everything before them. They are most compelling. Roebling's bridge had to be built. Roebling, in fact, had something to say about politicians, an aspect that, interestingly, has been absent from discussions here. Roebling once described the then mayor of New York as having suffered an acute attack of integrity — from which he quickly recovered.

We were carried for a long time in civil engineering with the power of doing things new and for the first time. In fact, that carried us up until the time maybe 15 or 20 years ago when something else apparently even more potent came along, and that is the power of modern analysis which has become a preoccupation in academic circles and with students because it is so much fun and because it does appear to give so much additional power to our work.

It is important, I think, now, as we try to understand what we do and why we do it, and what these things mean in the world of power, that until maybe 15 or 20 years ago, we were able to do a good deal without formal analysis. Closed form solutions were the only formal analyses available, and there were very few real-world situations for which those closed solutions worked. We nonetheless managed very well. As I think many of us remember, structural engineering was one of the few fields in all of engineering in which there was any pretense of mathematical analysis. Most of the rest was almost pure pragmatism.

Somehow the realism that was associated with the earlier modes of engineering is maybe lost to us today as we have become infatuated with analysis. Sure, we can invert matrices of 2000 by 2000 but also we can have disasters like the Westgate Bridge. Although that occurred a long way away in Australia, it is worth noting because I think it relates to this remarkable preoccupation with analysis that has now taken over both education and a lot of civil engineering design work as well. The Westgate Bridge was a multispan express highway bridge being built across part of the harbor at Melbourne. It was designed in Britain by some people with very big computers. They had a mathematical model of how the structure would behave. They sent out junior engineers to supervise the construction. As the subsequent Royal Commission Report determined when the investigation was taking place, this junior engineer first sent letters, then telegrams, then finally made desperate phone calls because the thing, as it was going up, was not behaving as the mathematical model in the computer predicted. However the people in London, looking at the computer printout, said no, everything had to be right. Finally the bridge collapsed killing, I think it was, three dozen men. In the subsequent investigation, this incredible story of the designers rejecting experience in favor of their analysis came out. It is a lesson for all of us engaged both in education and in the practice of designing.

En route then, something has been lost. We see the world as something to be analyzed, and we have perhaps lost sight of the nature of doing things successfully. The exultation with power has moved on to other areas a little more fashionable. The electrical engineers and computer scientists with their chips are now enjoying some of the intoxication of technical power that civil engineers held a generation ago with their tall buildings and long bridges.

But the infrastructure issue reminds us again of the importance of reality and the difficulty and limitations of dealing with such simple abstractions as we see in analytical work.

In looking then at reality, I think we can try to contemplate this sort of situation; the structure of power as it affects what we as engineers do. My own experience in government has led me to conclude that we as engineers do not acknowledge or do not discern that there are three kinds of rules of evidence. We all know about rules of evidence as they apply in a court of law. There is another set of rules of evidence that occur in a scientific laboratory or, for that matter, in an engineering analysis. There is objective fact, objective truth, even, that we believe, but naively, speaks for itself. The third domain, in which there are entirely different rules of evidence is, of course, in a political situation where there is no objective fact, where issues have no reality until they are defined by the political process as being compelling.

I think at the previous sessions we heard some confirmation of that—as the politicans told us that until the public becomes concerned, matters have no political reality.

Infrastructure issues, I think, relate very well to this because they show us that what we as engineers have always acknowledged and known to be so indeed had no political reality until very recently.

The story of the bond issues described here indicates why the politicians are prepared now to address issues, as the public has come to acknowledge the need to act. The kind of logic is, of course, alien to engineering. We like to see the world as a problem to be solved; lawyers and politicians see it as a game to be played. To an engineer, facts are paramount and speak for themselves. In politics, no fact exists without political support. Of all the people who spoke here, I think Richard Sullivan told us that most emphatically: if we want action people have to become excited.

Politics then deals with what is to us an irrational world. Who knows what issues will become the focus of media attention and of our political people tomorrow? Politics, in fact, deals in magic, offering solutions to insoluble problems.

Most fundamentally, of course, and the burden of all governments in democratic countries today, is that the public wants services that have been developed and expanded over the last couple of decades, but is really quite unwilling to bear their current cost. To an engineer that is irrational. To a politician it is reality.

In politics solutions can be, tend to be, compromises. In engineering, our culture is different; a compromise is never going to hold a bridge up, right or wrong. And I think this explains why — as Governor Cuomo said — politics tends to be reactive and not proactive. We used to joke, when I was in government, that long-range planning was anything with an outlook of more than 30 minutes. And why, as another wag said, in politics we tend to see the handwriting on the wall only when our backs are up against it.

I think that many issues that are now of increasing concern suggest that we have to somehow find ways to relate the technical knowledge of engineering to such political realities. Not only infrastructure, but environmental protection issues and particular problems such as the transportation of hazardous materials are still, I think, very tenuously understood. They pose enormous difficulties. There are trade-offs to be made, but we are not in any position yet to work these out rationally.

Engineers deal with objective risk — probability. The public, and therefore politicians and lawyers, seek absolute assurances. To engineers, the legal system is really quite incomprehensible. It is a kind of gladiatorial contest intended to produce a victor.

Derek Bok, the president of Harvard University, attacked the legal system in North America, early in 1983, for its contribution to inefficiency and waste. He attacked the law schools for preparing people to play those gladitorial games rather than preparing people to think about the resolution of differences.

Unfortunately, North America is increasingly in the hand of lawyers, courts, and politicians. In fact, North America leads the world in the production and employment of lawyers, accountants, masters in business administration — all people who help share wealth but not people who help create it. You have probably heard the statistic that Japan manages with about 10% of the lawyers, as a proportion of population, that we have in North America.

Although there are new signs of increased reality in North America, and certainly we have heard suggestions that there have been some improvements in industrial production and competitiveness, I do not think that we can soon expect any change in the real structure of power.

As we look at the future for our engineering curricula, I think, personally, that we need a good knowledge of some of those facts. Generally, both in our educational systems and in our practice, we engineers have tended often to overlook them because they seemed so irrational and so remote from our ordinary culture. We have to do many other things, of course, as you are going to hear about "expert systems" and other kinds of new techniques that will become extraordinarily important. But I think we need most of all to find some way to cope with these realities. They do have a logic, as Comptroller Regan described. I thought his address was remarkably cogent because he indicated very clearly why it is that politicians and governments do what they do.

It seems to me then that, from this, we have to find ourselves less frequently victims of these processes and that perhaps can learn more frequently to be players. I do not think we can ever expect to change completely our own culture, but I think we should try to prepare our students to understand these processes — and there are certainly ways to do it. I think that there should be studies of these things as systems, to be dealt with as we deal with other systems — soft systems at least — and that it would not be difficult to accommodate some such understandings in undergraduate curricula. I do not think one needs to spend much time talking about how that might be done. I think that case studies and examples that are used in other modes of analysis would be appropriate. The fact that the results are not quantitative but qualitative should not, I think, impose extraordinary difficulties — although certainly our culture in the last 20 years has taken us farther and farther from things that have to be dealt with qualitatively. But my feeling, already before I came here and very much more strongly as a result of hearing what was said, is that civil engineers will simply *not* find themselves in true positions of authority and leadership unless they find some way of understanding and dealing with those kinds of realities.

DISCUSSION OF THE PAPER

W. C. WRIGHT (*Metropolitan Studies Program, Syracuse University, Syracuse, N.Y.*): One of the things that I've noticed and that seems to be lacking is that there are not enough engineers who are pursuing careers in the public sector. Looking at some of the schools that are available for them, in my own institution, the Maxwell School is probably one of the leading institutions that has very prominent individuals in all levels of government — yet there are only 2 engineers out of 150 students who are involved in the program, of which I am one. I don't know if you have any ideas on how to get more students, more practicing engineers, young engineers, to go into these programs.

D. WRIGHT: Well I think that's a bit of a rhetorical question. Really, as I was suggesting, if engineers are interested, they will pursue these things. One of the ironies is that lots of schools of public administration and particularly studies of policy analysis tend to follow the same problem, that is, they become preoccupied with the mathematics. If you look at journals in the field, they're all mathematical, just like the engineering journals are these days, filled with second-class mathematics; the real problems are not acknowledged. It makes me think of the old joke about the drunk and the policeman: one night the policeman came along and found a man digging in some rubbish in the gutter under a street lamp. The policeman asked him what he was doing. The man said he had lost his watch. The policeman looked down with his flashlight and didn't see it, and asked, "Where did you drop it?" and the man said, "Up the street"; the policeman said, "Why are you looking here"; The man said, "There's no light up there."

UNIDENTIFIED SPEAKER: I was very fortunate in having a four-year liberal arts course before I studied engineering, and I was once asked what it did for me. And I said that I learned that people who could write poetry, could study the philosophers, and so on, were extremely smart; most of them led the class inevitably. The trouble with engineers as I've worked with them now for many, many years is that if they're dealing with a problem and if the person they're working against is not an engineer, well they consider him just a fool or stupid.

W. S. BUTCHER (*Division of Civil and Environmental Engineering, National Science Foundation, Washington, D.C.*): I don't think that needs a reply.

M. S. JETHWANI (*New York City Department of Environmental Protection, New York, N.Y.*): All of us have been saying for the past decade that the lawyers are taking over engineering. What can we do about it? The legislature is controlled by lawyers and many elected officials and politicians are lawyers. How can we reverse that trend?

D. WRIGHT: Well, not by retreating. I think engineers tend to retreat behind their mathematics, as that last gentleman really was intimating. I think the thing has to change. In Japan, you know, most senior people in public life have a background in engineering or science. I made my first visit there recently, and I talked to a member of a very senior body, the body that produces all of the policy directives for the country, general stuff, on science and technology. It's called the Prime Minister's Council on Science and Technology and comprises their prime minister, Mr. Nakasoni, four senior cabinet members, four chairmen of large industrial organizations, and a couple of other scientists. Talking with these people, someone asked the question, "Well you know, this stuff is pretty important but clearly the prime minister of a country like Japan has many things to worry about, and I guess you don't get much of his time for the work of this committee." The Japanese gentleman replied: "No we don't. He only meets with us about 12 days a year."

I don't think one could imagine any senior politician in North America at this stage giving that much of his time to the kinds of issues that really matter. But I do see signs, signs that in fact reinforce, I guess, some of what I was trying to say—that the public is now aroused about a failure to compete internationally, and they do believe that there are solutions possible. Those solutions will arrive from the use of science and technology, and, therefore, I think that we'll become essential to more people at senior levels of authority who need to acknowledge those matters and become conversant with them. Now, it may happen that lawyers will just learn some of the buzz words about technology and retain their present authority, but I think it's up to us to decide whether we wish to play those games as well. I think it can be done. Certainly in Canada, we have numbers of people with technical backgrounds who have found their way into government and politics. Sure they become politicians, but they don't lose that understanding — and I do believe that I see some signs of that happening in this country as well.

Educating Engineers for Rebuilding Rather Than Building

ROBERT D. HANSON

Department of Civil Engineering
University of Michigan
304 West Engineering Building
Ann Arbor, Michigan 48109

The subject of this New York Conference on the Infrastructure: Maintenance and Repair of Public Works is timely. The broad-based view represented by the speakers which covers government policies, public financing, influence of maintenance and repair on building codes and standards, and the recognition that reconstruction requires different technological innovations is particularly pertinent to this session on civil engineering education and research. The purpose of this paper is to discuss what civil engineering educators and researchers must do to prepare new engineers for these new challenges.

The United States has had a relatively unique position in the technological development arena. Many of our cities and public works were initiated and expanded while the new technologies were being created and improved. Our transportation systems evolved through waterway systems including canals, railroads, auto and truck traffic on dirt roads, and paved highways and expressways, and by air. In almost all of these cases the newest of the technology was applied as additions to or replacements for existing systems. Many parallels exist for water supply and waste treatment. The same is also true for our buildings. The evolution of building technology from timber, stone, and brick through iron, concrete, steel, aluminum, and prestressing has in general left us with a broad supply of building types and materials. Historically, when new facilities were needed the old facilities would be demolished and replaced by newer, bigger, better facilities.

Design analysis has had a similar history. Each step of the evolution from simple design analysis procedures through the more complex interconnected systems designs now common followed the development of new analytical capabilities. Even though we now need large digital computers to effectively use our analytical capabilities for the particular problem being studied, we should not forget that earlier designers faced the same decisions that we do now. Many public officials and engineers, not too many years ago, firmly believed that the results of a computer simulation provided the answer for their decisions. At the present time there is a growing recognition that computer modeling and input data are not sufficient to provide the final answer in all cases. However, reevaluation of our past experiences based on current knowledge is necessary. Interaction between our real nonlinear, nonelastic,

176

complex behavior and the variations of these behaviors over time and over operating conditions is necessary to improve the models for our sophisticated computer programs. All of this requires increased data storage and time for interpretation and evaluation of existing data.

Our design codes and material specifications have followed a similar process of development based upon actual practice and observational experience of systems during their effective lifetimes. Quality control and quality assurance in the construction process and increased trust in our analytical capabilities have continued to lower the factor of safety designed into these systems. It is important for us to recognize that over 150 years of engineering education has been built on the premise that we learn from the past in terms of material, analytical, and construction behavior characteristics for the design, specification, and construction of new facilities to serve specific objectives. I repeat, construction of *new facilities*. As stated by the speakers at this conference, it is not politically possible or economically beneficial to continue the previous policy of demolishing the old and replacing them by new facilities.

At this point I will narrow the focus of this discussion to buildings as a subset of the general topic of public works. A further focus will exclude buildings of historical significance because they allow (or require) decisions somewhat independent of economics. More specifically, let us look at one class of public buildings which is becoming more and more important to public officials — the public schools. The public school building may have been built in the late 1800s or early 1900s utilizing a single or mixed mode of construction involving brick, timber, reinforced concrete, iron, and roof tile. In many cases the building may have undergone a number of periods of remodeling in which hollow concrete block, plywood, sheet rock, wood studs, or metal studs have been utilized to change the function or to modernize certain spaces in the building. The windows may be single-paned glass in wood casements, and the stairways would be of wood or iron with tile, granite, or concrete treads. The human occupancy environment is excellent in terms of deterioration of the building materials, but the maintenance of the structure may have been poor or nonexistent, especially in recent years. Roof leaks may have allowed water to penetrate into the roof supports, the ceilings, and even into the masonry walls. This water intrusion causes a rapid deterioration of the building materials and, if not fixed in time, can result in failure of the building.

The architectural changes in the building may have been cosmetic in nature or in some cases may actually have provided local stiffnesses and strength to the building. The first problem the engineering designer is faced with is an assessment and evaluation of the building's current state. When was the original structure built? With that information a determination of the applicable building codes, material performance characteristics, and reputation of the original designer and constructor will provide an initial judgment of the structure. What changes have been made since initial construction? Again the applicable building codes, material performance characteristics, and reputation of the designer and constructor are crucial to the assessment of the current building. What environmental conditions, loading conditions, and maintenance has the building seen? This is needed to assess the probable deterioration of the building materials throughout the life of the structure. In some cases these effects may be small so that the original material characteristics can be used for the current evaluation. In other cases the effects of deterioration may be so major that an assessment of the original strength may have no effect on its current characteristics. Most cases are not at these two extremes.

A word of caution must be given to those who have not been involved in many cases of rehabilitation or strengthening. The official file plans, if they exist, may not accurately reflect the details of the actual construction. This is not to imply fraud by the constructor or building inspector, rather it reflects the difference between field conditions and those assumed by the designer. The differences are sometimes noted on the drawings. Some drawings may be nothing more than architectural plans with general dimensions and types of materials indicated.

In summary, what the structural engineer needs are techniques whereby the current structural characteristics can be evaluated. From this evaluation an assessment of the proposed rebuilding can be made. Not all of the tools needed to efficiently perform this evaluation and assessment are available at the present time. This will be addressed later when research is discussed.

There have been very few educational programs that have addressed the issues of rebuilding and rehabilitating existing facilities. The most common ones have been "short courses" directed toward the design professionals and taught by other design professionals. Most of our engineering colleges do an excellent job of educating their students for design of new facilities using the most up-to-date materials, processes, and techniques and incorporating the most recent of the national building codes and materials specifications. What cannot be taught effectively in the colleges is the performance experience that practicing engineers develop by observing their designs in practice and their observations of real building performance under different loading histories and maintenance conditions. I believe that most employers of recent graduates are reasonably satisfied by the content of the education provided. The fact that not all colleges approach the area of design in the same way is important so that each employer can obtain the diversity of backgrounds necessary for a strong organization. Nevertheless, there are a few philosphical concepts that every college can implement to significantly upgrade their graduates' capabilities to solve the complex problems created by the need to rebuild rather than build new.

The approach that has been used by the University of Michigan Civil Engineering Structures' Faculty to prepare their students for these types of problems has been twofold. First, the main emphasis for analysis and design is that the student develops an understanding for the real behavior of the structural system and the materials used in the system. One of the keys to developing this understanding is that the student is able to follow the behavior of the structure and its elements from the small deformation elastic response through its damage level behavior until failure. As much as possible these behavioral experiences come from real structures; that is, examples of real structure behavior are studied and correlated to behavior that would have been expected based upon previous experiences, theories, and laboratory studies. All of the faculty members have been involved with laboratory tests, at many scales, and to varying degrees with observations of real building failures. Earthquake-damaged buildings provide one of the largest groups of buildings for these studies. The major difficulty with using earthquake-damaged buildings is that the loading condition is not precisely known. However, from a series of studies an understanding of the sequential damage conditions becomes clear. Buildings subjected to other types of overloads are also valuable in this regard. Buildings damaged during construction or with damage caused by design or construction errors are not a very good source of data because most of the concerned parties wish to restrict the information.

These real building data are supplemented by laboratory test data. It is important for the student to have hands-on experience with damaged materials and structural systems. Without this experience the student does not have the ability to assess and interpret written and photographic descriptions of damaged real buildings. This hands-on experience has to be closely coupled with appropriate theoretical and computer model studies. Then both the physical and mathematical results are interpreted in light of the current building codes and specifications.

Second, research studies into the behavior of various methods of repair and strengthening of structural elements and systems need to be carried out. These studies serve two purposes. They provide data needed by the design professionals, and they provide physical observations needed by the students. It is unfortunate that many of the rebuilding systems are designed and constructed on the basis of theoretical investigations and without physical tests to verify the expected behavior.

Laboratory research as described above can provide valuable data as well as valuable educational experiences. It can also provide a means for evaluating various techniques for assessing field measurements of material properties. A number of research efforts in the repair and strengthening of buildings for increased earthquake resistance have provided data useful in material properties evaluation. Seminars that bring together design and construction professionals and researchers have proven to be an excellent method to quickly raise the state of the art.

If the question is, What should civil engineering educators be doing to prepare their students for the challenges of rebuilding the infrastructure? then the answer is, Provide the students with hands-on physical experience to couple with their existing theoretical and mathematical abilities. With a full appreciation of the real behavior of the physical system and how that compares with the mathematical simulations, the design professionals will be able to create innovative solutions to their problems. They will be able to develop solutions that may not literally satisfy the codes, but that can be demonstrated to more than satisfy the full intent of the codes. This physical experience will also encourage design professionals to use experimental research to answer questions and suggest solutions not conveniently solved by theoretical methods alone. Civil engineering education needs to reemphasize physical laboratory experiences and to tie those experiences closely to real operating system characteristics and to computer simulations of the same systems.

DISCUSSION OF THE PAPER

P. L. RINALDI (*Port Authority of New York and New Jersey, New York, N.Y.*): Before coming to the Port Authority, I taught civil engineering for several years. It seems that we do a reasonably good job in our engineering education institutions in teaching the basic tools we need to do engineering. When we couple that with application of those tools in the undergraduate curriculum we seem to focus on building new and putting systems in place that are new. Many of us now that are practicing engineering find that those tools have to be applied in a different way. Yet when we try and fall back on some of the examples that we learned in our academic days, they don't apply because we've been taught to look at building new systems rather than rebuilding systems.

You have mentioned that what can't be taught in the colleges is the performance experience that engineers get in practice. I differ with you in that we can do that. It seems that what we tend to do is recruit faculty for our educational institutions with an emphasis on academic credentials and to the exclusion of practical experience. And if anything, in rebuilding infrastructure, practical experience is a very key thing that should be shared with students as they go through the civil engineering curriculum. It's something that we haven't been doing. Adjunct professors with many years of experience teaching courses do lend themselves to this very well. What I ask Dr. Hanson is, What could you recommend or what have you done in your department and at the University of Michigan (1) to change the curriculum to focus the curriculum more on rebuilding and (2) in recruiting or putting in place a faculty that can adequately do that?

R. D. HANSON: I find your comments very appropriate. However, I disagree a little bit with some of the conclusions that you reach from those same observations with which I agree. Because the employers for which we are educating our students have a broad range of needs it is not always possible to give them the essential observational information in an academic environment. We do use adjuncts, we do provide our students with hands-on experiences as much as we can. However, there's a limited amount of time within any educational program. Our firm belief of what we want to do is to educate an engineer to have the capability of thinking and understanding the behavior of a system whether it be a structural system, a water supply system, or a transportation system so that an entire overview from the mathematical simulation aspects to the practical, physical interpretation is understood. We don't have the time to take very many specific examples and try to apply them.

The other aspect of engineering education, and one that I'm very strongly supportive of, is that not every engineering school should be doing the same thing. I think we need engineering schools that cover the entire range of the engineering profession. Those that are directed more toward research applications and those that are directed more for immediate engineering design applications. We need the whole spectrum of background and viewpoint, and that's why I have tried to emphasize that the firms hiring these engineers should hire them from many different sources so that they build a strong organization with different points of view and different experiences coming out of the educational environment. Not every school can cover the entire area in the way that both you and I feel it has to be covered.

Artificial Intelligence–Based Methods for Infrastructure Evaluation and Repair

STEVEN J. FENVES

Department of Civil Engineering
Carnegie-Mellon University
Schenley Park
Pittsburgh, Pennsylvania 15213

INTRODUCTION

The evaluation of the physical and functional condition of a bridge, pavement, or sewer segment bears a close analogy to diagnosing a patient: symptoms must be collected and evaluated by an expert analyst and compared to hypotheses of possible malfunctions. Recommendations of repair action are similarly analogous to prognosis: the prescription of remedies considered appropriate by the expert. There is a shortage of expert infrastructure diagnosticians. A recent outgrowth of computer science research in artificial intelligence, called knowledge-based expert systems, has shown the potential to produce computer programs that perform diagnosis and prognosis at the level of experts. Unlike conventional algorithmic programs, where all combinations of conditions and all sequences of decisions must be explicitly and deterministically defined, expert systems require only that the expertise be represented in the form of local if-then rules; they can also deal with inexact and incomplete knowledge. The purpose of this paper is to introduce expert systems, illustrate their potential application to infrastructure evaluation and repair, and discuss their implication on civil engineering education and practice.

It may seem preposterous to suggest that more or better computer programs have anything to contribute to the maintenance and repair of public works. While present-generation computer programs have provided invaluable help in the *well-formed* aspects of civil engineering, notably in analysis based on incontrovertible physical laws, these programs have been largely inadequate in the *ill-structured* aspects, such as design. As any user of a bridge-rating or infrastructure priority evaluation program will attest, computer programs have been even less adequate in dealing with evaluation and repair issues.

It is worthwhile to examine critically the cause of mismatch between user needs and conventional computer program capabilities. This examination will reveal that conventional programming imposes a mold—one could say a straitjacket—on the problem-solving process. A radically new problem-solving strategy will then be introduced.

ANATOMY OF CONVENTIONAL PROGRAMS

Every computer program consists of a set of *rules* in the form

IF (condition) THEN (action)

Thus, if (there is input) then (compute) is the overall model of any program, where (compute) is then further subdivided into hundreds or thousands of more detailed rules, e.g., a steel design program may contain the rule

IF (section is compact) THEN (allowable stress $= 0.66\ F_y$)

The conditions and actions are deeply intertwined, as the action of one rule becomes a component of the condition of another rule, thus

IF (a and b and c . . . are satisfied) THEN (section is compact)

IF (actual stress $\leqslant$ allowable stress) THEN (stress constraint is satisfied), etc.

It is clear that only a person knowledgeable in the field of application, an *expert*, can define the applicable conditions and the resulting actions. This is particularly true in any practical engineering application program, where a very large proportion of the rules are not necessarily based on the *causality* of physical laws, but represent the *heuristics* (assumptions, limitations, rules of thumb, or "style") of the expert or his organization. Thus, the program sketched may contain a rule such as

IF (trial section not compact) THEN (choose another section)

because the expert may want to take advantage of the 10% "bonus" in the allowable stress or, alternately, to insure that yielding is the governing limit state.

Developing a complete set of rules for any engineering application is a major undertaking. However, a person writing a conventional or algorithmic program, a *programmer*, incurs three additional major professional responsibilities:

1. He must determine the *sequencing* of the program, that is, the fixed order in which the rules will be executed.
2. He must guarantee *completeness* of the program, that is, that the program performs the correct actions for every possible combination of conditions — even if the action is only an error message for combinations not specifically provided for.
3. He must similarly guarantee *uniqueness* of the results, that is, that every combination of conditions leads to one action only.[a]

---

[a] This is not really an independent requirement, since the programmer's choice of sequencing automatically assures a unique set of actions — although they may not necessarily be the *correct* ones for each combination of conditions.

It is the discharge of these additional responsibilities that makes conventional program development so expensive. The expense is multiplied when programs have to be updated to reflect new situations; the programmer not only must modify or add a few relevant rules, he also must locate their appropriate place in the predefined sequence and frequently modify the sequence itself. It is no wonder, therefore, that many conventional programs appear inadequate and are often outdated.

EXPERT SYSTEMS

Knowledge-based expert systems have recently emerged from decades of research in artificial intelligence as practical problem-solving tools that can reach a level of performance comparable to that of a human expert in some specialized problem area or domain. Surveys of expert system concepts are given in References 5, 6, and 13 and in a recent textbook.[10]

The principal distinction between expert systems and conventional interactive programs is that in an expert system a clear distinction is made between the *knowledge base*, containing the model of an expert's problem-solving knowledge, represented in many expert systems by if-then rules of the type illustrated above, and the *control strategy*, or inference mechanism, which manipulates the knowledge base. Whereas the knowledge base is specific to a given domain, the control strategy is completely general.

The third component of an expert system is the *context*, akin to data in conventional programs, which represents the expert system's knowledge about the particular problem at hand.

These three basic components of an expert system are shown in FIGURE 1, together with a user interface. The process of using an expert system is as follows:

1. The user enters some known facts about the problem into the context (or is prompted to do so by the expert system).
2. Following its control strategy (to be discussed below), the inference mechanism locates the potentially applicable rules — those whose condition portion is *matched* by the facts in the context — selects one of these, and *fires* it, that is, causes its action to be executed.
3. The result of any action is to add to or modify some aspect of the context; thus, new rules become candidates to be fired, and Step 2 is repeated in an "infinite loop" until a goal is satisfied or there are no more rules remaining to be fired.

All expert systems possess, in some form, these three basic components. In addition, many contain three additional, highly desirable components.

Treatment of Imprecise or Incomplete Knowledge

Many expert systems provide the ability to deal with imprecise or incomplete knowledge, where rules are represented as

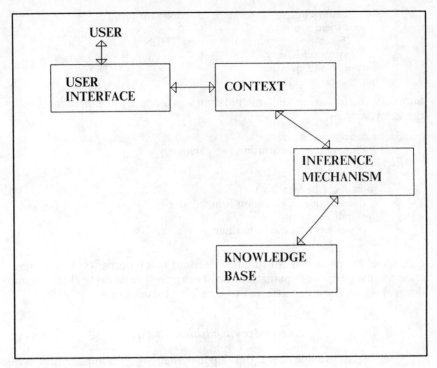

FIGURE 1. Functional diagram of basic expert system.

IF (condition) THEN (action) WITH CERTAINTY
e.g., IF (component exposed to salting) THEN (damage due to corrosion)
is very likely.

The inference mechanism can then propagate certainty measures about the inferences along with results of the inferences.

Explanation Facility

It is very important that the expert system explain to the user its inference process. A good explanation facility can provide both a priori and a posteriori explanations. The two can be illustrated using the last sample rule given above. The simulated dialogue below illustrates the use of an a priori explanation using the keyword *why*:

ES: is component exposed to salting?
User: why?
ES: you mean:
      why is component exposed to salting needed
      I am attempting to determine whether

>   damage due to corrosion is an important factor
> and there is a rule
>   IF component exposed to salting THEN damage due to
>   corrosion is very likely
> please answer question
User: yes

Similarly, the following dialogue illustrates an a posteriori explanation using the keyword *how*:

ES: I conclude that
>   damage due to corrosion is highly likely
User: how?
ES: you mean:
> (how did I deduce that)
>   damage due to corrosion is highly likely
> you indicated that
>   component exposed to salting = yes
> and there is a rule . . .

Of course, in any actual consultation session, much deeper chains of inference are involved; the explanation facility can then recursively chain up and down through the rules affected to provide explanations.

Knowledge-Acquisition Facility

Since the knowledge base is built up incrementally, it is important to have a facility that permits the addition of new rules. Ideally, the expert should be able to add to or modify the knowledge base as sessions on the expert system reveal gaps in the knowledge base.

An expanded expert system incorporating these components is shown in FIGURE 2. It is to be emphasized that only the knowledge base is specific to a given domain; all the other components are parts of a general purpose expert system building framework.

An *expert system building framework* is simply an inference mechanism with an empty knowledge base; the knowledge-acquisition facility is used to develop the knowledge base and to structure the context for a particular application domain.

COMPARISON TO CONVENTIONAL PROGRAMS

The above brief description of expert systems can serve as a basis for comparing them with the shortcomings or difficulties of conventional programs discussed earlier.

Sequencing

In an expert system, sequencing of the rules is entirely the responsibility

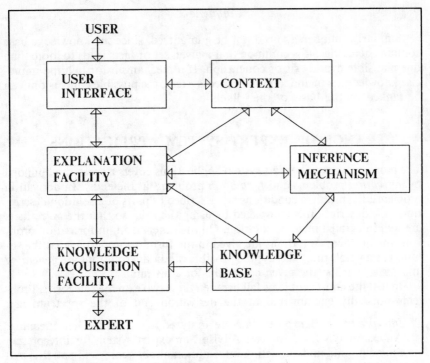

FIGURE 2. Functional diagram of expanded expert system.

of the control strategy. In many expert system frameworks, a single knowledge base can be manipulated or "executed" using two different strategies.

In the *forward chaining*, or data-driven, strategy, the system works from the known facts input into the context toward a goal state, that is, the most appropriate hypothesis or conclusion that fits the facts.

In the *backward chaining*, or goal-driven, strategy, the system starts from a hypothesis or goal, checking facts in the context to see if the hypothesis can be supported from the facts. If the necessary facts are not available, subgoals are set up to get them.

Completeness

In an expert system, completeness need not be guaranteed, at least not in the development stages. If the knowledge base contains no rules for the situation at hand (or if it leads to unacceptable conclusions), the user can switch to the knowledge-acquisition facility to supply additional rules to be added to the knowledge base.

Uniqueness

Similarly, uniqueness need not be guaranteed; since the knowledge base contains heuristics, it is common that a given set of facts leads to more than one plausible hypothesis or conclusion. If a mechanism for treating imprecise knowledge is included in the expert system, the possible conclusions can be ranked on the basis of their likelihood.

RANGE OF EXPERT SYSTEM APPLICATIONS

The range of potential expert system applications covers a spectrum bounded by *derivation* problems and *formation* problems at the ends.[1] In derivation problems, the problem conditions are described as parts of a solution description; this description is completed by using the rules so that the given facts are well integrated into the solution. On the other hand, in formation problems the problem conditions are given in the form of properties that the solution as a whole must satisfy; the possible candidate solutions are *generated* and *tested* against the given conditions or constraints.

In real life, most problems fall between these two extreme categories. Problems normally encountered at the derivation end of the spectrum are:

Interpretation. The given data are analyzed to determine their meaning. An example is the Dipmeter Advisor, an expert system for interpreting dipmeter data and extracting information about geological patterns and trends.[3] Another well-known example is PROSPECTOR, an expert system for identifying ore-bearing geological formations.[4]

Diagnosis. The problem consists of finding the state of a system based on the interpretation of data (which may be noisy, i.e., imprecise). In this category are several medical diagnosis programs, such as MYCIN for infectious diseases[15] and DIALOG for internal medicine.[14]

Monitoring. Signals are interpreted continuously and required changes are made depending on the state of the system being monitored. An example is the Ventilation Manager for monitoring patients' ventilatory therapy.[7]

Formation problems are usually examples of the *generate-and-test* paradigm. In the purest form of generate and test, a possible candidate solution is generated by one part of the system and is then tested for suitability by another part of the system. Formation problems fall into two subclasses: *constraint satisfaction* and *optimization* problems. In constraint-satisfaction problems, the solution need only satisfy a set of constraints, while in optimization problems an attempt is made to find the optimal solution.

Problems usually encountered at this end of the spectrum are:

Planning. The objective is to set up a program of actions that are required to achieve certain goals (i.e., create plans). An outstanding example in this category is MOLGEN, an expert system for planning experiments in molecular genetics.[17]

Design. Design involves the selection of a physical system to perform a certain function. A very successful example, in a limited definition of design, is R1, an expert system that designs VAX computer configurations, including selecting the needed components and determining their physical layout and interconnections.[12]

EXPERT SYSTEM DEVELOPMENT PROCESS

As already indicated, the development process of an expert system is incremental: a prototype system may be implemented and tested by the expert, and as a result new knowledge added to the knowledge base. The main reason for this evolutionary development is that a great deal of time must be spent on *formalizing* the expert's knowledge to a much larger extent than he or she had ever done previously.

At the present state of expert system development methodology, the generation of an expert system involves the cooperative efforts between one or more experts who possess the domain-dependent knowledge and a *knowledge engineer* who elicits the expertise and converts it into the system's knowledge base.[b] Several major research projects are aimed at improving the knowledge-acquisition process to the point where the expert can communicate directly with the system.

It is useful to identify the major stages of expert system development.[10]

Identification

The first stage is to identify the problem domain to be addressed. Some of the criteria of a "good" domain are:

- Algorithmic solutions are inappropriate, overly constrained, or over-specialized.
- There are recognized experts who perform tasks in the domain provably better than novices.
- The knowledge components are taught to novices or are available in textbooks — novices become experts incrementally through practice.
- Typical tasks take an expert from several minutes to several hours to complete.
- There is a high "payoff": the process could be significantly improved if an expert could be put to work on each occurrence of a task.

---

[b] This process is akin to the early days of computer programming, where an intermediate *programmer* was needed.

Formalization

The formalization stage involves the identification of key concepts, relations, and information-flow characteristics of the problem domain, and the mapping of these concepts and relations into the formal structure supported by an available expert system building framework.

Implementation

At the implementation stage, the initial knowledge base is built up from interviews with the expert.

Testing

The knowledge base is tested and validated using actual tasks, and modified or extended as needed.

POTENTIAL APPLICATIONS TO INFRASTRUCTURE PROBLEMS

Expert system methodology is still in its infancy. Expert systems specifically geared to civil engineering include:

- HYDRO, an expert system to aid a hydrologist in estimating values of input parameters to an algorithmic watershed simulation program.[9]
- SACON, an expert system to aid a structural analyst in selecting the appropriate modeling options in a large, general purpose, finite element program.[2]
- SPERIL, an expert system under development at Purdue University for the assessment of seismic damage to buildings.[11]
- HIRISE, an expert system being developed at Carnegie-Mellon University for the preliminary design of high-rise buildings.[8]

To the author's knowledge, there are no working expert systems specifically applied to infrastructure problems. However, there is considerable conceptual similarity between infrastructure problems and problem areas addressed by existing expert systems. Furthermore, many of the infrastructure problem areas exhibit most of, if not all, the characteristics of "good" problem domains discussed above.

Therefore, the following is presented as an exploratory list of potential applications, organized according to the range of expert system application areas presented earlier.

Interpretation

Much of the information about the state of infrastructure components has to be obtained from tests, visual and other inspection devices, and observations. The interpretation of all such information sources is a task well suited to expert systems. Among the potential applications are pavement and bridge deck condition interpretation based on nondestructive measurements, sewer and water line evaluation based on remote visual and other observations, etc.

Diagnosis

The evaluation of integrity or, more precisely, the diagnosis of actual or potential losses of integrity is again applicable to many infrastructure components, such as bridges, pavements, and water and sewer lines. Diagnostic systems could incorporate the heuristics of expert inspectors, and substitute empirical knowledge where factual knowledge is missing (e.g., if design data are not available, approximate parameters may be supplied for experts' recollections of practices used in the period). Diagnostic systems could identify most likely causes of deficiency and provide recommendations for remedial actions.

Monitoring

The information needed for many of the interpretation and diagnosis tasks described above is frequently time dependent, either because real-time behavior information is needed (e.g., dynamic behavior of bridges) or because changes over time are involved (e.g., gradual degradation). With inexpensive microprocessors and sensors providing input to expert systems, monitoring and time-dependent diagnosis may be performed in real time for critical structures or suspected emergency conditions, as well as long-term monitoring based on periodic data recording.

Planning

Expert systems are appropriate to consider for many of the planning functions pertaining to the maintenance and rehabilitation of the infrastructure, because of the large number of considerations, conflicting requirements, and contingencies involved. Such systems may range from microscopic ones (e.g., construction scheduling and traffic maintenance on a single site) to macroscopic ones (e.g., city-wide or statewide priority determination).

Design

The design of remedial measures for various infrastructure components also appears suited for expert systems. A large number of possible remedial strategies and techniques could be explored and the feasible ones ranked by several categories. Also, the implications of possible undetected flaws could be explored early in the design process.

Other possible applications will undoubtedly occur to the reader. While the development of a practical, operational expert system is not trivial (efforts of the order of 5–10 man-years are common), it is important that a start be made.

IMPLICATIONS

The emergence of expert systems as an additional component of the engineer's "toolkit" promises to introduce changes at least as far-reaching as the entire "computer revolution" to date. This new development has far-reaching implications for engineering practice and education.

In practice, the most direct implication is that computer assistance to engineers can be significantly extended into application areas that were previously intractable. More importantly, engineers will be able to operate *as if* the most expert person in a particular problem area were looking over each engineer's shoulder, providing advice and guidance based on long experience. Also, organizations will be able to "capture" and constructively use the expertise of senior people for many years after their retirement. This is particularly valuable in the infrastructure area, where the range of problems that may be encountered exceeds any one person's direct experience, and where much of the information about current conditions may be obtained only from the personal recollections and experience of individuals who participated in the design or earlier reconstruction of the facilities.

The implications for education are equally powerful. Expert systems can serve as training or teaching tools, providing the student or novice "synthetic experience" in dealing with ill-structured problems. The development of simple expert systems may be an excellent pedagogical tool, permitting the student to organize and formalize his thought processes. One such experiment has been reported.[16] Beyond this, experimentation with expert systems, particularly with the formalization of concepts and thought processes, may eventually lead to theoretical insights and discoveries that may obviate the need for heuristics.

REFERENCES

1. AMAREL, S. 1978. Basic themes and problems in current AI research. Presented at the Fourth Annual Artificial Intelligence in Medicine (AIM) Workshop, Rutgers University, June.
2. BENNETT, J., L. CREARY, R. ENGLEMORE & R. MELOSH. 1978. SACON: A Knowledge-Based Consultant for Structural Analysis. Technical Report STAN-CS-78-699. Stanford University. Palo Alto, Calif.
3. DAVIS, R., *et al*. 1981. The dipmeter advisor: interpretation of geologic signals. *In* Proceedings, Seventh International Joint Conference on Artificial Intelligence: 846–849. IJCAI. Tokyo, Japan.
4. DUDA, R. O. 1979. A Computer-Based Consultant for Mineral Exploration. Final Report SRI Project 6415. SRI International. Menlo Park, Calif.
5. DUDA, R. & J. G. GASCHING. 1981. Knowledge-based expert systems come of age. BYTE 6(9): 238–279.

6. DUDA, R. O. & E. H. SHORTLIFFE. 1983. Expert systems research. Science **220**: 261–268.
7. FAGAN, L. M., J. C. KUNZ, E. A. FEIGENBAUM & J. J. OSBORN. 1979. Representation of dynamic clinical knowledge: measurement interpretation in the intensive care unit. *In* Proceedings, Fifth International Joint Conference on Artificial Intelligence: 1014–1029. IJCAI. Tokyo, Japan.
8. FENVES, S. J. & M. L. MAHER. 1983. HI-RISE: An Expert System for the Preliminary Structural Design of High Rise Buildings. Technical Report. Department of Civil Engineering. Carnegie-Mellon University. Pittsburgh, Pa.
9. GASCHING, J., R. REBOH & J. REITER. 1981. Development of a Knowledge-Based System for Water Resources Problems. Technical Report SRI Project 1619. SRI International. Menlo Park, Calif.
10. HAYES-ROTH, F., D. WATERMAN & D. LENAT, Eds. 1983. Building Expert Systems. Addison-Wesley. New York, N.Y.
11. ISHIZUKA, M., K. S. FU & J. T. P. YAO. 1981. SPERIL I-Computer Based Structural Damage Assessment System. Technical Report CE-STR-81-36. Purdue University. Lafayette, Ind.
12. MCDERMOTT, J. 1980. R1: A Rule-Based Configurer of Computer Systems. Technical Report CMU-CS-80-119. Carnegie-Mellon University. Pittsburgh, Pa.
13. NAU, D. S. 1983. Expert computer systems. Computer **16**: 63–85.
14. POPLE, H. E., JR., *et al.* 1975. DIALOG: A model of diagnostic logic for internal medicine. *In* Proceedings, Fourth International Joint Conference on Artificial Intelligence: 848–855. IJCAI. Tokyo, Japan.
15. SHORTLIFFE, E. G. 1976. Computer-Based Medical Consultations: MYCIN. American Elsevier. New York, N.Y.
16. STARFIELD, A. M., K. L. BUTALA, M. M. ENGLAND & K. A. SMITH. 1983. Mastering engineering concepts by building an expert system. Eng. Educ.: 104–107.
17. STEFIK, M. 1981. Planning and constraints (MOLGEN 1). Artif. Intell. **16**: 11–140.

Fire Technology and Urban Systems

PAUL R. DE CICCO

Fire Research Center
Polytechnic Institute of New York
333 Jay Street
Brooklyn, New York 11201

BACKGROUND: SCALE OF THE FIRE PROBLEM

If there is anything more disheartening than seeing infrastructure die of old age, it must be to see it succumb to sudden and useless assault by fire. If time, weather, and hard use are the drivers of normal infrastructure decay, then surely unwanted fire, caused accidentally, through neglect, or by design, is the hobgoblin of its more acute demise.[14]

A sampling of some of the great fires of this century amply demonstrates that the most catastrophic incidents have been directed to our central cities, often at their most vital elements.

The Iroquois Theater fire in Chicago in 1903 killed 602 persons, which represents the greatest loss of life in a theater in United States history. In the year following, the excursion steamer General Slocum was devastated by fire in New York Harbor with 1030 dead. The Ohio State Penitentiary fire in 1930 killed 320, and 294 perished in the Consolidated School explosion and fire in New London, Texas in 1937. A train collision and the ensuing fire killed 43 persons in Cuyahoga Falls, Ohio in 1940; and two years later, the Coconut Grove fire in Boston caused the death of 491. In 1947, the Texas City fire and explosions cost 468 lives and destroyed several ships and a large part of that city's waterfront. Fires in public buildings, utilities, airports, subway cars, grain silos, wastewater treatment plants, and almost every other element of infrastructure are well documented in terms of frequency and incurred deaths, injuries and monetary losses.

To bring fire technology and urban systems into the context of infrastructure renewal, we should first consider scale, diversity, and certain attributes of unwanted fire that are particularly relevant to urban communities.

Each year, fire departments in the United States respond to over 2.8 million fire calls,[12] and it is estimated that there are over 10 times this number of unreported fires. The unreported fires do not appear in national statistics, but in the aggregate, these incidents have a profound impact on the physical condition, longevity, and esthetics of housing, transportation, waterfront environment, and other parts of public and private infrastructure.

Approximately 36% of all fires occur in structures (1,027,500), and of these, over 70% involve residential buildings. The five-year annual average for civilian deaths resulting from fire is over 6900. Almost 84% of these occur in structural fires, with the largest number (96.2%) in residential buildings. Approximately 30,400 civilian injuries resulting from fire are reported each year, and direct dollar losses exceed $5.7 billion. Indirect losses are placed at over twice this amount. The highest fire incident rates are associated with the larger urban communities (population over 500,000) and with the smallest ones (population under 2500), with the Northeast and South having both higher fire and death rates than other regions of the country.

Of all unwanted fires in the United States and elsewhere in the world, the problem is most serious in older, central-city communities where infrastructure is most in need of renewal.[13] Researchers from Johns Hopkins University report that in Baltimore, Maryland, 60% of fire deaths occur in the poorest neighborhoods, although only 40% of the population lives in these areas. The density of buildings and other structures and the extreme diversity of occupancy types and uses exacerbate issues brought on by worn-out and overloaded infrastructure.

A recent report on worldwide fire services indicates a wide range of figures for numbers of fire personnel, reported fires, and fire deaths in major cities (populations of 500,000 to 3 million).[11] Cities in the United States have from 1.5 to 2.0 times as many fire-fighting personnel per capita as do their overseas counterparts. At the same time, foreign cities have from 1.3 to 1.6 times the personnel per fire. The answer to the obvious question as to whether we in the United States have too few fire fighters or too many fires lies in the statistic that we have three times the number of fires per capita than does most of the rest of the world!

If we examine fires causing large loss of life (10 or more deaths in a single incident) during this century, we find that approximately 85% (139 of 164 incidents) involved elements of infrastructure. These included 65 in public buildings and other structures, 35 in transportation systems (land, air, and water), 9 in stores and office buildings, 7 in basic industry (including utilities and defense), and 23 in manufacturing (including storage and special structures).

Large-loss fires (fires in which over $1 million in losses are incurred) also appear to have particular significance and impact on infrastructure.[16] As in the case of fires causing large loss of life, these incidents are more likely to involve public buildings, places of public assembly, large commercial and manufacturing establishments, utilities, institutions, and transportation. In 1982,[16] large-loss fires accounted for only 0.01% of the fires in the United States but resulted in 14.4% of the total dollar damage for that year. In 1982, the K-Mart fire in Falls, Pennsylvania resulted in a loss in excess of $100 million. In that same year there were 32 other fires with losses of over $5 million each. At least one-third of these directly affected one or more infrastructure systems.

It is of interest to note that the percentage of these fires attributed to incendiary or suspicious origin (26.6%) is much greater than for smaller fires. Because there are really no limits to the potential for damage to infrastructure that fire can cause, arson for profit or as a "simple" act of vandalism stands, short of war, as perhaps the most serious of threats to urban communities.

FIRE EXPERIENCE IN NEW YORK CITY

Although we often call attention to New York City for its uniqueness in scale and diversity of infrastructure, because of this very scale and diversity, it is also reasonable to consider much of the fire experience of this city as representative of what goes on in many of the large urban centers of the nation. For example, when compared with four of the six largest cities in the country, we note that the borough of Brooklyn has about the same population as Los Angeles; the population of Queens is somewhat greater than that of Philadelphia; both Manhattan and The Bronx have greater populations than Detroit or Houston; and Staten Island, the smallest but fastest-growing borough, would rate within the 50 largest cities in the country.

These five boroughs are almost as different from each other (vis a vis fire experience and fire potential) as are the cities noted above. For example, nowhere in the world are there the number, variation, and occupancy levels in high-rise buildings of both commercial and residential types as are found in Manhattan. Nor does any other city have the extensive port facilities and related marine activities found in this same borough.

Brooklyn also has extensive waterfront facilities and in addition has a population housed in over one million dwelling units. This community undoubtedly contains more obsolete structures than any other place in the nation.

Queens, an immense bedroom community, also contains the John F. Kennedy and Laguardia airports; and Staten Island (borough of Richmond) varies from rural to suburban to densley populated communities. It is somewhat isolated, and fire forces must contend with longer travel distances.

It should also be noted that every one of the five boroughs of the city is physically older than most places in the United States and each has been heavily worn by generations of people, some who have come and stayed and many who have used the city as a jumping off place to other locations. Each wave of newcomers is always replaced by another. These immigrants have generally been limited in both funds and education, and the worst of New York City's housing stock never wants for occupants.

The city of New York contains over 900,000 buildings of which, at any given time, 15,000 to 20,000 are vacant and therefore extremely vulnerable to fire. There are over 389,000 one-family and 223,000 two-family buildings, most of these in the combustible class. There are also some 40,300 buildings, including old-law tenements (constructed prior to 1929), that contain three or four dwelling units. In addition, there are over 1,500,000 dwelling units distributed within the city's intermediate and high-rise apartment buildings.

Most of the structures of each of these types are older than 50 years, with electrical systems that did not anticipate television, air conditioners, home freezers, dryers, and myriad other power-consuming tools and appliances. From the perspective of fire risk, these buildings also contain dangerous light and ventilation shafts, open cockloft spaces which connect one building to another, and combustible siding materials.[4,5,7]

The city also has more than 1100 high-rise office buildings which house over 1,000,000 persons each working day. These structures, which range from 10 to 110 stories in height, together with residential high-rise buildings are estimated to have on the order of 4000 fire calls annually. Several hundreds of these turn out to be serious fires.

In its waterborne commerce, New York City receives 48,966,000 tons of cargo each year. This is almost twice that of the closest of the two dozen largest seaports in the nation. Fire hazards associated with combustible piers, warehouses, transit sheds, transfer yards, and container storage areas are difficult to quantify, but they obviously bring special concerns in terms of maintenance, inspection, and protection against fire.

The New York City Fire Department, with a force of some 12,000 fire fighters, protects approximately 7.1 million persons over an area of 303 square miles.[12] It uses approximately 210 pumpers and 138 ladder trucks operating from 221 stations. The department's annual budget is on the order of $400 million. A busy engine company might handle 6000 working fires in a year. A busy ladder unit will respond to over 4000 working fires, and all units will make over 1 million runs in a single year. No other major metropolitan fire department approaches this level of activity.

Approximately 250 persons lose their lives in fire in New York City each year,[15] and there are over 3000 injuries to fire fighters which result in almost 100,000 lost duty days. Each year, on average, six or seven fire fighters die in the line of duty.

If we examine this record for relevance to the fire-infrastructure issue, we find that of approximately 122,000 fire calls answered annually in New York City, over 30,000 are in structures. There are also as many as 10,000 "brush" fires, almost 8000 abandoned vehicle fires, and 35,000 refuse-related fires. An estimated 4000 fires occur in underground facilities.

While these statistics are somewhat awesome, they are not atypical of other urban centers. Actually, New York City compares extremely favorably with other large urban communities in the country in terms of number of fires per capita, number of fires per building protected, and number of deaths and injuries to civilians.

INFRASTRUCTURE-FIRE RELATIONSHIPS

Streets and Roads

The significance of accelerated wear on fire apparatus (as well as on other emergency and nonemergency service vehicles) due to neglect of street maintenance can easily be appreciated if we note that many cities consider replacement of fire apparatus after 25,000 runs or approximately 10,000 hours which (in New York City) amounts to from 9 to 14 years of service. If we consider single unit costs of $250,000 for ladders (overhaul cost of $65,000), $95,000 for pumpers, and $70,000 for a medium rescue truck, and allow that a street system in disrepair can halve the time for replacement or major overhaul, the additional cost to operate a fleet of 350 pieces of major apparatus becomes obvious and merits inclusion in the evaluation of benefit-to-cost aspects of street surface renewal.

When considering the condition of the street system and the effects of its state of disrepair on the delivery of fire protection services, it is of interest to note that in addition to fire calls, there are over 8 million responses to non-fire incidents each year in the United States. In New York City, the fire department responds to over 60,000 nonfire incidents annually. Relevant to the subject at hand, 7400 of these calls involve leaks of flammable liquids, 2900 relate to power hazards or failures, 78 to ships and vessels, and 19 to tunnels and bridges.

What about response time? This is extremely critical to both the "saves" that can be made at a fire and the property loss that will be sustained. For example, in examining the feasibility and benefit-to-cost aspects of McDonald Douglas' SMS (Suspended Maneuvering System or "Flying Fire Engine"),[9] approximately 50 high-rise fires were studied for which both dollar property loss figures and the times for fire fighters to control the fire were available. We found that for each minute of the fire (assuming an extremely conservative, straight-line relationship between time to control and damage suffered), losses grew at the rate of $27,000/minute. Allowing for inflation, this figure is estimated to be at least twice this amount in 1983. Decreasing the time to reach a fire by way of the street infrastructure can be extremely important.

In a number of full-scale fire tests conducted in a high-risk neighborhood in New York City,[4,7] we found (somewhat unexpectedly) that fires in two- and three-family row-frame buildings reach "flashover" in from 4 to 4½ minutes after ignition. If total response time of the fire department averages 5–6 minutes, we can see why they often arrive too late—with such a dangerous coincidence between flashover (in the occupancy type, which results in the greatest number of fire deaths and injuries) and response time, it becomes obvious that a minute or two of time lost en route, as a result of streets in disrepair, detours, or failure to clear snow, can be critical. Needless to say, dispatching fire units from more distant locations, which is the result of reduction in the number of fire stations, also results in greater response time with the same end result.

Further evidence of the criticality of rapid fire service response and the extreme hazard of street conditions that reduce fire apparatus travel speed can be found in the results of studies that examined the relationship between size of fire on arrival and time to control.[17] Findings indicate that while 94% of fires whose size on arrival was less than 100 square feet were controlled in less than 10 minutes, only 70% of those with areas between 250 and 1000 square feet on arrival were controlled in the same period.

Water Supply

When fire units do arrive on the scene, their principal weapon to bring the fire under control is water. Therefore, if they arrive and find the operating nut of the nearest hydrant sawed off, or the valve stem damaged, or all sorts of debris in the hydrant barrel, the consequences can be serious. Further, if they require four hose streams to make headway against a fire and the water supply available is inadequate in either quantity or pressure, they may be unable to halt extension, or even protect the egress routes for occupants and fire fighters. Based upon energy release expected, the water necessary to keep up with a fire involving 4000–5000 square feet in a typical high-rise office building (where a single floor may have an area of 15,000 to 50,000 square feet) would require on the order of four standard hose streams (250 gallons per minute each). Full-scale fire tests in this type of building, with typical fuel loading (6.5 pounds per square foot), also demonstrated the rapidity with which flashover and maximum temperatures and pressures may be reached (four minutes).[1] Needless to say, fires do not always occur in areas where the water distribution system is in the best condition, and supply problems are sometimes further worsened by illegal use of street hydrants in the summer months (in the most vulnerable neighborhoods). Aerial photographs taken during summer months indicate that when fire hydrants are opened for recreational purposes, they are often opened simultaneously on both grid elements of serving streets.[8]

High-Rise Buildings

In fire safety studies concerning high-rise commercial buildings in New York City, it was found that some structures still in use were constructed almost 100 years ago or, more significantly, over five building codes ago.[1-3] It should come as no surprise that older buildings are more susceptible to collapse under fire stress than those that are newer; and while high quality of construction is often associated with some of our older buildings, brick and mortar eventually succumb to the ravages of time. Perhaps more significantly, older converted or rehabilitated buildings frequently are called upon to withstand large changes in structural loading, in the number of occupants, and in the number of different simultaneous activities served.

Subway Systems

In a study conducted several years ago, it was estimated that the New York City subway system suffered over 4000 fires each year — most of these were considered "trivial" and were quickly controlled, but if we examine the locations of these fires on system maps, many can be considered as "near misses." That is, some of the fires that produced large quantities of smoke and toxic gasses could just as well have occurred in sections of the underground system more remote from exits and under specific aerodynamic conditions that could greatly reduce opportunities for escape of passengers while at the same time making it more difficult for fire fighters to access and control the fire and smoke.

It should be noted that repairing and renewing infrastructure systems to enhance their principal intended use does not necessarily bring commensurate improvements in life safety attributes. Faster speeds and enhancement of subway ventilation and air conditioning, unless developed with regard for related smoke control issues such as piston effect in tunnels and horizontal and vertical exiting, may in fact create greater risks to life during fire emergencies.

Waterfront Infrastructure

The protection of waterfront property is made particularly difficult by constraints on access of fire apparatus to piers and wharves and, in many instances and paradoxically, limited availability of water supply for firefighting purposes. If we further consider that most piers and wharves are constructed almost entirely of combustible materials (wood pile foundations, wood substructure and deck, and often, combustible superstructure), the vulnerability of this element of urban infrastructure becomes apparent.

In the case of New York City, approximately one-half of all piers are greater than 400 feet long and less than 10% are less than 200 feet in length. Add to this the fact that the largest single use (approximately 1/3) of piers and wharves is for the storage and handling of various types of fuels, and the need for special consideration of fire protection of waterfront infrastructure becomes obvious.

In a preliminary examination of piers and wharves in New York City, it was found that almost 50% have buildings or major enclosures on them. With regard to combustibility, 14% have foundations, substructures, decks, and superstructures that are combustible; 12% have combustible foundations and substructures; 51% have combustible foundations (pilings, wood cribs); and only 23% have all elements (foundations, substructures, decks, and superstructures) constructed of noncombustible materials.

Current trends in waterfront property development[10] indicate the probability of increasing use of floating structures as music barges, restaurants, and cultural and recreational activity centers such as museums and historic ships. These constructions, as in the case of piers and wharves, pose special problems for safe exiting of large numbers of people and for adequate access by fire fighters. They also represent significant changes in the way waterfront property is used.

CONCLUDING REMARKS: STATE-OF-ART FIRE FIGHTING

The Center for Fire Research of the Polytechnic Institute is housed in what was once the Brooklyn headquarters of the New York City Fire Department. On moving into the landmark building, we discovered an archived "day book" for Engine 207. One of the entries recorded a fire call made in 1909. In those days, with horse-drawn equipment, it took the company approximately four minutes to reach a residential building in the area under its protection. On arrival fire fighters, using a steel bar, forced entry into the building and fought the blaze with a 2½-inch hose line, which supplied water at the rate of approximately 250 gallons per minute. Now, in 1983, it still takes this engine company about four or five minutes to reach a building in the same neighborhood. Fire fighters carry a steel bar called a "halligan" for entering, and use a 2½-inch hose line, which supplies approximately 250 gallons of water per minute to cool the fire. Not much change in seven decades.

Despite a few noble attempts to advance the fire-fighting craft, there have, in fact, not been advances in fire protection and fire fighting commensurate with general gains in technology. It is true that computers and new communications systems have improved the process of dispatching units to the fire scene, and horses have been replaced by internal combustion engines, but these advances have had little effect on time in transit of responding fire forces or in what fire fighters do on arrival.

Essentially the fire fighter is still the key element in the municipal fire protection system. Rescues are made the way they always were—the fire fighter must enter the fire building, locate, and carry or drag the victim through heat, smoke, and toxic gasses, sometimes with the help of a self-contained breathing apparatus—often without. Fires are brought under control by application of water with approximately 1 gallon per minute needed for each 1000 BTU/minute of energy released (a single pound of cellulosic fuel will release from 6000 to 10,000 BTU). It is true that we know a little more about what levels of carboxy-hemoglobin in the blood will render the fire fighter ineffective or prove lethal, and we can attempt to estimate the time it will take for the fire environment to reach levels of carbon monoxide that will bring CO-Hb levels to the 30–40% of concentration considered dangerous, but we are still given only two choices from furniture manufacturers; a slow-burning, dirty fire or a fast-burning, clean fire.

We are still without noncombustible materials that people are willing to use to furnish and decorate the places where they live and work. We are still using flesh and blood men and women and not robots to break down doors and carry the first hose lines into fires (stress causes 41% of career fire fighter deaths), and we are still without early warning devices to alert fire fighters of impending structural collapse of walls, floors, and roofs, which accounts for approximately 25% of fire fighter deaths.

REFERENCES

1. DeCicco, P. R. 1973. Report on Fire Tests at Hudson Terminal Building, New York City. American Society of Heating, Refrigerating and Air Conditioning Engineers. Louisville, Ky.
2. DeCicco, P. R. 1973. Study of Fire Safety Aspects of Proposed Atrium Hotel for New York City. Report for Norman Portman Associates. Atlanta, Ga.
3. DeCicco, P. R. & C. Schaffner. 1975. Development of a comprehensive fire safety law for New York City. In International Symposium on the Control of Smoke Movement in Building Fires. Fire Research Station of the Building Research Establishment. Garston, United Kingdom.

4. DeCicco, P. R. 1976. What to do with existing row-frame residential buildings. Fire J. **70**(6): 23–29, 69. (Boston, Mass.)
5. DeCicco, P. R. 1977. Fire in the city—search for technological solutions. Lecture presented at the Brooklyn Engineers' Club, Brooklyn, N.Y.
6. DeCicco, P. R. 1978. Trends in fire protection. National Real Estate Investor (December): 30–32. (Communication Travels Inc.)
7. DeCicco, P. R. 1980. Fire hardening of old residential buildings in high-risk urban communities. Presented at the annual meeting, Society of Fire Protection Engineers, Boston, Mass.
8. DeCicco, P. R. 1980. Aerial photography in fire risk evaluation. Presented at the American Society of Civil Engineers Specialty Conference on Remote Sensing, Madison, Wis.
9. DeCicco, P. R. 1977–78. Suspended Maneuvering System Rescue Vehicle. Report for McDonnell Douglas Aerospace Corp.
10. DeCicco, P. R. 1981. Study for New York Waterfront Construction Code. New York Department of Ports and Terminals. New York, N.Y.
11. Banks, J. 1983. On fire services in the world. *In* Fire Technology. National Fire Protection Association. Boston, Mass.
12. 1984. The Fire Almanac. National Fire Protection Association. Boston, Mass.
13. Lauriente, M. & J. H. Wiggins. 1976. A national program for fire safety in transportation. Presented at the Fourth Intersociety Conference on Transportation, Los Angeles, Calif.
14. 1978. Highlights of Fire in the United States. U.S. Department of Commerce. National Fire Prevention and Control Administration. Washington, D.C.
15. 1978. General Statistics, 1977–1978. New York City Fire Department. New York, N.Y.
16. 1983. Fire Journal (November). National Fire Protection Association. Boston, Mass.
17. Schaenman, W., *et al.* 1974. Procedures for Improving the Measurement of Local Fire Protection Effectiveness. The Urban Institute. Washington, D.C.

DISCUSSION OF THE PAPER

B. N. Igwebuike (*Polytechnic Institute of New York, Brooklyn, N.Y.*): From your paper I'm able to gather (and of course all of us know) that most fires and disasters occur in buildings, both residential and commercial. Fire alarms are intended to protect lives, property, and the structure itself. But I have observed that most of these fire alarms are often misused. At times when there is no fire, you go on hearing fire alarms. In fact, I am staying at a dormitory in Brooklyn and very often I hear these fire alarms, but after all there'll be no fire. So I am of the opinion that misuse of these fire alarms does more harm than good. I would like to know if there is any law against the misuse of fire alarms.

P. R. DeCicco: There are definitely laws and penalties against false alarms. The answer is yes. New York City, up until a year ago or so, was having something like 420,000 fire calls of which 212,000, as I remember, were false alarms. And the problem that's posed here is a very, very significant one. Most certainly there are laws and regulations. In fact in New York City they experimented with, and we now have in the streets, alarm boxes such that when you call in the alarm you are expected to stay there and speak and give directions through two-way communication, in which case the dispatcher will ask you where you are and so forth. There have been times when if you didn't speak back to the dispatcher they would regard the call as a false alarm, even in that potentially serious situation.

In the United States, there are people who have suggested that we have lockable booths, so that when you go into the booth to call in an alarm, the booth locks behind you. There have also been suggestions regarding the use of handcuff devices so that you will have to wait there until somebody comes. We don't have a real good solution, but we're trying.

Rebuilding Bridges

A Different Engineering Problem

HERBERT ROTHMAN

Weidlinger Associates
333 Seventh Avenue
New York, New York 10001

Essential to any bridge rehabilitation project are its provisions to maintain traffic and community functions during the repair period. Traffic diverted from the span must be accounted for elsewhere in the corridor. A concept that does not allow for both peak and off-peak traffic flow, unimpeded ambulance, police, and fire fighter passage, access to homes and businesses, and the need for residents to sleep at night is not suitable. As a result a structural solution that is completely inappropriate when applied to new construction may be the best or perhaps the only one possible for rehabilitation. The relation between traffic flow, construction staging, and repair methods is so basic and so well established that further elaboration is unnecessary. Four other issues will, therefore, be discussed in this paper, not necessarily in order of their importance. The four are:

1. The remaining useful life of old material.
2. Realistic measures of safety.
3. Esthetic restraints.
4. Opportunities unique to rehabilitation.

The first three are intended to stimulate discussion leading to eventual resolution of questions that are still unanswered. The fourth issue is merely a reminder that traditional approaches are not the only ones available for rehabilitation. The few unique opportunities described are a small fraction of the total.

THE REMAINING LIFE OF OLD MATERIAL

Even after all visible damage is repaired, the remaining life of the old, presumed sound material may not be sufficient to justify its retention. We have little experience with the behavior of materials during their second 50 years of service, and considerable research-based information is needed. FIGURE 1 illustrates much of the problem. The fractured lower lateral bracing member can be easily repaired with a splice plate, but before designing the repair the following points should be considered.

FIGURE 1

- The crack demonstrates that the lateral has operated in a high-fatigue environment. Has fatigue weakened the material adjacent to the crack so that the old material will fail soon after the splice remobilizes it?

    The question could be made moot by replacing the entire member, but such a solution may be economically unjustifiable in a bridge with hundreds of such members. A more suitable decision can be reached if available tools are applied to estimate the accumulated damage and remaining life of the material. However, better research-based information and design techniques are needed for this to be effective. Especially needed is a field test that will determine accumulated field damage where no visible cracks are present.

- Will pitting, visible in the photograph, cause accelerated corrosion?

    Both the difficulty of maintaining a paint film over the rough surface and the existence of corrosion cells at each pit can make maintenance very difficult. Most engineers have some experience with paint performance on corroded metal and will make decisions based upon their experience and intuition. However, because these personal data bases are small, means for combining them so that less subjective judgments can be made should be developed.

- How good is the bolted splice if either the splice plate or the bolt proper must bear against a rough, corroded surface?

    Intimate contact is impossible; corrosion of faying surfaces and of the bolt surface within the faying surfaces must be prevented by paint and/or caulking. Moreover, the thinnest material may bend so greatly that the bolt will not develop its clamping force. Investigations presently under way may show whether these effects degrade joint strength or durability. Meanwhile, most engineers design such joints using procedures developed for new, undamaged material. In this interim period, when there is any doubt, tests made on material removed from the bridge should be used, or the pitted material should be removed.

• Can the 70-year-old steel in the photograph be asked to perform for at least 50 more years?

We know little about material nearly 100 years old, and there is no certainty that some latent second-order effect will not become first order at this advanced age. It is conceivable that with age, local metallurgical differences will develop that will result in corrosion cells and rapid deterioration. Perhaps there is a synergistic relationship between fatigue and age similar to the relationship between fatigue and corrosion. Present practice assumes that old material will continue to obey the same rules as new material.

These illustrations all dwelled upon a single steel fracture. Similar questions could be asked for other details and for concrete structures. What is the prognosis for a reinforced concrete pier that has spent 40 years in seawater? Will the properties of prestressing steel and highly compressed concrete change when the structure becomes 40 to 100 years old? In every case, present design procedure assumes that except where specific damage is observed, steel and concrete are immutable. Most engineers believe the errors due to these procedures are small. Nothing has yet surfaced to show otherwise, but confirmation would make us all feel more secure.

REALISTIC MEASURES OF SAFETY

When a bridge element is judged to be unsafe beyond any argument, it will be repaired. Often, however, the danger is marginal and a difficult decision must be made. In a new structure, marginally safe is nearly always made unquestionably safe by adding a small quantity of material at little additional cost. The cost for adding a small quantity of additional material to an existing bridge, on the other hand, could be considerable; and since the available resources are finite, we must make socially responsible decisions. The following three illustrations are not intended to show solutions, but rather to indicate the complexity of the question, "Is it safe?"

High Stresses, Low Risk

FIGURE 2 is a section through the suspended span of the Manhattan Bridge. Because of fabrication and erection methods used in 1909, the inner cables carry more load than the outer cables and they hang slightly lower. Therefore, the lower roadway floor beams are bowed downward and have a locked-in stress; a condition that could easily have been eliminated during construction by cambering.

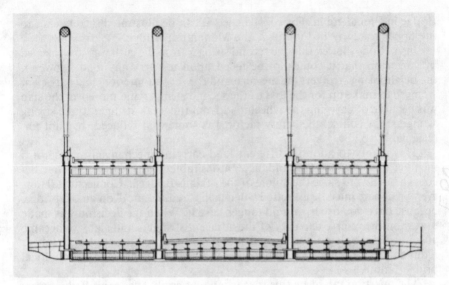

FIGURE 2

The locked-in stress, which was not considered in the design, produces an "apparent" overstress. It is apparent because it can be demonstrated that the overstress has no effect on the strength or serviceability of the bridge. Money spent on removing the overstress could better be spent on paint, or on repairing another structure.

The reason for the lack of significance is that the locked-in stresses are self-limiting. If the sum of locked-in stress plus live load is below the yield point, nothing happens. If the sum reaches the yield point, the temporary yield is followed by a rebound to a lower locked-in stress level. Temporary yield does not produce a hinge and is no different from the behavior of any structure assembled with components that are not perfectly accurate. Such readjustment has been tacitly (and often patently) accepted by engineers for nearly a century—since the mathematical techniques needed to analyze structures were developed. For the centuries before it was understood, readjustment was accepted unknowingly but no less successfully.

Within a few years after the bridge was opened, a few such redistribution cycles reduced the residual floor-beam stresses to safe, code-satisfying values. Ironically, the few heavy trucks that produce the "unsafe" total stress have not harmed the bridge, while the lighter, "safe" trucks are exacting a huge fatigue toll. Although residual stresses should properly be prevented in a new structure, it is not proper to eliminate them in this existing bridge. Society expects us to eliminate unsafe conditions, not high numbers.

Redundancy and Reliability

Another, less clear safety-related question arose on the Benjamin Franklin

Bridge in Philadelphia. For convenience, it can be illustrated by reference to the upper roadway in FIGURE 2, the Manhattan Bridge.

Inspections showed that the second stringer from the curb was so weakened by corrosion that it could not be relied upon to carry any load. However, the neighboring stringers (at the curb and the second interior) had sufficient strength to make up for the loss of the second stringer and moreover the slab was capable of carrying the wheel load from the weak stringer to the strong stringers. Of course, the safety factor was somewhat reduced, but not unreasonably so.

This ability to adopt a different load-carrying mechanism in case of a member loss is called "redundancy," a desirable characteristic that has become a buzz word since the failure of the Mianus Bridge in Connecticut. However, great care must be exercised when using "redundancy" on an old bridge, because once you use it, you no longer have it. When the decision was made to rely on the reserve capacity of the adjacent stringers and slab, we became absolutely dependent upon each of them. The modified structure is no longer redundant, and a failure of any of the three components will cause a local bridge failure.

The question raised by this scenario is not easily answered. Redundancy is basically a reserve for future deterioration. Are the years after 1984 the future for a bridge that was opened in 1924? Should a portion of the available resources be spent today to restore "redundancy"? No categorical answer exists, each bridge is different. When a nonredundant solution is adopted, we are completely dependent upon inspection to permit remedial steps to be taken before a member fails. Once a redundant member fails, the bridge becomes nonredundant and again dependent upon inspection. The decision therefore must include an evaluation of the owner's inspection capability.

This issue is closely related to the previous question of locked-in stresses. Locked-in stresses can only exist in redundant structures. If it is acceptable to consider a redundant bridge's ability to redistribute loads after fracture, we should also consider it under the more benign yield conditions.

Code Changes

What should be done when a sound, functioning structure that satisfied applicable codes when it was built no longer meets a revised code? The most startling example is the Severn Bridge in the United Kingdom. This 3240-foot-long span was recently declared to be in danger of collapse. This risk was considered so serious that two lanes were permanently closed and the government is considering a second crossing. The bridge has had problems with suspender wear and in some of its details, but these are repairable. The bridge has been declared unsafe essentially because the United Kingdom's wind and live load codes have become more stringent since the bridge was built. Interestingly, if the United Kingdom code were adopted in the United States many of our long-span bridges would become unsafe by the same token.

There is little risk that an abitrary or irrational decision will be made in connection with a major structure such as the Severn Bridge; the cost is simply too great. However, many lesser bridges facing similar problems will not have the benefit of evaluation by committees of distinguished engineers and public representatives. Worse, in many cases the responsible engineer may be forced to make his decision based upon what his insurance company and lawyers tell him his risks are. The failure to follow a code, even for the right reasons, assures a loss in any litigation.

There are two possible solutions to these three and similar safety-related questions. In the more desirable one, the engineer functions as a professional who interprets physical laws, the intent of the code, and the intent of society. He cannot be locked to the code as it is presently written. An eminently satisfying procedure would be to subject his conclusions to a peer review. Alternatively, the code can be rewritten to cover rehabilitation. It is possible to institutionalize nearly all of the rational procedures that should be used, although peer reviews of the more complicated cases will still be necessary. Such code changes will take years to bring about, but they will focus research on the most urgent problems.

While on the subject of lawsuits, it would be well to point out that rehabilitation offers exceptional opportunities for legal predation against engineers and bridge owners since construction is done under traffic, retention of substandard conditions such as narrow roadway lanes is often necessary and proper, and risks are inherently greater when reusing aging materials. Rehabilitation funds will go much further if engineers and owners responsible for making these judgments are protected from unreasonable and unfair lawsuits.

ESTHETIC RESTRAINTS

FIGURE 3 shows the Brooklyn Bridge. The inclined stays are in such poor condition that one fell from the tower and killed a pedestrian on the bridge. However, it is inconceivable that the stays will be removed to eliminate the problem. The stays are important to the appearance of the bridge, and the bridge is an important part of New York City, and indeed of the country. The stays must be repaired (and will be repaired) so that the bridge appearance is preserved.

There is however another side to this coin illustrated by FIGURE 4, the Bronx Whitestone Bridge. When built, it was considered to be one of the handsomest in New York City. The few inclined stays on this bridge and the truss on top of the plate girders were not part of the original design. They were added to stabilize the bridge when it exhibited excessive wind-induced motion. The changes were generally considered detrimental to the bridge appearance, but they were made anyway. When the engineer in effect said, "if you do not allow these changes, the bridge will be unsafe," there was no choice, and the change was made. Should the same condition arise today, the same conclusion would be reached, even if it were the Brooklyn Bridge.

FIGURE 3

The Brooklyn and Whitestone bridges, of course, represent two extremes where the solutions are obvious. Disagreements occur, and the difficult decisions must be made for intermediate cases where trade-offs are possible; where the engineer says, "I can save money if you allow me to change the appearance" and the preservationist says, "you can't change the appearance." Generally, when this happens both sides take extreme positions and meaningful give and take ceases. Although the problem has generally been well managed in New York, a procedure is needed that forces the opposite sides to communicate effectively and promote compromise. The solution will clearly be applicable to the rehabilitation of more than just bridges.

OPPORTUNITIES UNIQUE TO REHABILITATION

Rehabilitation introduces many new problems, but it also introduces opportunities. Community acceptability is already known; environmental effects both good and bad occurred long ago and the structure is now the environment. Solutions can be tried out, speeded up, checked, and compared before a commitment to an expensive construction program is made. Moreover changes to optimize operation, structure, and maintenance can be deduced from the structure's history; and equally important, changes that are *not* needed can be deduced.

Structural solutions can be simplified because there is an existing structure available for study. For example, calculated stress levels in critical parts of a bridge can never be better than the mathematical model of the bridge

FIGURE 4

they are based upon. But why use a mathematical model when the real bridge
exists? A few strain gages on the critical parts will show stresses sooner, at
less cost, and with greater accuracy than a computer analysis.

Comparison between analytic results and direct measurements often shows
substantial differences. This usually indicates that the engineer's understanding
of the bridge's properties, which he built into the mathematical model, did
not duplicate those that exist in the bridge. The necessary rethinking will then
produce a different and presumably more effective solution. In a striking example, analysis of the differences showed that contrary to the assumptions
used for the mathematical model, the sliding bearings on a bridge were not
sliding. Secondary stresses that damaged all parts of the deck were thereby
increased up to fourfold. The most effective part of the repair was the replacement of the bearings.

In another case, measurement showed that the roadway stringer details
did not fully isolate the deck from the trusses. As a result the deck, considered by the original model to be independent of the rest of the bridge, participated in the live load resistance, causing the stringers to fail in fatigue. This
behavior was demonstrated when it was observed that the time for the stress
to rise, peak, and fall was equal to the time for one truck to cross the bridge.
The instrumentation was not installed to demonstrate this but rather to confirm a completely different (and as the strain gages showed, less important)
mechanism that was assumed to be the cause of cracking. In both examples
the causes of damage were found quickly by field measurement. They might
never have been found without it.

Characterization of Traffic

Strain gages can also be used to characterize bridge traffic, by recording long segments of stress variation under actual traffic. These samples are then processed to produce a histogram. The histogram, which defines the fatigue environment for the specific detail on which the gage is mounted, can be expanded to show the fatigue environment for the specific bridge that contains the detail. Criteria based on such measurement are narrowly focused, and eliminate overly conservative factors introduced into design codes to make them universally applicable. It is, however, necessary to allow for future changes in traffic patterns.

Test Installations

By constructing a small portion of one or several possible solutions on the bridge, all of the following can be accomplished at a relatively small cost, before a commitment to the full solution is made:

- Unanticipated construction problems, frequently due to incorrect or unavailable drawings of the existing bridge, can be eliminated. More reliable schedules and estimates become possible.
- The performance of various solutions can be compared by observing their behavior for several months before final contract documents are completed. Possible candidates for competitive evaluation are pavements, overlays, curbs, barricades, joints, bearings, and drainage details.
- The proposed solution can be studied with strain gages, accelerometers, and vibration-measuring devices to confirm analytic procedures.
- Detailed records of construction can be kept for subsequent presentations to bidders. This should reduce the bidders' uncertainty and result in lower prices.

CONCLUSIONS

Bridge rehabilitation is not a variation of new bridge construction. New technologies are needed to describe the behavior of aging and damaged material; better definitions of the risks society is tacitly willing to assume must be derived; new professional practices are necessary to allow the engineer to make judgments on matters that are not codified; and present technologies should be applied in different ways so as to recognize the difference between a standing structure and a design still on paper.

DISCUSSION OF THE PAPER

P. C. WANG (*Polytechnic Institute of New York, Brooklyn, N.Y.*): I know you have been doing bridge design for a long time and now you are doing infrastructure work. Certainly you are very qualified for this kind of work. What I want to ask you is a question related to the academic field. I'm teaching now although I worked with you at one time 30 years ago. The question is, How can this infrastructure endeavor promote cooperation between the practicing engineer and the academician? For example, I understand that for bridge design, the impact factor on a structure is based on the design code. However, the impact factors on infrastructures are much more complicated: one simple fact is that many roadway bumps after a severe winter will change the impact effect on a bridge.

My feeling is that there is a need for more academic research to see how to account for these effects. I wonder whether you have thought about this.

H. ROTHMAN: I certainly agree with you, P.C., and perhaps I can discuss a relevant example. An evaluation of the Jamaica elevated rapid transit line in Queens depended heavily upon knowledge of impact forces. The history of the Transit Authority's impact formula was unknown, and it was feared that it understated the impact due to an offset or irregular rail joint.

As a test, we purposely built a rather large offset into one of the rails — I believe on the order of one-half inch — and made strain gage measurements of stresses in the stringers, floor beams, and columns. For that example at least, we found that the Transit Authority design formula was about correct for a single train, but it understated the effect (or probability) of loads on multiple tracks. It also showed that traction and braking requirements of the code were overly conservative.

However, that's one test on one span of a specialized structure. More work is clearly needed.

It might prove useful to study the possibly beneficial effect of high strain rate in partially offsetting the higher stresses caused by impact. I would also like to see a study of the effect of the vibrations set up by impact on the fatigue capacity of the structure. If vibration is significant, the impact factor should be a function of bridge damping.

Intuitively, it seems that the portions of the bridge most sensitive to impact are the deck and stringer, which feel the wheels most directly. A dynamic analysis will show that by the time impact reaches the major load-carrying components of a long-span bridge, it is greatly attenuated. This is, of course, considered at least partially in the AASHTO code, which reduces impact as the member span increases. However, were a long-span floor beam to frame into a short-span girder, the code would require greater impact on the girder than on the floor beam. You can see that the code is not completely rational.

One last piece of evidence implicating impact is, I believe, the deterioration of bridge decks. It is properly ascribed, in the snow belt states, to salt penetration, possibly abetted by acid rain. It does seem to me, however, that invariably the outer truck lanes are the first parts of the deck to break up. There may well be a synergistic relationship between moisture penetration, salt attack, and vehicle impact.

I agree, P. C., more work on impact is needed.

E. J. FASULLO (*Port Authority of New York and New Jersey, New York,*

N.Y.): I would like to just pick up on one of Mr. Rothman's points and that is the esthetic implication of this infrastructure issue. I think that's particularly obvious in relation to buildings. Public Law No. 5 requires owners to inspect their facades on a cyclical basis and make necessary repairs, and yet there've been all sorts of cases of people being injured by falling debris. The law is very fine and the goals are certainly things that we all agree to. However, the results have been that many fine architectural facades have been completely defaced by the owner in the process of repair because of the repair method. Of course if you want to restore these types of ornate decor, it is very expensive. I think we all have to be very, very sensitive to the social obligation of maintaining the visual aspect, whether it be bridges or buildings, in the retrofitting process. You go through New York and you'll see wire mesh attached to the face of a very beautiful building because of the issue of its facade. I don't think we can arbitrarily deface our structures. I do think posterity has a certain right to expect us to be very responsible.

I. VAMOS (*New York State Office of Parks, Recreation and Historic Preservation, Albany, N.Y.*): We sometimes have the difficult job of reviewing issues such as you describe. It's very often possible to replace certain surface features with different materials that are cast in the same style. Let's say using modern materials, a developer can leave the face of buildings or structures looking the same but composed of much lighter plastic or other materials. A responsible review agency should be able to help you put together a good-looking solution without the same load factors that were needed 70 or 80 years ago.

E. J. FASULLO: Again I do think it is extremely important. It's very easy for engineers to take the approach of solving the technical problems while not being sensitive to the impact on the social issue.

Pavement Rehabilitation

Evaluating, Recycling, and Extending Useful Life

ALFRED F. GRIMALDI

The Port Authority of New York and New Jersey
Design Division—72S
Engineering Department
1 World Trade Center
New York, New York 10048

INTRODUCTION

Comfort and safety are generally the two most important criteria that the traveling public will use when judging how bad a pavement is when driving over it. A lot of people also think that once a roadway is built it will last forever, or at least as long as some of the famous Roman roads that were built more than 2000 years ago, and in some cases still exist today. It is more realistic to accept the fact that roads and streets will wear out as they become older and are subject to more traffic, changes in the weather, and other environmental conditions. The rate of deterioration of the roadway is also dependent upon the level of maintenance that has been performed over its lifetime, and gradually it can lose its high level of serviceability. When this occurs, a decision must be made to determine whether the pavement can be saved before total replacement is required. How we evaluate the pavement system — and some of the methods used for rehabilitation — is the subject of this talk.

The two roadway pavement categories of major concern are flexible pavements and rigid pavements (FIGURE 1). Flexible pavements generally consist of a relatively thin asphalt concrete wearing surface, placed over a base course on a stone subbase course which rests on a compacted subgrade. Rigid pavements generally consist of a portland concrete surface course placed over an unbound aggregate base course, resting on a compacted subgrade.

Bridge decks represent a third category of pavement and will also be covered in this paper.

Highway pavements (on grade) will be discussed first.

PAVEMENT EVALUATION

A pavement evaluation can be as simple as driving over the roadway to make a visual inspection of the surface, or as sophisticated as employing testing devices to evaluate the structural properties of the pavement section. In ei-

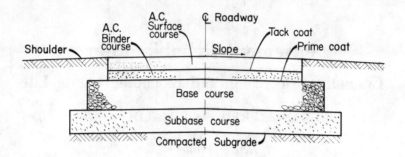

Flexible Pavement

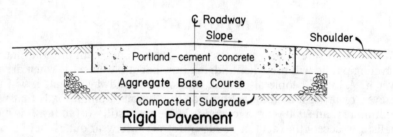

Rigid Pavement

FIGURE 1. Two main roadway pavement categories.

ther situation, an understanding of the types of pavement failure and why they occur will be helpful to the evaluator.[1]

The visual condition of the pavement surface will generally be a good indication of when a pavement is undergoing some type of distress.

Flexible Pavements

One of the first signs of pavement distress is the occurrence of alligator cracks. This condition is indicative of excessive movement of one or more of the underlying layers of the pavement structure, or it may be due to fatigue of the surface course. If not properly maintained, water will penetrate the foundation of the pavement and eventually cause potholes to occur.

Rutting, or surface distortion, can result from consolidation of one or more of the paving layers. This also can occur when axle loads exceed the allowable loading.

Longitudinal and transverse cracks are caused by shrinking of the bituminous concrete surface due to changes in atmospheric temperatures. Longitudinal cracks (or "cold joints") can be caused by poorly constructed paving joints that eventually open up.

Reflection cracking will occur in asphalt overlays of jointed portland cement pavements and generally reflect underlying joints or cracks in the concrete pavement.

Raveling of the pavement surface is caused by dislodging of aggregate particles and loss of asphalt binder.

Corrugation of the surface of asphalt pavements generally will occur in a transverse (right angles to traffic) direction. This type of distress is sometimes called "washboarding" and results from a lack of stability in the asphalt mix. As the surface is subjected to repeated wheel loads, the situation worsens as vehicle wheels bounce up and down on the pavement.

Frost heaving of the pavement will generally occur when a lower course or the subgrade freezes in winter, causing a volumetric expansion. In the springtime (as temperatures rise) the heave will thaw and result in a support weakness and pavement breakup.

These are but a few of the types of problems that can occur in asphalt pavements. If left unchecked, water will penetrate the pavement section and eventually result in a complete failure of the pavement.

Rigid Pavements

Distress in rigid concrete pavements can be brought about as a result of changes in temperature, inadequate or insufficient pavement joints, or warping of the slabs.

Corner cracking (or a corner break) is a crack that goes through the full depth of the slab, is triangular in shape, and generally extends from a longitudinal joint (or edge) to a transverse joint. Corner cracks are caused as heavy traffic loads pass over the pavement corners that have poor support. A lack of proper support may be created by curling or warping in the slab, or by a soft saturated base or subgrade. Frequently, the action of free water under the slab, when subjected to traffic loads, has removed a portion of the supporting material below the cracked corner.

Spalling of concrete generally occurs along joints or cracks and is characterized by cracking, breaking, or chipping of the pavement along the joint. The main cause of spalling results from excessive stress concentrations at the joint or crack. Stones or dirt may clog the joint opening and restrict the free movement of the joint.

Cracks in themselves do not necessarily constitute a failure; however, if not properly maintained they can cause breakup and necessitate a complete replacement of the slab.

Condition Surveys

Thus far, we have presented some of the more common problems one is apt to encounter on city streets and highway pavements. The list is by no means complete, as each geographic area has its own unique set of problems which can cause many other types of pavement failure.

Once the evaluator achieves a basic understanding of what to look for

ROUTE _____ LANE _____ LIMITS OF SECTION _____

TO _____ LENGTH _____

AGE OF PAVEMENT _____ COUNTY _____

DATE INSPECTED _____ DATE LAST RESURFACED _____

TYPE OF TRAFFIC _____

VOLUME OF TRAFFIC _____ MAINT. COST/MILE/YEAR _____

PAST PERFORMANCE ☐ GOOD ☐ FAIR ☐ POOR   PATCHING ☐ MINOR ☐ MODERATE ☐ EXTENSIVE

VISUAL RATING BY _____ NUMERICAL RATING BY _____

| 0 | 1 | 2 | 3 | 4 | 5 | 6 | 7 | 8 | 9 | 10 |
| VERY POOR | POOR | | FAIR | | FAIRLY GOOD | | GOOD | | VERY GOOD | EXCELLENT |

	TYPE OF FAILURE	YES	NO	REMARKS	NUM. VALUE
CRACKING	SLIPPAGE			_____	
	SHRINKAGE			_____	
	ALLIGATOR			_____	
	TRANSVERSE			_____	
	LONGITUDINAL			_____	
DISTORTION	RUTTING			_____	
	WAVES, SAGS & HUMPS			_____	
	PUSHING OR SHOVING			_____	
	CORRUGATIONS			_____	
	"CHUCK OR POT HOLES"			_____	
	RAVELING			_____	
SKID HAZARD	POLISHED AGGREGATE			_____	
	EXCESS ASPHALT			_____	

FIGURE 2. Pavement condition survey.

when inspecting the pavement structure, the next step is to put these findings in some logical recording system.

An example of one form used to gather the necessary information is shown in FIGURE 2. Basic information, such as road location, some history of the pavement, and a numerical evaluation of the pavement condition, is entered on the form. The visual survey can be supplemented with field testing depending on the depth of investigation to be conducted, time available, and the available funds.

ROADWAY REPAIR

After the pavement system has been evaluated, a plan of action is established for correcting the pavement problems. If the evaluation of the pavement has concluded that the section is structurally adequate and only isolated areas of distress are present, then these areas may be corrected by patching, seal coating, or cracked sealing.[2]

When the pavement cracking condition indicates that the problem is related to excessive repeated loading and deflection, then an overlay may be the only answer. There are many methods for determining the thickness of the overlay; however, the Asphalt Institute is probably the best guide.[3] If the problem is one of poor subsurface drainage resulting in frost heaves, it will be necessary to improve the drainage condition by installing underdrains or other drainage devices.

Maintenance problems associated with concrete pavements generally are concerned with the pavement joints or the texture of the pavement. Joints should be continually maintained by periodically cleaning them out and resealing with proper joint materials. If the joints have seized and no longer are working, it may be necessary to cut the joint out and rebuild it.

If the surface condition of the concrete pavement is rough but structurally sound, the pavement can be overlayed with asphalt concrete to restore the original ride characteristics.

When the texture of the surface has become polished and slippery in wet weather, it can either be overlayed or textured with a pavement profiling machine to restore its friction characteristics.

"PAVER" – PAVEMENT MANAGEMENT

The United States Army Construction Engineering Research Laboratory (CERL) has developed a pavement management system (PMS)[4] that has been adapted for city and country use by the American Public Works Association. The system is called PAVER and has a tested computer software package available; however, it can also be used manually.

This system can assist in arriving at the most cost-effective maintenance conclusions and greatly assist in assigning maintenance needs on a priority system.

BRIDGE DECK EVALUATION

Bridge decks generally consist of reinforced concrete slabs supported by the structural framework of the bridge.

Concrete bridge decks can deteriorate when subjected to deicing salts and high-density traffic. The salt penetrates the concrete and initiates corrosion of the steel reinforcement. This in turn causes cracking and rupturing of the concrete and spalling of the concrete surface.

The bridge deck evaluation should start with an investigation of the original construction of the deck and its performance to date. A field investigation of the deck can be similar to the procedures previously outlined for pavements-on-grade along with some additional field tests.

By tapping the concrete deck surface with a hammer, areas of delamination can be located. An instrument known as the "delamtec" can be used to speed up the process and record the variability in soundness on a tape. If the concrete deck has a waterproof membrane system on it, the permeability of this system can be evaluated by testing the resistivity of the system. This can be supplemented by other nondestructive testing devices to determine if there is corrosion activity in the reinforcement steel.

Other tests can be performed by obtaining samples of the concrete by coring in order to determine the salt content and compressive strength of the concrete deck.

The cores are also used to verify the nondestructive testing and provide a visual inspection of the deck section.

In summary, the steps included in a bridge deck condition survey are as follows:

1. Record of past history.
2. Visual inspection.
3. Sounding or delamination detection.
4. Compressive strength of concrete.
5. Chloride analysis.
6. Corrosion tests.
7. Resistivity test.

When these results are used collectively, an estimate of the true condition of the bridge deck can be made. This will assist the evaluator in determining the correct course of action for rehabilitation or repair of the bridge deck.

Selection of the Repair Method

There are many concrete patching materials on the market that are available for repairing bridge decks. The decision about which is best to use will depend upon the climatic conditions to be expected when the repair is made, the time available to perform the work, the anticipated life of the repair, and the cost. A decision must also be made as to whether it is economical to continue repairing the deck, or rehabilitate it, or in extreme cases replace the complete deck. A combination of the alternatives may also suit the conditions; for example, limited patching of the concrete deck followed by a concrete overlay, or placing an asphalt overlay with a waterproof membrane. Some of these rehabilitation schemes will be discussed later in this paper.

RECYCLING

Great advances have been made in the areas of pavement rehabilitation and repair using innovative construction techniques and newly developed materials. These advances have, in many cases, stretched the paving dollar while helping to conserve our natural materials and energy resources.

The recycling process for paving materials falls under this category. Some 15 billion tons[5] of recycled pavement materials have already been placed nationwide. Using today's prices and the average value of 1 ton of asphalt being equal to 100 pounds of asphalt cement and 1900 pounds of aggregate, this represents a $50 billion investment in our future. As natural resources become scarcer and more costly to obtain, their recycling takes on even greater importance.

Improvements in pavement removal methods and equipment have made the recycling process more economic and feasible. The two most commonly used methods for the removal of asphalt concrete pavements are:

1. *Ripping*—where a tooth-edge dozer blade or backhoe bucket is used to remove the pavement, which is then transported to a crushing plant for size reduction.
2. *Milling*—using on-site milling equipment, which results in an acceptable graded material that can be used directly as produced.

The graded reclaimed material from either process can be used in either a conventional batch asphalt plant that has been modified to handle the recycled material or in a drum mixer plant that has been designed to handle the recycled material to produce a high-quality of hot mix asphalt concrete. Reclaimed materials in proportions of up to 70% have (recycled to virgin materials) been successfully recycled in both types of plants without violating environmental standards.

Conventional pavers and rollers are all that is necessary to spread and compact the mixes containing reclaimed asphalt pavement materials.

Our experience in the Port Authority shows that hot mix recycling can be successfully accomplished in either the modified batch-type plant or a drum dryer plant. Monitoring of these installations has indicated that it is difficult, if not impossible, to detect any visual difference between finished recycled asphalt pavement and finished conventional asphalt. Test data, to date, also indicate that both products are structurally equal.

RECYCLING PORTLAND CEMENT CONCRETE PAVEMENTS

In some areas of the country, rapid depletion of the supply of quality aggregates for use in highway construction is becoming a major concern.[6] This coupled with the fact that dump sites for concrete disposal are becoming scarcer makes recycling an interesting alternative.

Equipment has been developed to effectively crush old concrete, remove the reinforcement steel for salvage, and then recycle the material back as aggregate for new construction. The resultant material can be used as crushed stone foundation course for pavements, or an aggregate for new portland cement concrete.

Rehabilitation and maintenance of roadways are costly, time consuming, and material intensive. Recycling of existing pavement materials has emerged as a viable rehabilitation and maintenance alternative that has the potential of also reducing construction costs.

EXTENDING USEFUL LIFE

There are many other systems that can assist in extending the life of pavements. These include simple maintenance techniques to sophisticated rehabilitation systems. I plan to briefly cover some of the schemes that have worked for us and are listed below. These are by no means the only systems available, and reference should be made to the publications at the end of this paper for a more complete list of systems.

PAVEMENT REHABILITATION SYSTEMS

Sulfur-Extended-Asphalt (SEA) Pavements

In the search for alternative paving products, the Port Authority participated in a demonstration project in 1979 with the United States Department of Transportation[7] to construct a test installation of sulfur-extended asphalt at one of its facilities.

For this test, a 70 to 30 ratio (by weight) of petroleum asphalt cement to sulfur was used.

A two-inch overlay was constructed on top of an existing asphalt concrete pavement, which also included a control section of normal asphalt concrete adjacent to an SEA overlay.

Environmental testing was performed throughout the test and yielded satisfactory results. The finished pavement has been monitored since completion and has indicated that the SEA pavement has performed as well as the conventional asphalt control section constructed next to it.

Hot Mix Membrane Waterproof System

Most bridges in the metropolitan area cannot be shut down for a prolonged period of time when maintenance or repair is necessary. Materials and methods of construction must have the ability to be placed with little interference to the traveling public as well as perform well during its lifetime.

For the past few years, we have been using a paving system on our bridge decks that provides reasonable waterproofing for the deck as well as a tough-wearing surface that can withstand the heavy traffic using our facilities.

The bitumen blend by weight of the membrane is 60% A.C. 20 and 40% natural asphalt. The asphalt cement weight is approximately 11%.

This top course can be applied as thin as 3/4 inches thick and consists of fine and coarse aggregates, mineral filler, and asphalt cement blended with refined Trinidad Lake asphalt cement and a liquid rubber additive. The material handles the same as any standard asphalt paving mix. However, special consideration is required to insure a homogenous mixture of the asphalt blend, as higher mixing and placing temperatures must be maintained for proper laydown and compaction of the mix. The design criteria for the membrane mix and asphalt wearing course are shown in TABLE 1.

The job mix formula for the wearing course is based on the New Jersey Interagency Engineering Committee Standard Mixture Design Table (the New Jersey Interagency Engineering Committee is a joint engineering committee made up of the Port Authority of New York and New Jersey, the New Jersey Department of Transportation, and the New Jersey Turnpike Authority).

The Bitumen blend by weight for the top course is 70% A.C. 20, 20% Trinidad Lake asphalt, and 5% latex rubber. Bitumen content by weight is 5%.

The asphalt materials are first blended together and then mixed in a conventional asphalt plant. The materials are then delivered to the site and placed on the cleaned deck surface with conventional asphalt paving machines. The membrane is applied at a temperature of 325°F.

After compaction, the top course is placed and then compacted, resulting in a smooth asphalt paving system that will provide many years of protection to the structural deck while affording smooth and safe passage to commuters and other travelers using the facility.

Latex-Modified-Concrete Paving System

One method of providing a more durable wearing surface for concrete pavements is in the use of latex-modified concrete.[8] This system can be used for elevated structures such as bridge decks as well as on-grade roadway slabs.

Our experience has been primarily with bridge decks where we were looking to rehabilitate the concrete slab and provide for future protection of the deck against chloride damage. The paving system consists of milling off approximately ¼ inch of the existing concrete surface, making spot repairs of unsound concrete prior to placing the new concrete.

The material is mixed in a mobile concrete mixer where sand, water, aggregates, and the latex modifier are blended and then deposited on the deck at a thickness of 1¼ inches. Workers broom the fresh concrete on the substrate to provide a bond coat, and this is followed by the concrete finishing machine which consolidates and finishes the modified concrete. The surface is then troweled and textured.

After texturing, the concrete is covered with burlap and polyethylene

TABLE 1. Membrane and Wearing Course Design Criteria

	Marshall Stability (ASTM 1559)	Flow Value (0.01 Inch)	Percent Air Voids (ASTM D3203)
Membrane mix	1000 minimum	15 to 40	0.5 to 1.0
Wearing course	1800 minimum	8 to 16	2 to 6

sheeting for a 24-hour moisture cure. An additional 48-hour air cure is also required.

The finished product results in a smooth, tough, durable, and impervious pavement that has successfully rehabilitated the deck.

Repair of Concrete Roadway Slabs by Epoxy Injection

A new technique of repairing delaminated concrete slabs has shown some promising results.

The technique consists of injecting epoxy resin into the subsurface deteriorated hollow areas in order to rebond them back into one monolithic form with strength equal to or greater than the original deck.

The concrete slab has generally deteriorated as a result of corrosion of the reinforcing steel, and this can cause major problems if allowed to go unchecked. For this reason, there is a need for a suitable repair method capable of reconstructing the damaged area before it results in further delamination and spalling of the concrete. Epoxy injection is a repair method that has been developed for the purpose of repairing delaminated concrete before spalls occur.

The procedure consists of locating suspected delaminated areas by sounding or any other appropriate method. A grid pattern is then set up on the slab, and injection holes are drilled down to the depth of the delamination which is generally at the top steel.

The holes are fitted with injection ports and then filled with a quick-setting cement, which anchors the port into the drilled hole. The injection equipment consists of an air compressor with two separate holding tanks, one containing the resin and the other the hardener. The mixing of the epoxy is performed in a separate chamber at the injection probe. Epoxy is pumped into the ports at a pressure of 14 to 20 psi. During the injection process, the pavement is sounded to determine whether the delamination is being filled. The delamination's hollow sound will change as the epoxy fills the cavity.

Our test results have indicated that cores taken through the delaminated concrete have been rebonded wherever a delamination existed. Our limited experience with this procedure, together with reported successes by some highway departments,[9] indicates that this method of bridge deck repair can be effective in solving some of the infrastructure needs.

Fiber-Reinforced Concrete

Historically, fibers have been used to reinforce brittle materials since ancient times; straws were used to reinforce sun-baked bricks, and horsehair was used to reinforce plaster.

The concept of incorporating discrete metallic wire segments into concrete is not new, and in fact many patents have been issued for various methods of doing so.

Modern research on the use of random steel fibers in concrete began in the late 1950s and was directed primarily toward overcoming the low tensile strength and brittle character of conventional concrete. Since that time, a great deal of work has been done in the United States as well as in other countries.

These results have shown that the addition of steel fibers to concrete results in a convenient and practical means of achieving improvements to many of the engineering properties of concrete, such as high flexural strength, increased toughness and energy adsorption, the ability to minimize cracking, added resistance to abrasion and spalling, and improved durability. These advantages, along with the ability to reduce pavement section thicknesses, can be very attractive for solving many pavement rehabilitation problems.

From 1974 to 1982, the Port Authority has placed over 7000 cubic yards of fibrous concrete at the three major airports in the New York metropolitan area.[10] These applications were primarily thin concrete overlays (5 to 9 inches) which were placed to correct asphalt shoving problems that occurred on specific areas of the airports.

Other maintenance and repair uses of fiber concrete have been tested and include the following:

1. Repairs to spalled concrete.
2. Bus stopping slabs.
3. Precast slab.
4. Steel fiber shotcrete.

After approximately 10 years of experience with the use of fiber-reinforced concrete, we had determined that it solved the maintenance problems previously experienced in the installations where it has been used by us.

CONCLUSIONS

An attempt has been made in this paper to cover some areas that are important for the pavement engineer to consider when faced with the challenge of rehabilitating the vast network of pavements included in the infrastructure.

New construction materials and improved methods of construction will help get the job done, when combined with the knowledge and experience of the many people involved in the paving industry. It is hoped that some of the ideas presented in this paper will stimulate others to further investigation, as well as provide input for the development of newer and even better materials and construction techniques.

REFERENCES

1. BARENBERG, E. J., C. L. BARTHOLOMEW & M. HERRIN. 1973. Pavement Distress Identification and Repair. Report No. AD-758447. Department of the Army. Construction Engineering Research Laboratory. Champaign, Ill. 61820. (Available through National Technical Information Services (NTIS), U.S. Department of Commerce, Springfield, Va. 22151.)
2. HARTVIGAS, L. 1979. Patching Flexible and Rigid Pavements. Report No.

FHWA/NY/RR-79/74. New York State Department of Transportation. Albany, N.Y. (Available through NTIS.)

3. 1981. Thickness Design, Asphalt Pavements for Highways and Streets. Manual Series No. 1 (MS-1). The Asphalt Institute. College Park, Md. 20740.

4. Corps of Engineers. 1981. Pavement Maintenance for Roads and Parking Lots. Report No. CERL-TR-M-294. American Public Works Association. Chicago, Ill. 60637. (Available through NTIS.)

5. 1980. Recycling Asphalt Pavements. Series No. 11. National Asphalt Pavement Association. Riverdale, Md. 20840.

6. Transportation Research Board. 1982. Pavement Recycling: Summary of Two Conferences. Report No. FHWA-TS-82-224. U.S. Department of Transportation. Washington, D.C. 20590. (Available through NTIS.)

7. GRIMALDI, A. F., L. G. MILLER & H. SCHMERL. 1981. Field Trial with Sulphur-Extended-Asphalt (SEA) Binders, Port Authority of New York and New Jersey. Report No. FHWA-TS-81-207. U.S. Department of Transportation. Washington, D.C. 20590. (Available through NTIS.)

8. KUHLMANN, L. A. 1980. A Performance History of Latex Modified Concrete Overlays. Dow Chemical Company. Midland, Mich.

9. STRATTON, F. W., R. ALEXANDER & W. NOLTING. 1978. Cracked Structural Concrete Repair through Epoxy Injection and Rebar Injection. Report No. FHWA-KS-RD-78-3. Kansas Department of Transportation. (Available through NTIS.)

10. GRIMALDI, A. F. 1983. Fibrous concrete used at Port Authority airports. In Proceedings of NJIT-ASCE-ACI Structural Concrete Design Conference: 31. Department of Civil and Environmental Engineering. New Jersey Institute of Technology. Newark, N.J.

DISCUSSION OF THE PAPER

P. C. WANG (*Polytechnic Institute of New York, Brooklyn, N.Y.*): One material I haven't heard mentioned in your discussion is polymer concrete. I understand that on several bridges, polymer concrete has been used to protect the surface. What is your comment on this matter?

A. F. GRIMALDI: We have experimented with the use of polymer concrete although I did not include it in the paper. The installations that we've put in have worked relatively well. One of the biggest problems that we seem to have is that equipment has not yet been developed to put the material down under mass production. It works very well in patching operations. A few years ago we put it on the Bayonne Bridge, on a 60-foot panel, and the difficulty they had—because the material does set up very quickly—is screeding it and finishing it in time. I think it's one of the materials that probably can be used very successfully in infrastructure repair. Actually latex modified concrete is also considered a polymer concrete.

P. C. WANG: I understand that the strength of the La Guardia Airport extension is under investigation. I also heard that the overhang slab is overstressed. It involves a relatively small area and I believe it can be polymerized without much problem.

A. F. GRIMALDI: I really can't offer any comments on the La Guardia extension since that really falls into the structural area. With regard to impregnation by polymer, we were going to do an experiment at one time with it. Quite frankly we got a little concerned when there was a similar job being done out on Long Island where I think they had an explosion. So the material is rather volatile.

That concept certainly is an interesting one, and I think more research should be done because if you can put a liquid material on a deck and just wait until it soaks into the deck and glues whatever delaminations you have in there, it's got to be a very cost-effective means of doing it.

E. J. FASULLO (*Port Authority of New York and New Jersey, New York, N.Y.*): I would mention that we have used polymer concrete in architectural panels. At the George Washington Bridge, you can see the new toll plaza building that was just constructed, with the panels on that particular facility being polymer concrete panels used for architectural purposes.

Changing Pavement Construction Techniques and Materials to Meet Changing Needs

JACK R. CROTEAU

Bureau of Transportation Structures Research
Department of Transportation
The State of New Jersey
1035 Parkway Avenue
Trenton, New Jersey 08625

Like most other transportation agencies, the work of the New Jersey Department of Transportation is increasingly directed toward preserving and maintaining the existing highway network, rather than making additions to the system. During the past year, for example, about 90% of the paving projects initiated by our Design Unit were concerned with resurfacing or reconstruction of existing pavements, and only about 10% involved new roadway construction.

This shift in focus of the department's work program from new construction to rehabilitation has resulted in parallel changes in our research efforts in the areas of materials technology and pavement construction techniques.

This paper outlines several of the major operational needs in these areas and briefly highlights selected department research studies undertaken to address those needs. The three issues discussed are the need for modified construction techniques on pavement rehabilitation projects, the need for a definitive solution to the reflection cracking problem, and the need for inexpensive and effective alternatives to resurfacing as a means of restoring pavement serviceability.

NEED·FOR MODIFIED CONSTRUCTION TECHNIQUES

Example 1: Longitudinal Construction Joints

The need for modified construction techniques on pavement rehabilitation projects encompasses two basic problems. The first of these is that certain techniques commonly used in new construction are inapplicable to the rehabilitation of pavements under traffic. As a consequence, alternative procedures must be used, some of which give rise to performance problems in the reconstructed pavement.

One specific example of this is the problem of providing distress-free longitudinal joints in the lane-at-a-time paving typically used in resurfacing work.

In placing a bituminous overlay on a heavily trafficked road, it is often impractical to pave the full width of the pavement in a single pass. The lon-

228

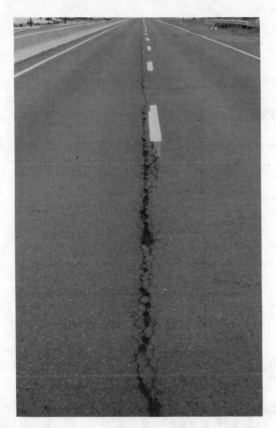

FIGURE 1. Typical distressed longitudinal joint.

gitudinal construction joints resulting from lane-at-a-time paving are often the weakest point in the finished surface. A poorly constructed joint inevitably leads to difficult to repair cracking and ravelling (FIGURE 1). This in turn permits water to infiltrate the pavement structure, thereby accelerating the deterioration of the pavement as a whole.

In the past, many methods of providing improved construction joints have been tried, often with little success.[1] In order to avoid a cold longitudinal joint and the associated subsequent cracking and separation, New Jersey's specifications limit the length of bituminous mat that may be placed before the paver must be brought back to the adjacent lane. On resurfacing projects, these drop-back provisions are generally not enforced due to difficulties in traffic control. The result is an almost vertical cold joint and a pavement drop-off condition which may exist for several days. This drop-off condition poses a possible hazard to drivers making lane changes in the construction zone.

In order to provide for better compaction of cold longitudinal joints and

ZONE OF INFRARED HEATING

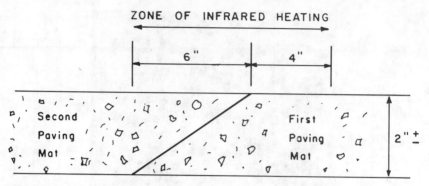

FIGURE 2. Wedge joint cross section.

to avoid the vertical drop-off problem, the department is experimenting with the use of a so-called bevel, or wedge, joint in combination with infrared heating. In this procedure, the unconfined edge of the first bituminous mat laid is formed into a triangular shape using a sloping metal plate attached to the inside edge of the paver screed. As shown in FIGURE 2, this inclined plane slopes from the usual 2-inch uncompacted mat thickness to 0 over a distance of 6 inches. When the adjoining mat is placed, an 8-foot-long infrared heater will be mounted on the side of the paver at a height of about 3 inches above the pavement. This heater is designed to preheat and soften

FIGURE 3. Wedge edge paving mat.

FIGURE 4. Cleaning and degreasing manhole frame.

FIGURE 5. Cleaning and degreasing extension ring.

FIGURE 6. Application of epoxy.

an approximately 10-inch-wide strip of the previously laid mat so as to increase the achievable density. While this infrared heating of itself may not yield a significant increase in joint density, we believe that the use of supplementary heat in combination with overlapping edges will indeed provide a monolithic joint of higher and more uniform density.

FIGURE 3 shows the appearance of the longitudinal wedge edge in some preliminary trials of the sloping plate device. This first work was undertaken to check the design of the metal plate and did not make use of infrared heating. The conventional vertical mat edge is shown in the far background, and the wedge edge is shown in the foreground. As shown in the photo, a neat, inclined edge was obtained in the initial mat. The second (overlapping) mat yielded a finished joint whose texture was indistinguishable from that of the surrounding pavement.

Example 2: Resetting Manholes and Inlets

A second aspect of the general need for modified construction techniques—and one that is certainly a paramount concern in a highly urbanized, heavily trafficked state such as New Jersey—is the need to develop techniques that will permit pavement rehabilitation operations to be accom-

FIGURE 7. Seating extension ring in manhole frame.

plished more quickly and efficiently so as to minimize interference with normal traffic flow.

As a result of a recently completed study,[2] the department has succeeded in shortening the required time of construction for one of the most common items of work on rehabilitation projects, namely, the raising of existing manholes and inlet frames to match the elevation of the overlaid pavement surface.

This seemingly simple operation is usually time-consuming, costly, and disruptive of traffic flow. In some of our urban areas, the number of manholes and inlets that must be raised prior to resurfacing can be as high as 120 units per mile. Depending on the number of units on a particular project, the contractor may elect to raise the manhole frames a month to six weeks before the paving operation, thereby creating a continuing obstruction in the traveled way. In the case of inlets, the resetting operation conventionally entails removing the concrete curbing on each side of the inlet, installing a new masonry course under the frame, installing a metal curb piece, and reconstructing the curb.

The improved practice developed in the research study involves the use of cast-iron extension frames. While the use of extension frames is not new, past experience with frames breaking loose and covers popping out caused the department to prohibit their use for any application other than raising inlets in shoulder areas.

FIGURE 8. Completed raised manhole.

The previous problems with extension frames were overcome by using an epoxy to securely seat and bond the extension element in the old frame. During the course of the research, the new procedure was successfully used to reset some 800 inlets and 200 manholes. Based on this experience, the department recently approved the use of the extension frame technique as an alternative to conventional resetting methods.

The procedure developed typically requires a three-man crew. As shown in FIGURE 4, the first step in the process is to clean the existing manhole or inlet frame with a wire brush (preferably power driven) and wipe it with a degreasing solution (e.g., trichloroethylene). The extension ring is then similarly brushed and degreased (FIGURE 5). A prepackaged, two-component epoxy (e.g., Sylvax 818) is applied to the old frame using a caulking gun (FIGURE 6). The extension ring is then seated on the epoxy bead (FIGURE 7), and the cover or grate is replaced (FIGURE 8). The entire operation takes as little as 15 minutes. A 1-hour set time is required prior to paving.

The new resetting procedure can save money as well as time. While the magnitude of savings will vary, depending on project conditions, the use of the extension frame technique to reset inlets can result in a construction cost savings of as much as $250 per unit. Although the new system does not result in substantial cost savings in resetting manholes, it permits them to be

FIGURE 9. Reflection cracking control section.

raised within a matter of hours before paving, thereby reducing the driver discomfort and possible traffic hazard associated with the conventional practice.

It is interesting to note that, out of concern for these potential driver discomfort and safety problems, our department is currently considering limiting the length of time manholes can remain raised prior to the completion of paving. If such a specification requirement were adopted, a significant increase in New Jersey's use of the extension ring technique could be expected.

NEED FOR A SOLUTION TO THE REFLECTION CRACKING PROBLEM

A second major need in pavement rehabilitation work is for a definitive solution to the problem of reflection cracking of bituminous overlays placed on portland cement concrete pavements. Reflection cracking occurs when the bituminous overlay material in the vicinity of the original pavement joints is overstressed due to the movement of the concrete slabs. This is, of course, a long-standing problem for which a variety of cures have been proposed.

FIGURE 10. Weakened-plane test section.

As early as the 1950s, for example, New Jersey experimented with the so-called cracking and seating technique (which involves breaking up the existing pavement prior to resurfacing) and the use of expanded metal mesh reinforcement between the bituminous layers as possible solutions. More recently, the department has experimented with the use of stress-relieving geotextile fabric underlays placed beneath the resurfacing. Each of these past efforts was unsuccessful. In one of the experimental installations of geotextile fabrics, for example, most of the transverse joints in the underlying pavement reflected through a 3½-inch overlay within three months after construction. After a year in service, all of the longitudinal and transverse joints had reflected through the overlay. Another geotextile trial installation delayed reflection cracking for less than a year.

One of the probable reasons for our lack of success in these past efforts is that New Jersey employs a unique concrete pavement joint design which poses a particularly acute problem with respect to reflection cracking. That is, the vast majority of our concrete pavements are of an expansion joint design with 3/4-inch-wide joints placed at approximately 78-foot intervals. As a consequence of this relatively long joint spacing, the temperature-induced joint movements that lead to reflection cracking are more pronounced than would be expected in a conventional contraction joint design.

While many of the department's past efforts to solve the reflection cracking problem have been unsuccessful, we now feel that we do have a workable solution, based on the performance of an experimental installation made some

FIGURE 11. Sawed and sealed longitudinal joint.

six years ago. This procedure—which was patterned after some early work performed by the state of Connecticut[3]—is referred to as the weakened-plane or saw-and-seal system. The procedure involves making a 3/8-inch-wide saw cut, 5/8-inch deep in the overlay over the prereferenced concrete joints, and sealing this joint with a rubberized sealing compound. The basic theory here is fairly simple: when the movement of the underlying concrete slabs induces cracking in the overlay, the weakened plane created by the saw cut will cause the cracks to occur in a straight line, beneath a joint that has already been sealed.

FIGURES 9 through 11 show the condition of the New Jersey test installation after six years service. FIGURE 9 shows the untreated control section, which has obviously developed the usual irregular, difficult to seal cracks in the vicinity of the longitudinal and transverse joints. FIGURE 10 is an overview of

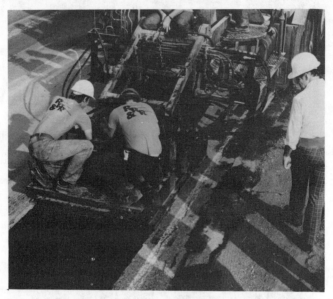

FIGURE 12. Placement of inlay to correct rutting.

the test section incorporating the weakened-plane system. This installation is about three-quarters of a mile long and has 116 saw-cut transverse joints. There are three longitudinal joints: one next to the barrier curb, one at the centerline of the roadway, and one adjacent to the shoulder. FIGURE 11 is a photo of the longitudinal sawed and sealed joint adjacent to the shoulder. As in FIGURE 10, the test pavement is seen to be free of any random cracks.

Based on the excellent performance of our test installation, as well as the favorable results reported by other states,[4] the sawing and sealing technique will be used next spring on a number of department resurfacing projects.

NEED FOR ALTERNATIVES TO RESURFACING

Another general problem area in pavement rehabilitation work is the need for effective, low-cost alternatives to resurfacing as a means of restoring pavement serviceability. The background underlying this problem is fairly obvious: since the infrastructure rehabilitation needs of highway agencies often far outstrip their resources, there is a need for the development of materials that can provide an effective "holding action" to arrest pavement deterioration until funds for complete restoration become available.

This is considered to be a particularly pressing need in New Jersey since certain of the treatments proposed as an interim solution to pavement distress problems are not suitable for our heavily trafficked roads. For example,

FIGURE 13. Finished wheel-path inlay.

it appears that at least on our higher volume roads, use of conventional slurry seals may generally be inappropriate due to potential skid-resistance problems.

As a consequence, the department recently initiated a study that involves an evaluation of materials that are basically an improved type of slurry seal. The study will examine both nonproprietary and proprietary products. An example of the latter is Ralumac,[5] which is a mixture of latex-modified emulsion, high-quality aggregate, portland cement, water, and an additive that triggers a chemical reaction. This material is applied with equipment similar to a conventional slurry seal machine and can generally be opened to traffic within an hour after placement.

Two basic applications are envisioned for these improved slurry seal materials. The first of these—the traditional sealing-type application—involves placing a thin (1/4- to 1/2-inch) overlay on a distressed pavement to prevent the entry of water and to restore skid resistance.

A second type of application—and the one that will be emphasized in the research study—is to use the slurry seal material as an inlay placed in the wheel paths of severely rutted pavements (see FIGURES 12 and 13). This inlay could be used either as a temporary solution to the rutting problem or as a preliminary to an immediate overlay. In the latter application, it would provide a low-cost alternative to the expensive process of milling and/or leveling course construction. These measures are normally required prior to resurfacing a severely rutted pavement so as to preclude differential compaction and the consequent early reemergence of rutting.

SUMMARY AND CONCLUSIONS

The task of restoring and maintaining the highway infrastructure with limited available funds requires the resolution of a number of long-standing problems in the areas of materials technology and pavement construction techniques. Procedures developed in two recently completely New Jersey Department of Transportation research studies—the weakened-plane system for controlling reflection cracking and the epoxy-bonded extension frame technique for resetting manholes and inlets—provide implementable, money-and/or time-saving solutions to certain of these problems. Two other department studies directed at developing improved pavement rehabilitation techniques and materials (i.e., the evaluations of the "bevel edge" paving technique for providing improved longitudinal joints and slurry seal inlays for remedying pavement rutting) are in the preliminary stage, and hence, no meaningful conclusions regarding their outcome can be drawn at this time.

ACKNOWLEDGMENT

Acknowledgment is made to Edgar J. Hellriegel, a colleague in the Bureau of Transportation Structures Research, for his assistance in preparing this paper.

REFERENCES

1. FOSTER, C. R., S. B. HUDSON & R. S. NELSON. 1964. Constructing longitudinal joints in hot-mix asphalt pavement. Highway Res. Board Rec. **51:** 124–136
2. Second Generation Pavement Overlays. Research Study No. 7778. New Jersey Department of Transportation. Trenton, N.J. (Final report pending.)
3. WILSON, J. O. 1962. Crack control joints in bituminous overlays on rigid pavements. Highway Res. Board Bull. **322:** 21–29.
4. NOONAN, J. E. & F. R. McCULLAGH. 1980. Reduction of Reflection Cracking in Bituminous Overlays on Rigid Pavements. Research Report No. 80. New York Department of Transportation. Albany, N.Y.
5. O'BRIEN, L. G. & W. BALLOU. 1982. Ralumac Latex Modified Emulsion Mix Overlay. SUR-TECH, Inc. Harrisburg, Pa.

Aging Water Supply Systems

Repair or Replace?

D. KELLY O'DAY

Peer Consultants, Inc.
1616 Walnut Street, Suite 2002
Philadelphia, Pennsylvania 19103

INTRODUCTION

There is a growing concern about the condition of our public infrastructure, including urban water supply systems. The Congressional Budget Office has estimated that for the 756 urban water supply systems in the United States, between $63 and $100 billion will be needed by the year 2000 to replace all water mains over 90 years of age and to replace other mains, as necessary. Extrapolations to all community water systems (adjusted for population variations) suggest that total replacement and rehabilitation needs for all communities could run as high as $160 billion by the year 2000.

How valid are these estimates? Are our public water supply distribution systems in a serious state of disrepair? How does a water utility evaluate the condition of its mains and make systematic decisions on maintenance and replacement?

DISTRIBUTION SYSTEM DETERIORATION PROBLEMS

Water distribution system deterioration problems (as opposed to growth-related problems) can be grouped into several general areas, namely:

- Water quality problems related to tuberculation and internal pipe corrosion.
- Low pressure and high head loss problems due to main tuberculation.
- Distribution system leakage due to joint leaks, main breaks, and service leaks.
- Main breaks due to main deterioration from internal and/or external corrosion.
- Valves and hydrants inoperable due to neglect and/or unavailable replacement parts.

Water main replacement is critical when mains deteriorate structurally to the point where they break frequently. The next section discusses the structural deterioration of mains and the relationship between deterioration and main breaks.

241

STRUCTURAL CAUSES OF WATER MAIN BREAKS

Water mains are structures that are stressed by both internal and external forces. As long as a main's strength exceeds the stresses caused by these forces, the main will give reliable, break-free service. When the stresses exceed the main's strength, the main will fail as a structure, which will result in a break. While this point may seem obvious, it is central to the required analysis and planning for water distribution system rehabilitation.

The strength of a main depends upon both the inherent properties of the pipe material used to manufacture the pipe and the thickness of the pipe wall. A main can be weakened by corrosion activity which reduces wall thickness, and if left unchecked this can lead to a main break.

The forces that act on a main include the following:

1. Internal pressure (both working and surge).
2. External loads from earth, truck superload, and frost in northern climates.
3. Beam loading if the main is not uniformly supported.
4. Thermal contraction if the main is restricted from expansion and contraction.

FIGURE 1 presents the set of factors that affect both the forces acting on the main and those affecting the loss of pipe wall from internal, external, and electrolytic corrosion.

Each factor indicated in FIGURE 1 can vary from main to main due to site-specific conditions such as soil characteristics, external loads, stray direct current electricity, temperature effects, soil moisture, pipe joint type, and pipe unit strength. The interplay of these factors in a given situation determines the structural condition of the main. Thus, a main of given unit strength and effective pipe wall thickness may break because the forces exceed its unit strength, while a weaker main at another location may function adequately because the forces on the main are less. It is necessary, therefore, to recognize the variety of conditions that exist across a water distribution system.

It is the combination of a main's environmental conditions, the time the main is exposed to those conditions, and the forces exerted on the main that determines its structural condition.

ROLE OF AGE IN WATER MAIN DETERIORATION

Age, or the year a water main was laid, represents several independent factors that should be considered, namely:

- Length of time the main has been in operation.
- Indication of design practice when built.
- Indication of construction practice when built.
- Indication of material strength and quality when built.
- Length of time the main is exposed to corrosion processes.

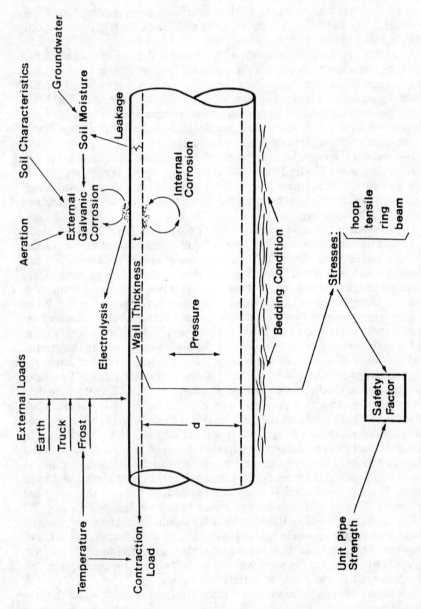

FIGURE 1. Conceptual model of water main structural condition.

A main does not deteriorate just because of age, it deteriorates due to corrosion and wear and tear. A main's age does not indicate the extent of damage caused by corrosion or wear and tear. One year of exposure in a corrosive clay soil may be worse than 30–40 years in a noncorrosive sandy soil. Therefore, soil conditions and the presence of stray dc current are more critical to a main's break rate than is its age.

As part of the Philadelphia Water Department Water Supply Infrastructure Study, the author has statistically evaluated the relationship between main age and main break rate, expressed as breaks per mile per year. The Philadelphia study included the development of a water main inventory and break history file, with complete information on main characteristics (age, diameter, etc.) and break history by water main segments. Segments constitute a stretch of pipe with uniform diameter, age, and material.

Two statistical models were prepared to relate main age to main break rate for six-inch mains. Model 1 related the main age to its break rate for 455 main segments, with segment lengths averaging 368 feet. Model 2 was an aggregated model based upon the mean break rate in five-year age groups related to the group's mean age.

The coefficient of determination is 0.0081 for Model 1 and 0.267 for Model 2, a 33-fold increase! How can the same set of data yield such different results?

There are both statistical and practical explanations for the differences in results. Correlation and regression analyses try to explain or account for the variation (sum of squares) between cases. When each main is the case, or unit of analysis, the model explains differences between each main. When the data were grouped into age categories and average values replaced individual main values, most of the variation was incorporated within groups and the regression model only explained the differences between the groups.

If the sums of squares of the two regression models are considered, the differences between these models become even more clear. TABLE 1 presents these data, which indicate that the total variation (SS) of the 455-case data set was 1079.79, of which only 8.75 or 0.81% of the variation is explained by Model 1. Model 2 reduces the total variation from 1079.79 to 2.01 because it only includes the 20 average values instead of the 455 data points. The amount of variation explained by Model 2 dropped from 8.75 in Model 1 to 0.54 in Model 2; however the portion of the Model 2 variation explained, or the coefficient of determination, increased to 0.267, 33 times the Model 1 value. There is less variation to explain in Model 2 because the variations from main to main of the same age group have been ignored.

This phenomenon of multiple correlation results from the same basic set of data is well known; many investigators refer to it as "ecological fallacy." Reviewers of correlation analysis must recognize that correlation coefficients only apply to the data at the particular unit of analysis. As data are aggregated, they often tend to yield higher correlation values.

The practical explanation is based upon the need to understand that the main segment level results are for individual mains, while the 5-year age group results are for a time period. Model 2 indicates that, on average, older mains have higher average break rates than do younger mains. The key word is

TABLE 1. Age vs. Break Rate Model Results

Model	Cases	Sum of Squares			Coefficient of Determination
		Residuals[a]	Regression[b]	Total[c]	
1	455	1071.05	8.75	1079.79	0.0081
2	20	1.47	0.54	2.01	0.267

[a] Variation not explained by the regressional model.
[b] Variation explained by the model.
[c] Total variation between individual main cases.

average. On average, 80-year-old mains have higher break rates than do 50-year-old mains; however, there are many 50-year-old mains with greater break rates than in 80-year-old mains. Age cannot be used to predict individual segment break rates, it can only be used to roughly indicate average break rates by age group.

The critical break rate determinants are the factors that control the internal and external corrosion process and the structural forces on the main. Time is only one of several factors that influence the corrosion process, it is not necessarily related to the structural forces acting on the main. This explains why different main segments, built at the same time, can have such different break rates. The next two sections examine the role of corrosion and leakage in main deterioration.

ROLE OF CORROSION IN MAIN DETERIORATION

The literature reflects a wide diversity of opinion on the relationship between corrosion and main breaks. Fitzgerald states:

> It has been recognized, however, by water utility personnel that the majority of breaks occur at locations where the pipe wall has been weakened. Such weakening is the result of graphitic corrosion of cast iron and, although the actual failure may be due to stress, corrosion can be shown to be the real cause[1]

Fitzgerald's statement can be contrasted to statements in the U.S. General Accounting Office's Report to Congress:

> External corrosion of cast iron mains does not appear to be a major problem. . . . According to the Cast Iron Pipe Research Association, most of the soil in the United States is not corrosive to cast iron pipe. A survey by this association in 1970 showed that only 5 percent of 121,500 miles of pipe in 229 cities in 48 states was affected by corrosion. Pipe age ranged from new to 149 years old. An earlier survey, in 1960, by the American Standards Association (now the USA Standards Institute) disclosed that of 83,000 miles of cast iron installed by 110 utilities, less than 2 percent was in areas where serious corrosion had been encountered.[2]

These statements reflect considerable differences of opinion. Which is correct? In order to reconcile them, it will be necessary to review the corrosion process to provide background information on corrosion, its rate of development, and measurement. The following paragraphs briefly describe water main corrosion.

Water Main Corrosion Process

Corrosion of cast-iron water mains is caused by an electrochemical reaction between the pipe metal and its environment, in which the pipe loses its ferritic constituent, leaving behind the graphite. The three sources of corrosion are galvanic reaction between the pipe and its surrounding soil, internal corrosion caused by tuberculation, and electrolytic corrosion in which a stray dc current migrates onto the pipe.

Each source of corrosion involves the flow of an electrical current along the pipe wall. In tuberculation and galvanic corrosion, the current is self-generated by the pipe and its surrounding soil, while electrolysis involves the impression of an external dc current onto the pipe which causes metal loss at the point where the current returns to its proper circuit.

The detrimental effects of tuberculation have been reasonably well handled by the water utility industry. Cement lining of water mains has been used commercially in the United States since the 1930s to eliminate tuberculation and the resulting internal corrosion of water mains. Generally cast-iron and ductile iron mains laid since the 1935–1950 period have been cement lined. Older unlined mains can be mechanically cleaned and cement lined, often at a fraction of the cost of installing a new main.

Electrolysis can be a serious problem where it occurs; however, sources of stray dc current tend to be restricted to specific locations and situations. The primary sources of concern in the water industry are from mass transit rail systems, cathodic protection systems, and some special situations such as radio transmission facilities.

Galvanic corrosion is more common; it occurs in all situations where a bare metallic pipe is buried in soil. The pipe and soil act to generate a low voltage battery or corrosion cell. A simple galvanic corrosion cell has an area serving as the anode (area losing iron) and the cathode (area protected). The pipe wall acts as the wire, in which current will travel from the cathode to the anode. The current leaves the pipe at the anode and travels through the soil, returning back to the pipe in the cathodic area. The pipe loses iron at the anode where the current leaves the pipe.

Iron loss is proportional to the current flow, with approximately 20 pounds of iron lost for each ampere-year of electrical current.

Corrosion Measurements

Galvanic corrosion follows the basic Ohm's law which is reproduced in Equation 1.

$$I = \frac{E}{R} \tag{1}$$

where I = current (amps): E = potential (volts); and R = resistance (ohms).

The units in galvanic corrosion are expressed in millivolts, milliamps, and ohm-centimeters because the absolute magnitudes are small, but significant. The actual resistance of a pipe/soil galvanic cell cannot be defined because of the multiple pathways the current can follow in the soil; thus the soil's electrical properties are expressed in ohm-centimeters, which indicates the soil resistivity in ohms per centimeter.

The metal loss from a galvanic pipe/soil corrosion cell can be estimated by Equation 2.

$$W = 0.02 \times \frac{E}{(r \times L)} \times T \tag{2}$$

where W = pipe metal loss (pounds); E = pipe to soil potential (millivolts); r = soil resistivity (ohm-cm); L = effective corrosion cell length (cm); and T = time (years).

Equation 2 shows that there are three variables that determine metal loss in galvanic corrosion, namely, (1) pipe to soil potential difference, (2) soil resistivity, and (3) time. The potential difference between pipe and soils varies over a relatively narrow range; the major source of variation in metal loss from galvanic corrosion is differences in soil resistivity and time. Soil resistivities vary from as low as 500–1000 ohm-cm for some corrosive clays to as high as 30,000 ohm-cm for some noncorrosive sands. Thus the loss of iron is highly influenced by the soil and length of time the pipe is exposed to that soil. Ten years exposure to a corrosive clay may be equivalent to 70–100 years exposure to a noncorrosive sand.

Corrosion Rates over Time

Studies by the National Bureau of Standards show that soils' corrosion rates differ over time. In one soil the corrosion rate may be constant or increasing over time, while in other soils it may decrease over time.

In general, the rate of corrosion in well-drained soils with high electrical resistivities is high initially, but becomes insignificant after a few years. Conversely, in poorly drained, low-resistivity soils, the rate of corrosion is nearly linear after 1–2 years. The actual corrosion rate for a main depends upon the soil environment around the main, and whether the corrosion products are removed from the anode and cathode or build up to inhibit the process.

To accurately define the corrosion pattern for mains it is necessary to conduct a sampling program to collect samples of mains of various ages and that are surrounded by various soils. While time is a factor in corrosion, the soil characteristics are more important. The soil moisture plays an important part in the soil resistivity. As water main leakage can increase soil moisture levels, its role and relationship to leakage control are discussed in the next section.

ROLE OF LEAKAGE IN MAIN DETERIORATION

Water distribution systems leak because of undetected breaks, joint leaks, and defective services that carry water from mains to individual properties. Control of leakage is important for water utilities because the costs involved in treating and pumping water are often greater than the costs of finding and correcting leaks. In the following discussion the relationship between leakage and main breaks is of special interest.

Distribution system leakage can affect water mains through (1) disruption of the main's bedding, and (2) increasing the soil moisture around a pipe. The first and second factors directly affect the structural loads the main must withstand. It is clear that undermining of mains does occur; the severity and prevalence depend upon many factors including soil type, drainage characteristics, and construction practices. Frost conditions result in greatly increased break rates in northern climates. Leakage may contribute to that increase by providing artificially high soil moisture which can freeze and exert substantial loads on the main.

The impact of soil moisture on soil resistivity warrants further discussion because it has not been widely considered. Equation 2 above shows that soil resistivity is a primary determinant in the pipe/soil corrosion cell. The soil resistivity variable, however, can be significantly affected by soil moisture. TABLE 2 relates soil resistivity for one clay to its soil moisture. As shown in TABLE 2, the change in soil resistivity with change in soil moisture is dramatic.

In the example of clay soil, an increase in soil moisture from 5% to 10% increased the corrosion rate by 16.6, while an increase in soil moisture by a factor of four increased the corrosion rate by a factor of 200. Obviously, the soil moisture has a major bearing on a given soil's resistivity, which in turn affects the overall corrosion rate.

Soil moisture varies with climatic and seasonal groundwater changes. In addition, it can be artificially increased by leakage from mains and services. Very little research has been directed toward the relationship between water distribution system leakage and its influence on soil moisture and corrosion. That is unfortunate. Leakage control could serve to both eliminate water waste and provide preventative maintenance for mains.

ANALYSIS OF WATER MAIN MAINTENANCE RECORDS

The previous discussion has focused on the causes of water main deterioration. It is now time to turn to a discussion of what a water utility can do to plan and manage its distribution system rehabilitation.

Most water utilities collect and store extensive data on main breaks, leaks,

TABLE 2. Relationship: Soil Moisture and Resistivity (One Clay Soil Sample)[a]

Soil Moisture (%)	Resistivity (ohm-cm)	Relative Corrosion Rate[b]
5	2,000,000	1.0
10	120,000	16.6
15	30,000	66.0
20	10,000	200.0
25	6,000	333.0

[a] Source: Melvin Romanoff, National Bureau of Standards.
[b] Ratio of corrosion rate at given moisture to that at 5% soil moisture.

and routine maintenance activities. These data can be very useful in (1) assessing the overall condition of the utility's water distribution system: (2) evaluating the condition of specific mains; and (3) developing a comprehensive rehabilitation program.

There are five levels of analysis that a water utility can employ to evaluate the condition of their water distribution system. These analyses are as follows:

- Analysis of break trends over time.
- Analysis of break patterns by main type.
- Analysis of break patterns by break type.
- Visual inspection of break samples.
- Microscopic inspection.

The methods and benefits of each analysis level are briefly described below.

Trend Analysis

Trend analysis can be used to determine whether water mains are deteriorating at an accelerating rate. This analysis can identify which areas within the distribution system are experiencing the greatest increase in breaks over time. The result of this analysis is a clear understanding of the trend in main deterioration and an indication of the likely future pattern. It is the first step that a utility should undertake in evaluating its water distribution system condition.

Analysis by Main Type

Analysis by main type is undertaken to determine which main types have the greatest incidence of breaks and/or leaks. Failure data are summarized by main diameter, age, material type, joint type, area of the system, and other combinations to define those main types that experience the greatest rate of failure. This is generally the second step a utility should undertake in assessing its rehabilitation needs.

Break Type Analysis

The type of main break varies with the structural cause of the failure. The principal break types and their causes are summarized in TABLE 3.

The break type should be recorded in the field at the time of the repair since it indicates the ultimate break cause. Analyses of break patterns by break type can indicate the extent of circumferential, longitudinal, blowout, and crack bell breaks that the utility experiences, by main diameter, age, material, and location.

Most utilities experience a majority of circular breaks on small-diameter mains (10-inch and less) and longitudinal breaks on larger-diameter mains. This pattern can be explained structurally because small mains will fail under beam loads while larger mains will fail from crushing loads. Variations from this pattern can indicate specific patterns that the utility should investigate.

Visual Inspection

The condition of the pipe wall can be determined by visual inspection of a polished section of the main. The inspection can determine the corrosion source (internal or external), degree, extent, and depth. This provides specific information on the source and extent of corrosion for the test sample. The inspection results can be used to assess the structural condition of this main.

Microscopic Examination

While visual inspection of a pipe wall can identify the source and extent of corrosion, microscopic examination can provide additional information through analysis of the microstructure of the metal. It can identify selective corrosion on specific metallurgically definable areas which may not be apparent from visual inspection. The microstructure of the pipe wall can be defined by examination of etched specimens under a microscope. This can reveal the thermal-mechanical history of the metal and possibly the underlying cause of the corrosion.

These five levels of analysis can yield detailed information on the condition of a utility's water distribution system. While utilities routinely record data on main breaks, many do not record the break type, few perform visual inspections of break specimens, and very few perform microscopic examina-

TABLE 3. Main Break Types and Structural Causes

Break Type	Structural Cause
Circumferential	Thermal contraction beam failure
Longitudinal	Excessive ring load
Hole	Internal pressure blowout
Bell crack	Thermal contraction joint material expansion

tions. The level of analysis a utility can perform is dependent upon the extent of the data that are collected at each main break. Without main break type analysis it is not possible to determine the structural cause of the break; without visual inspections it is impossible to determine the source and extent of corrosion; without microscopic examinations it is not possible to determine whether different groups of mains are more prone to internal or external corrosion because of microstructure differences.

DISTRIBUTION SYSTEM MAINTENANCE

There are many actions that are taken to maintain the water distribution system, including:

- Repair of main breaks.
- Leakage survey and repair.
- Cathodic protection facility maintenance.
- Stray current survey.
- Main cleaning and lining.
- Valve maintenance.
- Main relaying.
- Abandoned service removal.
- Service leak inspection.

These activities usually are funded through the operating budget with the exception of the main cleaning and lining and relay work, which often are funded through the capital budget. For many utilities the dual funding mechanisms complicate the process of defining the "best" maintenance program. While best can be defined in various ways, one reasonable definition is one where the total annual cost for both operating and capital expenses is minimized. Therefore, the objective of distribution maintenance should be to meet target performance levels at the least total annual cost including operating and capital debt service.

Funding levels for all maintenance activities should be based on their contribution to the performance of the system, rather than on their funding source. This requires an assessment of the impact of each maintenance activity on the system's overall performance, a difficult task which should be done to improve budget allocation and management of the distribution system.

To see the implications of this approach, consider the decision on the proper level of funding for leakage surveys. Under the present approach, no consideration is given to the impact of leakage control activities on future main break trends. The consolidated budgeting approach would determine the level of leakage control by recognizing the dual benefit of leakage control in reducing water loss and preventing the undermining of the main bedding and reducing the main's corrosion condition, both helping to reduce causes of main breaks. From a cost analysis standpoint, it is likely that a substantial leak control program could be very cost effective in limiting main breaks.

Similar situations occur for cathodic protection, stray current surveys, abandoned service removals, and service inspection programs as well as valve maintenance. The critical point to recognize is that each mile of main relay costs approximately $500,000. Each mile represents a small portion of the overall system. In many cases, the benefits of main relay may not be as significant as an investment in other maintenance actions that could provide dramatic improvements.

Distribution system maintenance planning does not adequately address the interplay of routine maintenance actions like leak control and the capital program items like replacement, primarily because of independent budget planning and because of limited information on the relationship between more aggressive field maintenance and reduced capital needs. For many utilities, the capital costs for widespread replacement may be too costly, and so improved maintenance to prolong main life and selective replacement in critical areas will prove a better course of action. As an example of the benefits of an accelerated maintenance program, it will be useful to review the economics of leak control and main replacement.

ECONOMICS OF LEAK CONTROL

In 1981 a major United States water utility undertook a comprehensive leak correction program for approximately 200 miles of its distribution system. The program resulted in the location and correction of 596 leaks and the elimination of 12.2 million gallons per day of leakage.

The leak detection costs for the utility staff, consultant fees, and equipment costs were approximately $204,000, equivalent to slightly more than $1000 per mile for the 200 miles in the survey area. The total costs for repair were $243,000, for a total detection and repair cost of $447,000.

The value of the future water losses saved by this leak control program is equivalent to the present value of future water and wastewater treatment and pumping costs. The net present worth for these savings is estimated to be nearly $6,600,000 over a 30-year period. That is, the $447,000 leak detection and repair program will save an estimated $6,000,000 in treatment and pumping costs over a 20-year period.

The economic benefits of this program are quite remarkable, indicating that the savings from the leak detection program are 14.42 times the costs, an incredible return on investment.

While there is no way to measure the actual impact of these benefits on future main breaks in the area, it is safe to say that they will have a positive benefit which will tend to reduce the number of breaks in the area. It is hard to imagine a more effective program for preserving the life of a main without completely replacing it. For a cost of $2000 per mile, significant water loss was eliminated, 60–200 future main breaks were corrected, the causes for potential future breaks were eliminated, and the value of the saved water in the first year paid for the entire survey. The $447,000 spent for the detection and repair work would provide slightly less than one mile of main relay, only 0.5% of the 200 miles of main in the survey area.

ECONOMICS OF MAIN BREAKS AND MAIN REPLACEMENT

There are several criteria that need to be considered when evaluating whether to replace a specific main. The following criteria, developed by Stacha,[3] represent the major items to be evaluated:

- Projected future costs of continued repair.
- Cost of main replacement.
- Public risk from future breaks.
- Frequency and severity of public inconvenience from future breaks.
- Hydraulic adequacy of main.
- Future plans for street and/or utility construction that could affect break patterns and alter costs through joint construction.
- Severity of disruption caused by main replacement construction activity.

In reviewing the costs, it is important to distinguish between the direct costs versus the indirect social costs involved in water main rehabilitation. The utility must pay the costs for continual main repairs, the costs for main relays, and damage claim costs from individuals, businesses, and residences that experience damage from main breaks. Damages can vary widely, from minor to very severe. Generally, breaks on larger mains (24-inch and over) cause more serious damage, while those on smaller mains cause service disruption and local inconvenience.

The social costs on many breaks can be much greater than the direct repair costs. Thus it is necessary to recognize both in addressing the economics of main break repair versus rehabilitation.

The economic trade-off of replacing a water main rather than continually repairing it must compare the initial cost of replacement with the projected annual cost of continued repair. If a particular pipe section has more than the break-even rate of breaks, it is economically advantageous to replace it. Conversely, segments with less than the break-even rate are not economical candidates for replacement.

ROLE OF RISK ANALYSIS IN REHABILITATION PLANNING

Utilities face two sets of risk, the probability that a given main will break in a specified time and the potential damage caused by a failure from that main. The damage will vary depending upon many local conditions such as type of development, time of day, season of year, time it takes to shut off the flow, drainage facilities, and other nonpredictable factors.

As an example, consider New York's water main break pattern. The city experiences approximately 600 breaks per year, actually less than that experienced by many considerably smaller water systems. Of the 600 breaks per year, only a relative few receive widespread notice — those generally on large-diameter mains that cause flooding of a subway station, disrupt traffic, or cause a fire. The break in the garment district of Manhattan in 1983 is a good example. That break caused a major fire, disrupted business for a week, and potentially caused businesses to lose millions in revenues.

In establishing maintenance and replacement priorities, utilities must recognize the risk of a main failing and the risk of damage from the failure. Not all breaks are equivalent. A break on a 48-inch main may cause more damage than 10–20 breaks on 6-inch mains. On the other hand, a break on a 6-inch main near a subway station may disrupt the commuter system, impacting thousands of riders.

Utilities should develop a maintenance and rehabilitation priority system that recognizes the different risks associated with different elements of the distribution system. Mains in high-risk areas and those with critical roles should receive higher rating than those in lower-risk areas. In this way, mains are evaluated for both their structural condition and the risk of major damage from a failure.

CONCLUSION

Conditions vary within a given water distribution system and from city to city. It is difficult, therefore, to generalize on water distribution system conditions either by state or across the United States. It is clear, however, that water utilities must improve their maintenance and rehabilitation planning to protect the major investment in water distribution networks.

This paper has presented techniques for analyzing the condition of the distribution system to define the situation. It is essential that utilities develop sound information on the condition of their systems, and routinely evaluate the information to ensure that they control the deterioration process.

Maintenance and replacement planning should be integrated to provide the best mix of preventative maintenance and long-term replacement. In this regard, utilities should reevaluate their approach to leakage control. They should assess whether they can use leakage control as a preventative maintenance technique in addition to its water loss saving benefits.

Replacement priorities should be established based upon a realistic assessment of the probability of main failure and an examination of the risk of damage from such a failure.

REFERENCES

1. FITZGERALD, J. H. 1968. Corrosion as a primary cause of cast iron main breaks. J. Am. Water Works Assoc. 68(8): 882.
2. U. S. General Accounting Office. 1980. Additional Federal Aid for Urban Water Distribution Systems Should Wait until Needs Are Clearly Established. Report to Congress, November 24.

3. STACHA, J. H. 1968. Criteria for pipeline replacement. J. Am. Water Works Assoc. (May).

DISCUSSION OF THE PAPER

M. KARAMOUZ (*Polytechnic Institute of New York, Brooklyn, N.Y.*): I was wondering how you monitor leakage. Is there any way the inspector can monitor leakage?

D. K. O'DAY: Yes that's an area that is quite well established, that's been going on for a long time. There are two components to this: one is the flow monitoring into an isolated area where you can actually measure the flow going into that area over the days and look at the nighttime flow to come up with an estimate for what you think the leakage may be.

The other method which goes hand in hand with that is sonic listening. Leaks on a water distribution system make a noise, a vibration actually. By going along listening with electronic listening devices, these noises can be picked up quite well. I might mention that New York is one of the cities using a new unit that's been out for a couple of years called the noise correlator. With this equipment you bracket the leak, and the noise correlator will give you a very precise location for that leak so that you can then excavate at that location. It's improved the pinpointing of leaks quite well.

Leakage detection technology is well practiced, it's well known, it's just not done nearly to the level I think it should be as a preventive maintenance technique in addition to its water saving value.

M. KARAMOUZ: Do you have any idea of the percent of water loss in Philadelphia each year?

D. K. O'DAY: That's a whole other ball game. Let me go to Boston, because I'm living in Philadelphia. You may have read in the press that Boston has 50% leakage in its pipes. That statistic, somewhat outdated, has been badly misinterpreted. It reflects the metered ratio, which is a number that you compute by figuring out how much you bill customers and how much you deliver to the system. That 50% includes losses due to meter problems; it includes the computer system, which may have all kinds of problems; it reflects whether the municipal buildings are metered; and so forth. The actual leakage itself is considerably less than the unaccounted for water, it probably is around 10 to 15%. It's not really 50% in Boston, or in the Philadelphia case 35%. The leakage is probably around 10%.

M. KARAMOUZ: How often do you calibrate those meters?

D. K. O'DAY: The master meters are calibrated routinely. It's the half a million residential meters that are neglected for a long time, and they tend to underregister and that's really the concern. That's one of the components of the unaccounted for water problem, and you've got to be careful of those statistics.

UNIDENTIFIED SPEAKER: You didn't mention anything about relining pipes as a method instead of just replacing. Do you have any comments on that?

D. K. O'DAY: There are a lot of issues that I didn't mention because of the time limit. Relining is a very useful technique. You saw the tuberculation problem — it's a very serious hydraulic problem, and of course, it contributes to the loss of metal for iron mains.

The caution I have on relining — and I must say that these are preliminary findings from a number of the samples in Philadelphia — is that metal loss from internal and external corrosion in some areas of the city proved to be very, very serious and in fact would mean that relining may not be a wise solution. In any kind of a relining program you've got to do a structural evaluation of the pipe wall thickness at several points along the pipeline to make a determination of whether or not you should in fact invest in the relining or if you need replacement. So I think relining is a tool, but it's not a wholesale tool unless you've really done a good level of analysis on what the structural condition of that pipe is. And the only way you can do that is by getting samples of it. One point here is that coupons should be used and analyzed. You've got to take the opportunity to get information on what the condition of the main is.

UNIDENTIFIED SPEAKER: You only touched on it very briefly, but these problems are much greater with heavy traffic. Have you reached any way of measuring this vibration, the effects of force, because it seems to me that's where the worst breaks come from — heavy trucks, buses, things of that kind.

D. K. O'DAY: Yes, obviously heavy truck traffic is in some situations a serious problem. From the design literature, the assumption is that much of the truck load will be dissipated if the main is three to four feet deep. There's very little research going on with older water mains and the conditions to which they are subjected. That's one of the areas that I would put on the research agenda.

I might add this. From the analysis we've done in Philadelphia by looking at the type of paving, we found that on the state highway network, which tends to be rigid pavement, the break rate is considerably lower even though it has higher truck traffic. We partially attribute that to the value of rigid pavement in protecting the main by isolating and reducing these loads.

P. L. RINALDI (*The Port Authority of New York and New Jersey, New York, N.Y.*): Carl Turkstra touched on this at a previous session and you mentioned it briefly at the end of your presentation, that is, the area of risk analysis. In the area of water mains as opposed to sewers and other utilities, the consequences of failure are rather explosive and they do interact with other facilities. We saw this with the Canal Street water main break, which shut down our transit system, and we saw this earlier, where a water main break flooded an electrical substation and put power out in the center of the city for about a week. It comes to the point of risk analysis. In all of these assessments we have tools to assess the conditions, look at the hydraulic quality of the pipe, and the water quality itself, but when it comes down to dealing with 3000 miles of piping in Philadelphia or 6000 miles of pipe in New York, you have to start using some rational process as to what mains you are going to repair first. Have you looked at a kind of risk analysis process that can also be implemented as a tool to take into account the consequences of the failure to a surrounding area?

D. K. O'DAY: The answer is yes. I believe I mentioned that a main on a major arterial or next to a subway station has a much higher risk of damage associated with it than does a main on a side street. There's also the concern that as the diameter of the main goes up, the flow that comes from a failure goes up by the square of the diameter. Obviously a 12-inch or a 24-inch failure causes greater damage than a 6-inch.

What we're doing in Philadelphia is developing an evaluation of the structural condition of the main. Then we're looking at the damage risk, and we will classify by block what the likely consequences of a failure would be and we're going to do this by category. Areas near a subway system, near a major arterial, underpasses, and places like that will get a very high damage risk assigned to them. We're not going to be able to say what exactly the dollar damage would be, but we recognize that any disruption of the transit system or the arterial system would be very serious, as would be failures in the commercial districts.

My suggestion is to make a structural evaluation of the mains and then make risk determinations of the consequences of failure and then in fact have a composite of those factors. In developing a rehabilitation plan, consider the number of active services involved, vacant and abanded housing, and the main condition. In many cases it may be wise to accelerate the leak detection component of maintenance. In those areas with high housing abandonment it may be more cost effective to survey for leaks routinely to both save water and reduce the role of deterioration. I recommend that cities dovetail their maintenance and replacement plans. Those areas with high probability of failure but low risk should increase leakage control. Accelerate the replacement of mains in the high-risk areas because of the main break damage potential.

There's a limit to the amount of money that's available from the capital side, so I'm trying to give you two answers at the same time. That yes, you've got to evaluate the risk of damage, you've got to look at the consequences of the failure, and I'm also saying that you've got to tie together the maintenance and replacement components into an integrated plan. In the past, cities that I've looked at tend to have a capital budgeting program and an independent maintenance budget and they are not tied together. The truth is, whether it comes out of capital or maintenance budgets, you really have to tie both together to have a consistent coherent approach.

That's what can be done using risk analysis as part of the decision process. This approach is in the process of being developed, and I must say there are some legal concerns that have to be considered. It's a process that needs to be done.

UNIDENTIFIED SPEAKER: What is the speed of closing down valves when you have a main break?

D. K. O'DAY: The trouble with the valve is that you never use it till the critical time and it may or may not work for you when you most need it.

Valve maintenance is absolutely essential, and I should also say that as part of leak detection, one benefit you also get is in exercising valves. Cities need programs to provide annual testing of valves. Properly done, valve inspection can help to build a good information base: Which way do the valves turn? How many turns? Is the valve open or closed? Basic information that's critical is actually missing for the field personnel. That's why as engineers we've got to get much, much more involved in the maintenance side and improve how we're operating and maintaining these facilities.

UNIDENTIFIED SPEAKER: When main replacement is done in Philadelphia, do they replace the water service lines at the same time? And if they do or don't, does the city own the water service line or does the private homeowner?

D. K. O'DAY: Philadelphia is similar to New York in that the city owns the water main and the ferral connection, that is, the connection from the main to the service. The property owner actually owns from the ferral into his property. As part of water main replacement work, Philadelphia is putting in a new service to the curb stop as part of the replacement. They do that actually as a way to help to protect the main. You don't want to put a new main in and have a plumber come in six months later to have to repair an old service connection.

UNIDENTIFIED SPEAKER: And is that paid for by the city as part of the water main?

D. K. O'DAY: Yes it is. Up to the curb stop is part of the construction of the replacement of the main to try to insure the integrity of the main.

Breathing New Life into Aging Transit Systems

ERLAND A. TILLMAN AND GIRARD L. SPENCER

Daniel, Mann, Johnson & Mendenhall
1200 Gramercy Park Building
257 Park Avenue South
New York, New York 10010

Last year the American Public Transit Association (APTA) celebrated its 100th anniversary. As an outgrowth of its predecessor, the American Street Railway Association formed in Boston in 1882, APTA membership now includes over 350 systems throughout North America. Of the systems incorporating rail, bus, or both that are currently in operation many have been in existence since the turn of the century. Those with the most extensive infrastructure are, of course, rail transit systems.

In this presentation, we discuss several systems that have operated for a number of decades. These older systems are experiencing similar problems and should be considered in any discussion of needed improvement of transit infrastructure. Thus, the scope of this paper has been confined to those older systems—the Port Authority Trans Hudson system (PATH), connecting New York and New Jersey, and those located in Boston, Chicago, and in particular Philadelphia and New York. Most started as horse-drawn rail streetcar service before giving way to cable cars and elevated lines in the 1860s and 70s, followed by parts of them at least being located underground near the turn of the century. The systems as we know them today started rail transit operations in the following years: Boston, 1897; Chicago, 1897; New York, 1904; Philadelphia, 1905; and PATH in 1908. While they have been expanded up to the current time, almost without exception, the major portion of their rail segments were completed 30 or more years ago.

As with all undertakings, the passage of time brings with it technological advances along with the normal wear and deterioration of component elements. For this reason, if for no other, there is the obvious need for repairing and upgrading the infrastructure belonging to these systems. Moreover, in the case of significant segments of older rail transit systems, the need for rehabilitation, improvement, and revitalization of their fixed facilities—their infrastructure—is particularly acute because of many years of neglect or deferred maintenance.

Although rail transit infrastructure has not received the attention given to other infrastructure elements such as roads, bridges, sewer systems, and water systems, for those cities largely dependent on transit systems, the viability and condition of this infrastructure is just as vital to their economic well-being.

To bring things into perspective, let us review how rail transit systems came to be in their current state of disrepair and try to obtain a sense of the magnitude of the problems. In the early years, rail transit systems were developed and run by private entrepreneurs. These operators varied the quality of service they provided to the riding public and the extent of maintenance of their facilities primarily as a function of economics. Some provided very little in the way of passenger amenities, as indicated by an operator in St. Louis who complained that if passengers were given heat during the winter, next they would want fans in the summer.[1]

But the problems only originated at this point. To a large degree public policies promulgated over the years compounded the financial difficulties facing transit operators which often had a direct impact on the severity of deteriorating conditions. Chief among these policies was the politically popular low fare, which affected and still affects the availability of funds for adequate maintenance. Low fares became far more important to political leaders than the slow and hidden deterioration of the system that would become the problem of future administrations. While it is true that the fare was what people cared about most, the public seems to be losing on both counts as recent decades have seen fares rise at accelerated rates while the quality of service has fallen off dramatically due to system deterioration and obsolescence.

Yet, while politicians may be largely to blame, they are not fully at fault. During the early 1900s transit operators leased facilities built and financed by cities. Typical of these agreements was New York's Dual Subway Contracts (dual because there existed at this time only two transit operators — IRT and BMT). The term of the lease between the city and the transit operators was for a period of 49 years and included the requirement that operators maintain a five-cent fare for the life of the contract. The operators agreed to these terms believing that innovations would lower operating costs and protect their profits. However, the operators did not anticipate the rapid rise in inflation after World War I which led to terrible financial pressures.[1] System maintenance was the first target for deferrals instituted during a financial shortfall.

As transit systems grew older more problems evolved. Because of the numerous transgressions against patrons brought about by the lack of sufficient revenue, there was a greater outcry for public control of mass transit systems. As a result, municipalities stepped in and bought out the bankrupt private operators. Now, however, the public operators find themselves in much the same situation as did the private owners, and are turning to the states and to the federal government to take up the slack.

While recent decades have seen sharp increases in fares, the fare box revenue has been insufficient to meet transit costs. The federal government initiated the operating assistance program in 1974 and, by 1980, provided 15% of transit's total operating revenues. Even though the older systems receive a percentage of their operating revenues from government sources, including state and local funds (currently, Boston receives only 33% from the fare box while New York receives 55%), the revenue and operational subsidies do not approach the amounts needed to refurbish, rehabilitate, and modernize systems suffering from almost a century of neglect.

So we get back to the reality that rail transit infrastructure has been allowed to deteriorate to an alarming extent. Fortunately, transit operators are recognizing the need to bring a halt to this deterioration and are making efforts to secure the funding to initiate massive rebuilding programs for inner city mass transit and commuter lines. The New York Metropolitain Transportation Authority has arranged for $8.5 billion for its current 5-year revitalization program, Boston has raised $1.4 billion, and other systems have received varying amounts (from a combination of local, state, and federal sources).

One of the initial problems for any system is to determine the extent and cost of work that is required and the manner in which the work must be accomplished to provide safe, attractive, and comfortable travel for the patrons of transit systems. This task is not an easy one. Identifying the work to be done and prioritizing it is a major effort, which includes separating certifiable needs of transit operators from "wish lists."

Fortunately, the identification problem has been recognized by the federal government. The 98th Congress has charged the Urban Mass Transit Administration (UMTA) with the task of performing a condition survey of all transit systems to obtain a better handle on the existing conditions and to prioritize the needs. This survey requires the establishment of minimum transit standards and an assessment methodology.

The study has begun and the challenge is to establish realistically what has to be done to provide essential rail transit service, what improvements in productivity can be achieved through a modernization program, and what the financing requirements will be to achieve the resulting benefits.

The study identifies three levels of improvements, defined as modernization, rehabilitation, and refurbishment. *Modernization* is upgrading, which will involve the use of materials, components, or subsystems to achieve higher standards of productivity than are possible with the original equipment or materials. This effort should meet changed requirements in a service area and result in meaningful improvements in system performance for a period ranging from 10 to 30 years. *Rehabilitation* involves the substitution of worn or weakened materials, subsystems, and components with replacement subsystems having basically the same fit and function as the original equipment and capable of achieving the original levels of service and reliability. Rehabilitation should result in an improvement in system performance for a range of 5 to 20 years. *Refurbishment* entails the restoration of equipment and facilities to adequate standards of performance to enable operations to continue without further degradation. The existing system performance should be sustained for at least 5 years. The levels of improvements and exactly how much money should be invested to obtain those improvements are determined by measures of effectiveness, that is, "how well" improvements to the system elements and subsystems meet the objectives or designated standards.[2]

Overall, the efforts to modernize, rehabilitate, or refurbish the various elements of mass transit systems are directed to produce increased system productivity, employee productivity, and maintenance productivity, resulting in better service. Obtaining the funds and determining the needs and priorities are only the first steps in the process.

As the work proceeds new problems evolve which require unique solutions. Anyone involved with the rehabilitation of a transit system knows that a major consideration is to accomplish the work while keeping the facility operating as efficiently as possible. Unlike constructing a new system, rehabilitating an existing system must be done while continuing to operate and to serve the patrons, insofar as possible without diminishing the quality of this service.

Each transit system is different and has its own problems. Let us look at specific elements of a couple of systems as examples of what is being done and the problems and difficulties inherent in rehabilitating the various system elements while maintaining adequate passenger service.

One of the more demanding efforts in this regard is the one that has been undertaken by the New York City Transit Authority (NYCTA) in their $472 million rehabilitation and modernization program for upgrading their car barns and shops. This is only one segment of the MTA's $8.5 billion current 5-year program. Utilizing the funding effectively required a comprehensive analysis of the needs and the development of an overall maintenance policy directed to the many diverse items of this program. Work involved research of records, site visits and physical surveys, interviews with management and maintenance personnel, study of consultant reports, observations of facility operating conditions and the elements needing improvement, inquiries into operations of other transit systems and visits to these systems for information gathering, and the development of the priorities for the program. Among the many aspects evaluated were:

- Upgrading the physical condition of the facilities, providing for a more suitable work environment.
- Investigating existing procedures and practices on inspections and repairs and the capability of a facility to carry out planned maintenance and repair functions.
- Identifying the more important improvements to existing maintenance and repair components; for example, blowout of cars, cleaning of air conditioning, exterior and interior cleaning, wheel trueing, truck overhaul.
- Evaluating existing work areas and storeroom space and determining additional areas and arrangements at each location.

In evaluating the facility improvements, a detailed study also was called for to assess the adequacy of track arrangements and pit configurations, lighting, heating, ventilation, plumbing, safety systems, and provisions for security. This had to be done for the 13 barns and 2 major repair shops to arrive at how best to devote the available funding to the improvement needs. In the case of the NYCTA barns and shops, it became evident that the preponderance of the spending had to be allocated to repairs and rehabilitation of the neglected facilities themselves, all to be accomplished while maintaining daily operations. In this regard, more than $360 million of the progam has been devoted to physical structure upgrading.

The areas of improvement include a new system of blowing out cars, chemical and water washing of trains, air-conditioning cleaning and maintenance, a new organization and refurbishment of the wheel-trueing facilities, a new 600 volt direct current stinger system in the barns, and renovation of electric power and distribution systems. One of the significant changes made to existing practices is a new concept developed for installing a utility track at each barn for use in making periodic inspections. The utility track, which houses an entire train, embodies posted rails (in lieu of pits) to make the undercar more accessible to the inspection staff. It is planned that the blowout area (the entire track) will be equipped with a powerful movable vacuum exhaust collection system to provide a cleaner atmosphere by collecting the dust and dirt during the blowout operations. Air-conditioning cleaning will also be done on the utility track. In addition, trains will be given a chemical cleaning each time they receive a B or C inspection using the car-wash installation at the end of each utility track. All of these new improvements must be installed in an operating facility with minimum effect on continuing operations.

When completed this new facility will allow maintenance forces to perform cleaning, inspection, and maintenance in a 24-hour cycle, without having to move the train during this period as previously was necessary. New chemical car-wash equipment will allow graffiti removal phased in with a water wash program. Additional water washers will be installed throughout the system so that cleaning of the train with a mild detergent can be done every 3 to 4 days. Heavy duty chemical wash cycles will be reduced to about every 10 weeks (coinciding with the inspection cycles). The separately enclosed chemical car washers will permit the cleaning of trains all year round and will be equipped with air blowers to strip the water from the cars as they leave the utility track.

Thus, not only will the physical plant be brought up to a state of good repair, but each of the 13 barns will be specifically designed to operate as inspection barns and equipped to accommodate a variety of maintenance and inspection operations so that maintenance and the appearance and cleanliness of cars will be greatly improved.

In another program, four existing wheel-trueing machines will be upgraded by scheduled replacement and some relocation of equipment 15 to 20 years old with new or refurbished machines and will include the addition of one more to the system. Thus, by 1987 five wheel-trueing machines will be in operation, spread throughout the system, substantially reducing the number of miles of "deadhead" travel required under the present procedures.

The two large repair shops which deal with heavy repair and overhaul of almost all car systems, i.e., bodies, trucks, propulsion motors, brakes, heating and ventilation equipment, doors, electrical systems, etc., will be modernized to incorporate newer, more advanced machinery, thereby increasing car equipment reliability. A major goal is to reduce the number of car failure delays and increase the mean distance between failure (MDBF) which is a major indicator of train service performance. The MDBF, now averaging 7000 miles of operation, will be increased to 15,000 by 1988 through the barn and shop improvement measures and the purchase of new cars. In this connection industrial engineering studies have been made to evaluate shop work flows and procedures aimed at increased productivity and cost effectiveness. Efforts have been directed to bring about a number of reliability and capability improvements.

In addition to modernizing individual elements and the support shops within the shop complex, the industrial engineering analyses have resulted in revised layouts and machine placements to improve work flow, repair procedures, material handling, and the movement of personnel. A key instance of significant shop improvement is that of providing the truck shop with a progressive flow line to replace the work station concept currently in use. Also an important step in shop modernization is the structural expansion of the Coney Island shop to handle the new 75-foot-long cars which will gradually increase in number as the procurement contracts are implemented.

Other items of work included in the program of barn and shop rehabilitation which are expected not only to restore the physical structure and improve operations but add to employee morale as well are:

- In all facilities, the employee welfare elements (locker rooms, toilets, lunch rooms) will be modernized.
- New heating systems will ameliorate a number of adverse conditions in the facilities resulting from the harsh New York winters.
- New overhead lighting, using both high-pressure sodium vapor lamps and metal halide lighting fixtures, will create better working conditions and safer operations.
- Ventilation will be upgraded to improve the worker's environment.
- Water supply systems and drainage will be refurbished or replaced as necessary.
- New fire protection systems and equipment will be installed.
- Machine tools and material handling equipment will be upgraded and, where called for, replaced by special or more modern equipment with greater output capability.
- Pit lighting will be improved.
- Public address systems will be refurbished or new ones installed as appropriate.
- Air-conditioning will be provided in certain areas.
- Electrical services will be upgraded to serve the increased electrical needs.
- Walkways and roadways around the facilities will be improved, as will be security measures.
- New motorized doors will be provided at many of the shops and barns.
- Defective or deteriorated windows will be replaced.
- Leaking roofs will be repaired.
- Floors will be done over where necessary.
- The general appearance of the facility exterior and interiors will be upgraded by appropriate selection of architectural finishes and painting.

All of this must be done while still keeping all of these barns and shops operating at a total level equivalent to that currently existing. This requires careful planning and scheduling based upon close coordination between the designers and the maintenance operators. Detailed schedules based upon availability of work space must be incorporated into construction contract documents. These schedules must be based on an overall analysis of the complete maintenance picture taking into account the ability to move work between barns and between shops. This is an entirely different set of problems than those that exist in planning and executing the construction of new facilities.

Another system element for which upgrading will have an impact on passenger service is the renewal of the line structure. Here the problem is different and probably even more complicated. To give you an idea of the complications involved in rehabilitating a rail structure while still keeping the transit system in operation, let us look at plans for the reconstruction of a portion of the Southeastern Pennsylvania Transportation Authority (SEPTA) Frankford elevated line in Philadelphia along its existing alignment. The Market Frankford line is a heavy rail rapid transit line connecting the 69th Street Terminal in Upper Darby with downtown Philadelphia, and with the Bridge Street Terminal in northeast Philadelphia. The portion of the line being rehabilitated is elevated from Bridge Street to Spring Gardens for a distance of slightly under six miles. The line operates at very high densities 24 hours a day, 7 days a week.

The work generally includes superstructure reconstruction of approximately five and a quarter miles of two-track elevated structure; repairs to the three major bridges over Lehigh Avenue and the Amtrack and Conrail tracks; and the reconstruction of all 11 existing passenger stations. Limited signal and traction power improvements will be required north of the Bridge Street Terminal and south of the Girard Avenue Station to the Fifth Street Station to interface facilities.

A portion of the Frankford elevated was replaced during the Interstate 95 relocation, leaving only the stretch from Girard Avenue to Bridge Street (approximately five miles) as existing steel structure. This structure has been examined and tested in a series of studies made by more than 23 consultant and in-house entities over the last 20 years. In general, it has been determined to be in a seriously deteriorated, though safe condition. Various reconstruction schemes have been examined, and the basic conclusion is that replacement of the complete existing steel structure is not cost effective. Accordingly, a series of alternative plans were formulated and a final decision has been made in the last few months to proceed with a limited reconstruction program as opposed to total replacement.

This limited reconstruction program takes full cognizance of the fact that the existing foundations and columns are in good condition and can be quite economically repaired or rehabilitated to provide a minimum of 30 years of additional life. The remainder of the structure has certain attributes that lend themselves to allowing virtually total reconstruction to be undertaken while maintaining daytime weekday peak and off-peak service.

The existing structure primarily is made up of either single- or two-column bents with transverse girders. The transverse girders, in turn, support three longitudinal trusses, which in turn, support I or wide flange floor beams on approximately five-and-a-half-foot centers. The floor beams are connected with a concrete track slab; the track type is mostly ballasted deck with timber ties and either jointed or continuous welded rail, except in stations where the track is modified; that is, stub tie in concrete construction.

The reconstruction scheme calls for the existing columns and transverse girders to be retained. New longitudinal girders will be installed under the floor beams to provide an alternative support for them. Four of these girders will be installed roughly below the rail on each of the two tracks. Upon installation of these girders, the outside trusses will be removed and the center truss essentially will be disabled or cut away. To replace the catwalks, which are now mounted on the outside trusses, new precast concrete longitudinal members will be installed with a self-contained duct assembly catwalk and railing.

Next in sequence will be track replacement. The existing deck is in poor condition. It has laminated and separated in general, and a series of experimental grouting tests led to the conclusion that repair of the deck through rock bolting or grouting would be prohibitive in cost and unacceptable as to the time required. As a result the track-replacement method that has been devised allows for elimination of the existing deck. While the design has not yet been completed, the concept calls for construction of precast, prestressed concrete longitudinal track beams of a rough trapezoidal shape, tailored in length and sufficient in strength to match specific bents that will not be replaced. Generally, bents on this elevated structure average 50 feet in length; however, there are major variations at intersections and at other special locations. By working nights and weekends on a specified number of bents, the existing tract and ballast can be completely removed, and the concrete decking under the rail area broken away. The longitudinal beams, complete with resilient track fasteners and rail, will then be dropped into position and anchored to the floor beams and service will be restored. Using an assembly line sequential program, the remaining deck will then be removed and replaced with a safety floor. During this process the third rail support system will be replaced and air lines and signal cables will be relocated or replaced as necessary.

This particular scheme is the only one that fully meets the need to maintain weekday service during this reconstruction. In addition, the method of construction will cause a minimum of disruption to the street below and to the residential and commercial areas, some of which are extremely valuable along this route. Because the Frankford Elevated is the essential transit artery of northeast Philadelphia, any substantial period of shutdown of this line would seriously disrupt transportation in the entire northeast Philadelphia area. With a total of 11 stations, the elevated serves some of the city's oldest and most densely populated neighborhoods and encompasses areas of great economic need with large minority populations.

These two examples of rapid transit infrastructure rehabilitation show the types of problems involved in such undertakings. All of the other system elements in the older transit properties need attention. In addition to the barns and shops and the aerial structure, which we have covered, are the stations, the tunnels, the line track, the yard tracks, the traction power system, the signal-control system, the communication system, and the fare-collection system. Each of these has its unique problems, but they all have the common underlying problem — to accomplish the repair, rehabilitation, or replacement while still operating the system and providing service to the traveling public. This along with the distinct need to remember and consider the infrastructure maintenance, rehabilitation, and improvement needs of rapid transit systems is the message we want to leave with you.

REFERENCES

1. CUDAHY, B. J. 1982. A century of service: the story of public transportation in North America. Passenger Transport Suppl: 10, 65–66.
2. 1982. Rail Modernization Study Design. Urban Mass Transportation Administration. Washington, D.C. (Final report.)

DISCUSSION OF THE PAPER

C. TURKSTRA (*Polytechnic Institute of New York, Brooklyn, N.Y.*): Have you made a study of the graffiti problem in the New York subways, and have you taken this into consideration in redesigning the yards?

E. A. TILLMAN: I won't say that we studied the graffiti problem, but we certainly have taken it into consideration in the rehabilitation of the barns because that's one of the reasons for these chemical wash facilities. It will increase the number of facilities that the transit authority has and would be able to use hopefully in cutting down on that problem.

C. TURKSTRA: Just as a supplement, if I may, my understanding is that most of the graffiti work is done in the yards and that the security of these yards has historically been very poor. If my information is correct, some of the yards where the cars are parked are not enclosed. If this is correct, it would suggest a major effort to enclose these yards and defend them.

E. A. TILLMAN: I think most of the yards are now completely fenced. One of the problems of course is that there's not space enough in the yards to take care of all of the trains and all of the cars. There is a yard program, in which we are not involved, where they are expanding the yards also with a view to doing away with that problem so that they will be able to store all of their trains within a secure yard.

Nondestructive Evaluation of Infrastructure Conditions

GEORGE A. MATZKANIN, LEWIS S. FOUNTAIN,[a]
AND OREN TRANBARGER

Southwest Research Institute
Post Office Drawer 28510
6220 Culebra Road
San Antonio, Texas 78284

In rapid transit systems, the integrity of subway structures must be known for the benefit of public safety. New and innovative surveying techniques are required to overcome limitations of inspection methods presently used for determining the integrity of structures in aging subway systems. Nondestructive evaluation (NDE) techniques have been successfully developed and applied in a project funded by the Office of Technical Assistance in the Urban Mass Transportation Administration (UMTA) to assess the structural integrity of brick tunnels and concrete inverts in the New York City area. Promising results have been obtained so far in tests on a brick wall and concrete slab which simulated the subway structures of interest and in initial field tests conducted on a New York City Transit Authority (NYCTA) concrete floor.

In subway tunnels over 70 years old there is an increasingly urgent need to develop NDE inspection methods to detect the degradation of structural materials and the presence of voids that could potentially cause failure. Brick-lined tunnels require information on axial and radial variations and material properties, such as density and strength, in order to assess the overall structural integrity. Some of the brick tunnels being studied were originally built with an exterior boiler plate for maintaining the proper dimensions of the traffic passageway. Silt infiltration into gaps between the brick and the boiler plate shell could conceivably lead to deterioration of the outer layer of brick over the years. In this type of structure, there is interest in a method for determining whether the outer metal shell exists and whether the brick in the outer portion of the wall is structurally sound. In the case of the NYCTA subways, the primary structural integrity concern is the existence of voids and cavities under the concrete inverts. Voids can form when cracks occur in the invert and the underlying soil is washed out as a result of changes in the water table and the pumping action associated with passing trains. Reconstruction to replace the invert is very costly and involves substantial diversion of traffic. Therefore, identification of voids or cavities under the inverts is important in guiding rehabilitation procedures.

[a] To whom correspondence should be addressed.

Present inspection methods of brick-lined tunnels involve visual inspection of the condition of the brick walls and monitoring of water seepage. A sounding technique based on tapping the walls is sometimes used, but this technique is essentially an art and requires an individual with considerable training and experience to interpret the response of the walls. This manual sounding technique is slow, subject to considerable error in interpretation, and may only be sensitive to shallow flaws. Present inspection of NYCTA subway tunnels also relies on visual methods which involve the observations of cracks in the concrete invert along with the presence of water and silt on the surface of the invert to identify washouts below the invert. Water seepage flow rates are also monitored to identify those areas where water flow is abnormally high.

Because of the absolute necessity of maintaining the structural integrity of transportation system tunnels for public safety and protection of substantial capital investments, there is strong justification for the identification and development of better, more rapid and reliable NDE methods than are presently available for evaluating tunnel structures. Rapid survey methods are especially desirable because of the length of tunnel to be inspected and the traffic disruption difficulties associated with slower inspection methods.

The general approach taken by Southwest Research Institute to address these problems involves three phases: (1) assessment of the available NDE technology for tunnel inspection; (2) laboratory evaluation of selected candidate methods on simulation test structures; and (3) field evaluation of the most promising methods in actual subway tunnels. In the following sections, results obtained during phases 1 and 2 are presented along with preliminary results obtained during the phase 3 field evaluation studies which are still in progress.

TECHNOLOGY ASSESSMENT

The technology assessment of available and applicable NDE techniques for inspecting tunnel structures comprised a comprehensive literature search, document review, personal contacts with experts in the field, evaluation of potential NDE methods, and ranking of the most promising candidate methods.

As a result of the literature review and other related information gathered during the information-acquisition efforts, the following 12 state-of-the-art NDE methods emerged as the most viable candidates for accomplishing the program objectives:

1. Acoustic emission.
2. Sonics.
3. Vibration analysis.
4. Ultrasonics.
5. Acoustic holography.
6. Short-pulse radar.
7. Frequency-modulated continuous-wave (FM-CW) radar.

8. Photon backscatter.
9. Photon (backscatter) tomography.
10. Neutron interactions.
11. Electrical resistivity.
12. Infrared thermography.

These methods were subsequently evaluated and assessed in the context of the specific tunnel inspection problems. Criteria used for rating and ranking the candidate NDE methods were divided into the following four categories:

1. *Sensitivity.* Sensitivity refers to the effectiveness of the method for detecting or sensing the various conditions of interest. In the case of the brick wall, the defects and influencing conditions of interest included voids, delaminations, cracks, density variations, potential interference from metal, and the influence of nonplanar surfaces. For concrete inverts, the parameters of interest were cavity detection and sizing.
2. *Adaptability to field use.* This category pertains to factors associated with applying the method under field conditions. These factors include (a) equipment operation; (b) safety; (c) power requirements; (d) ruggedness; (e) accommodation to the field environment (temperature, humidity, vibration, surface conditions, etc.); and (f) accessibility to the region to be inspected. For the concrete inverts, a useful inspection methodology must accommodate interfering features such as floor I-beams, the presence of steel tracks, electrified rails, wood ties, gravel ballast, and possibly water on top of the concrete invert.
3. *Instrumentation.* The instrumentation category is composed of factors related to characterizing the inspection system based on its complexity, potential for automation, degree of operator dependence for routine operation, and ease of data interpretation.
4. *Survey capability.* This category refers to the capability of the NDE method to be applied in a continuous survey mode for tunnel inspection.

Based on the information from the literature review and technical interchange with various NDE experts, the 12 state-of-the-art NDE methods were rated and ranked according to 25 parameters in the four categories listed above. The methods ranked highest for the brick wall and concrete invert inspection problems are listed in TABLES 1 and 2, respectively. Practical considerations eliminated the photon backscatter method because of (1) safety factors associated with the use of radioactive sources; (2) limited penetration depth in geologic materials; and (3) difficulties associated with implementing the method in a rapid survey mode. Thus, the principal approaches chosen to be evaluated further were FM-CW radar, electrical resistivity, and electromagnetic conductivity. Laboratory results obtained on simulated test structures are described in the next section.

TABLE 1. Ranking of NDE Methods for Inspecting Brick Walls

Ranking	Method (material conditions)	Survey Capability (brick wall)	Remarks
1	FM-CW radar (density, flaws[a])	good	very good overall
2	Photon backscatter (density, flaws)	fair (slow scan only)	poor capability for crack detection
3	Electrical resistivity	fair (requires development of adequate moving electrode contacts)	poor capability for detecting cracks and delaminations
4	Neutron interaction (porosity)	fair (slow scan only)	no capability on delaminations and cracks
5	Ultrasonics/sonics (modulus, flaws)	fair/poor (requires development of adequate transducer coupling for scan)	reduced sensitivity to low density
6	Vibration analysis (modulus, stiffness, flaws)	poor (possibly only very slow scan rate)	reduced sensitivity to low density

[a] Flaws refer to voids, delaminations, and cracks.

TABLE 2. Ranking of NDE Methods for Inspecting Concrete Inverts

Ranking	Method (capabilities)	Survey Capabilities (concrete invert)	Remarks
1	Ultrasonics/sonics	none	Use of compressional and shear waves can provide good cavity detection but transducers must be directly coupled to top of invert
2	Photon backscatter (detection, sizing)	none	Method is probably limited to penetration of about 1 foot of concrete invert thickness. Both source and detector, although noncontacting, must have direct access to upper invert surface
3	FM-CW radar (detection)	good	Penetration of cross-ties and ballast limited by conductive water. Cavity detection beneath invert is primarily limited by penetration which is a function of moisture present in invert concrete
4	Electrical resistivity (detection, sizing)	fair (requires development of adequate moving electrode contacts)	Sensitivity probably limited by the placement of electrodes on the subway walls which will be necessary to implement a survey mode

FIGURE 1. Brick wall test structure. (a) Back side of test wall (top). (b) Wall with two additional courses of loose brick and a 15 inch × 13 inch hole (bottom).

FIGURE 2. Concrete invert test structure. (a) Bare slab (top). (b) Slab with built-up section of railroad track (bottom).

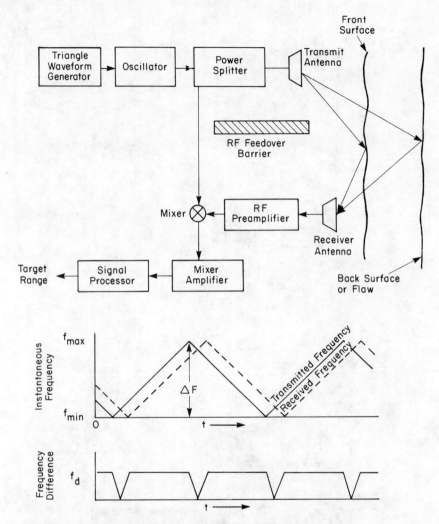

FIGURE 3. Nondestructive inspection using FM-CW radar.

LABORATORY EVALUATION

Test Structures

Test structures were built in an open field at Southwest Research Institute. The objective was to build structures that would simulate brick tunnel walls and concrete inverts and be suitable for evaluating the selected NDE methods. The shape and size of the test structures were determined by the instrumentation parameters of the laboratory equipment used in the study.

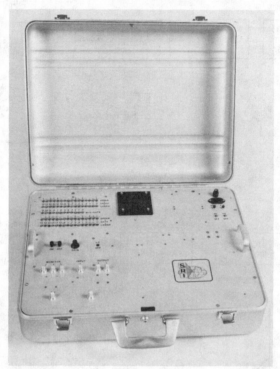

FIGURE 4. FM-CW radar. (a) Operating panel (top). (b) Electronic circuitry (bottom).

For example, the lateral dimensions of the structures were made large enough to accommodate the radar antennas without introducing edge effects.

For the tunnel studies, a brick wall was erected 12 feet long × 8 feet high × 6 courses of brick (approximately 2 feet) thick. The wall was erected on a concrete slab approximately 16 feet × 10 feet × 8 inches thick to serve as a foundation. The brick was D'Hanis common brick, and the mortar used was a standard mix. In addition to the 6 mortared courses of brick, 2 additional courses of loose brick were stacked against the rear of the wall to simulate loose or deteriorated courses of brick. A rectangular hole approximately 15 inches × 13 inches was left in the center of the loose brick courses to simulate a cavity at the rear section of the wall. Photographs of the test brick wall are shown in FIGURE 1. A steel plate 4 feet × 8 feet × ⅛ inch thick was used to simulate the boiler plate at the back surface of the brick tunnel wall. This plate could be removed to evaluate the absence or presence of metal on the performance of the NDE methods investigated. Toward the end of the laboratory evaluation phase, the two loose courses of brick were mortared to the back of the wall to increase its thickness to 8 courses. The rectangular hole was left in the two extra courses.

For the concrete invert studies, an unreinforced concrete slab 8 feet × 12 feet × 18 inches thick was cast on leveled ground. The slab was cast in two pourings with a waterproofing layer inserted at the 6-inch depth between the two pours. The waterproofing layer consisted of four thicknesses of 15-pound asphalt-impregnated felt. Also cast into the test concrete slab were 2-inch inside diameter lifting eyes so that the slab could be lifted with a crane, providing access to the ground under the slab. Voids of various dimensions and configurations could be formed in the ground below the slab for evaluation of the NDE methods. The bare concrete invert test slab is shown in FIGURE 2a. Initial performance of the NDE methods was evaluated with air voids, water-filled voids, and mud-filled voids, under the bare slab. After thoroughly characterizing the NDE responses on the bare concrete slab, a short section of running track consisting of gravel ballast, wooden ties, and rails was erected on the concrete slab as shown in FIGURE 2b. This configuration provided an opportunity to evaluate the influence of the ballast, ties, and rails on the NDE methods under evaluation. Results of these evaluations are described in the next sections.

Radar

Description of Approach

In the FM-CW radar approach evaluated, the transmitted signal has a linearly swept frequency vs. time function over a finite bandwidth. The received signal is displaced in time from the original transmitted signal. When the two signals are mixed together, a difference frequency signal results which is a linear function of the target echo range,[1-3] as illustrated in FIGURE 3. Since a portion of the transmitted signal is mixed with the received signal, there

FIGURE 5. Bistatic radar antennas.

are no short-range limitations with the FM-CW method as there may be with pulse radar.

Typically, FM-CW radars utilize low-power, voltage-tuned oscillators that operate at 1 GHz or above, with bandwidths that can vary from 1 GHz to 10 GHz. This frequency range may be lowered so that sweep frequencies are obtained with frequency components as low as 30 MHz for good penetration into high-loss materials. Since the bandwidth of the linear FM-CW oscillator is easily controlled, different bandwidths and operating sweep ranges may be achieved for optimizing the depths of penetration and range resolution of the radar system. A sweep range from 50 to 500 MHz was used in most of the laboratory studies.

For the studies reported, a pulsed FM-CW radar system was designed and built. The completed field system is shown in FIGURE 4. The bandwidth-determining component of the system is a yttrium iron garnet–tuned transistor oscillator sweeping from 2 to 6 GHz. A digitally controlled radio frequency (RF) switch selects a programmed frequency window out of the overall sweep range which is down converted to lower frequencies and then amplified to a 1-watt level for penetrating the structures of interest. The time-gated difference signals are amplified in the receiver and displayed by a fast Fourier transform spectrum analyzer to obtain information on defects and characteristics of the inspected structures.

The system was designed for a bistatic antenna configuration. The two radar antennas shown in FIGURE 5 are resistively loaded transverse electromagnetic wave horn structures filled with titanium dioxide powder. The dielec-

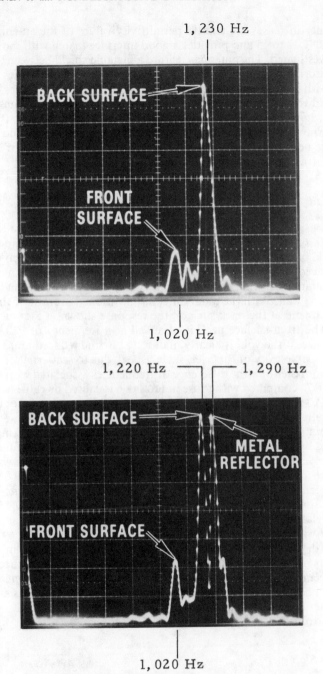

FIGURE 6. Radar signals from solid brick wall. (a) Front and back surface return signals (top). (b) Radar return from metal reflector behind wall (bottom).

tric powder increases the relative permittivity values of the antennas to approximately 12 to 15 and provides a good interface match with the materials being investigated. The antennas feature a metallic shield between two layers of RF absorbing materials to improve side-lobe suppression. Studies were conducted with the antennas oriented in horizontal and vertical planes, and with the E-field vectors cross polarized. In field applications, the antennas are cumbersome; however, these antennas were originally developed for the United States Army for pulse applications. Considerable design work and improvements are necessary before a final system is developed capable of operating on a rail-transportable platform.

Brick Wall

The basic FM-CW radar response from the air-dry brick wall is shown in FIGURE 6a. There is a weak front-surface peak at 1020 Hz and a large-amplitude back-surface peak at 1230 Hz. A metal reflector, such as a steel plate, spaced 26 inches behind the wall is easily detected as shown in FIGURE 6b. This dramatically illustrates the penetration capabilities of the radar signals through the wall. With the radar antennas positioned in front of the 15 inch × 13 inch void at the back surface, the response shown in FIGURE 7a is obtained. The front-surface peak is observed at a frequency of 980 Hz while the presence of the void is clearly manifested by the reduced amplitude and increased complexity of the back-surface peak due to scattering of the radar signals from the void (the difference of frequencies associated with the peaks in FIGURE 7a compared with those in FIGURE 6 is caused by cable length variations). A small metal plate inserted into the void space increases the back-surface reflection as shown in FIGURE 7b; however, the scattering effects due to the void are still distinguishable. The influence of water soaking was investigated by placing hoses on top of the wall and letting water run over and down the wall for prescribed periods of time. After soaking the wall for 20 hours, the attenuation factor increased from 10 dB/m to 13.5 dB/m and the relative permittivity increased from 5.76 to 8.6. After three-and-one-half days of water soaking, the attenuation of the wall increased to only 15.4 dB/m and the relative permittivity factor remained constant at 8.6. Radar responses from the water-soaked wall were similar to those shown in FIGURES 6 and 7 for the dry wall; however, the front-surface reflection was diminished and the effects of the metal reflector spaced behind the wall were reduced. These results occur because the relative permittivity value of the wall increases. This provides a better match with the dielectric material in the antennas and results in a greater wall-to-air interface reflection at the back surface, obscuring the response from a metal reflector.

Concrete Slab

A number of radar measurements were made to evaluate the capabilities of FM-CW radar for detecting voids beneath the concrete slab. One-way

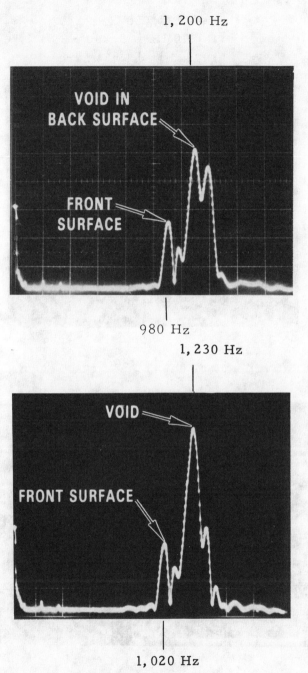

FIGURE 7. Radar signals from void in brick wall. (a) Fifteen inch × 13 inch void at back surface (top). (b) Metal plate in void (bottom).

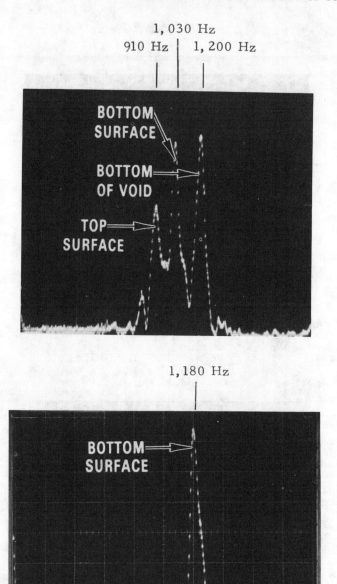

FIGURE 8. Radar signals from air void beneath concrete slab. (a) Radar antennas located to one side of void (top). (b) Radar antennas centered over void (bottom).

propagation measurements showed the concrete slab had an attenuation factor of 39.5 dB/m and a relative permittivity value of 4.6. Despite the high attenuation factor measured for the concrete slab, the dielectrically loaded antennas provided a good interface match with the concrete which diminished the effect of the front-surface reflection that might otherwise mask signal reflections from targets below the slab.

Large air- and water-filled voids were readily detectable. FIGURE 8 shows the presence of an air-filled void measuring 2 feet × 3 feet × 1 foot. With the radar antennas located to one side of the void, a triple-peaked spectrum was observed as shown in FIGURE 8a. This results from one of the antennas being directly above the edge of the void. A geometrical analysis of the signal reflection paths involved for this antenna offset condition indicates that three possible reflections should occur. These correspond to the front surface, the back of the slab, and the bottom of the void at the edge nearest the antennas. However, when the antennas are moved directly over the void, only a single peak associated with the bottom surface of the slab is observed as shown in FIGURE 8b. The trailing edge of this signal reflection is distorted by a weak reflection from the back of the void. Two peaks are not present because the air-space distance of the void is not fully resolvable for the effective bandwidth of the system, which includes the antenna and concrete frequency responses.

Increasing the sweep bandwidth of the radar system from 50 to 700 MHz improved the system resolution capabilities for detecting mud-filled voids and small, shallow voids. For this increased sweep bandwidth, the attenuation factor of the concrete slab was found to be 43.7 dB/m and the relative permittivity was computed to be approximately 4.95. Although the effective bandwidth is limited by the frequency response of the antennas in addition to the attenuation vs. frequency characteristics of the media, there is a significant improvement in the system resolution capabilities for detecting shallow voids. With the increased frequency sweep, the response of the concrete slab to radar signals becomes more complex as shown in FIGURE 9a. As the antenna array is scanned across a 12 inch × 18 inch × 4 inch deep void area, the combined effects of the slab-air interface are detected as shown in FIGURE 9b. The presence of a shallow, mud-filled void is also shown in FIGURE 9c.

In tests conducted after the ballast, ties, and rails were added to the slab, good resolution was obtained for the distance through the ballast as shown in FIGURE 10. Although there is evidence in this display that the target at 1252.5 Hz is the back of the slab and the shallow 4-in-deep air void, reliable radar detection of voids below the slab is inconclusive at present. On the other hand, the ties, ballast, and rails do not preclude the application of FM-CW radar techniques for inspecting concrete subway inverts.

Electrical Resistivity

Description of Approach

A variety of electrical resistivity exploration methods have been consid-

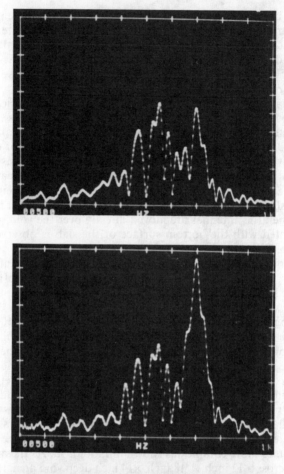

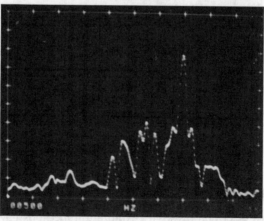

1,050 Hz ⎯⎯⎯   ⎯⎯ 1,100 Hz

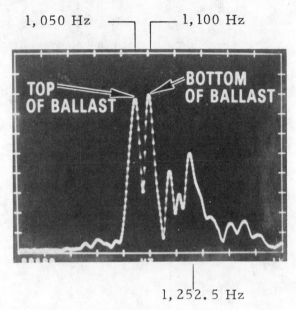

1,252.5 Hz

FIGURE 10. Radar signal from concrete slab and track section.

ered as potential approaches to detection of subsurface material changes. The use of electrical resistivity measurements for detecting subsurface material variations involves establishing an otherwise predictable electrical current distribution within a relatively large volume of material. Any observed perturbations in the current distributions, measured as potentials or electric fields at the surface, may be interpreted in terms of possible subsurface structural or material resistivity anomalies. The degree of perturbation in the current distribution is dependent upon the resistivity contrast between the anomalous subsurface structures and the surrounding material; and, equally important, the detectability of such perturbations is dependent upon the size and shape of the anomaly and its orientation relative to the current flow.

Various electrode arrays are used to establish the subsurface current distributions and to measure the potential differences at the ground surface. In particular, dipole-dipole electrode arrays have proved to be useful for detecting subsurface cavities and structural anomalies. They are convenient to use and have good spacial resolution.

Two dipole-dipole arrays evaluated for tunnel inspection are illustrated in FIGURE 11. FIGURE 11a shows an in-line or polar dipole electrode array. The distances a between current electrodes C_1 and C_2 and between potential

FIGURE 9. Radar signals from small voids beneath concrete slab. (a) No void (top). (b) Twelve inch × 18 inch × 4 inch deep air void (center). (c) Twelve inch × 18 inch × 4 inch deep mud void (bottom).

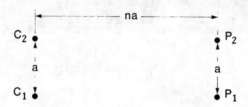

C_1 and C_2 = current electrodes (current dipole)

P_1 and P_2 = potential electrodes (potential dipole)

$$\rho_a = \frac{\pi na \, \Delta v}{I} \, (n+1)(n+2)$$

a. IN-LINE DIPOLE ARRAY

C_1 and C_2 = current electrodes (current dipole)

P_1 and P_2 = potential electrodes (potential dipole)

$$\rho_a = \frac{\pi na \Delta v}{I} \, \frac{\sqrt{(na)^2 + a^2}}{\sqrt{(na)^2 + a^2} - na}$$

b. EQUATORIAL DIPOLE ARRAY

FIGURE 11. Dipole-dipole resistivity arrays for tunnel inspection. (a) In-line dipole array. (b) Equatorial dipole array.

electrodes P_1 and P_2 are generally significantly smaller than the distance *na* between electrode pairs. Current is applied through electrodes C_1 and C_2, and potential is measured between electrodes P_1 and P_2. The apparent resistivity associated with the geometrical spreading of the current can be calculated by the equation

$$\varrho_a = \frac{\pi na \Delta V}{I} \, (n + 1)(n + 2) \tag{1}$$

where ΔV is the measured potential and I is the current injected into the medium.

FIGURE 11b shows another dipole-dipole electrode array called an equatorial array in which the two dipole pairs are parallel. With this electrode array, the resistivity is calculated using the equation

$$\varrho_a = \frac{\pi na\Delta V}{I} \frac{\sqrt{(na)^2 + a^2}}{\sqrt{(na)^2 + a^2} - na} \tag{2}$$

Most of the evaluations for subway tunnel inspection were conducted using the in-line electrode array. The equatorial array was used where obstacles on the test structure precluded use of the in-line array.

Two types of resistivity measurements were made during the evaluation phase, electrical sounding and horizontal profiling. The electrical sounding approach provides depth information. The basis for the measurement is that the farther away from a current source the measurement of potential is made,

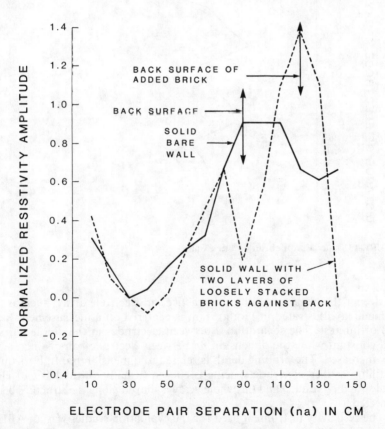

FIGURE 12. Electrical sounding measurements on brick wall.

LOG OF APPARENT RESISTIVITY

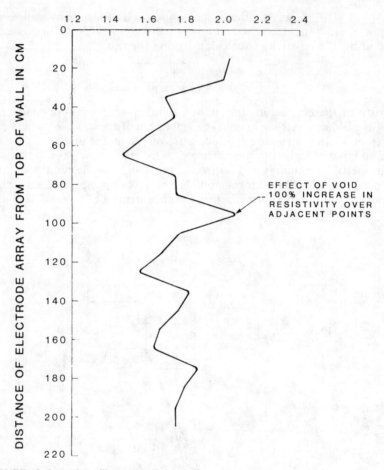

FIGURE 13. Lateral profile scan on brick wall.

the deeper the probing will be. In practice, an electrode array, such as the in-line array illustrated in FIGURE 11a, is centered on a measurement location of interest. The separation *a* between electrodes in the dipole pairs is held constant while the dimension *na* between electrode pairs is incrementally increased. The probing depth is related to dimension *na*. In horizontal profiling, a fixed electrode spacing is chosen (usually on the basis of electrical sounding results) and the whole array is moved along the structure being inspected.

The resistivity instrument used for the evaluation studies was an ABEM Model SAS 300. It is a signal-averaging system and, thus, can operate in

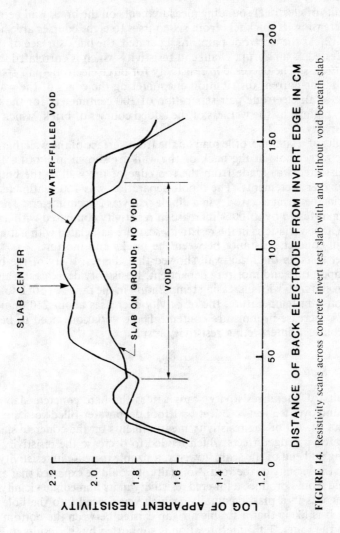

FIGURE 14. Resistivity scans across concrete invert test slab with and without void beneath slab.

electrically noisy areas. It uses a commutated transmission current that is programmed at 0.4 Hz.

Brick Wall

Results of electrical sounding measurements on the brick wall before and after increasing its thickness from six courses to eight courses are shown in FIGURE 12. As the electrode pairs are separated, the back surface of the wall is manifested as an abrupt change in resistivity which is correlated with the wall thickness. The decrease in resistivity for large electrode-pair spacing is caused by the current distribution encountering the edges of the wall. The decrease at an electrode pair separation of 100 centimeters for the thicker wall is explained by the wetness of the added courses of brick, which lowers the resistivity.

Results of a lateral profile scan on the front surface of the wall that passed over the target hole at the back of the wall are shown in FIGURE 13. The scan illustrated was made from the top edge of the wall to the bottom in 10-centimeter increments. The dipole separation was 160 centimeters, and the spacing between electrodes in a dipole pair was 20 centimeters. The target hole is manifested by a 100% increase in resistivity compared with adjacent points. Other variations in the resistivity scan are associated with natural variations in contact resistance between the bricks and mortar.

Other tests on the brick wall showed that the resistivity of the brick is very temperature and moisture dependent. Resistivity decreases at a rate of 13 ohmmeters/°F with increasing temperature in the range of 50°F to 120°F. For a constant temperature, the resistivity decreases about 250 ohmmeters for a 1% increase in moisture content. These variations need to be taken into account in interpreting resistivity results.

Concrete Slab

Results of lateral resistivity scans across the bare concrete slab on the ground and over a 3 feet × 2 feet × 1 foot deep water-filled void are shown in FIGURE 14. All of the resistivity measurements on the concrete slab were complicated by edge effects which tended to decrease the resistivity at the beginning and end of the scan; however, a sizable increase in resistivity is obtained in the vicinity of the void. Normally, it would be expected that a water-filled void would produce a lowered resistivity in its immediate vicinity. Since the water was in a plastic container which was placed into the hole under the slab, it is likely that a sizable air gap existed between the bottom of the slab and the water. This interpretation is supported by the results in FIGURE 15, which show that both water-filled and mud-filled voids produce resistivity increases similar to an air void. Voids as small as 18 inches × 12 inches × 4 inches deep could also be detected, but produced smaller increases in resistivity.

Additional evaluations showed that reinforcement rods substantially

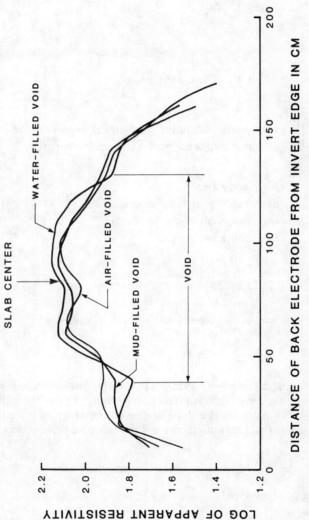

FIGURE 15. Resistivity scans across concrete invert test slab with various voids beneath slab.

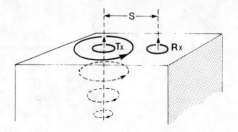

$$\frac{H_s}{H_p} \simeq \frac{i\omega\mu_o\sigma S^2}{4}$$

H_s = secondary magnetic field at the receiver coil

H_p = primary magnetic field at the receiver coil

ω = $2\pi f$

f = frequency (Hz)

μ_o = permeability of free space

σ = ground conductivity (mho/m)

S = intercoil spacing (m)

i = $\sqrt{-1}$

$$\sigma_a = \frac{4}{\omega\mu_o S^2}\left(\frac{H_s}{H_p}\right)$$

FIGURE 16. Basic principle of electromagnetic conductivity inspection.

lowered the apparent resistivity so much that variations associated with voids were difficult to resolve. Similar effects were observed after the ballast, ties, and rails were in place on the slab. In general, conducting material in the proximity of resistivity measurements will probably mask detection of voids.

Electromagnetic Conductivity

Description of Approach

The basic principle of the electromagnetic conductivity method is illustrated in FIGURE 16.[4] A transmitter coil, T_x, is energized with an alternating current at an audio frequency, and a receiver coil, R_x, is located a short distance away. The time-varying magnetic field, H_p, associated with the alternating current in the transmitter coil, induces small currents in the material being inspected. These currents generate a secondary magnetic field, H_s,

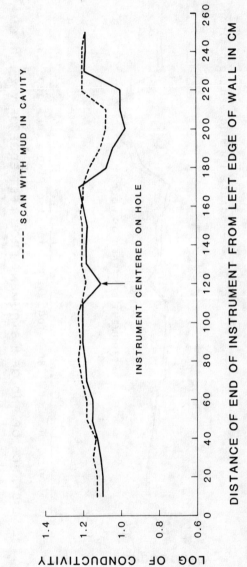

FIGURE 17. Conductivity scan across brick wall with air void.

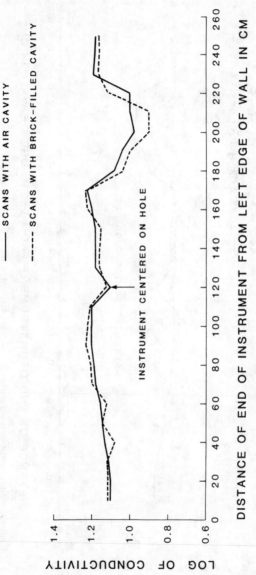

FIGURE 18. Conductivity scan across brick wall with brick-filled void.

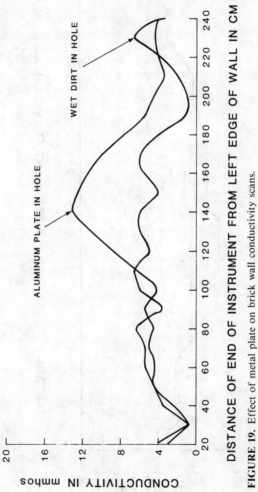

DISTANCE OF END OF INSTRUMENT FROM LEFT EDGE OF WALL IN CM

FIGURE 19. Effect of metal plate on brick wall conductivity scans.

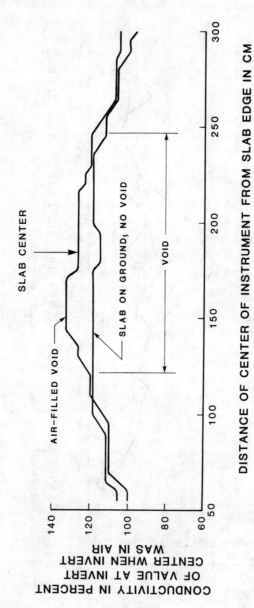

DISTANCE OF CENTER OF INSTRUMENT FROM SLAB EDGE IN CM

FIGURE 20. Induction conductivity scans across concrete invert test slab with and without void beneath slab.

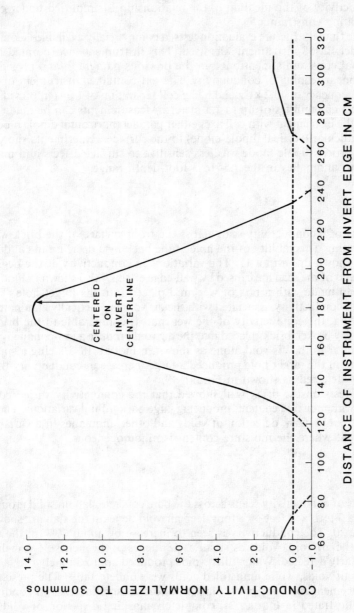

FIGURE 21. Effect of reinforcement rods on concrete slab conductivity scan.

which is sensed together with H_p by the receiver. Although, in general, H_s is a complicated function of intercoil spacing s, operating frequency f, and the conductivity of the medium σ, the relationship is simplified under certain operating constraints.[4]

For the tunnel structure evaluation tests, a commercially available Geonics, Ltd. Model EM38 instrument was used. This instrument incorporated the operational constraints mentioned in the previous paragraph and provided a direct, linear reading of conductivity. The self-contained instrument operated at a frequency of 13.2 kHz and had a coil separation of 1 meter, providing penetration capabilities of up to 1.5 meters. Measurements can be made by scanning the instrument with coil axes either parallel (horizontal dipole mode) or perpendicular (vertical dipole mode) to the surface. Experiments showed that the vertical dipole mode was less sensitive to surface effects and more sensitive to anomalies in the 1.5- to 3-foot depth range.

Brick Wall

Results of a conductivity scan across the front surface of the brick wall demonstrating detectability of the hole at the back by a decrease in conductivity are shown in FIGURE 17. The variations in conductivity at the beginning and end of the scan are caused by wall-edge effects. Also shown in FIGURE 17 is a scan made with a box of wet mud placed into the target hole. The decrease in conductivity associated with the air void is practically eliminated, implying that the conductivity of the wet mud is comparable to the brick. However, dry broken bricks placed into the air void produce a low-conductivity region similar to the air void alone as shown in FIGURE 18. Placing a small metal plate in the target hole produced a large increase in conductivity that was easily detected as shown in FIGURE 19.

Other tests on the brick wall showed that the conductivity varied considerably with moisture content, producing large background variations. These variations could mask detection of voids and other anomalies in a variable environment where the moisture content is inhomogeneous.

Concrete Slab

Results of conductivity scans across the bare concrete slab on solid ground and with a 3 feet $\times$ 2 feet $\times$ 1 foot deep air void beneath the slab are shown in FIGURE 20. The conductivity is seen to increase by about 10% in the vicinity of the air void. Voids as small as 18 inches $\times$ 12 inches $\times$ 4 inches were similarly detected. Water-filled voids produced approximately the same results as air voids, while mud-filled voids were undetectable. The presence of reinforcement rods under the slab produced a large increase in conductivity as illustrated in FIGURE 21, completely masking detection of voids.

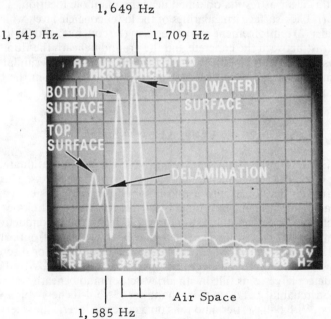

FIGURE 22. Radar signals from NYCTA concrete floor. (a) Manhole opening showing slab and void (top). (b) Response from manhole region (bottom).

FIELD EVALUATION

Preliminary field evaluation studies of the FM-CW radar were performed during October 1983 at the Coney Island barn in New York City for NYCTA. This facility is a large maintenance shop used by NYCTA for rebuilding subway cars. In some locations, the earth under the subway floor is sinking, resulting in a number of voids under the floor. In the initial field tests, calibrating radar measurements were made in a section of the floor near the location of a manhole. As illustrated in the photograph in FIGURE 22a, the floor consists of two slabs of concrete. The top layer of the floor is approximately 8 inches thick. The bottom layer was originally poured on the ground and has a very irregular back surface. At the point where the radar measurements were made, the bottom layer of concrete is approximately 12 inches thick and the air distance from the slab bottom to a water-filled void below the floor is approximately 18 inches. A delamination is evident between the two concrete layers shown in FIGURE 22a. The radar signals readily penetrated the floor and the air space below the floor, resulting in the display shown in FIGURE 22b. The front surface, delamination between layers, back surface, and air space are clearly identifiable. The signals at 1700 Hz reflected from the water-filled void surface could be reduced in amplitude by holding a metal plate under the floor. In tests conducted on the floor in other areas of the building, results were not as clear as results obtained near the manhole location. This is because of (1) back-surface irregularities of the lower concrete layer, which scatter the signals; (2) reinforcement rod patterns in the concrete; and (3) low dielectric contrast between the concrete and the ground beneath the floor at those locations free from water-filled voids. However, radar signals similar to those shown in FIGURE 22b were observed at six other locations in the building, suggesting the existence of air spaces under the floor.

CONCLUSIONS

Pulsed FM-CW radar is the most effective NDE method evaluated for inspecting brick walls and concrete slabs for infrastructure defects. This method can be further developed into a rail-mounted surveying system capable of rapidly assessing tunnel conditions. Electrical resistivity techniques are also applicable for inspecting tunnel structures. Electromagnetic conductivity measurements are not practical where there may be interference from conducting materials. In brick walls, FM-CW radar is capable of detecting discrete flaws such as voids and internal dielectric property changes. FM-CW radar can be used to detect large voids filled with air, water, or mud beneath concrete slabs with good reliability and smaller, shallower (3 to 4 inches) voids with less reliability. With ballast, ties, and rails on a concrete invert, the interpretation of radar responses becomes more difficult; however, the application of FM-CW techniques to the invert problem is still feasible through signal processing and data analysis. Radar measurements of the concrete floor at the NYCTA

Coney Island maintenance facility show the presence of numerous voids under the floor.

REFERENCES

1. TRANBARGER, O. & M. B. TREUHAFT. 1981. Evaluation of Potential Coal Interface Sensing Techniques for Extended Depth Guided Auger Cutterhead. Southwest Research Institute. San Antonio, Tex. (Final technical report. Department of Energy Contract DEAC 01-76ET12213.)
2. JERSCH, R. L., R. B. JOHNSON, D R. BELSHER, A. D. YAGHIJIAN, M. C. STEPPE & R. W. FLEMING. 1979. High Resolution Sensing Techniques for Slope Stability Studies. Report No. FHWA-RD-79-32. Federal Highway Administration. Washington, D.C.
3. OWEN, T. E. & O. TRANBARGER. 1977. Volume II — Investigation and Development of a High-Resolution FM-CW Radar System for Residual Coal Thickness Measurement. Southwest Research Institute. San Antonio, Tex. (Bureau of Mines Contract No. H0262055. Interim Report — Phase I.)
4. McNEILL, J. D. 1980. Electromagnetic Terrain Conductivity Measurement at Low Induction Numbers. Technical Note TN-6. Geonics, Ltd. Mississauga, Ontario, Canada.

DISCUSSION OF THE PAPER

A. S. GOODMAN (*Polytechnic Institute of New York, Brooklyn, N.Y.*): From what I can see from your paper, these methods indicate that something is wrong, but they really do not provide direct information on what needs to be done in correcting the defect. Does more research need to be done to, for example, develop calibration graphs and things of that nature?

O. TRANBARGER: Calibrating methods are required for the radar to aid in the interpretation of the signals obtained from the structures being investigated. The floor test at the Coney Island barn is a good example of how the radar is calibrated. In that test, the physical conditions could be correlated with the radar data and used in comparison to test other sections of the floor that could not be observed from the back side. One of the goals of the laboratory phase of the project described in this paper was to observe the responses from the test concrete slab and brick wall in an effort to provide some basis for calibration. Although research could be continued in building test structures and calibrating the radar, more information will be learned in conducting field tests. Additional calibration efforts are not recommended.

A. S. GOODMAN: I think my point was that you already knew what the problem was so that you could make an interpretation based upon that knowledge. Now in inspection work, we really have another situation; we could use an instrument like this and so we would see that something was wrong, but the question concerns determination of just what the problem is.

O. Tranbarger: In the case of studying the tunnel walls, waveform comparisons would be made. For instance, suppose there is a section of wall with a different kind of response than some other representative section; then the next step would be to core the wall and examine the material to fully interpret the test results.

P. L. Rinaldi (*Port Authority of New York and New Jersey, New York, N.Y.*) You mentioned 12 areas and said you chose three of those areas for further research. More specifically, you said you were looking at tunnel walls, concrete, and brick. Have you experimented with the other methods that you did not investigate, such as infrared and acoustic emission, and found applications for other parts of infrastructure testing? Also, you seem to have limited yourself to these three areas. Was the limitation to these three areas because you were looking specifically at the tunnel walls and concrete inverts? And are there other applications for the other nine techniques that you did not investigate?

L. S. Fountain: Our work was directed toward the tunnel wall and tunnel invert problem. The other inspection methods are used in a large number of applications, but in our judgment the three methods that we described were more applicable to the tunnel inspection problem and could more readily be developed into a safe, mobile detection system.

C. H. Luebkeman (*Cornell University, Ithaca, N.Y.*): Obviously the radar techniques you've been looking at have been to find large-scale voids. What about for stalls on bridge decks?

We're dealing with a 16th, a 32nd of an inch as far as a detection phase. Have you done any work with that?

O. Tranbarger: The present FM-CW system may be used to scan bridge decks with good results; however, there are resolution problems in detecting voids, cracks, or delaminations as small as 1/16th or 1/32nd of an inch because of the limited sweep bandwidth. To fully resolve structural defects this small would require a very wide sweep bandwidth that is not practical in present FM-CW or pulse radar systems; furthermore, microwave frequencies contained in such a wide sweep bandwidth do not propagate effectively in bridge decks. However, small defects below the theoretical resolution limits of the system may still be detected in some cases as an anomaly in the receiver display. This was true for the floor tests at the Coney Island barn. Also, some of the data presented on the concrete slab imply that a bistatic antenna arrangement may enhance void detection below the resolution limits of the system by altering the geometry of reflected path lengths.

T. R. Cantor (*Port Authority of New York and New Jersey, New York, N.Y.*): Would you think that the next phase of radar development is to develop a library of traces so that then you could computerize and identify the defect?

O. Tranbarger: Yes. The goal of this project is to ultimately develop a rapid-scan surveying system that is capable of collecting and processing data. A data base will be established once equipment is implemented to collect and store the test results. In this process, each point surveyed in the tunnels must be identified in location. Point-by-point comparisons may then be made with data collected in an ongoing surveying program. This will be an effective way of monitoring and evaluating deteriorating processes that may be affecting the structures.

Our Water Infrastructure

Luncheon Address

S. RUSSELL STEARNS[a]

Office of the President
American Society of Civil Engineers
345 East 47th Street
New York, New York 10017

It is a pleasure to represent the American Society of Civil Engineers here. We in the ASCE, the oldest national engineering society in the United States, welcome the opportunity to cooperate in this important conference on the infrastructure—a subject of vital concern, and a challenge, to our 91,000 members. The discussions here have included a wide array of important topics including: government policies and perspectives, financing, maintenance, education, research, technology, and innovative solutions. The committee is to be commended for organizing such a comprehensive conference.

This subject has received a great deal of attention in the national press this past year, and the "maintenance and rehabilitation of the infrastructure" was chosen by ASCE's past president John Wiedeman as the society's theme for 1982–83. I have continued this emphasis with specific concentration on the subject of "water resources." In addition to applying our resources to the solution of technical problems, it is our goal to bring to the public's attention the seriousness of the situation, particularly as it affects future generations. This past year members of ASCE have testified in federal, state, and local hearings on infrastructure needs. Also, we placed a full-page ad in the *Washington Post* about the 5-cent gas tax at the time of the United States Senate debate, and recently placed ads in the *New York Times* and New Jersey's *Star Ledger* in regard to the New York and New Jersey Infrastructure Bond Referenda.

We all know the details of the infrastructure condition in our own regions, and generally in the other parts of the United States, from press and television reports. Papers in this conference have discussed these conditions and suggested remedial solutions: technical, financial, legislative. But I wish to emphasize that, in the words of the Los Angeles section of the ASCE, the term "infrastructure" includes "the whole interwoven network of highways, streets, railroads, drainage, underground facilities, water supply, flood control, sewage and waste disposal systems, and public buildings." These are the lifeline facilities and services on which modern civilization depends for its continuing existence.

The question has been raised, Is there really an immediate crisis? Because

[a]Address correspondence to Thayer School of Engineering, Dartmouth College, Hanover, N.H. 03755.

of a new public awareness, because of the impressive progress in New York
City since 1978 as documented yesterday by Mayor Koch, because of the 5-
cent gas tax increase (the first since 1958), and because of local bond issues
and projects, perhaps the answer is no—for the immediate future.

But the problem seems to be more acute for our water-related infrastructure. In fact, our nation's water resources picture as a whole may well be
reaching a "crisis" stage.

Older water systems are in a critical state due to age and lack of maintenance. Breaks occur in New York City water mains every week (remember
last summer's garment district water main break and the break that occurred
just yesterday).

The dubious condition of the city's two water supply tunnels, steady
leakage from old pipes, not just in New York but in every major Northeastern
city as well as in others around the nation, and the intrusion of wastes, salt,
chemicals, and other dangerous substances into soil surface and groundwater
supplies all point to a growing crisis. In many areas of the country, depletion
of major aquifers due to well drawdown for industry and especially for
irrigation—a huge percentage of the nation's water is used in agriculture—
combined with rapidly growing demand in low-rainfall areas of the West and
Southwest, also points to a growing crisis in water.

In addition, a number of governmental reports indicate a growing water
resource shortage, if not a crisis. For example, the Congressional Budget Office reported in April 1983 that inadequate sewer pipes and sewage treatment,
as well as insufficient system capacity to handle storm runoff, characterize
many of the nation's 1500 wastewater treatment systems.

It is this life-supporting part of the infrastructure that I wish to discuss
with you today. The "ASCE national water policy" advocates, and I quote,
"that water, a natural and all important resource of the Nation and its people,
be wisely and effectively conserved, protected, controlled, and used to the
end that optimum benefits may accrue to all." The policy also points out that
"the role of the civil engineer in water resources management is to provide
the leadership, technical knowledge, skill and creative judgment required in
the planning processes and for execution of the implementing works."

America has been blessed with adequate sources of water and the facilities to transport it to where it is needed. Water is the nations's most boun-
tiful resource; trillions of gallons are stored in reservoirs and lakes; subsurface aquifers hold trillions more. The reservoirs, distribution systems, and
treatment plants built by America's civil engineers in the latter half of the
nineteenth and early twentieth centuries assured supplies of clean drinking
water for most urban Americans—supplies that are unknown in many parts
of the world.

Our nineteenth and twentieth century engineers were almost too successful.
Modern Americans have forgotten that as recently as the end of the nineteenth century, mortality rates from waterborne diseases in the United States
were very high. Typhoid and cholera remain a scourge for the majority of
the world's population. But in the United States, we have been conditioned
not only to believe that pure water is plentiful, but that it is virtually free.

We take unlimited supplies of clean water and our water, sewer, and storm drainage systems for granted.

We water our lawns, fill our swimming pools, wash our cars, and leave faucets running with little thought of where all the water is coming from. Not all parts of the country receive their water directly from the sky; yesterday's tunnels, canals, and other water distribution systems transport it to irrigate farmland and to supply urban and industrial consumers. But now the condition of these systems, particularly the older water mains and sewer pipes in the northeastern cities, has deteriorated seriously and major leaking is occurring. To keep the costs of operating and maintaining the water and sewage systems minimal, we have postponed maintenance.

In the West, we are depleting the subsurface aquifers that supply our farms and cities there. Pollutants of various types—fertilizer, salt—have intruded on groundwater supplies. Land subsidence is also a problem, due to years of pumping water from the ground.

Unfortunately, we are starting to learn the value of water the hard way. We are beginning to learn that water is not unlimited; like any other valuable resource, it must be managed and protected. It cannot be given to industry and agriculture—not even to us, ourselves—at ridiculously low cost. Government subsidies and the use of general tax funds have made this appear to be possible—until now.

What should be done to prevent further deterioration of water supply and wastewater treatment systems, and to bring them up to par to meet growing demand and resist contamination? Do we have the necessary technology and construction management to provide a long-term solution? Where will the necessary funds come from?

The answers to these questions will come from an interdisciplinary attack involving scientists, civil engineers, economists, educators, business managers, government officials, and legislators at all levels. A team effort will be needed.

First, more manpower will be required. Bright, capable young people must be attracted into educational programs, especially civil engineering. These programs will prepare them for management of public facilities, public and governmental service, and positions of leadership in their profession and community.

Most required technology is already available. However, it will be necessary in each case to decide whether to repair or replace. Local conditions, costs, and resulting performance will govern. Inventories of performance, cost, and condition must be established with a timetable for projects.

Support must be provided for research into the causes of deterioration, and means of preventing it, including new materials and designs; research on methods to determine benefits and costs of repair or replacement; research on how to establish priorities for selection of projects, and research on financing mechanisms and the proper federal role in the rehabilitation of the nation's infrastructure.

As always, the bottom line is funding. Professor Brian Quinn of Dartmouth's Tuck School of Business Administration places the cost of necessary water and sewage system construction at $10 billion per year for 20 years, and growing at 6.5% per year. The United States Environmental Protection Agency says that by the year 2000, $118 billion will be needed to bring the country's sewerage systems up to standards. The Associated General Contractors estimates about $140 billion for water supply facilities and $510 billion for wastewater treatment, just to put them back in shape. To this must be added the cost of cleanup of lakes, rivers, aquifers, and leaching solid waste and chemical deposits. Much has been said and written on this subject, in this conference and previously. It is clear that, with present policies continuing, the amount of federal participation will continue to decrease, but not disappear. The federal gas tax, and the proposed water resources bill with its loan provisions and local participation are examples of continuing federal assistance. A national infrastructure corporation or bank, capital planning and budgeting, low-interest loans, block grants, revenue bonds, and taxation have all been noted.

One general conclusion is that the user who benefits will have to pay the lion's share, one way or another. In the case of water, excluding irrigation where the farmer pays almost nothing, the American consumer pays anywhere from 50 cents to $1.50 per 1000 gallons. We use the expression "dirt cheap," but a load of topsoil, delivered, would cost about 100 times an equal volume of water at the faucet. I said previously that we Americans take water for granted. Well, the user price must go up if the water infrastructure is to be put back in shape, and maintained that way. Though higher user fees will cut down on consumption and help conserve water, even this will not be enough to protect supply. We will also have to promote conservation aggressively to maintain water resources for the use of future generations.

Dr. Robert White, president of the National Academy of Engineering, said at the ASCE National Convention in Houston last October, "The United States has entered a new age of environmental realism and civil engineers must face up to and accept the challenge." We do accept this challenge of leadership with optimism for the future. Through cooperation between government officials, professionals, industry, academia, and the engineering societies, the research, technology, management, and financing so necessary to put the infrastructure back in shape will be obtained. The civil engineering profession stands ready to share in the reconstruction of the nation's infrastructure.

Highlights of the East River Bridge Rehabilitation Program

GEORGE ZAIMES

Office of the Director of Engineering
Department of Transportation
The State of New York
Two World Trade Center, Room 5454
New York, New York 10047

Engineering history was made on May 24, 1883 when the Brooklyn Bridge was opened to traffic in New York City—100 years ago!

I will share with you here some highlights of our equally "historic adventure" now under way in restoring, strengthening, and revitalizing the magnificent structures spanning the East River: the Queensboro, Williamsburg, Manhattan, and Brooklyn bridges!

There are 2013 bridges in New York City. In 1977 (only six years ago), the New York State and New York City Departments of Transportation mutually pledged to join forces in a gallant and much-needed program to inspect, rate, prioritize, and rehabilitate all of these bridges in New York City.

This talk will cover only four of the 2013 bridges. But they are the most magnificent, historic, and challenging of the lot. The oldest of these bridges, the Brooklyn Bridge, is nearing its centennial celebration. The youngest—the Manhattan Bridge—is now in its 73rd year of service.

They have all served us well— and have withstood tremendous traffic burdens, windstorms, snowstorms, drenching applications of salt, scorching sun, and pigeons for all these years without complaint. They have suffered and need our help—they are showing their age.

The Queensboro Bridge was under the general design supervision of Gustav Lindenthal, and was opened to traffic in early 1909. This 74-year-old bridge is a unique and historic structure crossing the East River at Fifty-Ninth Street in Manhattan, and connecting with Queens Boulevard, Thompson Avenue, and Bridge Plaza South in Queens.

The bridge is an unsymmetric cantilever truss structure spanning 1180 feet over the west channel and 985 feet over the east channel of the East River. The cantilever ends are connected by shear links which render the bridge a "continuous structure."

The Queensboro Bridge—the most massive structure of the four East River crossings—is 7600 feet long with the approaches, and an additional 5400 feet long with the ramp connections. Its 11 lanes carry 150,000 cars daily, 7 lanes in the lower roadway and 4 lanes in the upper roadway. Tension eyebars on the bridge are of nickel steel, and the remainder is carbon steel. Dye-penetrant testing and close examination of the eyebars found no cracks. Considerable corrosion between eyebars had caused pitting. This does not at this time affect the structural integrity of the eyebars.

The shear link pins, however, were found to be badly worn, and the holes receiving the pins were enlarged and elliptical from movement. They are now being replaced and adjusted.

The I-beam-lock concrete-filled deck of the main spans was in relatively good condition, but the reinforced concrete deck approaches were riddled with potholes. This concrete deck — only 26 years old — had chloride contents as high as 20 lbs. per cubic foot.

Drainage on this bridge as well as the other three East River bridges and most bridges built more than 10 years ago was clogged and poorly designed. The uncontrolled leaking of water contaminated by deicing salts through the deck and joints is literally eating the steel away throughout the structure. Debris buildup on the flanges and connecting angles acts as a corrosive blotter. Deferred maintenance on drainage cleaning and painting has taken years of life away from this bridge.

We have now scheduled eight rehabilitation contracts to update the structural integrity of the Queensboro Bridge for a total of $152.4 million spread out over a period of 15 years. The first two contracts are already under way with the third being let this spring. The last contract will be let in 1994. The biggest headache on this bridge is maintenance and protection of traffic during rehabilitation! There is very little room to put 150,000 cars a day when you are demolishing two lanes and you have the Commissioner of Traffic Operations on one leg of the bridge! The firm of Steinman, Boynton, Gronquist and Birdsall is designing the rehabilitation of the Queensboro Bridge.

The Williamsburg Bridge was designed under the general supervision of Leffert L. Buck and Gustav Lindenthal, and was opened to traffic on December 19, 1903. The structure is a four-cable suspension bridge with separately supported side spans. The total length of the bridge is 7308 feet with a main span of 1600 feet and 135-foot clear height above mean high water. The bridge presently carries two inner and two outer roadways in each direction for a total of eight travel lanes, two sets of railroad tracks, BMT subway, and one footwalk on an upper level above the north roadway.

The general problems of poor drainage and corroding steel similar to those of the Queensboro Bridge also plague this bridge. But the big problem with the Williamsburg Bridge is the cable system. The main cables are made up of 7696 no. 6 gauge ungalvanized "bright steel wires" coated with a "hydrocarbon compound mixed with graphite." Cable samples were taken throughout the structure. In almost every sample, the cable was found to be uniformly rusted — not just on the exterior wires, but six to eight inches into the core. Cleaning and testing of these wire samples indicated a significant loss of metal and cross section to a point where the factor of safety (FS) is now approximately 2.2, from an original FS of 4.0. Loss of ductility has also been detected.

The research firm of SRI (Stanford Research Institute of Sacramento, Calif.) was engaged to support the staff of our general consultant, Amman and Whitney, in conjunction with the American Bridge Company. We are now experimenting with encapsulating cables and injecting a vapor rust inhibitor to maintain the cables in their present condition.

Another problem with the cable system is the poor condition of the suspender ropes and connections. Significant rusting was found in clamp and truss connections; but even more serious, the suspender wire ropes have been found to be approaching a "brittle" condition. Cable research is now under way, and the replacement of one-third of the suspender ropes is on a crash course.

The total estimated cost to rehabilitate the Williamsburg Bridge is now at $109.5 million, and that assumes that we can successfully rehabilitate the main cables. If we eventually have to replace them, the total cost will go over $200 million for this structure. The consultant firm of Ammann and Whitney is designing this project.

The Manhattan Bridge was designed by Leon Moisieff, and was opened to traffic in 1909. The bridge connects Canal Street, Manhattan, to Flatbush Avenue, Brooklyn. The bridge has four main cables, each supporting a stiffening truss. The suspended center span is 1470 feet, and there are two suspended side spans of 725 feet each for a total of 2920 feet between abutments. With approach spans, the total length of this bridge is 6200 feet.

The major problem with this bridge is excessive torsional deflections. This was recognized soon after the bridge was opened, but the situation worsened as a four-track subway system grew into larger, heavier trains, and at more frequent loading. Such eccentric loading is resulting in torsional deflections of four foot magnitude, which produce fatigue stresses and secondary stress throughout the structure in excess of the original design parameters.

Findings during our inspection in 1979 were unexpected and serious. Floor beams and stringers of the upper roadways installed new in 1962 (making them 17 years old) were found to be cracked in a widespread pattern. Cracked steel members were clustered near anchorages, towers, and the center span.

Emergency-type repairs were executed, and an intensified analytic investigation was launched developing a three-dimensional computer model to fully analyze the distribution of stress and stress reversals during the deflection cycles. The following are some examples of the emergency repairs already in place:

1. At the upper floor beams, hundreds of failures of connecting angles were rectified by floor beam stiffening and construction of bearing support brackets under the floor beams.
2. At the towers, vertical link hanger cracks and separations necessitated temporary construction of a bearing grillage under the truss for vertical support until new hangers can be designed and installed.
3. Worn-out sole plates from upper strings have been replaced by Neoprene "elastmeric" bearings.
4. Rapidly expanding cracks in the webs of track floor beams were quickly addressed by drilling holes at the leading of a crack and then placing ¾-inch steel sandwich plates on both sides of the web secured with high-strength belts.

We have arrived at a recommended stiffening system, and that is the forming of two torque tubes in the plane of the truss connected by strengthened floor beams at the lower level. The torque tubes are formed by stiffening some of the truss members and primarily by the addition of new diagonal bracing to reduce deformation of the rectangular truss shape during torsional stress. New strengthened floor beams tie the torque tubes in place.

A 72-foot section of test panel was installed at the most critical area on the bridge, and strain gauge instrumentation was installed on the test panel; this confirmed computer model analysis.

The Manhattan Bridge design is being handled by Edwards and Kelcey, with Weidlinger Associates being the major subcontractor doing the computer model and the stiffening scheme recommendations. Steinman, Boynton, Gronquist and Birdsall is assisting in the cable restoration design and stiffening scheme.

The total rehabilitation cost for the Manhattan Bridge is $93.1 million (including the stiffening described). The bulk of the work can be done during nonpeak travel hours and at night with stiffening diagonals placed in the early stages, and floor beam and deck replacement as the final contract. We have scheduled all work to be completed by the end of 1994.

The Brooklyn Bridge, designed by John Augustus Roebling, was opened to traffic on May 25, 1883. The main structure is a suspension bridge with a center span of 1595.5 feet and two equal side spans of 933 feet each. The use of this bridge went through several transformations, but it is now a six-lane structure with a raised middle pedestrian promenade.

The Brooklyn Bridge is surprisingly sound for its age. The masonry and mortar joints need little work. The main cables, except for the anchorage, are clean and as good as the day that they were installed. There is obviously need to rehabilitate some steel and the concrete approaches.

Some minor structural repairs were executed early on the Brooklyn Bridge because they were easy to design and implement, and would serve to "dress up" the bridge for its 100th birthday.

Bulkhead protection at the Brooklyn tower had collapsed and was threatening the erosion of the tower foundation. A new steel cofferdam was installed, and a new bulkhead and platform were constructed over it for a more permanent and pleasing protection to the Brooklyn tower.

The timber deck promenade had been replaced many times—but the steel supports were ready for rehabilitation and the timber deck needed a face-lift for the centennial celebration, which was expected to bring a pedestrian traffic count similar to that experienced during the city transit strikes—the pedestrian count then topped 5000 per day.

A temporary overhead promenade was constructed prior to permanent rehabilitation of the existing deck to accommodate the constant flow of pedestrian and bicycle traffic on this bridge during that repair project.

The most pressing structural needs of the Brooklyn Bridge are the rebuilding of the rusted cable at the anchorage and the replacement of the suspender ropes and diagonal stay wires, primarily because of the socket corrosion and the original type of construction.

Let us look at the Brooklyn Bridge anchorage. The main cable at the splay band branches out into 19-eyebar anchorages; the bottom rows have been covered with concrete and debris. It is also impossible to examine and make repairs of the broken wires in the confined area.

Columbia University research developed a splay clamp design that was successfully tested and jacked to simulate the total tension in a splay wire grouping. A current project will install the splay clamp and jack toward the eyebar assembly until all tension is relieved in the corroded portion of the splay wire. It will then be carefully opened up at the eyebar shoe and examined. If needed (and we believe that it will be), we will cut the entire splay wire group, clean up the anchorage, install new cable, and socket a complete new fitting which was designed and tested by Columbia University. The new coupling socket will have mechanical bonding and then be solidified by pouring in molten zinc at 700°F.

The original sockets for suspender and diagonal stays are also rusted. Steel wedges driven into original sockets have rusted out. In addition the socketing material was lead, which did not properly fill or seal the sockets. The suspender and diagonal stay work is scheduled for 1985 at a cost of $40.0 million.

In all, we estimate the rehabilitation of the Brooklyn Bridge to cost $111.8 million with all work now fully identified and scheduled for completion by the end of 1995.

The design of the Brooklyn Bridge is being performed by the firm of Steinman, Boynton, Gronquist and Birdsall.

Clearly, you can see that a new technology is emerging with these bridges, and it's called bridge geriatrics. As you may know, working in geriatrics requires tender loving care, a good case history, a complete physical examination, and much innovative and creative thinking—much like, if not more than, what went into the original design. There were few design manuals then, and not many to cover the renovation requirements of today.

Let us examine some of the traits of the original designers. John Augustus Roebling has been described not only as a brilliant engineer, but also as a "visionary," a "spiritualist," a metaphysician, an inventor, and a businessman. Surely such traits were needed to design and create the historic monuments of steel that span the East River.

In order to keep these old timers standing and functioning into the next 100 years, we will require all of the traits and blessings listed for John Roebling plus metallurgist, chemist, traffic engineer, historian, environmentalist, tightrope walker, financier, and politician!

I salute the engineering profession, for I know that we are up to the task ahead, and that *we* are at the forefront of rebuilding America—a task so desperately needed.

DISCUSSION OF THE PAPER

T. R. CANTOR (*Port Authority of New York and New Jersey, New York, N.Y.*): Could you expand on the magnetic detector for detecting broken wires in the main cables?

G. ZAIMES: I really can't expand on it. There are two scientists that now work for Brookhaven Laboratory, and when Project "Isabelle" was slowed down, they approached our consultant and offered their services. They are now developing a magnetic wire discontinuity detector. I can describe it as being about four feet long and it has two longitudinal sectional parts that have been made to fit over the main cable. A very low electric current is fed into the detector, and by moving this device along the cable itself, you can detect breaks in the cable wire by discrepancies of electromagnetic flow within the wires themselves. The scientists feel very confident that it can be developed. They are now putting it together. We will have it available certainly for the state of New York, and once it is available to us it will be available to the engineering community. We hope to have this magnetic detector operational by the end of the year.

F. E. MATUSKY (*LMS Engineers, Pearl River, N.Y.*): Can you tell us anything about the metallurgy of the cables and of the major bars that are in these bridges? They are some 100 to 75 years old, and there's been lots of vibration and exposure. What has been found regarding metallurgical condition, such as crystalline cracking problems, things of this sort?

G. ZAIMES: We're still doing a lot of research on that subject and probably the critical elements are the "eye" bar tension members of the Queensboro Bridge. I mentioned that they were constructed from nickel steel and that we were very much concerned with the eyebars, a lot of the other members, and certainly the rolled section and some of the steel sections of the Brooklyn Bridge are over 100 years old. There is now real concern that there may be built-in stresses just from the rolling before any loads were even applied, and we are now proposing a testing program utilizing blind-hole drilling. I think I mentioned it; it's a technique that was developed by a Canadian firm and has been proved to work, permitting you to establish critical points throughout the structure. Strain gauge rosettes are applied to the metal in question, at assumed areas of stress; they are wired into a computer and very slowly you drill right through the strain gauge rosette removing about an eighth of an inch of metal. Once that's done, the surface stress will relieve itself, actually record itself, and you'll get a good measure of the built-in stresses, the dead load stresses, and also the applied stresses to that structure. We would actually get a great handle on what is happening. We are moving ahead primarily on the Brooklyn Bridge and the Queensboro doing that specific research.

As far as the general metallurgy, we've taken some coupons from all of the bridges and we've analyzed those and primarily found A-13 type steel. While these days we have refined our steel specifications, the standards of providing structural steel 60–100 years ago were still adequate; and thank God, our old designers used a fairly thick brush when they computed their designs, they didn't use the fine pencil points that we do today. So that old designs were still on a conservative basis, but that's to our benefit today.

H. TAFAGHODI (*PITS International Technology Corp., New York, N.Y.*): Was there anything done about the substructure of these bridges?

G. ZAIMES: Well certainly all I hit was highlights today. If we were to go through a complete, in depth inspection of each of these bridges we would be here until next week. We did an underwater inspection of all of those foundations in water, we actually took borings throughout. Most of the old bridges, we found, were in excellent condition and the Brooklyn Bridge foundation which is on a rock caisson was found to be undisturbed. We built some protective steel sheeting around it to further preserve it. We found some cracks in the foundation of the Williamsburg Bridge and that is now being repaired in a current program. But we found no serious problems with any of the foundations of any of these four bridges.

UNIDENTIFIED SPEAKER: The preceding speaker spent some time on the overall dollar cost of the program and the length of the program. I wonder if you have some overall figures on what the rehabilitation of these four bridges will cost and who is going to pay?

G. ZAIMES: Without getting into precise numbers, the rehabilitation as we see it now for all four of these bridges will run somewhere around $450 million, and the reason we have the work spaced over 15 years is so that we can do it in pieces; there's no way that we could rehabilitate one bridge in total. It would be impossible to take all the traffic that's on any one bridge now at 110,000 cars and say, "Good-by, find another way to cross the East River." So we're doing it in pieces, but we're doing it in priority need and we're doing it so it can be easily funded. Even before the bond issue, even before the five-cents-a-gallon tax, we had clearly worked out a strategy where we would make application for discretionary bridge rehabilitation funds to do these four bridges and that application would be somewhere in the tune of $30 to $40 million per year—we are still on that schedule. The federal government has accepted all of our applications, and as you can see we're moving right along with that program. So the funding is in place. The only "kicker" would be if our research and development on the cable of the Williamsburg Bridge proves to be faulty and we cannot rehabilitate that cable; then I'm looking for another $100 million. That again can be found in the time frame that we have.

E. J. FASULLO (*Port Authority of New York and New Jersey, New York, N.Y.*): Have you considered the reduction of dead load as a way of increasing your load factors on the basic structural elements? I mean the dead load is probably I would guess 80% of the total load these bridges carry. Have you considered or evaluated the use of aluminum in some exotic form so that you could replace the deck with a much lighter system, thereby increasing the carrying capacity, or reducing the actual stresses in the cable, or increasing the load factor, depending how you want to look at it?

G. ZAIMES: An attempt has been made to go along those lines and it's very difficult indeed. The Queensboro Bridge probably is one of the most critical because it is the most massive bridge. There we have removed certain elements of the bridge that were up there initially but are no longer needed. In replacing some of the heavy fascias, we put back steel shape half-section barriers rather than concrete barriers. We're utilizing the I-beam lock deck device, which I think is a little lighter than full depth concrete decks, and we're putting the I-beam lock decks wherever we can.

It's very difficult to a take weight off of these structures, basically because we're doing a rehabilitation rather than bridge replacement. But certainly your point is well taken and is kept in mind in all cases — whenever we can use a lighter structural element or a structural section, we do that. We have not been too successful though. Utilizing aluminum and other exotics may very well give us a problem in the maintenance end. Clearly maintenance, not only on these bridges, but on all the 2013 bridges in New York City, has been a problem. We are designing for zero maintenance, and anything I do, anything that we design, has got to be with that primary in mind rather than reducing weight.

J. ROWEN (*State Capitol, Albany, N.Y.*): Is it desirable or feasible to go to some toll-generated financing for funding part of this rehabilitation program that you're going to have to do?

G. ZAIMES: For a long time, the city of New York has gone through an evaluation of considering tolling, and it's a matter of an annual study that they continually review this possibility. If tolls are imposed, our studies have indicated that we indeed would develop long queues at the toll booth, the toll booths themselves would occupy a tremendous amount of right of way, the air pollution at the toll booths would be a problem, and we would generate tremendous additional congestion. And if we did impose a toll, we would certainly lose the federal participation that we're getting now. I don't believe it is an advantage to the city. At any rate, the city did decide several years ago not to pursue the tolling of these bridges and to keep them free, and with that we have had to go through a whole clean air process and redefine our clean air application to the Environmental Protection Agency. So the city's policy right now is to continue to review the possibility of tolling, but certainly pursue a toll-free East River bridge policy.

Development and Use
of a Geographical Data Base
for Houston, Texas

CHARLES H. DRINNAN

Synercom Technology, Inc.
10405 Corporate Drive
Sugar Land, Texas 77478

INTRODUCTION

In the fall of 1978, the Houston City Council approved the development of a mapping information management system called METROCOM (metropolitan common data base) under the direction of Public Works. Later in the fall, the City Council authorized the city's tax department to maintain a permanent digital record of the cadastral data in the METROCOM data base. The record would include results of a complete reappraisal of all exempt and nonexempt property that was then being conducted within the territorial limits of the city of Houston and the Houston Independent School District. After three years, the result is an immediately accessible, complete digital map and attribute data base including planimetric, facility management, and mutlipurpose cadastral data for more than 550,000 parcels and 575 square miles. The system is used as a source of detailed planimetric maps; a repository of cadastral information including not only property lines and dimensions but also attribute information about each parcel centroid; a facilities management system for Public Works facilities and a small city-owned gas company; and city planning.

METROCOM is the latest stage in the development of accurate mapping for the city which has been ongoing for over 16 years. Most of the development of the computerized mapping and the management of the stages prior to computerization were done by one of the city's private consulting firms, Turner Collie and Braden (TCB). The computer system utilized for METROCOM is the INFORMAP™ software developed by Synercom™ and implemented on PDP 11/70®s with Synercom-provided graphics work stations.

The first part of this paper reviews the development of the METROCOM data base and relates it to the source material developed over the years before automation. The remainder of the paper describes the unique features required of a mapping information management system (MIMS) to support an effort this size.

The resulting data base is, in the author's knowledge, the largest of its kind in the municipal arena. Other cities have developed multipurpose computerized data bases, and several joint-use (multiple corporate and municipal entities sharing the cost) data bases have been attempted. One of the most successful joint-use projects is BJUMP in the corporation of Burnaby, British Columbia.[1] All of the cities larger than Houston in the United States have an automated mapping project of some kind under development. However, the scope of these projects is either less than the city of Houston's or considerably less progress has been made. Systems that have completed the conversion of a significant portion of a multipurpose mapping system and distributed the results are smaller, usually less than 100,000 parcels.

The INFORMAP system selected by the city of Houston offers unique advantages to facilitate the capture and maintenance of a large mapping information management data base. The geographically organized data structure provides functionally a continuous digital map of the entire city. The user perceives that he has a single map of the entire area, with the scale and content he requires for his application. The INFORMAP software accomplishes this at essentially no loss in speed of access. The representation of an element in the data base is determined by the user at the time he makes a display or plot. This is done by defining representational tables external to the data base. By changing display modes with a single command, the user may change the representation of the entire continuous digital map without changing a single element in the data base. This has obvious application in a multipurpose mapping system. However, since the representation of the data is not stored in the data base (as well as other overhead items which have been removed by careful design of the system), the disk storage required to store the data base has been minimized. This produces a manageable data base size even for the extensive content and area represented by METROCOM. Systems not designed to minimize storage often require 8–10 times more disk space.

A MIMS requires an integrated graphical and attribute data base so that the user can relate an element to more extensive attribute information than can ever be displayed on a map. The user perceives, for example, that a manhole has a representation, geographical location, and associated attribute information as a single entity. The alternative is the maintenance of a graphical data base and a separate data base (typically on cards) and all the problems inherent with dual data bases (missing data, misplaced data, partially updated data, longer access time, etc.). The user needs to be able to produce immediate reports for analyses such as comparative value studies, Public Works facility availability, and planning summaries.

Interface with the data base is important since most of the attribute information is more effectively entered in key-to-disk type systems than at a specialized mapping station. This means that the user should be able to bulk load data from disk or tape into the INFORMAP data base. The format and content of the data will not be known to the INFORMAP developer. Conversely, the INFORMAP data base is a rich source for analysis using other programs. Neither the programs nor the format and content of data required will be known to the INFORMAP designer or perhaps the data base administrator at the time the data base structure is determined. Thus the user must have a flexible and easily used interface with the data base. The INFORMAP programmers library of user subroutines (PLUS) provides an easy access via FORTRAN programs written by the user.

CITY OF HOUSTON MAPPING PROGRAM

In 1967, the city of Houston Public Works Department undertook a long-term mapping project. The city was divided into sections and planimetric maps of the detail shown in FIGURE 1. This figure is derived from the digital METROCOM data base. It is representative of the level of detail of the original map except that it does not include trees and contours which were not captured by METROCOM. The process included densification of monuments to approximately every 2000 feet.[2] The coordinates of these survey markers were computed from second-order, class II horizontal and vertical surveys using National Geodetic Survey procedures and specifications.[3] The area was then flown to produce 1 inch to 500 feet color aerial photographs using cartometric quality cameras. Using classical manual stereo compilation techniques, the planimetric maps at a scale of 1 inch to 100 feet were developed by scribing on an emulsion-faced mylar, forming a negative. Positive mylars were produced by photo techniques. Periodically the maps were revised using 1 inch to 1000 feet color photography. The resultant planimetric maps meet national horizontal map accuracy standards. Some of this work continued throughout the METROCOM project and is now being computerized using the direct stereo compilation capabilities available with the INFORMAP system. These maps formed the basis for the planimetric base of the METROCOM data base.

Concurrently, the tax department of the city, as required by law, maintained plat maps of each subdivision of the city. These are similar to FIGURE 2 in content. These and other sources, when deemed more reliable, were the basis for the cadastral segment of METROCOM.

Public Works maintained a variety of facility maps of varying accuracy, content, and scale. Over 40,000 sets of plans (usually at a large scale) and thousands of land development plats were accumulated by the time METROCOM began.

Pilot Study

In 1977, Public Works contracted for a study and pilot to determine the feasibility of automating the planimetric and Public Works facility management maps into a single multipurpose data base called METROCOM. After a thorough evaluation, TCB was selected to perform the study.[4] With the city's participation, the contractor did an extensive evaluation of available computer graphics mapping systems and selected the Synercom INFORMAP software and related hardware as the computer system foundation. TCB purchased a minimal system from Synercom and converted a mixed residential and com-

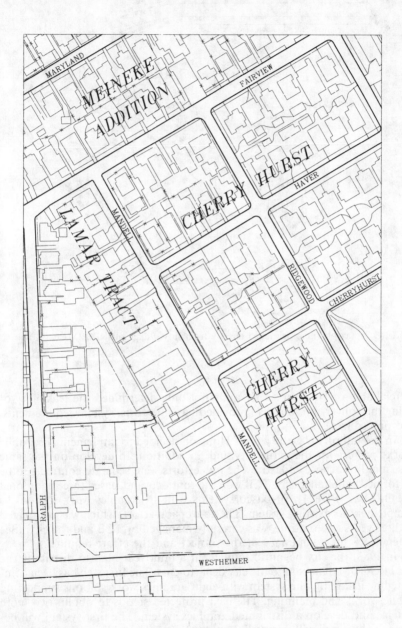

FIGURE 1. Planimetric map from METROCOM digital map series.

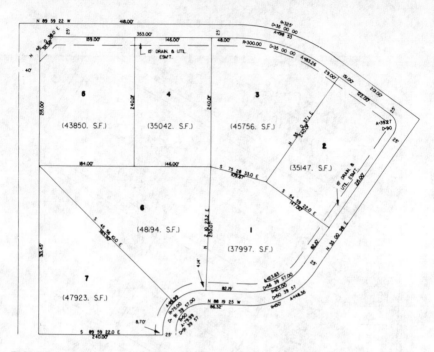

FIGURE 2. Tax plat map developed directly from survey data on INFORMAP.

mercial area of Houston. This study not only determined the feasibility of doing the conversion, but also provided baseline costs, system requirements, and procedures.

In the fall of 1978, the city of Houston decided to implement the Public Works project for the entire city and, in addition, to develop on the same base a multipurpose cadastre. The two efforts were separate contracts to be performed simultaneously. TCB won the contracts and leased three additional INFORMAP PDP 11/70–based systems with 16 graphics work stations to complement its existing system. The conversion effort, which was completed in three years and on time, was carefully managed by TCB and the city. (See Reference 5 for a summary of the project and the effort required.)

In 1983, the city began to implement a multiyear plan to distribute the METROCOM data base to the city departments. The first step has been completed by installing one system with eight graphics work stations supporting public works and planning. The next projected step is to obtain two more systems and develop a distributed graphics system. The first system will become the host and will retain all the shared data. The additional systems connected to the host via DECNET® will have the data that are particular to the applications they support. A further projected step is to upgrade the host to a VAX® and further distribute the system. The VAX will perform modeling and analysis of the Public Works facilities as well as data base management. New raster work stations will also be implemented.

METROCOM CONVERSION PARTICULARS

It is beyond the scope of this paper to describe the conversion procedures in detail; therefore, only an outline will be presented.

Most of the planimetric data were captured first using the 1 inch to 100 feet mylar base as a source. Direct digitizing was performed by laying the map on the digitizing table and occupying each point. Areas that were not previously mapped were stereo compiled. Data were organized into data types so that they could be rapidly selected to provide the different output content requirements. All maps were captured in the Texas state plane system, matched together, and rectified across the boundaries. The result was a geographically coordinated data base covering the entire city. Data captured included:

- Roadways.
- Railroads.
- Drainage.
- Sidewalks.
- Fences.
- Driveways.
- Parking lots.
- Buildings.
- Cultural features.
- Annotation.

The entire land base requires one 300 megabyte disk for 575 square miles.

In *Need for a Multipurpose Cadastre*,[6] the components of a multipurpose cadastre are defined as:

1. A reference frame consisting of a geodetic network.
2. A series of current, accurate, large-scale maps.
3. A cadastral overlay delineating all cadastral parcels.
4. A unique identifying number assigned to each parcel that is used as a common index of all land records in information systems.
5. A series of land data files, each including a parcel identifier for purposes of information retrieval and linking with information in other data files.

The METROCOM system meets all the requirements of a multipurpose cadastre, although the original impetus was to support a mass reappraisal rather than develop a multipurpose cadastre. The planimetric maps with the extensive existing monumentation provide the first two components. The remaining components were developed to support the reappraisal activity. The city was not producing a legal cadastre but did require accurate results.

Since the sources for cadastral data are varied, automated mapping users have taken many different approaches including:

1. Developing the maps from original deeds using precise coordinate geometry (COGO) survey commands.
2. Developing the maps from plats using precise COGO commands.
3. Fitting manually or digitally the plat maps to the planimetric base.

Using plat maps and deeds as a sole source of information is a tedious, time-consuming, and expensive process. Aerial photography on an accurate planimetric base is required to help identify errors and to localize the effect of small errors. The developer immediately encounters political and legal problems of what to do with significant discrepancies. For METROCOM, both the interpreted dimensions and the recorded dimensions are available in the data base for access when significant discrepancies occur. However for most applications, the recorded values are displayed.

TCB used the full capability of the INFORMAP software to develop the cadastral base. Where practical, they manually or digitally fitted the plat maps to the planimetric base. Coordinate geometry commands[7] and MACROS, sequences of INFORMAP commands stored in a file and accessed as a single command, were used to place regularly spaced lots. FIGURE 2 was developed entirely from coordinate geometry commands within INFORMAP. Alternatively a nonlinear transformation was used to digitize the property lines from existing maps. If these approaches were not practical, plat maps or original deeds were used in conjunction with coordinate geometry survey commands to enter the data.

The individual lots were not collected as polygons nor were the parcel attributes, associated with the lots, topologically encoded with the parcel lines. Instead an apparent parcel centroid was digitized, the state plane location used as a unique identifier, and the attribute data associated with the centroid. This is the most cost-effective approach. With the ability to use different symbology for the centroid based in an *ad hoc* fashion on the attribute parameters, the advantages of polygon data (i.e., cross-hatching based on attribute data) are essentially duplicated. FIGURE 3 represents symbolically the number of bedrooms for each centroid. This figure was developed after the data were digitized based on symbol modes and centroid attributes. With modern Geographic Information System capabilities (available with the INFORMAP software), topological polygons can be determined automatically from the existing parcel lines. Thus cost-effective capturing procedures may be utilized with all the benefits of capturing polygon data.

The attribute information includes:

- Land-use classification and neighborhood code.
- Tax account number.
- Names of all property owners and their percent interest.
- Service address of all parcels.
- Legal descriptions such as subdivision name, block, and lot number.
- Deeded and calculated acreage.
- Square footage of improvements.
- Date and price of last sale.
- Assessed value for land and improvements.

FIGURE 3. Number of bedrooms derived from parcel centroid data and symbolically represented.

- Reference to appraisal review history.
- Number and type of rooms (residential).
- Style and type of residence.
- Existence of carports, garages, swimming pools, easements.
- Type of foundation and exterior walls.
- Type of heating and cooling system.
- Roofing material.
- Commercial structures: frontage, location, and parking availability codes.
- Year constructed and/or remodeled.
- Reference to outstanding building permits.

The data were bulk loaded from data obtained by a local title company (Stewart Title) and from city-approved data provided by the city's contracted mass appraisal firm (Cole Layer and Trumble) based on keys stored as parcel centroid attributes.

For the Public Works facility data, more than 40,000 generally large-scale plan-profile and thousands of plat maps were the source of the data. (Street and bridge data were provided by the State Department of Highways and Public Transportation and bulk loaded into the METROCOM system.) Classifying these disparate data and geographically indexing the data were a major effort.

The INFORMAP software was used to support the indexing and classification. The GBF/DIME file for the city was loaded as a geographically orientated, digital map, and each facility map source was located on the map. An entry was made at the location including attributes indicating the location and identification of the source and the confidence level placed on the source. Using this index, the user could define a polygon enclosing the area to be converted and obtain a list of all the source maps required. These were then gathered by a clerk. Each selected source was then placed on the digitizer at a work station, the source referenced to the planimetric base using the nonlinear transformation, and the data digitized or entered using coordinate geometry. Confidence levels were associated with each facility item. Representative information for the facilities include:

- Manholes: various invert elevations, type of construction, size of manhole cover, utility serviced.
- Lines: flow elevations at each end, type of material, shape, size, status (proposed, existing, abandoned).
- Devices: number, type, size.
- Bridges: deck material, design load, reference number, length, width, number of spans, span material, span type, and vertical clearance.
- Roads: classification, curb status, number of lanes, agency responsible for maintenance, width, and type of pavement.
- All: date digitized, source document number, evaluator's confidence level.

FIGURE 4 is a wastewater engineering map from the same data base. The property lines are shown in place of the back of curb lines.

The INFORMAP software allows the user to incrementally develop the data base structure as the richness of the data base increases. The structure can be expanded without reallocating data storage or converting existing data. Thus the structure of the planimetric data was determined and a substantial part completely converted before the structure and content of the cadastral and facility data were determined.

MAPPING INFORMATION MANAGEMENT SYSTEMS

The result of the conversion effort is a very large (1.2 gigabyte) data base with many diverse users. The system, to manage and access the data base effectively, requires unique solutions designed specifically for mapping data bases. These systems are distinctly different from CAD/CAM/CAE systems and are broader than geographic information systems (GIS). (GIS systems are generally used to do thematic and polygonal analysis on small-scale maps.) The mapping data base industry is benefited by distinguishing these systems from CAD/CAM/CAE. Mapping information management systems describes the capability succinctly.

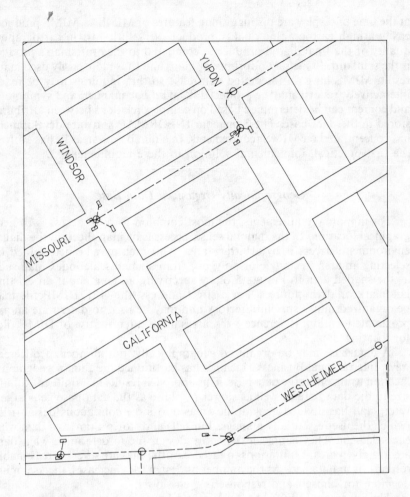

FIGURE 4. Wastewater engineering map.

A MIMS is a specialized system combining interactive graphics, entry, display, storage, and analysis techniques with a data base capability into a single integrated system. A MIMS is designed for mapping. It readily supports a continuous map over a large geographical area (easily a major city). Map sheets, or the equivalent design files organized by map sheet, are functionally gone. If the user wants to view the data across a boundary of a map or in the corner of a map with a MIMS, the user merely points at the desired area and the system determines how to retrieve the data. MIMS are not confined to a single scale of map but provide specialized techniques to support a range of different scales. User-selected content, symbology, and relative scale at the time of display are distinguishing features of MIMS. A MIMS produces easily a high cartographic quality product. Very little loss in cartographic quality of the final digital product as compared to the draftsman's product is the standard. In fact, a uniformity of maps and thus more easily used maps result. MIMS have an integrated data base so that inquiries may be made interactively, reports may be produced in an *ad hoc* manner, and symbology and content can be determined based on complex relations between attributes stored in the data base. The Synercom INFORMAP software development has concentrated on MIMS requirements. In a number of areas, it has evolved the first practical, implemental solution to these requirements.

Geographically Organized Data Base

For mapping requirements, the most common form of access is by geographical location. In the manual sense, access is by map sheet; in the digital environment, access is by arbitrary area. This area may be determined by selecting an area (rectangle or polygon) from a small-scale index map such as the shaded area in FIGURE 5 or by specifying an area about an existing landmark or street address. For a street address, the GBF/DIME file may be organized into a special directory and may be used to determine an approximate location. Reference 8 discusses more extensive use of DIME files for locating data.

A data base may be organized geographically in a number of different ways. International Business Machines has partitioned the data by geographic location using one large data base. This approach results in a finite maximum size to the data base as well as slower response as the data base gets larger. Intergraph has divided geographic areas into large contiguous design files (which the user essentially manages himself) and stores a range of data with each element. They can scan the entire design file to determine what data are in a given area. Limitations to the size of the files are severe if reasonable response is maintained. As the number of design files increases, the user must do more for himself and response is even slower.

The Synercom INFORMAP software divides the data base (both graphic and attribute) geographically into facets. Facets are rectangular areas of arbitrary user-determined size with algorithmically determined names. Thus, the system can determine automatically the facets that cover a desired geographic area. The data are further partitioned by types of data (property lines, sewer mains, manholes, etc.). The result is a collection of files (two for each data type) for each facet. For a large, dense area a lot of files result. However, they are well organized, handled effectively by the operating system, and offer distinct advantages in backup and security. The response is essentially independent of content and geographical extent over a much larger data base domain. The most popular theoretical approach is a "quad tree" approach, but the approach is not widely available in the commercial market. This approach could be considered a generalization and regularization of the facet approach.

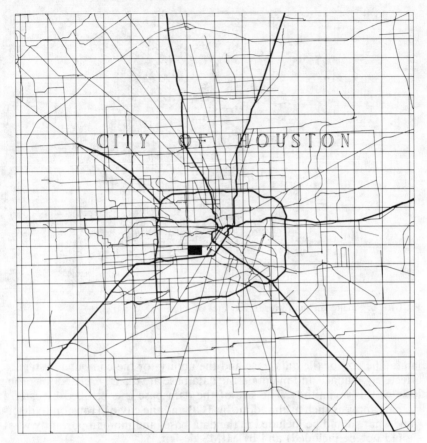

FIGURE 5. Index map of city of Houston.

The INFORMAP facetization approach realizes the concept of a continuous digital map. The continuous digital map is perceived by the user not as a collection of map sheets or files but as a single map. The shaded area indicated in FIGURE 5 may be immediately displayed as in FIGURE 6, with scale and content determined by the user at the time of display. A further window as indicated in FIGURE 6 may then be displayed as in FIGURES 4 and 7. Note that the level of content is entirely different because the application is different. The underlying facetization is immaterial to the user of the data. Facets are a physical data base structure, not a logical file access method.

Storage Techniques for Line and Symbol Representation

The number of entities in a data base the size of METROCOM is very

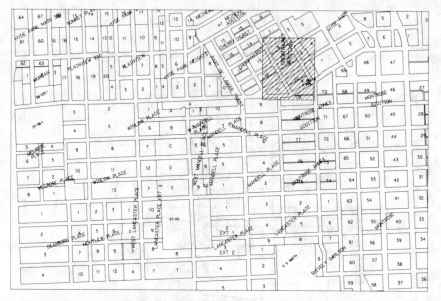

FIGURE 6. Small-scale map with further area of interest shaded.

large. The size of the data base and the ability for the computer system to effectively manage and maintain the data base are directly related for problems of this magnitude. The size of the data base is controlled by careful systems analysis such as that done by TCB and the city of Houston to determine what should be included in the data base (and more importantly what should not be included) and by MIMS design.

The MIMS must control the number of bytes used to represent each entity in the data base. Symbol, line, and annotation representation have been stored in the digital data base by either storing the individual strokes that make up the element directly in the data base ("stored stroke") or by storing representations of the symbology in tables and selecting the appropriate representation at the time of display ("table driven").

The advantages of the stored-stroke approach are improved display speeds (assuming that the increase in size of the data base does not reduce display speeds) and slightly more control since the user could change the symbology in special circumstances (i.e., remove strokes from the picture with possible loss in understanding). The disadvantages are the order of magnitude increase in disk storage required for the image and the inflexibility of producing different scale maps or different symbologies for different applications. FIGURE 8 provides examples of the line symbology required in a typical mapping application. The line examples in FIGURE 8 require 541 strokes to display or plot. Often, to produce different scales or symbology, different representations must be entered and stored in the data base, thus compounding the disk utiliza-

tion and maintenance problems. Additional care must be taken to maintain
the relationships between the various representations and the attribute data.

In the table-driven approach, a reference to a representational table is
stored in the data base and the representation is stored in a table. The representation can be changed for the whole map by changing the table. The representation may be easily changed to generalize the data for different scales and
purposes without changing the data base or adding to the data base size. The
lines in FIGURE 8 can be represented by 21 points. This is substantially less
than 541 strokes.

Disadvantages of the table-driven approach are a reduction of display

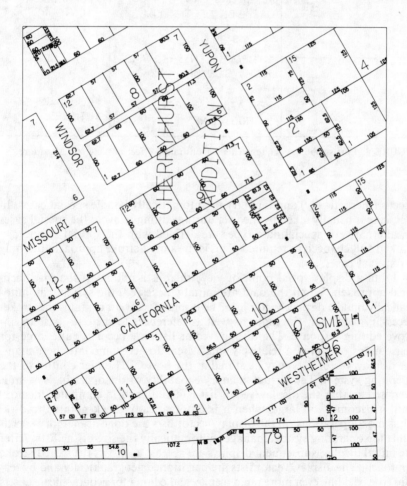

FIGURE 7. Land registry map.

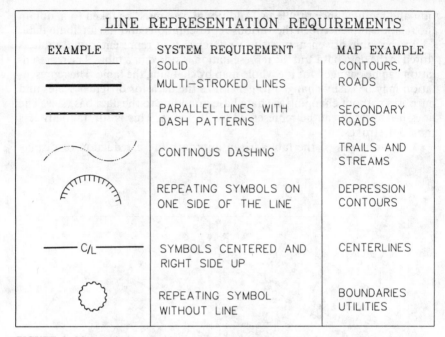

FIGURE 8. Line symbology requirements demonstrating effect of table representation.

speeds (theoretically) and inability to automatically handle special cases. In fact, care is usually taken by the user during editing to avoid the special cases or, alternatively, special data types are defined with the special symbology stroked and changed as required. This is the stored-stroke approach, but only for special cases.

From a display speed point of view, there is a middle-of-the-road technical approach. When the data are initially accessed, the system can automatically build a display/vector list. The display/vector list contains the strokes necessary to display the maps as well as references to the data base to improve editing response. The display/vector list may become quite large for dense maps over even a relatively small area. To accommodate these maps, the display/vector lists may be stored at the host CPU under control of the operating system. The virtual memory capability of the operating system is exercised so that the display/vector list is maintained in computer memory until it becomes too large, when it is automatically check pointed to disk. Thus most operations on the display/vector lists are done at memory speeds while the operating system manages automatically the size of the lists. After the initial display, subsequent displays are at least as fast as the stored-stroke approach. The display/vector lists are partitioned geographically and by feature type, yielding even more rapid display and editing for geographical subsets of the data. As the drawing is edited, the display, the display/vector list, and the data base are immediately updated. The table-driven display/vector list approach is unique to the Synercom INFORMAP software. The virtual display list technology has been implemented on the VAX-based raster graphic work station, GWS-III. The city of Houston is evaluating this technology for future implementation.

Multiuse Cadastral Data Base Representation Requirements

To support different uses from the same converted data base requires that maps at different scales, different content, and different symbolic representation be effectively supported. This is a distinguishing feature of MIMS systems. The table-driven approach allows the user, at the time the plot or display is produced, to select the relative scale as well as the representation of each symbol, line, and string of annotation. With the INFORMAP software, the user can even change the selection of attributes retrieved from the data base and displayed.

SUMMARY

The city of Houston has developed and is distributing a large multipurpose cadastral and facilities management data base. The INFORMAP system offers the unique data base structure and representational table approach that make the system feasible. Users may access the entire operating area as a continuous digital map with the appropriate scale and content.

REFERENCES

1. GARTH, S. L. 1977. Experience with computer-assisted mapping in Burnaby. *In* Proceedings of the Fifteenth Annual Conference of the Urban and Regional Information Systems Association. URISA. McLean, Va.
2. GALE, P. M. 1970. Control surveys for the city of Houston. Surveying and Mapping **30**(1): 95–101.
3. 1975. Federal Geodetic Control Committee Specification to Support Classification Standards of Accuracy and General Specifications of Geodetic Control Surveys. U.S. Department of Commerce. National Ocean Survey. Rockville, Md. (Reprinted 1977.)
4. STRANGE, K. B. & S. E. MANGUM, JR. 1980. Data management for a metroplex. *In* The Planning and Engineering Interface with a Modernized Land Data System: 202–214. American Society of Civil Engineers. New York, N.Y.
5. HANIGAN, F. L. 1983. METROCOM: Houston's interactive graphic municipal management system. *In* Proceedings of the Fourth Annual Conference of the National Computer Graphics Association: 359–369. NCGA. Fairfax, Va.
6. Committee on Geodesy, National Research Council. 1980. Need For a Multipurpose Cadastre. National Academy Press. Washington, D.C.
7. DRINNAN, C. H. 1981. Implementation of survey commands in an interactive graphics mapping system. Tech. Pap. Am. Congr. Surveying Mapping: 94–105.
8. BITKOWER, J. 1983. The geosupport system: geoprocessing in New York City. *In*

Proceedings of the Twenty-First Annual Conference of the Urban and Regional Information Systems Association: 313–322. URISA. McLean, Va.

DISCUSSION OF THE PAPER

M. KARAMOUZ (*Polytechnic Institute of New York, Brooklyn, N.Y.*): How can this data base be adapted to other cities?

C. H. DRINNAN: The data base structure, concepts, and procedures are applicable to any medium to large city. The specific user may modify the data base schema to fit the specific requirements. The INFORMAP system with a similar data base and similar purposes is being used by Oklahoma City, Vancouver, Salem, Bellevue, and others. The approach has been proven in the field. Differences in procedures occur because different users have different source maps, different budgets, and different schedules. The technological issues have been addressed successfully, and only issues of obtaining commitment to efforts of this size remain.

M. KARAMOUZ: Would they have to start from scratch, or can Houston's data bank be used as a guideline?

C. H. DRINNAN: They can start from scratch (i.e. from aerial photography, deed records, and/or survey) or from currently existing maps. The decision depends on the quality and accuracy of their current maps. Clearly the process of monumentation followed by stereo compilation and then followed by adding facilities and cadastral information is a slower, more expensive process, but it does lead to reliable accurate maps.

You know this technology is coming and it will be in use in every major city in the world. In fact every city larger than Houston in the United States has a system somewhat like this. The city of Houston's project is the most ambitious and the only one that has reached this level of accomplishment. However, all the major cities including New York are making progress.

P. L. RINALDI (*Port Authority of New York and New Jersey, New York, N.Y.*): I have two questions. First in looking at this system and based upon your experience with Houston, can you share with us the cost of putting such a system on line for a city like Houston? And second, can you give some examples about the Public Works Department and the engineers within that department. What kind of use have they made of this system to date and how has it helped them out?

C. H. DRINNAN: The cost for such a system varies with the amount of data you are capturing, the status of your current records, and other factors. The cost to the city of Houston was between $20 and $25 million. Generally for a little less comprehensive project, municipal data can be captured for $10 to $15 per parcel with a relatively high quality cartography and geographic accuracy. This is for a typical United States city, not necessarily New York City. New York has different problems relating to the density of facilities under the streets compared to parcels.

The primary usage is supporting construction and inventory work. Where are all the pipes installed between 1950 and 1960 that are cast iron, for example? Planning, tax equalization, and network analysis are other uses. For network analysis, the facility data base provides the model input and a medium for display of the results of the flow analysis.

New York
Metropolitan Transportation Authority
Infrastructure Program

JOHN M. KAISER

Engineering and Program Management Division
Metropolitan Transportation Authority
347 Madison Avenue
New York, New York 10017

INTRODUCTION

The development of the Metropolitan Transportation Capital Program for 1982 through 1986 began in the summer of 1980 when the chairman of the Metropolitan Transportation Authority asked the staff to prepare a full analysis and report on the status of MTA's capital plant. The result of this effort was the MTA's *Staff Report of Capital Revitalization for the 1980's and Beyond*, issued in the fall of 1980. The purpose of that report was to highlight the physical condition of the MTA systems and to determine the need for an expanded capital investment strategy for MTA and its agencies. Each of the physical components of the various systems was evaluated by analyzing its useful life and developing an optimum replacement schedule and the likely replacement cost. In aggregate, this analysis provided a 10-year program whose objective was to restore the various public transportation systems to a "state of good repair."

Based on the findings of the report, it was determined that the accomplishment of the recommended program would require some $14 billion in 1980 dollars. Of course, that would be a much larger sum in current dollars over the decade.

In addition to establishing the needs, MTA evaluated the funds available at the time and projected their probable continuing availability. Those funds consisted of the contributions from established sources: federal grants, matched periodically by state bond issues and small direct state appropriations, and a continuing level of contributions through the city of New York's capital budget. On a continuing basis, these sources were expected to provide, at best, some $300–$400 million per year, while the projected requirements on a continuing basis were well over $1 billion per year.

In order to close this gap, the chairman of the Metropolitan Transportation Authority proposed a series of new state and federal financing mechanisms that would add to the funds available for financing capital improvements to the infrastructure. Most importantly, these included bonding to be secured in three ways:

1. Through the expanded use of surplus revenues of the Triborough Bridge and Tunnel Authority.
2. Through a program of service contracts with the state of New York whereby state appropriations could be pledged to support bonds.
3. Through the use of MTA general or special operating revenues, fares and/or subsidies, to support MTA bonds.

MTA clearly understood that some of these mechanisms would have the impact of putting additional pressure on operating budget requirements in the future. Nevertheless, it was concluded that the historic undercapitalization of the systems had contributed to the deteriorating quality of service and that riders would be willing to pay more if they felt that such payments would contribute to improving the quality of service.

In retrospect, it was generally agreed that the capital needs of the transit commuter rail systems have been seriously underfunded since the earliest history of these systems. And, of course, the most serious consequence of undercapitalization is the deterioration of service. The policy of disinvestment led to the deplorable condition of the systems that many of us experience today.

In January of 1981, state legislation was introduced (at MTA's request) to expand the capital program of the Metropolitan Transportation Authority and its affiliated agencies. This bill not only provided new funding, but dealt also with the process by which capital projects are carried out. That process had become burdened with a multiplicity of required reviews and approvals for nearly every aspect of every capital program. At that time, most MTA contracts had 80% of their cost provided by the federal government. The balance of funds came from the state and, in the case of transit system projects, from the city of New York. Each of these funding entities has its own policies and procedures relating to approval of contracts. In many cases, these could only be dealt with one after the other, rather than simultaneously, and meeting them consumed much valuable time between the conception of a program and its implementation. In fact, so much time was being consumed that the original value of funds provided was seriously eroded by inflation.

The Transportation Systems Assistance and Financing Act of 1981, an extraordinary piece of New York State legislation, removed many of the approval steps required by statute and provided funds directly to the Metropolitan Transportation Authority, subject to audit by appropriate public bodies.

Of primary importance, that law provides MTA the ability to raise its own capital through the three financing approaches mentioned above. Taken together, these new funding sources are expected to generate more than $3.5 billion in bond funds over the next five years. Together with the continuing availability of city and federal funding, the MTA agencies have been able to undertake a capital program totaling more than $8.5 billion over a five-year period. This financing represents the largest single infusion of capital funds in our history. For the first time, it is possible to anticipate funding available for use over an extended period for an integrated high-priority capital-improvement program.

As MTA worked to secure passage of state legislation, it also began to work with representatives of the federal government toward improving the usefulness of the federal contributions by enhancing their purchasing power. Specifically, MTA proposed that private investors who wished to enter into sale-leaseback arrangements for any of MTA's capital assets be permitted to avail themselves of the investment tax credit. This would enable MTA to benefit from a tax advantage that would accrue to the private investor thus expanding the scope of the MTA program.

Additionally, MTA proposed that the Urban Mass Transportation Administration (UMTA) be authorized to commit by long-term contract a continuing level of funding through its Section 3 Capital Grant Program. Such long-term commitments could then be pledged to bondholders or to contractors. This would make possible substantially larger, early commitments for major purchases and projects.

Without the administration's active support for these proposals, we have been unable, as yet, to secure in full their adoption. However, Congress did enact a portion of MTA's tax proposal as part of the Economic Recovery Tax Act of 1981, thus opening new opportunities to marry, through a lease transaction, the proceeds of MTA's own borrowing with private capital to generate additional levels of resources for the program as a whole—a device used for years by airline and shipping companies.

MTA estimated that this process would yield savings in excess of 20% of the cost of rail cars and more than 10% of the cost of buses.

While this plan is defined in terms of funding that is now likely to be available, additional funding will continue to be sought from existing as well as new sources. The availability of such new funds would make it possible to achieve further progress toward fulfilling the aggregate needs of the system.

Let me now turn from the funding aspects to the substantive capital project elements of our five-year plan and our approach in developing the capital plan.

As primary source documents available to us in developing the five-year plan, we had the *Ten Year Revitalization Report* which listed all system needs and realistic estimates of the funds that we would receive over the next five years.

With these as inputs, we began the complex task of developing a specific, detailed five-year capital program of the highest-priority projects.

While this may seem a simple task, it was a relatively new process for the MTA, which had to that time been too seriously underfunded to be concerned with anything but the most critically needed emergency projects.

As a guide in evaluating capital projects, MTA developed what it calls a "capital value matrix." This was originally developed by the New York City Transit Authority (NYCTA) in order to augment an existing, informal project-selection process. The procedure has now been adapted, with some modifications, to meet similar needs in the commuter rail program.

The capital value matrix considers such factors as safety, reliability, security, maintainability, passenger comfort, economics/cost control, and public and employee concerns. A numerical value is assigned for each factor, including a weight for its relative importance. Their sum becomes the project's rating. While the ratings are an important guide in project selection, the final priority order of projects is further refined by the incorporation of the judgment of the system managers and their key staff.

Based on the combination of funding availability and the final rating of projects, MTA has developed its five-year program. These projects reflect what are believed to be realistic expectations for construction scheduling and projected inflation over the construction period. Each year's program level is designed to represent the value of commitments, i.e., contracts, that will be entered into in that year. This is closely correlated with the perceived annual availability of all funding sources. Program priorities also suggest what areas can be curtailed if funding is reduced.

HIGHLIGHTS OF THE MTA FIVE-YEAR CAPITAL PROGRAM

Overviews of the program are given in TABLES 1 and 2.

New York City Transit Authority

The capital plan for the Transit Authority begins with a program emphasis on the purchase of new subway cars, and calls for an expenditure of $1461 million to purchase 1150 new IRT cars and 226 new IND/BMT cars.

TABLE 1. Overview: Capital Project Elements (Millions of Dollars)

Projects	NYCTA[a]	Railroads[b]	Total	Percentage
Rolling stock	$2404.0	$ 506.7	$2910.7	34.08
Passenger stations	499.6	167.1	666.7	7.81
Track	403.4	28.0	431.4	5.05
Line equipment	142.9	–	142.9	1.67
Line structures	237.0	171.0	408.0	4.78
Signals and communications	454.0	152.4	606.4	7.10
Power equipment and substations	306.6	190.8	497.4	5.82
Shops, yards, maintenance facilities, depots, and terminals	1342.1	429.2	1771.3	20.74
Service vehicles	63.0	–	63.0	0.74
Security	20.3	4.0	24.3	0.28
New routes	171.0	–	171.0	2.00
Electrification	–	232.3	232.3	2.72
Automatic fare collection	100.0	50.0	150.0	1.76
Unspecified, miscellaneous, parking and emergency	344.9	121.0	465.9	5.45
TOTALS	$6488.8	$2052.5	$8541.3	100.00

[a] Includes MaBSTOA and SIRTOA.
[b] Includes Long Island Rail Road and Metro-North Commuter Railroad.

TABLE 2. Overview: Capital Plan Funding Sources
(Millions of Dollars)

Funding Source	NYCTA[a]	Railroads[b]	Total	Percentage
Federal	$2315	$ 534	$2849	33.35
Bonds	2592	1225	3817	44.69
City	604	–	604	7.07
State	319	169	488	5.71
Lessor equity	394	106	500	5.85
Port Authority	92	–	92	1.08
Other	173	19	192	2.25
TOTAL	$6489	$2053	$8542	100.00

[a] Includes MaBSTOA and SIRTOA.
[b] Includes Long Island Rail Road and Metro-North Commuter Railroad.

The reliability of the system is further enhanced by a program to rehabilitate existing cars. This portion of the program calls for an expenditure of $624 million, and includes $30 million for car door modernization, prototype for an air-conditioning retrofit program, and an overall car safety program for existing 75-foot cars.

The bus-replacement program projects an expenditure of $339 million to purchase 1605 buses. At the completion of the 5-year program, the number of buses of 12 years or more of age will have been reduced from 1500 to 573. Fifty percent of the fleet will be accessible to people in wheelchairs.

Five hundred and eighty million dollars are allocated for a program to begin to improve the passenger environment in subway stations—$419 million of this are to accomplish the total rehabilitation and modernization of some 80 stations throughout the transit system; $81 million are to replace overage escalators and elevators and to replace roofs, canopies, turnstiles, lighting, and signage and to complete the installation of abrasive warning strips at all stations. The balance of $80 million are for automatic fare collection equipment and installations.

The track and rail section of the program represents a proposed expenditure of $403 million to rehabilitate main line track, contact rail, and track switches and to continue the noise-abatement program by the installation of welded rail and rubber rail seats.

The line equipment program, totaling $143 million, will begin a long-range campaign to extend tunnel lighting and to rehabilitate pumping facilities, ventilating facilities, and power facilities.

The program relating to the line structures of the system calls for an expenditure of $237 million to repair elevated and on-grade structures and deal with adverse water conditions as well as for the replacement of wooden platforms and fire and water lines.

The program also calls for an expenditure of $454 million for signals and communication requirements.

The section of the program dealing with the power distribution system calls for a total expenditure of $307 million to replace and modernize antiquated substations on the IRT/BMT system, some of which date back to the early 1930s, and to reequip IND substations with more modern and reliable equipment.

The proposed expenditure of $472 million will advance a continuing effort at rehabilitating shops, replacing outmoded and inefficient mechanical equipment, maintenance-of-way machinery, and the rehabilitation of employee and shop facilities.

Subway yards represent an expenditure program of $443 million, to initiate a yard-expansion program (so all cars will be in yards) and to rehabilitate and generally upgrade existing yard facilities.

Bus depots are among the major constraints to improving the reliability of the bus fleet. This program calls for an expenditure of $427 million, of which $225 million are to construct 5 new depots. The balance will be used to rehabilitate, modernize, and reequip 10 existing depots.

Sixty-three million dollars will be used to replace maintenance equipment machinery, automotive trucks, service vehicles, and required work trains, and $20 million are to continue the program of station communications and making improvements to "protected" waiting areas.

The rapid transit extension program will be brought to the point where subway operations will be possible on two new segments of the rapid transit system: $171 million will be used to complete the Hillside Avenue connection and the Archer Avenue connection in central Queens and to complete the Sixty-third Street line to Twenty-first Avenue in Queens.

The total program calls for an expenditure of $345 million for miscellaneous and emergency needs including the upgrading of management information systems throughout the Transit Authority and improvements to security systems.

Staten Island Rapid Transit Operating Authority

There is a total of $34 million for station improvements and various track work and shop improvements for the Staten Island Rapid Transit Operating Authority.

The Long Island Rail Road

The Long Island Rail Road five-year plan totals $1.014 billion — $196 million of that amount will purchase 174 new electric cars, with an additional $10 million to rehabilitate diesel coaches.

The goal of providing the new cars is ultimately to relieve the overcrowding that currently exists; and we continue to experience increasing ridership on the LIRR. It is interesting to note that in terms of peak-hour arrivals at Penn Station, there has been a 37% increase over the last 10 years. It is estimated that some 9500 commuters now stand for from 20 to 65 minutes.

The five-year program calls for $76.3 million for passenger stations. Those improvements will include rehabilitation of escalators, improved signage and lighting, access for elderly and handicapped persons, and platform extensions.

In addition, $23 million will be spent on Penn Station passenger facilities — $8 million from other sources will also be used for added Penn Station improvements. These improvements will include air-conditioning, installation of new escalators, elevators, and a new west end concourse to relieve overcrowding at the west end of all LIRR platforms.

The railroad will spend $168 million to extend electric service into outlying areas.

Improvements to the existing infrastructure (track, switches, structures, signals, communications, and security systems) will entail the expenditure of $187 million. This effort will include installation of centralized control as well as the installation of reverse signaling between Jamaica and Penn Station as well as the upgrading of Harold Interlocking.

The five-year program also allocates $192 million for shop and yard improvements on the LIRR and $162 million for construction of the new west side storage yard complex.

The shop program will complete the first 3 phases and begin the 4th phase of a 10-phase shop program. The initial efforts of this program will be directed toward improving the comfort and reliability of the diesel car fleet. The west side storage yard, a major part of the shop and yard program, will make it possible for the LIRR to operate as many as 25% more trains into and out of Penn Station and to eliminate the wasteful practice of shuttling empty trains back and forth across the length of Long Island each day.

Metro-North Commuter Service (Totals $868.9 Million)

The Metro-North Commuter Service has allocated $281.7 million for the purchase of new cars and locomotives. Of this amount, $171 million are to purchase 142 new electric cars for Hudson and Harlem service and $71.6 million are allocated for the purchase of 44 new electric cars for our New Haven service. In addition, 10 SPV rail diesel cars at a cost of $12 million have been ordered using funds from the 1979 Bond Issue.

Nineteen million dollars have been allocated for rebuilding cars. This program includes the replacement of the 4400 series cars and seven FL-9 locomotives. This equipment will be used to improve service on the Upper Hudson. In addition, in conformance with U.S. Environmental Protection Agency regulations, money has been allocated for the replacement of transformers on existing M2 cars. In the event that regulatory changes permit the transformer program to be deferred, it is our intention to use this money to rebuild surplus electric cars to service our ridership more adequately.

Passenger station improvements will total $68 million, which includes construction of high-level platforms as part of the Upper Harlem electrification project. The balance of funding is for other improvements including access facilities for senior citizens and disabled passengers.

One hundred and sixty-eight million dollars will be used to make improvements to interlockings and track, to continue general bridge and tunnel rehabilitation programs already under way, and to install cab signaling on the

Harlem and Hudson Lines. With the completion of this program, the entire signal system will have been rehabilitated and modernized with the exception of the section between Grand Central Terminal and Mott Haven, which will be done during the next five-year period.

Among the most significant elements of the Metro-North plan is a program to modernize the power-distribution facilities. Totaling $191 million, this program will permit the construction of 30 new substations to replace the existing antiquated and obsolete ones we now have.

Sixty-four million dollars will be used to electrify the Upper Harlem Line, and $49 million have been allocated for shop and yard improvements.

Fifty million dollars have been set aside to automate the fare-collection systems of the two railroads.

In conclusion, I believe it is important to add that the analytical and planning effort that supported the development of the capital program will continue and be expanded as the plan is implemented. Given the size and complexity of the program and the number of external factors affecting its implementation, it is necessary to retain a basis for tracking progress and making adjustments as appropriate. Recognizing also that there will be substantial needs unmet at the completion of this five-year plan, the program management process will provide the basis for planning additional phases of what should be a continuing renewal program.

There are three key elements in the program management process. First is the capital program tracking system. The tracking system identifies the myriad projects being undertaken by the various operating agencies under the capital plan, reporting on their physical progress and budget performance. As an MTA-wide system, it is integrated with the particular tracking systems in use in the particular agencies so as to assure compatibility. It identifies problems in meeting construction milestones at an early enough time to take corrective action, and monitors financial performance as the basis for allocating funds from various sources, particularly those involving bonds that must be marketed on schedule.

Second, the MTA has initiated a system of annual capital budgets for the various agencies in the revitalization program. This process permits the annual review of the capital program status, the identification of projects to be initiated in the coming year, and any adjustments required to the five-year program to meet such problems as cost overruns or funding source shortfalls. This annual budget affords the MTA board the opportunity to retain flexibility in dealing with unforeseen conditions.

Third, the MTA is in the process of developing a basis for regular reporting of system activity and progress through the use of performance indicators. This system ties directly to the call for service and operational standards in connection with the capital program. It is our intention to use the performance measurement system in conjunction with the capital and operating budgets as a basis for allocating resources so that results can be measured. Development of this system is being supported through a UMTA technical studies grant. The various measures identified as standards in this capital plan will be tracked through the system, along with other indicators more directly oriented to operational and financial factors. In total, the performance measurement system is intended to provide various levels of MTA management, culminating with the Board of Directors, a comprehensive status report on MTA operations and the progress that is being made in meeting management goals and objectives.

Clearly, MTA has embarked on a most enthusiastic and comprehensive program to bring our systems into "a state of good repair." The magnitude of the program is *much* greater than we are used to. We see its implementation as an exciting challenge; one that we must succeed in.

Modifying Operational and Structural Components of Existing Water Supply Systems to Increase Capacities

JOHN P. LAWLER, FELIX E. MATUSKY, FRANCIS M. McGOWAN, AND JOHN F. LARKIN

Lawler, Matusky & Skelly Engineers
One Blue Hill Plaza
Pearl River, New York 10965

The history of the development of water supply for New York City, as well as for many large metropolitan areas throughout this country, is characterized by cycles of surplus or shortage. Political maneuvering and the perceived high costs for new water sources, during the city's rapid growth period in the early nineteenth century, resulted in the available supply lagging demand until "the twin scourges of fire and disease"[1] forced the building of the original Croton system. Similarly, immigration, industrial growth, and the rapid expansion of the city, including the extension of its boundaries to encompass Brooklyn, Queens, Richmond, and more of the Bronx, resulted, toward the end of the nineteenth century, in consumption outstripping the expanded capacity of the Croton system. These pressures resulted in the formation of the Board of Water Supply and the building of the Catskill system. Before the Catskill system was completed in 1927, the Board of Water Supply, as early as 1921, was already investigating the potential for development of a Delaware system. Interstate competition for the water resources of the Delaware basin (eventually resolved by the Supreme Court), the Great Depression, and World War II contributed to the delay of completion of the initial stage of the Delaware system until 1955. Meanwhile, in 1949, consumption outstripped rainfall and by December 1949 the combined storage of the Catskill and Croton systems had fallen to 33% of capacity, causing numerous restrictive water-use measures, including voluntary dry ("shaveless") Tuesdays.

The Hudson River pumping station at Chelsea, capable of injecting 100 million gallons per day (MGD) into the Delaware aqueduct through shaft 6, was built to provide some emergency protection for the city. The Delaware system was finally added to the water supply system in 1965 with the completion of the Cannonsville reservoir. New York City now had a safe yield of approximately 1300 MGD, and a normal demand that exceeded that amount.

Nearing the end of the twentieth century, New York City still needs additional water supply protection, but under circumstances different from the days of rapid growth. Faced with a loss of its residential, commercial, and industrial population, and committed to substantial welfare and other costly social programs, the city nevertheless continues as the country's major commercial and financial hub, thereby causing a water-related shortage to have consequences that reach out nationally. Expenditures for water supply infrastructure continue to impact heavily on the city's budget. An expected average annual commitment of $200 million, or approximately 10% of the average annual capital budget, through the year 1992, has been made to continue work on city tunnel no. 3, to repair and replace mains, and to build the Croton treatment plant. These capital commitments make it unlikely that the city will engage in any new capital-intensive water supply projects for developing long-term additional yield within the next 10 years. However, the city is investigating the possibility of increasing its emergency supply from the Hudson River to 300 MGD. The additional 200 MGD would be drawn from an expanded facility at Chelsea or from a new facility further upstream.

In today's climate of delay, occasioned by tight money and legal skirmishing, involving environmental and other regulatory procedures, long lead times are required, even for implementation of emergency protection. For example, though the city clearly recognizes the need for expansion of the Chelsea pumping facility, the expectation of considerable opposition to the concept of using Hudson River water as part of the city's supply, even on an emergency basis, has caused city and state officials to proceed cautiously. First, the city is moving toward the completion of a comprehensive environmental impact assessment before even seeking authorization to reactivate the existing 100 MGD facility. Reckoning time from the 1980–1981 threatened shortage, it could be 10 years before the additional 200 MGD supply is available. What happens in the meantime if another drought occurs?

Emergency planning should include, as a minimum, development of procedures that can be implemented in time to avert a threatened disaster. Obviously, this is difficult to achieve if the potential disaster is viewed as one causing random losses of portions of the system, such as might occur as a result of military action. Drought-caused water shortage, on the other hand, can be planned for to a much greater extent. Effective plans must include provisions for obtaining critical equipment and facilities, e.g., high-volume, high-lift pumps, and provisions for occupying highway, railroad, and other types of right-of-way so as to avoid long delivery time.

An approach to emergency water supply planning is presented herein that can resolve some of these issues and that may be useful nationally. The history of its development began with a series of ideas expressed to the staff of the New York City Division of Water Resources in February and March 1981, at a time when city officials were wrestling with the possibility of running out of water before year's end. The ideas are presented to illustrate the magnitude of the problem of providing emergency water supply to a large metropolitan area. In this case, the supply is from the Hudson River at Chelsea and the large metropolitan area is New York City. A concept of a national approach to emergency water supply planning is included and illustrated by several water supply emergency scenarios set in the New York–New Jersey metropolitan area.

EMERGENCY USE OF THE HUDSON RIVER
AT CHELSEA

The Hudson River pumping station at Chelsea can pump 100 MGD of Hudson River water into the Delaware aqueduct through a vertical connection in shaft 6. Shaft 6 joins the tunnel at a low point some 600 feet below sea level and was left accessible after completion of construction to permit dewatering of the tunnel. In 1950, prior to the tunnel's completion and while it was still

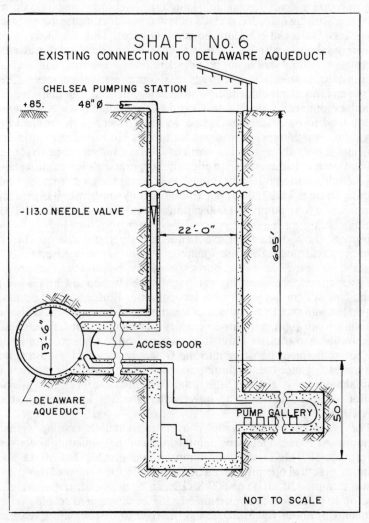

FIGURE 1. Shaft no. 6. Existing connection to Delaware aqueduct. (Ø means diameter).

dry, a 48-inch diameter concrete-encased steel riser pipe, originally designed to convey water from the aqueduct to neighboring communities, was connected to a booster pumping station as shown in FIGURE 1. High-lift pumps, capable of discharging Hudson River water into the tunnel against the 250 psi pressure at that point, and a Hudson River intake structure are the basic components of that facility.

The Chelsea Environmental Impact Statements (EIS) has not yet determined whether existing treatment will be adequate or whether additional treatment will be required. The quality of Hudson River water at Chelsea for emergency purposes appears acceptable. Though salt levels may climb into the range of 100 mg/l during extended periods of low flows [5000 cubic feet per second (cfs) or less], such salt concentrations rarely occur. They are likely to occur contemporaneously with droughts in the Delaware and Catskill watersheds. Nevertheless, salinity should not be a block to using water from Chelsea. Given that substantial detention time exists in holding reservoirs between Chelsea and the city, and that chlorination would be practiced, the delivered water would be biologically acceptable. Chemical contaminant levels in the water column tend to be at trace levels and do not pose a health problem in the short term. Poughkeepsie withdraws and treats Hudson River water for its municipal supply about 10 miles north of Chelsea and has done so for years.

The Central Hudson Gas and Electric Corporation's Roseton steam electric generating station is located immediately across the river from the Chelsea pumping station. This 1200 MW two-unit facility condenses its spent steam by means of a four-pump, 641,000 gallons per minute (gpm) (920 MGD) circulating cooling water system which draws water from the Hudson River. In the process, the cooling water experiences a temperature rise of 10 to 18°F before it is returned, otherwise unaltered, to the Hudson River.

In the context of an emergency response, the possibility of utilizing this intake structure for transmitting water across the Hudson to Chelsea was proposed. This system is very flexible in operation. Both generating units can be operated with two, three, or four of the circulating water pumps. This means that one or two pumps, in an emergency water supply situation, could be made available to transfer water from the Hudson to Chelsea or other locations for subsequent boosting into the Delaware aqueduct. Booster pumps are a necessity, since the maximum practical head available from these low-lift intake pumps is about 50 feet total dynamic head (TDH), while some 600 feet of head is necessary to inject water into the Delaware aqueduct in this vicinity.

The potential bypass capacity of the circulating cooling system is enormous. At 50 feet TDH, one pump bypassing the circulating water system will provide 190 MGD and two pumps would provide 340 MGD. At the minimum practical operating head of about 10 feet for one pump and 20 feet for two pumps, 320 MGD or 600 MGD can be delivered, respectively. This range of 10 to 20 feet is approximately the head required to pipe water in increments of about 160 MGD across the river to Chelsea using reasonable pipe diameters and velocities [6 to 7 feet, 9 to 6 feet per second (fps)]. Even if the generating station were to require operation of all four pumps, the 920

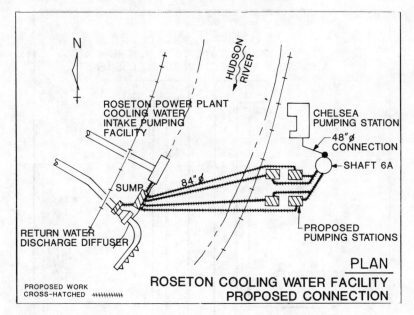

FIGURE 2. Plan for the Roseton cooling water facility proposed connection.

MGD plant discharge flow, or any portion thereof, altered only in temperature, could still be piped across the river.

Recognizing the potential of this fortuitously located pumping capacity complete with screen-protected intake at Roseton for bringing substantial volumes of detritus-free Hudson River water to the suction side of the nearby high-lift booster pumping plant at Chelsea, the possibility of utilizing this system was proposed to city water supply officials in early 1981. The basic plan is illustrated in FIGURE 2. As many as four 7-foot diameter steel pipes, each carrying about 160 MGD at low pressure (<10 psi), would be buried in the river's bottom, protected by a 5-foot blanket of sand and rip rap. The sump at the Roseton facility would be capable of receiving water directly from one or two Roseton pumps, or heated water directly from the plant discharge line, just above the discharge seal well. On the Chelsea side, as many as four booster pumping stations were envisioned, each containing a wet well into which an 84-inch diameter river crossing pipe would discharge, and eight 20 MGD, 250 psi high-lift vertical pumps.

Introduction into shaft 6 could either take place directly by pressurizing the shaft or through one or two 78-inch diameter steel downcomers (depending on whether a total of 320 or 640 MGD was selected as the design flow). The latter, illustrated in FIGURE 3, was suggested originally to preserve the present dewatering system, to avoid potential erosion of the shaft walls, and to eliminate construction of the massive cap that would be required to seal the 22-foot diameter shaft at ground level. To connect to the aqueduct, an existing

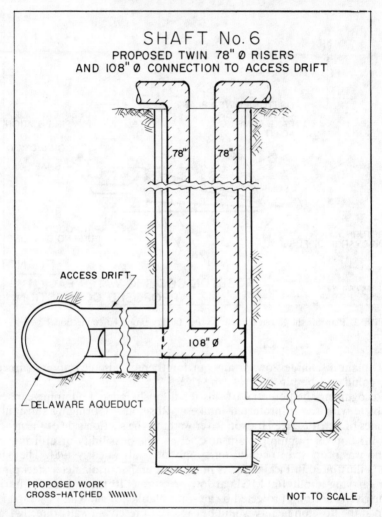

FIGURE 3. Shaft no. 6. Proposed twin 78-in. Ø risers and 108-in. Ø connection to access drift.

9-foot diameter bronze access door must be opened. This could be done by shutting the aqueduct down to permit a dry tap, a scheme that might be feasible if the Delaware reservoirs actually emptied. An alternative scheme would fill the new downcomer and equalize pressures, and remove the door by employing a previously installed track-mounted hydraulic robot. The robot would permit replacement of the door if it became necessary to shut down the facility and dewater the shaft.

This is a quick thumbnail sketch of the concept. The cost to provide the total capability is estimated to be on the order of $50 million. A particularly attractive feature was its role as the first stage of a possible long-term yield supplementing project. Treatment facilities and perhaps an east shore intake could make this a permanent installation.

In early 1981, during the course of a series of presentations and correspondence, an outline was developed of the substantial engineering considerations that would be necessary to bring such a plan to fruition. A day and night design/construct "fast track" program was envisioned, in light of the possibility of complete depletion of the city's reservoirs if the drought were to continue. It was recognized that wartimelike mobilization would have been required to achieve the completion of even part of this project within the time available (nine months). During this period of discussion, the rains came to relieve the drought, resulting in a reduction of the effort first to a feasibility study and finally to a low-priority project, a position it occupies today.

Certain features of this experience stand out and have led to the development of a planning approach to provide contingency protection for any city's water supply. One is the recognition that waiting until only six months of water supply remains causes the risk of being unable to achieve any protection at all. By example, early in February 1981, after a year of unusually low precipitation on its watersheds, New York City's reservoirs were down to 27% of capacity. Though water conservation had reduced normal demand by more than 15%, New York City water supply officials, recognizing the potential for disaster of a continuing drought, were evaluating a variety of emergency measures to contend with a situation of little or no water in the city's reservoirs. These measures ranged from severe curtailment, such as shutting down the water supply in every third block, to introducing New York Harbor salt water or treated sewage effluent into the distribution system, a scheme that, notwithstanding the severely degraded quality of such water, was recognized as only marginally useful because of the limited ability for introducing large volumes into the small piping of the downstream end of the supply and distribution system. Articles in the press spoke of "doomsday scenarios," and people became aware of the vital role of water in the maintenance of social and economic order, by its necessity for drinking, food preparation, hygiene, sanitation, and most importantly fire protection. In late February, the rains came, and another in a long series of threatened water shortages became history.

An enormous amount of planning, development of selected alternatives, basic engineering design, and hardware selection is clearly necessary to achieve results in the example provided; other situations will always have their own comparable planning and engineering problems. Even without breaking ground, or ordering a single piece of equipment, a substantial amount of the required effort can be achieved by having detailed planning and engineering available. Such plans might be carried through the signing of contingency contracts, all before an emergency befalls.

Another observation is that much of the equipment required to move large volumes of water is not available off the shelf. Manufacturing and construction time can exceed the time available to install the necessary contingency facilities before disaster can be averted. An effective emergency preparedness plan must recognize this and circumvent it.

Such planning can be effective, when it is recognized that drought-induced shortages provide more advance warning for the need of corrective action than virtually any other type of interruption of the water supply. Conversely, a dam failure, aqueduct failure, reservoir contamination, loss of a major interconnection or river intake, whether due to earthquake or a man-made act, deliberate or accidental, can all create an instantaneous emergency of the first order.

A NATIONAL APPROACH TO WATER SUPPLY EMERGENCY PLANNING

The emergency plan discussed herein is presented to satisfy the objective of providing methods and means of response to a major failure of water source or transmission in any large metropolitan area. The criteria to be met in achieving this objective include (1) reasonable costs with a potential for cost sharing among users; (2) limited time required for response, on the order of one calendar month; and (3) minimum requirement for new fixed facilities.

To be practical, the equipment and facilities required by the emergency plan should be available and ready for installation. The details of the installation may differ for each case, but the equipment should be modular and field adaptable to varying situations.

The limited response time requirement precludes permanent, fixed installations, and directs the design to portable, self-sufficient, and self-supporting facilities that may be transported and erected using readily available construction equipment, materials, and construction personnel. The emergency facilities will be placed above grade, preferably on a public right-of-way, and should include the capability for bridging at highways, railroads, and similar obstacles. Pumping equipment should be prime-mover driven, with diesel power a reasonable choice. Each engine-pump-control module should be skid mounted, for ease in handling and erection.

The concept can be summarized as emergency response planning, connoting a continuing evaluation of potential disaster scenarios and associated responses. Included are the purchase and stockpiling of pumps, pipes, valves, and assorted hardware; all with the potential for rapid movement of such to the affected site by air, highway, or barge; supplemented by data-base management for the identification and location of stockpiled materials, construction equipment, movable standby pumps, and the identification of the need for the installation of pads, anchors, and other critical elements that can materially reduce response time. Identification of backup contractors and contingency contracts and such matters would all be organized and managed by a core emergency planning and response unit.

Fixed facilities having the capability to respond to infrequent drought events are extremely costly, when viewed on a unit basis of additional protection (insurance) provided. Further, no amount of fixed, long-term facilities can guard against randomly occurring disasters such as seismologically caused dam or aqueduct failures, explosions, accidental or purposeful contamination, or other unpredictable events. The cost of a viable emergency response plan, capable of rapid response to a variety of major disasters, should become reasonable for the protection provided because:

1. Surface placement of portable equipment would avoid expensive land purchase, excavation, foundations, and elaborate instrumentation, all of which escalate costs of permanent facilities.
2. Costs may be allocated among the potential beneficiaries; since response capability to any event that disrupts water supply for any purpose is envisioned. Events include disruption of public water supply by drought, dam failure, aqueduct failure, and civil defense related occurrences. Disruption of industrial water supply and irrigation supplies by similar events could be included in the response capability.
3. The emergency response concept of a core unit, stockpiled equipment, rapid mobilization, and continuing evaluation of worst-case situations is national and even international in scope. A core unit and equipment located in Omaha, for example, could be available for rapid response to emergencies throughout the country. The concept, if developed, could provide emergency assistance to other nations in a water supply distress, via military airlift capability.
4. The reduction of expenditures for replicated long-term fixed facilities would free funds for use elsewhere in the economy.
5. Rapid relief and intervention in the rare disaster event eliminate costly damage that can exceed the cost of the emergency plan alternative.
6. Costs for providing the emergency response capability would appear to be appropriately funded by broad-based taxation. Costs of providing a specific response, depending on the nature of the event, may be appropriately charged, at least in part, to those benefiting from the response.

The national scope of such a plan, as well as the nature of emergency response, argues for a federal function in financing, administration, and implementation. Response to local and regional emergencies has historically been a role of the federal government. The ability to mobilize rapidly for use of stockpiled equipment in response to emergency and disaster lends to central command. It is suggested that the Federal Emergency Management Agency (FEMA) or the U.S. Army, acting through the Corps of Engineers (COE), could have a role to play in the administrative implementation of such a plan. Regardless of the agency assigned this task, a primary responsibility could be the continuing evaluation of potential disaster scenarios for vulnerable cities and heavily populated regions, to enhance the ability to respond quickly and effectively when such disasters occur.

ILLUSTRATION OF THE CONCEPT IN THE METROPOLITAN NEW YORK REGION

For the metropolitan region, the major water supply with sufficient volume to serve as a supply source is the Hudson River. Preferably, withdrawal should be upstream of the salt front to ensure fresh water, but in an extreme emer-

TABLE 1. Primary Hardware Necessary to Be Stockpiled to Permit Rapid Mobile Response to Emergency Water Supply Needs in the Metropolitan New York Area

1. Pump(s), 1000 horsepower (HP) diesel engine drive(s), 1200 rpm, delivering 15 MGD at 300 ft TDH, at approximately 80% efficiency. Weight of pump(s), engine, and valves, skid mounted, approximately 20 tons (T). Unit suitable for transportation by rail flatcar or flatbed semitrailer. (Approximate purchase cost per unit = $250,000.)

2. Force main pipe, steel, coal-tar enamel coated, 60-in diameter, ⅜-in. shell thickness, in 40-ft lengths. Weight 250 lb/linear foot (lf), 10,000 lbs per length. Each length tapered to allow nestable storage and shipment. 6 lengths = 30 T load; 22 loads per mile of main. Capacity at friction loss of 2 ft/1000 ft (10 ft/mile approx.) = 88.8 MGD. (Module = 6 pump drive units and one 60-in. main with approximately 90–100 MGD capacity.) (Approximate material cost per mile = $800,000.)

3. Force main appurtenances—jointing materials, joint ties, thrust anchors, support and bridging materials. (60-in. pipe is self-supporting at 40-ft span. Bridging needed for longer spans.)

4. Fuel storage and handling facilities—diesel fuel storage in 5000 gallon semi-trailer units, with fuel distribution piping to engine installations. Provide for multiple tanker units at feed connection.

5. Intake facilities—screened intake pipes for suction from the river, together with piping required to connect to pump suction fittings. Alternatives—connect to existing steam electric generating station intake or a barge-mounted intake screen and suction structure.

---

gency, brackish water would have to be accepted. To serve as an alternative source, based on the Hudson River, pumping equipment and transmission mains suitable for high-volume flow against high head are required, and the equipment must be conveniently portable.

The emergency facilities required are listed in TABLE 1. These items would provide, in a modular combination, items suitable for delivering 90 to 100 MGD against a head of 300 feet, a module being made up of six pumps and a 60-inch force main. For higher capacities or higher heads, additional modules may be added in parallel (to increase capacity) or in series (to increase head).

The following discussion presents three applications of the proposed emergency approach as a demonstration of its possibilities. The first two examples are based on supplying an additional 400 MGD to New York City while the third provides for an additional 115 MGD to New Jersey. For each of the examples it is assumed that emergency planning has progressed to the following levels:

- An emergency planning and execution agency has been identified and established to develop and direct the emergency program.
- Emergency equipment and facilities in the required quantities have been acquired and stored in a central location, and are ready for field service.
- Module components are complete with all auxiliary items, such as fuel systems for the diesel-powered pumps, pump valving and connection fittings, pipe joint rings, gaskets, and joint ties for the force mains, and the like.
- Speciality items, such as portable bridging sections and piers, thrust anchors and cables, and similar equipment are available in appropriate quantities.

- Administrative authorizations have been given for construction on normally restricted rights-of-way. In many instances, the specific authorization will be unique to the emergency, requiring prompt drafting of authorizations in accordance with a general outline developed from the emergency planning process.
- Listings of construction organizations, key personnel, and equipment are available, allowing prompt assignment of construction forces.

The prompt execution of the type of emergency water supply project under discussion would be possible only if the preliminary planning is accomplished with objectives clearly stated and understood by those responsible for the decisions.

The objective of the emergency plan is to meet minimum water requirements for residential use, for movement of sewage, and for fire fighting. In order to provide for this minimum, enough additional water has to be provided to offset leakage losses. Commercial and industrial demands would not be met. The assumptions used to estimate minimum demand requirements in the following examples are:

- Actual residential use averages of 60 would be cut to 30 gallons per capita per day (gpcd). (It is assumed that in-house residential leakage would be eliminated.)
- System leakage is 15% of average annual demand flow, and would continue at this level during a drought emergency.
- In northern New Jersey the example covers the five major utilities serving the Hackensack and Passaic basins: Hackensack Water Company, Jersey City Water Department, Newark Water Department, North Jersey District Water Supply Commission, and Passaic Valley Water Commission. Commonwealth, Elizabethtown, and Middlesex water companies are served by water from the Raritan basin, augmented if necessary by Delaware River water transported via the Delaware and Raritan Canal.
- Contingencies beyond the estimated emergency demand in New Jersey are met by transferring Raritan basin water through the existing interconnection between the Elizabethtown Water Company and the Newark Water Department system.
- New York City's existing Chelsea pumping station would provide about 30 MGD of the emergency demand and about 70 MGD for contingencies.

These figures lead to the following required demand:

	New Jersey	New York
Population served (1980)	1,966,000	7,071,000
Residential use (30 gpcd)	59 MGD	212 MGD
System leakage (15% avg)	53 MGD	218 MGD
Chelsea contribution	0 MDG	−30 MGD
Total	112 MGD	400 MGD
Say	115 MGD	400 MGD

The *New Jersey Statewide Water Supply Plan,*[2] in an alternative approach, based on supplying a fraction of previously experienced drought demands, leads to a New Jersey demand of 123 MGD and a New York demand of 432 MGD.

The examples developed herein provide 115 MGD for New Jersey and 400 for New York with additional contingency supplies possible from the Raritan Basin for the Passaic and Hackensack purveyors and from other sources for New York City, e.g., the Brooklyn-Queens aquifer.

NEW YORK CITY—REPLACE AND/OR AUGMENT DELAWARE AQUEDUCT SUPPLY

The Delaware aqueduct operates as a pressure conduit, conveying about 750 MGD. It may discharge to the West Branch reservoir at an elevation of 503 feet (at shaft 9) or to the West Branch–Kensico tunnel via the bypass tunnel.

The Chelsea pumping station is designed to draw water from the Hudson River and discharge to the Delaware aqueduct at shaft 6. The Chelsea input at shaft 6 is limited to 100 MGD; the station discharges to a connection originally intended to serve local communities, and capacity cannot be increased without modifying the structures of the shaft and aqueduct. An earlier example explained how this could be achieved; for purposes of this illustration, it is assumed that this expanded capacity has not been provided and, for the period of interest, cannot be.

A failure of the Delaware aqueduct between the West Branch reservoir and the Hudson River would preclude use of the existing Chelsea pumping station, but such an event would be unlikely to coincide with a drought condition, so that the Catskill and Croton supply systems would remain operational. Under such circumstances, delivery of 400 MGD of river water to replace the normal aqueduct flow would relieve the emergency significantly.

For either scenario, the flows delivered by the emergency facilities cannot be discharged to the aqueduct, but must be delivered to the system upstream of the West Branch reservoir. The emergency facilities assumed to be available are the items listed in TABLE 1, consisting of modules with capacity in the 90 to 100 MGD range. The emergency plan discussed below is designed to deliver 400 MGD of Hudson River water from an emergency intake in the vicinity of Chelsea, discharging to the West Branch through Black Pond and interconnecting streams.

The routing of the emergency plan aqueduct system is shown in FIGURE 4, and the profile of the routing (taken from U.S. Geological Survey Quadrangles) is shown in FIGURE 5. The routing is based on Interstate Route 84 right-of-way, with the emergency aqueduct located in the median. The hydraulic characteristics of the emergency facilities are shown in TABLE 2. Routing details of each stage are shown in TABLE 3. The emergency aqueduct installation described in TABLES 2 and 3 would require the major equipment listed in TABLE 4. TABLE 4 estimates the total cost to provide 400 MGD to be over $100 million, with the cost of 16 miles of transmission being the major cost

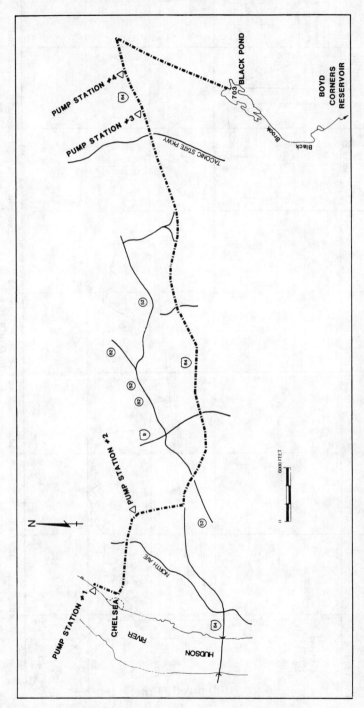

FIGURE 4. Route of emergency connection from Chelsea to Boyd Corners reservoir.

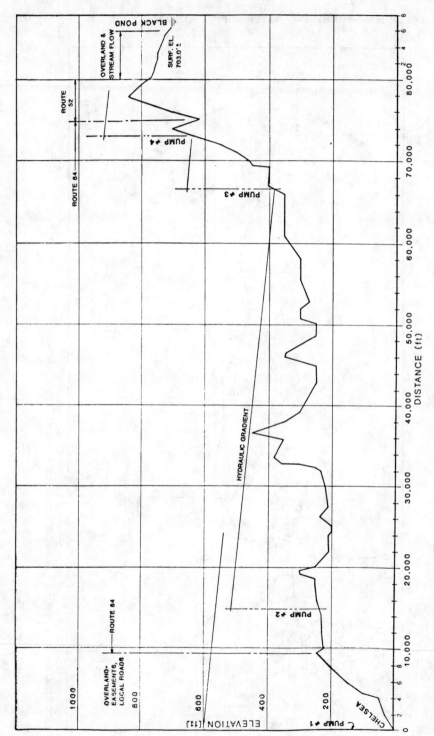

FIGURE 5. Chelsea-Black Pond profile.

356

TABLE 2. Emergency Project to Replace/Augment Delaware Aqueduct Flow: Hydraulic Characteristics

Item	Description
Pumping module	Six 1000 HP diesel-driven pump units to operate at 16.7 MGD and 273 ft TDH, discharging to one 60-in. diameter force main. For 400 MGD, 4 modules required
Force main characteristics	Diameter = 60-in. per module Flow = 100 MGD per module Velocity = 7.9 fps Velocity head = 7.97 ft Friction loss = 0.0254 ft/ft
Length of force main	76,000 lf (per module) (14.4 miles per module) (57.6 miles total length for 400 MGD)

Head required
  Static lift
  Friction loss
  Allowance for fittings
  Total head
	
	850 ft (to saddle north of Black Pond)
	193 ft
	29 ft
	1072 ft

Pumping stages	3.93, say 4

contributor. Comparing this to the estimated $50 million cost to provide some 600 MGD by utilizing shaft 6 shows the relative merit of injecting Hudson River water into the aqueduct at that site.

The emergency facilities described are not intended to replace the fixed facilities required to meet normal water supply demands. They are intended to provide a relatively prompt, high-capacity replacement or augmentation to fixed facilities in the event of extreme drought or supply system and/or transmission failure. The plan recognizes that the relief of an extreme water supply emergency will justify inconvenience in highway use and the diversion of construction equipment and personnel from normal programs.

It should be noted that the modular emergency facilities are not unique to the illustration given but would provide redundant water supply capability for any large metropolitan area that has access to a water source. For example, a single module would suffice to supply a population of one million persons, while the force main, equipped with an appropriate number of pumping units, would be adaptable to serve smaller communities.

CONNECTION TO THE CATSKILL AQUEDUCT

An emergency water supply system to utilize the 555 MGD capacity of the Catskill aqueduct could be constructed utilizing the Roseton power plant intake to transfer screened water to Newburgh, 5 miles south. The transmission line would consist of three 72-inch diameter low head force mains laid on the Conrail westshore railroad right-of-way. The force main pipe could

TABLE 3. Emergency Project to Replace/Augment Delaware Aqueduct Flow: Routing Details by Stage

Item	Description
River intake — stage 1 pumps	Six 24-in. diameter screened suction lines, (1 per pump) drafting from area enclosed within floating curtain fish barrier (Alternative: barge-mounted pumps, discharging to pile supported 60-in. force main.)
Stage 1 force main	From intake in vicinity of Chelsea pumping station, south to Chelsea hamlet, east parallel to Chelsea Road to Rte 9D; continue east parallel to north fork of Bantertown Road to second stage pumps.
Stage 2 pumps	South side of Bantertown Road, east of fork junction.
Stage 2 force main	South from stage 2 pumps across open land to Interstate Route 84; bridge over I-84 westbound lanes; continue east in I-84 median to stage 3 pumps located east of Taconic State Parkway interchange.
Stage 3 pumps	Approximately 2500 ft east of Taconic State Parkway interchange, in I-84 median.
Stage 3 force main	In I-84 median, east to stage 4 pumps.
Stage 4 pumps	In I-84 median, west of NY Route 52 crossing.
Stage 4 force main	East in I-84 median, to NY Route 52. Bridge eastbound lanes of I-84, then south parallel to Route 52 (east of Hosner Mountain) and continue south over saddle to Black Pond drainage.
Stream flow	Flow in Black Pond Brook (via Black Pond) to West Branch Croton River, to Boyd Corners reservoir, with outlet to West Branch Croton River and West Branch reservoir.

be made up of sections several inches smaller or larger than the nominal 72-inch diameter to allow nesting three pipes within one length. The transmission line would be installed immediately as delivered by rail.

The train-mounted booster pumping station, powered electrically from Roseton or by diesel as in the previous illustration, would be required at Newburgh to pump an additional 5 miles westward to the Moodna downshaft on the Catskill aqueduct at Brown's Pond in New Windsor. At this point, the gravity portion of the aqueduct becomes a pressure tunnel until a crossing of the Hudson River is made at Cornwall (West Point). The Moodna downshaft drops some 637 feet from elevation +419 to elevation −218. The booster pumping stations located at Newburgh would be required to lift water to an elevation of about +450 to reach the shaft. FIGURE 6 shows that nearly all of the transmission line between the Moodna downshaft and Roseton would be in existing railroad or power line right-of-way, thus allowing surface placement of the force main; exceptions would be made for crossing of the New York Thruway and other roadways — about five in number. These would be tunneled and sleeved or bridged. A modification of this connection would take water from the Hudson at Newburgh via a barge-mounted intake screen

TABLE 4. Emergency Project to Supply New York City Project Cost Estimates

Item	Number Required	Item Cost ($1000)	Installation Cost ($1000)	Amount ($1000)
Intake fish barrier	400 lf	$ 40	$ 20	$ 60
Pump Suction Lines—24 in.	750 lf	40	20	60
Pump units (all stages)	96	24,000	960	24,960
Force main (400 MGD)	57.6 miles	46,080	11,520	57,600
Structural bridges:				
WB I-84 (50-ft span)		40	20	60
Rte 52—I-84 (50-ft span)		40	20	60
Fishkill Creek (2 @ 50 ft spans)		80	30	110
Rte 9—I-84 (70-ft span)		60	40	100
EB I-84 (50 ft span)		40	20	60
Pipe Bridges (40-ft span)				
Chelsea Road		20	10	30
Route 9D		20	10	30
Bantertown Road		20	10	30
Taconic Parkway—I-84 (2)		40	20	60
Route 52		20	10	30
Stream and culvert improvement	4		200	200
Miscellaneous details		3,000	3,000	6,000
Acquisition and installation		$73,540	$15,910	$ 89,450
Contingencies @ 15%				13,420
Subtotal—construction cost				$102,870
Engineering, legal, administration @ 10%				10,290
Total—project cost				$113,160
			Say.........	$113,000

and suction structure, thus saving about 5 miles of transmission line. Costs for each alternative are given in TABLE 5.

This plan would not have the permanence of a Roseton-Chelsea connection to the Delaware aqueduct because of the temporary nature of the surface-placed transmission line and the train-mounted pumping stations. This plan would offer, however, an alternative means for supplementing the Delaware system in the event of a failure of the safe yield or upstream structural elements of the Catskill system. It would also provide a temporary bypass to permit dewatering the extensive surface cut and cover sections of the Catskill aqueduct north of the Moodna pressure tunnel for inspection and possible maintenance needs.

EMERGENCY SUPPLY TO NORTHEASTERN NEW JERSEY

Northeastern New Jersey communities are served by several water purveyors and distributors, who rely primarily on surface water supplies from the areas

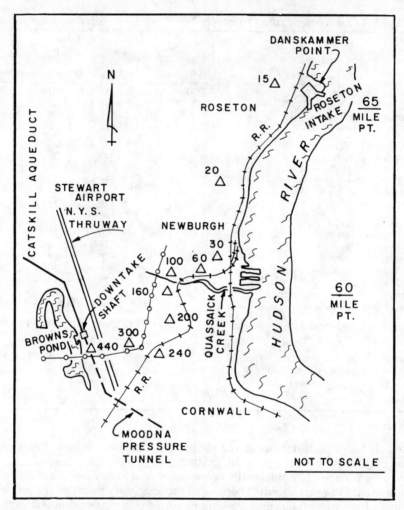

FIGURE 6. Hudson River connection to Catskill aqueduct at Browns Pond.

to the north and west. As a result of previous drought emergencies, the several systems are interconnected at a number of locations, allowing effective sharing of available supplies at moderate rates of flow. The several aqueducts of the North Jersey District Water Supply Commission (NJDWSC), the city of Newark, the Passaic Valley Water Commission (PVWC), and the city of Jersey City are in close proximity to existing interconnections at Great Notch, New Jersey. Under emergency conditions, delivery of a supplementary supply at an appropriate location to the aqueduct of the NJDWSC system would allow allocation of the supplementary flow to other purveyors through the existing interconnections.

TABLE 5. Costs of Discharging 500± MGD of Hudson River Water to the Catskill Aqueduct at the Moodna Downshaft

Roseton connection to Moodna downshaft	
1. Transmission line (540 MGD) 10 miles, 3 @ 72 in. diameter	$60,000,000
2. Booster pumping stations 5 modules @ 100 MGD/module	7,800,000
3. Roseton intake/pumping modifications	2,200,000
4. Contingencies	10,000,000
Total	$80,000,000
Newburgh connection to Moodna downshaft	
1. Transmission line (540 MGD) five miles, 3 @ 72 in. diameter	$30,000,000
2. Booster pumping stations 5 modules @ 100 MGD/module	7,800,000
3. Barge-mounted intake screens and suction intake system	2,200,000
4. Contingencies	6,000,000
Total	$46,000,000

The Hackensack Water Company (HWC) system is supplied primarily by the Hackensack River and its tributaries. The HWC is interconnected with the Jersey City and Passaic Valley Water Commission distribution systems, with each interconnection rated at 10 MGD. The HWC is now constructing a pipeline across Bergen County from the NJDWSC aqueduct system near the Pequannock River to deliver water eastward to the HWC Oradell reservoir in the Hackensack River basin. The cross-Bergen pipeline consists of 41,000 feet of 60-inch prestressed concrete cylinder pipe (PCCP) force main from the pumping station near the Pequannock River to the ridge line, and 55,000 feet of 48-inch PCCP for gravity flow from the ridge line to Oradell reservoir.

The emergency plan presented below is based on delivering 115 MGD of Hudson River water to the Lake DeForest reservoir of the HWC from which the flow may enter the Oradell reservoir via the Hackensack River. The emergency supply to the HWC will provide about 35 MGD for the HWC system and 10 MGD each for Jersey City and the PVWC systems via their interconnections with the HWC system. The remaining 60 MGD may be delivered to the NJDWSC aqueduct via the HWC cross-Bergen pipeline, operated to flow westerly from Oradell reservoir using emergency pumping facilities.

The Commonwealth Water Company and Elizabethtown Water Company systems are interconnected adequately, and, under emergency conditions, a supplementary supply would be available from the Round Valley and Spruce Run reservoirs in the Raritan River basin using the existing fixed facilities. These two purveyors are assumed to have no need to draw on Hudson River water delivered through the cross-Bergen pipeline. Any additional emergency water required in the Passaic and Hackensack river basins would be obtained from the resources of the Raritan River basin through the interconnection

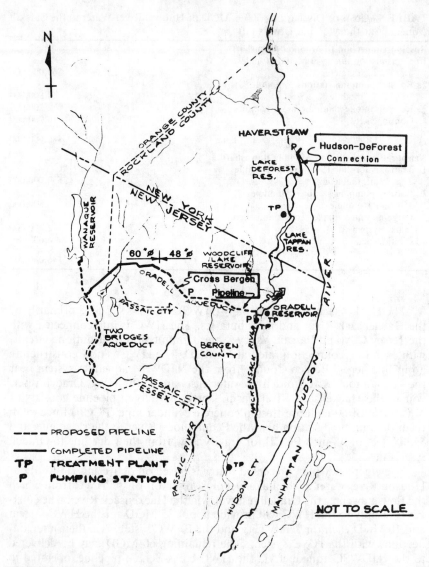

FIGURE 7. Cross-Bergen pipeline.

between the Elizabethtown Water Company and the Newark Water Department. This interconnection in Newark is referred to as the Virginia Street interconnection. It has a transmission capacity of 70 MGD. While it is uncertain just how much water would be available from the Raritan River basin, some surplus beyond basic needs should be available even in extreme drought. The basin has considerably more yield than is required by current demands.

TABLE 6. Emergency Project to Supply Northeastern New Jersey

Item	Description
(a) Hudson River water to DeForest Lake reservoir: (115 MGD)	
Pumping module	Seven 1000 HP diesel-driven pump units to operate at 16.4 MGD at 273 ft TDH, discharging to one 60-in. diameter force main. One module required.
Force main characteristics	Diameter = 60 in. Flow = 115 MGD Velocity = 9.08 fps Velocity head = 1.28 ft. Friction Loss = 0.00335 ft/ft
Length of force main	12,000 lf
Head required Static lift Friction loss Allowance for fittings Total head	 200 ft 41 ft 13 ft 254 ft
Pumping stages required	1
River intake	Seven 24-in. diameter screened suction lines, (1 per pump) drafting from area enclosed within floating curtain fish barrier (Alternative: barge-mounted pumps, discharging to one pile-supported 60-in. force main)
Force main	From intake at north end of quarry in Haverstraw to Conrail (NY Central) West Shore RR right-of-way via Hook Mountain tunnel; bridge RR (1 track) approximately 1000 ft south of tunnel portal, westerly across Kings Highway to Toms Brook.
Stream Flow	Flow in Toms Brook to Lake DeForest reservoir, then via Hackensack River to Oradell reservoir.
(b) Reverse flow direction of cross-Bergen pipeline—Oradell reservoir to Pequannock River connection to NJDWSC aqueduct: 60 MGD	
Intake	Treated water from HWC Milford water treatment plant.
Pumping module	Four 1000 HP diesel-driven pump units to operate at 15 MGD and 250 ft head, discharging to 48-in. diameter cross-Bergen pipeline.
Force main (existing) characteristics	Diameter = 48 in. Flow = 69 MGD Velocity = 7.40 fps Velocity head = 0.85 ft Friction loss = 0.0030 ft/ft
Length of force main	55,000 lf (existing 48-in.)
Head required Static lift Friction loss Allowance for fittings Total head	 227 ft 225 ft 40 ft 492 ft
Pumping stages required	2
Stage 1 pumps	Four 1000 HP emergency units. (Existing HWC pumps may be adaptable to provide some capacity.)
Stage 2 force main	Pump discharge header connection to existing 48-in. diameter cross-Bergen pipeline.
Stage 2 pumps	Break into existing 48-in. diameter cross-Bergen pipeline at approximate elevation 250, provide connections to suction

TABLE 6. (*continued*)

Item	Description
	and discharge headers of pumping module. Four 1000 HP pump units.
Stage 2 force main	Existing 48-in. diameter cross-Bergen pipeline to ridge line, approximate elevation 450.
Gravity main	Existing 60-in. diameter cross-Bergen pipeline from ridge line to NJDWSC aqueduct at Pequannock River. Required slope at 60 MGD = 0.00091 ft/ft, available slope approximately 0.005.
Discharge connection	Modify aqueduct connections to allow discharge from cross-Bergen pipeline to NJDWSC aqueduct.
Distribution	Flow in NJDWSC aqueduct to existing interconnections with PVWC, and city of Newark systems and via Newark system to Jersey City aqueduct.

The routing of the emergency plan aqueduct is shown in FIGURE 7. The emergency system is composed of two physically separate projects, one delivering Hudson River water to Lake DeForest reservoir, and the second delivering water from Oradell reservoir to the NJDWSC aqueduct system. The installations are described in TABLE 6. Costs are provided in TABLE 7.

Several alternative methods of drafting water from the Hudson River are available. The water quality of the Haverstraw intake may be saline, particularly in the event of a severe drought. An intake located upstream, in the vicinity of Newburgh, would be more likely to draft fresh water.

Several power-generating stations are located along the west shore of the Hudson River, and all have high-capacity cooling water intake systems. The Roseton station has redundant pumping units rated in excess of the 115 MGD required. At 115 MGD, one Roseton station pump would deliver at about 50 feet of head, enough to satisfy the friction loss in about 3 miles of 60-inch pipe. However, the distance from Roseton to Haverstraw is about 31 miles, and one additional pumping stage would be needed in addition to the force main routed along the west shore of the river. The Conrail (West Shore RR) right-of-way would offer the preferred route, but the cost of the project would increase sharply. Similarly, the cooling water intake and pumps at the Bowline generating station in Haverstraw could replace the emergency intake facilities but would require an additional mile of force main. The emergency project, as described above, would provide a basic water supply for northeastern New Jersey in the event of an extreme emergency.

Each of the foregoing plans has four elements in common: (1) use of *Hudson River water*, generally above the salt-intrusion zone; (2) use of *existing* public or private *rights-of-way*; (3) use of existing or readily implementable intake structures; and (4) use of diesel-driven pump modules and mobile transmission lines. All of the physical elements required for implementation of these large-scale water supply emergency response plans may be made available from a national water emergency stockpile.

The time for planning the physical needs and the time for establishing the institutional mechanisms have been made available by the record rain-

TABLE 7. Emergency Project to Supply Northeastern New Jersey Project Cost Estimate

Item	Number Required	Item Cost ($1000)	Instal- lation Cost ($1000)	Amount ($1000)
(a) Hudson River to DeForest Lake reservoir:				
Intake fish barrier	400 lf	$ 40	$ 20	$ 60
Pump suction lines—24 in.	875 lf	45	25	70
Pump units (1 stage required)	7	1,750	100	1,850
Force main	2.4 miles	1,920	720	2,640
Structural bridges:				
RR X-ing (40-ft span)	—	40	20	60
Pipe bridges:				
Kings Highway (40-ft span)	—	20	10	30
Stream and culvert improvement	4		200	200
Miscellaneous details	—	200	200	400
Subtotal (a) Acquisition and installation		4,015	1,295	5,310
(b) Cross-Bergen pipeline work:				
Intake piping	—	200	200	400
Pump units (all stages)	8	2,000	160	2,160
Stage 2 connections	—	50	100	150
Discharge connection	—	100	100	200
Miscellaneous details		200	200	400
Subtotal (b) Acquisition and installation		2,550	760	3,310
Subtotal (a) + (b)		6,565	2,055	8,620
Contingencies @ 15%				1,293
Subtotal—construction cost				9,913
Engineering, legal, administration @ 10%				992
Total project cost				$10,905
			Say	$11,000

falls experienced this year. If we miss the opportunity to act before the next drought disaster is upon us, we really should not blame the weather!

REFERENCES

1. BLAKE, N. M. 1956. Water for the Cities: a History of the Urban Water Supply Problem in the United States. Syracuse University Press. Syracuse, N.Y.
2. 1982. The New Jersey Statewide Water Supply Master Plan. New Jersey Department of Environmental Protection. Trenton, N.J.

DISCUSSION OF THE PAPER

M. KARAMOUZ (*Polytechnic Institute of New York, Brooklyn, N.Y.*): During the last two decades there has been a lot of thought given to mathematical model operation of reservoirs or water supply systems. In your study did you consider any of those mathematical models using optimization simulation techniques to come up with a kind of operating rule?

J. P. LAWLER: The original studies that I referred to, which we did for the Corps of Engineers back in the late 60s, were heavily into simulation modeling, using synthetic hydrology and simulating the systems of reservoirs and interbasin transfers in a variety of different ways, and were generally directed at coming up with optimal operating rules. And there are a lot of constraints that you have to take into consideration; you know, you're talking optimum, subject to the constraints that are imposed on the system. What I was talking about here, my findings in that whole area, is that you can usually show how you can increase your yield but you're usually not talking substantial percentage increases in your yield simply by changes in your operating rule or institutional changes. You've got to do something to add more water. You usually find that your operating people know how to operate their systems pretty well. They have learned by experience how to get the most out of them. What I was leading to here is that in my judgment there is a gap, and the gap is what do you do when you're really in trouble? It hasn't happened yet, but what do you do if you literally run out of water? No amount, no optimizing of the existing system is going to help you in that.

M. KARAMOUZ: How practical are those models used in real-time operation?

J. P. LAWLER: The types of models we used were extremely practical. First, the whole notion of using synthetic hydrology or operational hydrology allows you to put some kind of probabilistic interpretation on what your yield is and that's important at least from a planning standpoint. Secondly in the simulation of the reservoirs, you can run that down to a day-by-day basis if you want and that's practical from the standpoint of operating it. I don't know what particular models you have in mind. What I'm saying to you is those that we used for this study I found to be eminently practical, even from an operating standpoint.

M. KARAMOUZ: We have expert operators who know what to do. Do you think they can use an analytical method as a guideline at least to help them in operation of the water resource systems?

J. P. LAWLER: I'm sure you could find and train people to use these as a guideline. There's no reason why you shouldn't be able to do it.

M. GOLDSTEIN (*White Plains, N.Y.*): One thing you didn't discuss was the control over the use of water. That is, you mentioned the fact that water systems are capital intensive, and a purveyor of water tries to recover his capital by getting his customers to use as much water as possible. Therefore, inevitably you are going to have a draw down at the beginning of each season. The thing to do therefore is to facilitate a rate structure that will minimize the amount of water used and still provide an adequate return to the purveyor.

J. P. LAWLER: I don't disagree with that notion, at all.

UNIDENTIFIED SPEAKER: We studied a bit about these water problems, and we find water a very inflexible commodity with the country-wide exceptions of lawn watering and car washing. Situations of that sort can be dealt with by price fixing water. Some industrial processes are price sensitive, but generally the bulk of the water used is not sensitive to price. You can double the price, you can invert the price structure, you don't seem to change the usage.

Your basic water usage needs of the city start with the leakage. You've got to contain your leakage or you're going to get no water up to the house. Once you get into the house, you've got to satisfy your civil structure. We have developed a civil structure that has bathtubs and water closets that are prodigious water users. Nobody drinks much water — you get more water in scotch than you take out of the tap for personal use. The effect of civilization can be seen from use of a water closet which has caused a dramatic increase in water over the decade from numbers of the order of 38 gallons per capita in New York City in early 1900 to now where we're talking about 238 gallons per capita. There are things that can be done, and the New York City drought experience showed that a conscious public can reduce the water supply use on a billion gallon plus system by as much as 20%. That 20% isn't the kind of number that's going to save us in a disaster situation, where you lose the entire Croton system for instance or the Catskill system for New York City. We came very close to that situation in northern New Jersey in 1981, where you had reservoirs with 15-days supply, and then the weather got us off the hook.

There are things that can be done internally such as to start looking at the water conservation picture. There are water closets that can use vacuum in association with water to drop the use of that type of facility to possibly 10% of what a water closet fixture uses. There are some regulations in the state of New York right now looking toward conserving water by mandating such structures. This will take decades to really become accomplished unless we get pressed to the wall in an emergency. Therefore, that is just one single element to the overall problem.

J. P. LAWLER: I think what we're starting to look at is a need for a physically based insurance policy, and that is to divide the cost of an emergency situation over the total Northeast area by providing stockpiling of major pumping machinery, identifying right-of-way — railroad right-of-way, highway right-of-way, powerline right-of-way — that can be pressed into use for an emergency type of water system. We've seen these civil defense systems based on agricultural piping of only 6 and 8 inches diameter, very successful for small communities.

In the air raids of World War II, the city of London survived on an emergency stockpile of major water works equipment. They had water, they would rebuild a system overnight, because of planning in advance. That's the direction this paper is taking.

Index of Contributors

(Italicized page numbers refer to comments made in discussion)

369